DAGGER JOHN

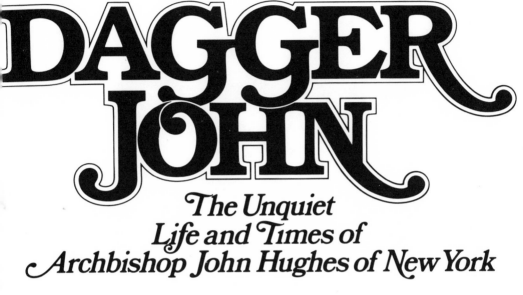

The Unquiet
Life and Times of
Archbishop John Hughes of New York

RICHARD SHAW

PAULIST PRESS
New York / Ramsey, N.J./ Toronto

Library of Congress
Catalog Card Number: 77-80799

ISBN: 0-8091-0224-2

Published by Paulist Press
Editorial Office: 1865 Broadway, New York, N.Y. 10023
Business Office: 545 Island Road, Ramsey, N.J. 07446

Printed and bound in the
United States of America

CONTENTS

v

To

J. R. S.

R. M. S.

PREFACE

John Hughes was ordained a priest in 1826 and died as archbishop of New York in 1864. His career spanned the nativist era in American history. The point has been well made that Church histories are oftentimes a view of the world as seen from a bishop's desk and not a social history of the Church's people. This story is about a bishop and his life's work. Yet he was very much one of the people, not simply in a pastoral sense but in his origins and character. His career reflected the American dream of the self-made man and of the battle of the immigrants to make the United States their own country.

Nineteenth-century American bishops were generally chosen from the ranks of European bishops or missionary priests. John Hughes arrived in the United States shortly after the War of 1812, half boy-half man, an uneducated Irish laborer. He possessed the sort of aggressive ambition that would have made him a leader in any career he might have forced his way into. He forced his way into the Catholic priesthood. He became a bishop, not because of Church politics but because of his unquestioned ability to command and because he made himself famous as a champion of the immigrant Catholics.

Both as a priest and bishop his life's work involved two main concerns:

He had left Ireland, ruled by Protestant England, expecting to find in the United States a land owned by no man's religion. When he arrived here he was informed hundreds of times over, in the newspapers and in popular oratory, that

1

"this is a Protestant country." He hurled this claim back in the faces of those who made it. He let them know that the United States would belong to the Irish Catholic immigrant as much as it ever belonged to any native-born Protestant. Other bishops conducted a gentlemanly defense of the Church and the immigrant. John Hughes was never so happily alive as when he was fighting. He returned in kind what the nativists gave out, and whether he won or lost his battles he earned the love of the little man, the immigrant, for whom he was a champion.

The second concern of his life's work was to teach Catholics as well as native Protestants that the Roman Catholic Church could exist in a democracy and retain its essential character. It would not become, as many Catholics hoped, a democracy itself. Hughes had an unshakable devotion to the proper chain of command. He demanded absolute fealty within the realm of his own authority, and he gave it in turn to those who were his superiors. To establish this as accepted Church discipline in the United States involved a constant struggle that stretched throughout his career.

There is a problem with sources when writing about priests. Celibacy leaves a man with no heirs and leaves a researcher with fewer remembrances about that man's personal life. Moreover, as with any organization determined to maintain a proper image both collectively and for its representative individuals, churchmen have tended to preserve only that which fit the image they felt was proper. John Gilmary Shea, the nineteenth-century Catholic historian, expressed his frustration about this in response to a question concerning the preservation of historical data. Shea said:

> Not only has little been done but some of that little has been destroyed. A Father Ulrich, one of the early Benedictines of St. Vincent's Abbey, kept a diary for many years, so that the volumes formed a pile several feet high, recording every event in the community and in the Church in that part of western Pennsylvania. They were all destroyed by order of the Abbot Wimmer. Bishop de St. Palais ordered all the papers of Vincennes diocese, collected, bound and indexed by his predecessor, to be destroyed. These were cases

of deliberate destruction, while of those resulting from ignorance or indifference it would be impossible to make a
record. The Archbishop of New York has really no archives, no papers of Bishops Connolly or Dubois, Archbishop Hughes and McCloskey. The relatives of Archbishop
Hughes, I find, destroyed all his letters. The papers of V.
Rev. John Power, V.G. and twice administrator of New
York, were placed in a religious house for preservation. In
time they were in the way and were all destroyed.

It is greatly to be regretted that priests do not write, at
least, the edifying and interesting events in their ministry.
There are few priests who could not relate many, but alas
they are seldom recorded.

The only important attempt at a biography of John
Hughes is that of John Hassard, who served as an amanuensis
for the archbishop. Published shortly after Hughes's death, it
includes all the major events of his life. Unfortunately, Hassard
was overly selective with his sources—even to the deletion of
paragraphs from letters—and carefully presented only what
would exhibit Hughes in a totally favorable light. This tends to
cast suspicion on any intimate portrayal of the man in those instances where Hassard is the only source.

This, by default, is a public view of John Hughes, moving
no closer into his inner personality than reliable sources allow.
Yet, because his career was so public and so frequently political, newspapers are the best source of information about him.
And none was better or more reliable than James Gordon Bennett's New York *Herald*. Bennett was both a Roman Catholic
and a fiercely independent man. No institution, including his
own Church, was sacrosanct to him. He printed news about the
activities of all the religious denominations to whatever extent
he felt the public was owed information about them, and he
praised and condemned the activities of the clergy in much the
same way he did the activities of politicians. John Hughes, who
had little use for any Catholic whom he could not control, had
almost no use for the editor of the *Herald*. The two men fought
an acrimonious battle in the 1840s, and thereafter Hughes
coldly ignored Bennett's existence. Bennett was too good a
newsman to ignore Hughes. He remained fascinated with him:

lauded him when he felt it was deserved and thrashed him when he thought the bishop was acting foolishly. He stuck to the facts. Hughes could never acknowledge Bennett's veracity publicly. Nonetheless, in 1858, when he was sending a report to Rome, the archbishop included a story that Bennett had written about the Catholic school system. "His object was merely to publish an article of general interest for the benefit of his newspaper," Hughes wrote. "I confess that I could not, myself, have furnished such an article, either for want of time to examine into the accuracy of details, or because the work is still going on. I shall send you the article as it was published by him on the 22nd of January." This researcher likewise acknowledges an indebtedness to James Gordon Bennett.

John Hughes is an important figure in American Church history. Another bishop, such as John England, might have been better at integrating the Church into a democracy. Another such as Francis Kenrick might have been a better example of a gentlemanly pastor of souls. It was Hughes, however, both autocratic and devoted at the same time to democratic principles, who as New York's bishop for the quarter of a century of the nativist era set the style for what Americans came to expect in a Catholic bishop for a century after his death.

PRELUDE:
THE BATTLEGROUND

Charles Whelan was born without social graces. Of Spartan exterior, he seemed incapable of making himself pleasing to others, and when he opened his mouth to speak, little came out that was worth listening to. He was, however, a young man of generous faith; he had an enormous capacity for enduring hardships, and he had a desire to serve. In the 1760s when he was in his twenties, that faith he desired to serve was systematically persecuted in his native Ireland by English law. Catholics were barred from holding office or voting in parliamentary elections. Commissions in the army and navy were closed to them. It was against the law for them to run schools or seek Catholic education for their children. A complex code of statutes all but negated their rights of ownership. They could not own a house worth more than five pounds, and it was not difficult to dispossess a Catholic of land (a son could take his father's property by turning Protestant). Higher ecclesiastics were barred, and only a limited number of licensed priests were allowed in the country. To seek admission to the Catholic priesthood, Charles Whelan left his homeland and set out for France.

Accepted by the Capuchins, he was ordained and advanced his way in that order until by 1779 he was serving his province as master of novices. There he might well have spent the remainder of his life, never venturing far beyond friary walls, except for the War for American Independence. Before

5

he had been novice master for a year, a call came from King Louis XVI asking the Capuchins to supply chaplains to the French Navy for the duration of hostilities. The Irishman was sent by his superiors, thus being separated from his religious community, as matters turned out, for the remainder of his life.

For the next two years he sailed with the French fleet, surviving fourteen engagements without mishap. In April 1782, after the defeat of the Count de Grasse in the West Indies, Whelan was taken prisoner along with 7,000 Frenchmen, 1,500 of whom were wounded. In Jamaica where they were shipped the heat and humidity quickly added to the casualty lists of battle.

Tirelessly, for thirteen months, Whelan spent each day going through the military prisons performing a service that did not require a pleasing personality to ensure its success. When the treaties of peace set the prisoners free, Whelan decided to return, not to France, but to the new country he had visited during the fighting, to serve the people whose independence had already cost him so much suffering. He would become a missionary to Catholicize the United States.

New York City had been a safe Loyalist stronghold for most of the Revolution. Still, a large area of it had been ravaged by fire, burned not by either army but by accident. Because of that, along with the great turnover in property and the departure of the British, the city was in many ways starting anew, both physically and socially, when Charles Whelan stood on the city's docks in October of 1784 contemplating his immediate future. The New York Legislature only months before had done away with a law of 1700 condemning any priest found in the province to perpetual imprisonment. He could enter the town without concealing his identity, something that technically, at least, he could not have done while serving in the cause of American Independence.

The colony had never been friendly to Catholics. Early in the war, Philip Schuyler had cleared out a group of Scottish Catholics who had settled in the Mohawk Valley, sending them and their priest emigrating to Canada. When the state convention in 1777 decided upon a policy of full religious freedom, John Jay fought to exclude from such those who followed "the wicked and damnable doctrine that the Pope has power to absolve men from sins."[1] Failing in this, he had managed to have included in the oath for taking office promises that would bar any believing Catholic.

The alliances with Spain and France, however, had already brought visiting Catholic notables into the young nation's main port of entry. The presence of these prestigious Romanists called for at least a polite toleration of the Church and in some circles made acceptance of it almost fashionable. Numbers of Catholics already in the city began to emerge into the light of day. Some of these found a newly discovered social advantage in their half-forgotten ancestral affiliation; others were people who had held quietly but stoutly to their faith while it was under proscription in the colony. This latter group had been cared for by the occasional visits of an itinerant priest named Ferdinand Steenmeyer, who went under the alias of Farmer, apparently to make himself more acceptable to the English colonists. The most that Farmer had been able to do was to gather the handful of practicing Catholics into shuttered attics in order to celebrate the Mass. Now, newly liberated, these people could await the arrival of a resident priest to start the city's first real Catholic parish. Whelan's appearance seemed almost providential.

A prominent Portuguese merchant immediately set out to secure him as his own chaplain, but the French Consul General, Hector St. John de Crèvecoeur, acted for the Catholic citizens of the city and took Whelan in hand. He introduced him to the right people—the governor, the local magistrates, the Marquis de Lafayette who was still in the city—and then set him up to serve the Church.

The consul general had previously published a book, *The Letters of an American Farmer,* in which he reflected the attitude of the Enlightenment by discounting revealed religion. From all evidences a Catholic in heritage alone, he was a proper spirit to represent a laity so long cut off from the mainstream of the Church's life and discipline. He was thoroughly republican in his views; the Roman Catholic Church was not. To supply a place for worship he applied to the city for the use of the Exchange, an ancient building on Broad Street, then used as a courtroom. Angry when permission was refused, de Crèvecoeur, acting on his own authority, legally incorporated himself and several other prominent laymen as the trustees of the Roman Catholic Church in New York. These men directed Whelan to buy several lots on Barclay Street, and the building of St. Peter's church was begun.

Catholics in New York were understandably sensitive about their image. The city had just been named as the capital of the nation, and they could easily have felt that the whole country would judge their Church by comparing it unfavorably with the long-established Protestant sects boasting accomplished orators. They had been raised in a world where the art of preaching was the prime criterion for judging the worth of a clergyman. To their dismay they discovered that Charles Whelan was the very worst of preachers.

When Farmer arrived in the city on a routine visit the next year representing the Prefect Apostolic John Carroll, a steady stream of Catholics called upon him to complain of the colorless Whelan. They wanted to know if he was to be considered as settled where he was. They would not have him. If need be they would apply to the state legislature for a law stating that no clergyman could be forced upon them. In vain, Farmer tried to convince them that having a drab but dedicated priest was better than having no priest at all. It was in vain as well that he appealed to Whelan to make himself more attractive to his parishioners. As willing as the man was, the task was beyond his ability. When Farmer left the city no one was happy. And then Father Andrew Nugent arrived.

Nugent was a Franciscan and was, as well, an early type of the vagabond priests who were to plague the Catholic Church in the United States throughout the first half of the next century. Having been suspended in his diocese of Dublin, Ireland, he had wandered to the New World to seek his fortune. Within a month's time, people were smoothing a path through the cobblestone streets to hear him speak. Parishioners of St.

Peter's were proud to point him out as a representative of their religion. Unfortunately for Whelan this only made their efforts to get him out of view a more pressing matter. Shortly after Christmas in 1785 they voted to oust their official pastor and replace him with the more than willing Father Andrew. With Father Andrew's ambitious support the parishioners withheld the church collection from their pastor and threatened to have the civil courts remove him if he would not leave. Early in February, Charles Whelan could stand the public scandal no longer. He resigned from the parish and sailed up the Hudson to stay with his brother on a farm west of Albany.

Father Farmer had come to firmly admire Whelan's dedication. Angrily he wrote of "the arbitrary and ungenerous manner with which they forced poor Father Whelan to depart, who though he was not very learned, yet was ready to ask and take advice . . ." (The trustees, he worried,) "have the principle that they can choose for themselves whom they please, whether approved by the superior or not . . ."[2]

The Catholics of New York had won the initial round in deciding who would manage the young Church in the Republic. Yet it was not a total victory. More wily as well as more colorful than his predecessor, Father Andrew measured the opportunities of supply and demand and then coolly announced to the shocked trustees that he would accept no less than $100 more than the annual salary they had agreed to pay him. With no alternative but to leave the new church on Barclay Street bereft of a priest, they resentfully paid the Franciscan his demand.

Still the victory in principle was theirs. For another twenty years Father Whelan went about serving the Church wherever he could as missionary, preaching as far west as Kentucky, and finally ending his days in Maryland where he died at the age of sixty-five in 1806. Even when Father Nugent had been deposed after a later fracas with the same trustees, Whelan never had the heart to return to the battlegrounds of New York. If Catholics in the United States were ever going to learn Church discipline, it would take a stronger man than Whelan to teach them.

PART ONE

The Priest

1

THE PRICE
OF A
BAPTISM

In early nineteenth-century Ulster County, neither the weather nor the Protestant overlords were especially kind to Catholic tenant farmers. It was in Ulster that Patrick and Margaret Hughes cared for a small farm and worked to raise their four sons and three daughters. Though of limited means, they were of strong ambition. They placed a high value on education, and they kept their sons in grammar schools as long as possible. When the third son, John, showed an inclination toward the priesthood they allowed him to study, at no small sacrifice to themselves, well after his two older brothers had been called home to work. The Hugheses were all but alone as Catholics in their area, and religious hatreds in Northern Ireland were as strong then as they would be for at least another century and a half. Once when John was fifteen he was set upon by a Protestant gang who apparently had every intention of stabbing him to death. He was turned loose only because one of his attackers knew the boy's father and announced that he should be let go.

In 1814 a ruinous farm year ended John's education at the age of seventeen.* He was heartbroken, but obedient to his parents' need for help. With a strong wiry build, the boy should have settled down easily enough to routine farm labor.

_____
*He was born April 24, 1797.

13

Yet it was obvious to his family that he would never be happy in that occupation. Perhaps to give his disappointed son the feeling that he was still being educated, Patrick arranged for him to become the assistant to the gardener at a nearby estate.

There was family tragedy to add to the bitterness of poverty. Peter, the fifth child, died, and was followed by Mary, next in age to John. At her burial a galling humiliation imposed upon Catholics was added to the grief. By law their priest was forbidden to enter the cemetery gates. The best he could do to comfort the mourners was to bless a handful of earth and give it to someone else to sprinkle upon Mary's coffin after it was lowered into the grave.

It was too much to bear. Patrick had begun to think of moving westward to America, as many of his countrymen were beginning to do. Now he took action.

In 1816 he sailed with his second son to find a new home for his family. The voyage consumed almost all of his funds, and there was no chance of buying into the rich farmlands he found in Pennsylvania. But it was rich green territory filled with promises of success for those with the courage to work for it. He rented a house in Chambersburg, not far from the Maryland border, and sent word back to his sons to come with the rest of the family.

This message arrived in the late spring of 1817. Owing to its timing the move was not easily accomplished. The Hughes's landlord refused to give them credit for the planted and growing crops. Michael, the eldest, unwilling to lose money, remained for the year with his mother and sisters. He sent his younger brother ahead in the company of an emigrating neighbor. Just twenty, John left his homeland smoldering with a strong sense of anger and exile. He would always thereafter speak with bitterness of what it meant to be a Catholic in imprisoned Ireland.

"They told me when I was a boy," he would remember, "that for five days I was on social and civil equality with the most favored subjects of the British Empire. These five days would be the interval between my birth and my baptism." After that he lived under a caste system of "civil degradation" because of his religion. Now, free at last, he bore with him across the Atlantic a hatred deep enough to last a lifetime for all things English and for the Protestantism that had been an integral part of the English state. As he sailed westward he focused his sharp, almost fierce, blue-gray eyes in the directions of a young nation whose Constitution provided that the land belonged to no religion. He dreamed of "a country in which no stigma of inferiority would be impressed on my brow simply because I professed one creed or another."[1]

Protestantism wasn't the only religion that had left him embittered. He bore no small amount of resentment toward his own Church as well. Ireland needed leadership, and her natural leaders in a fight against the oppression under which he had grown should have been, so he felt, her priests. He judged that because they were doing nothing effective to this end they were to a good measure responsible for conditions in that hapless land. The young man who had wanted to be a priest left his homeland solidly anticlerical.

All that ugliness, however, was to be of his past. In mid-summer of 1817 he landed in Baltimore. Instead of traveling to Pennsylvania to be with his father, he remained in Maryland with his brother Patrick. His experience as a gardener was an advantage. He obtained a job working on a plantation, and although half the growing season was gone, he worked mightily in the hope that his perseverance would earn him the right to be kept over the winter. He wasn't kept. As soon as the heavy harvesting was done, his employer curtly informed him that he had no more need of extra help. It was no more than any migrant farm worker might have expected to hear, but John, still breathing the air of promise in his adopted free land, was crushed and disillusioned. It was, he would recall long afterward, "the hardest blow I ever received in my life."[2]

The Hugheses were an independent lot. They were a strongly united family and would always remain so. Yet they never stifled one another by holding to a single destiny. The boys had remained away from the father to find work on their own, and now, penniless, and with farming prospects done with for the year, John looked about for regular employment. There was one advertised call for cheap labor answered by a large number of Irish immigrants that year. Work was just beginning in New York on DeWitt Clinton's Erie Canal, and the most tempting aspect of such a job must have been the opportunity for immediate and prolonged employment. But John Hughes was still young. Such a job would have taken him hundreds of miles from his family, and he was not yet that independent. Instead he went to Pennsylvania, moved in with his father, and for the next two years, during which the rest of the family arrived from Ireland, he worked as a day laborer, building roads and bridges, digging in stone quarries, and taking an occasional job as a gardener. Had it not been for the accident of geography, by which his father had chosen to live not far from Emmitsburg, Maryland, this might have been the pattern of John's career for the remainder of his life.

2

A MOUNTAIN
WHERE MEN MET GOD

Many problems of the young and growing Catholic Church in the United States reflected conditions in Europe. The Irish immigrants, who quickly came to be the greater part of the laity, found themselves served by French priests who had escaped the Revolution in their own native land. Because the French tended to dominate the ranks of the clergy, the Irish, sensitive to having escaped the rule of one foreign people, began to resent the idea that they should be under the authority of yet another while living in a democracy. The result was internal tension that was to endure for almost half a century.

"Americans have a repugnance to the clerical state." Thus wrote John Connolly, New York's first resident bishop in 1818. "If bishops continue to prefer priests from the continent to those of Ireland it will harm the Church." He warned Rome, "The Catholic population consists chiefly of Irishmen; they build the churches and expect priests who understand them."[1]

In the same year that Connolly wrote those words, his next two successors as bishops of New York met for the first time. One was a Frenchman, the head of a backwoods seminary and boy's school; the other was a twenty-one-year-old Irish day laborer. The personal relationship between the two men over the next quarter of a century was to reflect much of the lack of understanding between their respective nationalities in the American Church.

The repugnance to the clerical state that young John

Hughes had developed before he set foot in a democracy had begun by this time to fade. After a year in the United States, Hughes found work in Emmitsburg, Maryland, some thirty miles from his parents' home. A fellow Irishman he met in a tavern hired him to help build a mill in that town; then Hughes obtained some road work there. The employment came steadily enough for him to take lodgings with a local schoolmaster, and it was in this situation that he began to be affected by the presence of the two remarkable priests who were the spirit of Mount St. Mary's Seminary.

John Dubois and Simon Bruté were absolute opposites. Physically they looked like a fat man-thin man comedy team in a theater, and in fact there was something slightly comic about the day-to-day clashes caused by their very different personalities. Both were heroic; both had suffered during the French Revolution. Dubois had been a stolid young assistant at the large parish of St. Sulpice in Paris when the Terror broke out. He had continued as long as he could, working as chaplain at a Sisters of Charity orphanage and lunatic asylum. Only when the lunacy of his compatriots had gone beyond that of his charges did he flee to the United States, unable to speak a word of English. Someone had given him a letter of introduction from Lafayette, and this, along with his native intelligence, earned him a temporary home among the Virginia aristocracy. James Monroe gave him bed and board. Willing neighbors, notably Patrick Henry, helped him learn English while he in return pleased their yearning for education and helped them to improve their French. Dubois might have created a lifetime position from this. He was, however, a worker by nature. He regularized himself with the Church authorities and spent the next twenty years riding about Maryland on horseback serving Catholics wherever they could be found. In 1808 he chose a spot off the well-traveled road that led to Emitsburg, Maryland (and, going on a little farther, to Gettysburg, Pennsylvania). With little more than a prayer in his possession, he began an institution for the purpose of educating a native American clergy. There was no reason for it to have succeeded; but the man who in looks and personality resembled Napoleon enough to be nicknamed "the little corporal," brought it to success by strength of his will. In ten years' time it was well established and growing.

Frail looking Simon Bruté, whose large sensitive eyes dominated the whole of his expression, had lived an unfrail existence. He had been a child when the Reign of Terror broke out. His iron-willed, pious mother, in danger because she was the widow of an old regime government official, hid proscribed priests in her home. Simon grew in the shadow of the guillotine. The boy went to the courts and quietly watched the trials of the Revolution's enemies, sometimes slipping close enough to lean against the benches of the accused. He witnessed the sentencing to death of two elderly ladies along with the priest they had hidden, a crime these ladies shared with his mother, and he listened to the command that the toys of Roman superstition be burned alongside them while they were killed. He watched one of his former school professors, a priest, refuse to leave his underground ministry. The man was eventually forced out by a trick (a message sent that a priest was needed) and then shot through the head. He watched a discovered priest loudly praying the "libera" for himself and his companion as a declaration of faith, while the two were pushed through the streets to their execution. At fourteen, dressed as a baker's boy, he carried the Eucharist about his neck and visited the prisons with a priest disguised as a baker. Inside the priest would gather the condemned about him to clandestinely distribute Communion.

When the Revolution cooled down, Simon grew to adulthood in Napoleon's world. He went to school in Paris and became a physician. Only then, fully grown, did he decide to enter the priesthood, which the Revolution had determined to stamp out. He was ordained in 1808 and promptly volunteered for the American missions. Since he was too exceptional a man to be wasted in anything but education, his superiors, after tugging him back and forth between the competing seminaries of St. Mary's in Baltimore and Dubois's upstart Mount St. Mary's in Emmitsburg, finally settled him in the latter. Not that he was an unalloyed asset; his brilliant mind was often all

light and fire with no form. His lectures sailed through unchar-
tered courses in streams of consciousness. For all his genius he
never quite conquered the English language, and besides all of
this he was studded with the eccentricities shared by those who
live in a world quite apart from the reality in which they are
confined.

It is a wonder that he and the very down-to-earth Dubois
got along at all. Only the cement of their mutual, total devotion to the priesthood kept these two selfless men in any kind
of harmony. Bruté feared the methodical way that Dubois
pitched the infant school into debt for construction of buildings. The man built as if looking into the next century instead
of the present, and Bruté feared that creditors would move in
and take his only material treasure: his much-used library. He
found the dictatorial Dubois hard to talk with, and so he
scratched out long memos at night rather than walk into the
next room to face his intimidating superior.

Dubois concurred with the popular belief that Bruté was a
saintly madman, and treated him as such. When Bruté gave his
only coat to a beggar, Dubois railed at him, insisting: "We are
as poor as that man," and for months let Bruté pay for his generosity by wearing the ill-fitting clothes of a deceased student.[2]
Yet, the otherworldliness of Bruté could work to the advantage
of others. The archbishop of Baltimore once sent word to Bruté
that a reference was needed from his library, and was startled
at breakfast when this absentminded professor arrived, having
walked the fifty miles through the night to deliver the book.
Bruté had a habit of reading while he walked or rode a horse
and would measure a journey not so much by the miles as the
hundreds of pages covered. When Dubois made the mistake of
lending him a new gift saddle with Dubois's name engraved on
it in silver letters, Bruté returned, drenched, the horse in tow,
to report that he had lost control while crossing a log bridge.
Both beast and rider had plunged into the turbulent stream,
and the new saddle, torn off, had not been recovered. With
galling simplicity Bruté recounted that he last caught sight of it
swirling away in the foam and had seen the bobbing silver let-

ters flashing repeatedly, "John Dubois, John Dubois, John Dubois."[3] John Dubois was not amused.

And yet each man realized the value and need of the other. When Bruté was ordered to St. Mary's in Baltimore both men longed and worked to reunite themselves as a team in Emmitsburg. Bruté may have been an eccentric, but there was a strong ray of sanctity that shone through him so that people profited by his presence. The priest who took Bruté's charge at the village church near the seminary complained that some of the parishioners were so attached to "poor crazy Bruté" they were waiting for him to return in order to go to confession.[4] While in Baltimore Bruté was continually homesick for the mountain school and the community of people who had become a great part of his life. When at length he was allowed to go back he returned to the hills of Emmitsburg at roughly the same time that John Hughes took lodging in the town.

"Poor Crazy Bruté" must have enchanted the young immigrant, for John developed a worshipful awe for him that he was never to accord to any other man and which lasted until Bruté's death. Knowing prosperity and freedom for the first time in his life Hughes had begun to pick up pieces of dreams that had been dropped during the adverse fortunes of his childhood. He had gone to Dubois at Mount St. Mary's several times already, told him that he intended to become a priest, and pleaded for admission as a student. Dubois had turned him down. The small school was overcrowded. Moreover, Hughes was twenty-one years old, and his lack of schooling would have placed him on a level with boys who were still children. Dubois was not a man given to romantic possibilities. He judged the rawboned Irish lad to be a dreamer and waved him off.

John Hughes was not one to let another man's will stand in his path. He was persistent and called upon Dubois at regular intervals to see if conditions at the college had altered any decisions about acceptance, no doubt diminishing his prospects with Dubois by making himself a nuisance.

For almost a full year Hughes got nowhere, and if he approached Bruté for help in persuading Dubois, he must soon

have realized how little influence this slight man had in affect-
ing Dubois's decisions. Then in the fall of 1819 he sought work
at the convent of Sisters who ran St. Joseph's school, a short
distance from Mount St. Mary's. Dubois had been a rock for
these sisters to lean upon from the day of their arrival ten years
earlier. The founder of the community of nuns, a convert from
the Episcopal Church, was in many respects a strong third missionary partner to the two priests. If she depended greatly upon
their strength, it was equally true that neither of them could refuse a request from her. She got to know the young laborer.
Leaving the subject of whatever digging needed to be done, he
opened his heart to her, told her of his applications to Mount
St. Mary's and of Dubois's refusals. She looked beyond the
rough hands, the aggressive stance of the born fighter, and saw
something deeper than Dubois had in the light blue eyes that
confronted her. Mother Elizabeth Seton sat down, wrote
Dubois a note, and asked him if some sort of accommodation
might be made for this exceptional and intent young
man.[5] Dubois was grudging in his reconsideration. He
looked about at the needs of his school and struck a bargain in
which it would seem he had the advantage. He could use a
gardener and an overseer for the college's handful of slaves.
Hughes might have the job. In lieu of wages he would live in a
tiny cabin, a distance from the main house, and receive occasional tutoring. It was a good compromise to get the persistent youth off his neck and acknowledge the favor asked by
Mother Seton.

Hughes saw it as no special favor. It was "a regular contract between us, in which neither was required to acknowledge
any obligation to the other."[6] If it were a game he would beat
it; the door having been opened an inch, he could force it the
rest of the way himself. Still heady with notions of American
freedom, he resented caring for the Frenchman's slaves, even
though slavery was commonplace in Maryland, and there was
no social stigma attached to even a seminary owning its ser-
vants.

Hughes wisely kept his thoughts to himself. Only after he
gained full entry into the institution did he write a long, bitter

(and badly composed) poem on the shamefulness of black slavery. For nine months he worked with the gardeners and spent each night studying alone in his one-room cabin. He was a determined man with no time to waste. He devoured knowledge at every opportunity. In the late summer of 1820 Dubois came upon him at dinnertime and saw him using his time off to study rather than eat. He spoke with him, plied him with questions and, as the young man answered, Dubois began to perceive the potential that Mother Seton had discerned in a moment's time the year before. As always Dubois was a fair man. The day laborer had proven himself to be more than a dreamer. He had earned his right to study, a man among boys in Dubois's school. Immediately Dubois enrolled him as a full student for the fall term of 1820.

John Hughes was twenty-three years of age when he joined the sixty or so students of Mount St. Mary's. It was labeled a college, but the title was misleading. It was a boarding school for boys of all ages. Only a handful of young men there could properly have been called collegians, let alone seminarians. The student body included Protestants as well as Catholics. Dubois ruled over the place almost like a military commander, getting as much labor out of everyone as he could. What he imposed upon others, however, he demanded equally of himself. He could be seen working the grounds or taking his turn waiting on tables alongside the youngest boys. The older students he appointed as teachers in the basic subjects, but this was impossible for Hughes who was still being tutored while having to study with the younger classes. So Dubois placed him in charge of the study hall.

It was no easy assignment. The youngsters were quick to see the vulnerability of Hughes's position. The uneducated laborer who was a decade older than most of them had continually to switch roles—from being their peer in classes, to assuming authority over them in the study hall. He was overly stern and a constant butt of pranks such as hanging an effigy from the rafters on St. Patrick's Day and charging his desk candle with gunpowder.

The students weren't the only ones who found Hughes

hard to take. His age and taciturn personality made him a threat to the younger professors. They could and did react strongly to him. The first time Hughes ever spoke before an audience it was to read a speech to his younger classmates. He became nervous, stammered and dropped the paper from his hands. The presiding priest, John Hickey, was newly ordained and barely older than Hughes. He pounced upon the novice orator: "That's pride, sir," he threw at him, "nothing but pride! Put it under your feet. Pick up your essay and go on!"[7]

Hughes's transition from laborer to student was impeded by Dubois's reluctance to lose an overseer with a knowledge of gardening. Hughes was kept in charge of the slaves and often-times had to leave class to go out to direct the farm workers. Nor would the workmen let him forget from whence he had risen. When he berated one of the hired hands who was drunk, the man turned and accused his accuser of assuming a high and mighty air: "Who are you I should like to know? You are nobody but John Hughes. Don't I remember when you used to work with your two hands as do I?"[8]

Hughes remained, nonetheless, unflinching in his resolve. Slowly he began to pull himself up intellectually. At the end of his first academic year, an entry about him scratched into the college records comments: "Mr. Hughes would be at least equal to McCaffery [the school's best student] if he had the same chance—excellent judgment in translation—but does not know equally the meaning of words."[9]

When the game of being a student was interrupted by an emergency, Hughes could be quick to assume the role of leadership that belonged to him by nature. Once a raging forest fire eating its way downward on the mountain threatened the school. Hughes quickly mobilized the students into crews to cut a clearing between the college and the fire, then started a back-fire. He worked the boys throughout the day and well into the night until the threat to the school was averted. He himself had worked so close to the heat that a large hole was burned into the back of his coat. Having no money to replace it he walked about for a long time afterward with a black patch sewn across his shoulders to cover the burn mark.

All this while he remained close to his family and often-times on a Saturday walked the thirty miles to Chambersburg to be with them, walking back the next day after Mass. On one of these trips he brought back his younger sisters Margaret and Ellen. He enrolled them in the Sisters of Charity's school. Either from shrewdness, knowing the piety of the girls, or from knowing Ellen's intentions, he made an arrangement with the sisters whereby should one of them ever enter religious life, the Hughes family would be credited with whatever tuition was already paid.

As he grew more comfortable in the world of academics he took to composing poetry, none of which was very good but which was pleasing enough to the editor of the weekly Gettysburg *Adams Centinal* to be deemed printable. For over a year's time while he thought himself a budding poet Hughes contributed to the paper. In quoting these poems at length, Hughes's first biographer would note that it was "a curious fact that out of seventeen pieces only one is distinctly religious."[10]

It is not that curious a fact. Neither then nor at any time in his life would Hughes be a man to allow others to see into his soul. He was essentially a loner—a man who no matter how much faith directed his life could not expose that attitude of faith to even his close contemporaries. He could be a defender of the faith but never one of its mystical witnesses.

His defense of faith began during this period. Fourth-of-July oratory in that age often included a recital of the ills of a decadent Europe from which the United States had been so happily freed. A stock inclusion in this litany was the liberty-destroying temporal power of the Roman papacy. In Chambersburg when one such speech was given, along with the customary slur upon the Church, Hughes reacted. He wrote an angry response and presented it to the local paper, the *Franklin Repository*. According to one contemporary source, what he had written was so strong that the editor had to be argued into printing it.

A search of the paper reveals several letters that might have been Hughes's. The custom of publishing letters under classical names (Hughes signed his poetry as "Leander") makes any positive verification difficult. One thing is clear: As a reader of the newspaper, Hughes was well informed about the Philadelphia fracas that had given the Catholic Church a far worse image than any being offered by anti-Catholic propagandists.

The entire comedy is important to the Hughes story for it lasted long enough for him to be thrown into its final act and for him to be involved with all its main characters. This school for scandal would afford him an education about the American Church that would be as important as anything he would learn at Mount St. Mary's.

3

THE EMPEROR OF CHINA
AS A BISHOP

> Here no church, Catholic or Protestant can possess
> temporal goods nor income to its name. If it is built by
> public money the congregation must yearly elect trustees to
> administer the property and priests as such have no right to
> interfere with this property.[1]

With these words New York's Bishop John Connolly
attempted to educate Rome to the new realities it faced in the
United States. More concerned with matters in post-Napoleonic
Europe, Rome chose not to face this reality and relegated the
American Church to a limbo where it was left to work out new
situations for itself.

When Philadelphia's first bishop died in 1814 the See was
left vacant for six years, during which time prominent Catholic
laymen became increasingly more jealous about their prerogative of hiring and firing the wandering priests who turned up in
their diocese. In 1820, slight, dapper Father William Hogan arrived in New York City concealing the minor fact of his suspension from the priesthood in Dublin. Accepted by Bishop
Connolly, he was assigned to the wilds of Lansingburgh, as far
up the Hudson as a good-sized vessel could sail. Such primitive
conditions were not to his liking. In March of that same year
he turned up in Philadelphia at the fashionable red brick
church of St. Mary's, a short walk from Independence Hall.
With his boyish, handsome face he immediately charmed the
trustees and was hired. He was a Catholic clergyman the likes

of which the city had not seen since the stay of Talleyrand. Thoroughly secular in lifestyle, he hired a different dwelling than that provided for the priests and soon became the darling of society. Even the astute publisher Matthew Carey praised Hogan as a colorful preacher who might well revive a dormant Catholicism. Carey declared him "the most popular clergyman who had been at St. Mary's in years."[2] The only recorded exception to this initial admiration came from one masculine member of the parish who observed the cleric's foppish taste for dress and decided: "The price of pomatum must have risen since William's arrival."[3]

Rome, meanwhile, was concerned about filling the Irish See of Armagh in the county next to where John Hughes was born. The job should have gone to Henry Conwell who at seventy-three had held the office of vicar general for longer than John Hughes had lived. However, the delicate political situation with the English government called for a man of tact, and the other bishops of Ireland petitioned that the primal See be given to someone other than Conwell. To remove him diplomatically from the scene he was given the diocese of Philadelphia. Hearing of this appointment the man who did succeed to the primal See commented upon Conwell's qualifications for his new post. "I would not have been more surprised," he said, "if he had been made Emperor of China."[4]

Ordered by the newly arrived Conwell to assume the lifestyle of a priest, Hogan declared from the pulpit that no one, not even a bishop, had the right to dictate to him where and how he should live. The bishop then announced Hogan's suspension. There was no question in the old man's mind but that this would be accepted as due process enough. After all, Conwell had been a priest since before the American colonies had written their Declaration of Independence, let alone any Bill of Rights. His right to act thusly would never have been questioned on the eastern side of the Atlantic. He was soon educated to the manners of a democracy.

Public protests, pamphlets and formal delegations took up the campaign for Hogan's rights. When Conwell remained adamant he found himself fired from St. Mary's parish. He might be their bishop, but the trustees would not have him as their pastor. While the stunned ecclesiastic was evicted to the small chapel of St. Joseph's a short distance away, the trustees then declared William Hogan to be in charge of spiritual matters at their church. When Conwell then excommunicated Hogan, a resolution was issued by the parishioners deciding that the worst that Hogan had been guilty of was a "hasty and inconsiderate breach of pastoral courtesy" in regard to the bishop. Conwell in contrast was assailed as being "ignorant, acrimonious, censorious, vindictive, prone to ire, too mindful of petty offenses, stubborn in error and inflexible to forgiveness."[5] Rather a strong portrait of a man who had been in town a scant half year.

The tug of war for possession of St. Mary's dragged out over several years, with occasional minor characters arriving to add confusion. A Friar Rico, a vagabond Spanish Franciscan, entered the scene claiming to have been vicar general to the armies of Spain as well as a canon lawyer. He supported Hogan. Unfortunately for his credibility, he had also supported a wife in Alabama and since being vicar general to the armies of Spain had earned a living as a cigar salesman. He didn't remain long in town.

William Vincent Harold, a friar who, a decade earlier, had been almost as popular in Philadelphia as Hogan was now, did remain long. Conwell, without checking into the background of this priest, who had played almost the same role against his predecessor as Hogan now played against him, invited Harold to return from Ireland. It was a move to divide and conquer but none too wise a move. Once upon the scene Harold used the old man as a front for his own ambitions. The battle thus shifted and became a contest between two vain and self-seeking clerics out to win, through democratic appeals, the most prestigious Catholic parish in the United States.

The 1822 election of St. Mary's trustees was prepared for with an intensity to befit a national convention. By election day the flurries of pamphlets, news articles and demonstrations had divided the parish into bitter camps of enmity: one behind Hogan, the other backing Harold. Lathered to intensities of conviction the parishioners arrived to cast ballots and ended up treating their fellow citizens to a full-scale brawl in front of their church. For three hours the two parties, or mobs, battled. While bricks and fists flew, the doddering bishop, flanked by a calmly observing Harold, stood trembling in fear, ready with oils and a pyx to attend any who were greviously wounded. Hogan stood at another distance, and according to one contemporary account, "with the delicate ladylike daughters of the rebel Catholics raised shouts of laughter that could be heard over the shrieks."[6]

At length the police arrived and the unruly believers scattered, a good number of them—including the delicate ladies— scaling the high churchyard walls to avoid arrest. In all, the damages amounted to a few broken railings, heads and windows, along with a further dishonor to the Catholic Church's reputation in Philadelphia—if indeed that was by this point possible.

The parish-sized schism bogged down into its third year while the trustees sought an assistant for Hogan. They hired a vagabond priest, Angelo Inglesi, who made his predecessor, Rico, look like St. Francis. In and out of the priesthood, Inglesi had been a mime performer, fought as a British private in the Napoleonic wars, picked up a wife, surfaced again as a priest in New Orleans and had been exposed as a fraud while on a money-raising European tour for the American missions.

Even Hogan was losing favor with the trustees. He was twice brought into court, once on charges of bastardy and again on a charge that he had offered indignities to some female members of the congregation. Both times he was acquitted, but he was no longer Philadelphia's fair-haired priest. Just about everyone at St. Mary's was tiring of him when he suddenly disappeared from the city in November of 1823. This left the schismatic parishioners with only a drab, newly arrived assistant whom Hogan had hired from Ireland. Hogan finally returned in June of 1824 and fought to resume his position. He was rebuffed, however, and when he advertised his presence in the newspapers the trustees announced publicly that he was no longer in any way connected with St. Mary's. For another month he remained in Philadelphia. Making a decisive step, he began to preach in Protestant churches against the whole Catholic system. Then he departed for North Carolina. Within two weeks it was reported that he had married. The report was true. It was the first of two marriages, and both were to widows of property.

The Hogan phase of the Roman Catholic Church's education to democracy was dead. The basic arguments fought for by the opposing sides, however, were still alive and kicking.

4

TRANSFORMATION

The day laborer transformed into a student was being transformed into a cleric. While the seat of his home diocese was being disrupted by self-seeking men who fought over church buildings, the transformation of John Hughes remained under the direction of Bruté and Dubois whose vision of the Church was more clearly one of service to God and to man.

Dubois, like the Catholics of Philadelphia, was interested in buildings. With carefully drawn plans he organized his students into a task force and for a year with a hired crew they constructed a handsome three-story edifice. At last Mount St. Mary's was beginning to look like a civilized school. On the night of Pentecost Sunday in June of 1824, at the time when Philadelphians were going through their last scenes with William Hogan, a fire broke out in the almost-completed structure. The alarm was sounded and the students cleared out into the yards. One young man carrying two buckets of water, enough to quench the small fire, tripped and fell. It was a moment lost. The flames took over. This time not even John Hughes's talent for leadership could save the situation. It was work enough to save the surrounding log buildings. Gangs of students kept blankets drenched with water spread on the roofs. After a long night made bright by the conflagration, a gray dawn approached and there was time at last to stand and to look at the scorched stone shell of a building, and let reactions set in. Dubois, however heavy his heart may have been on this morning after Pentecost, turned to the students to give them what must have been the greatest lesson that life had taught him to teach. No one had been hurt and that was cause for rejoicing. Revolutions, exiles, fires, and buildings—they all meant little. What mattered was the fire of the Spirit that was in a man's heart. "The Lord gave and the Lord hath taken away," he quoted to them, "Blessed be the name of the Lord."[1] Then this indomitable man whose life had been measured by hard work and setbacks calmly pointed to another terrace: "I will place the new building here. I have all along felt that it was a mistake to build on the upper terrace."

Two weeks after this he took a pickax and marked out the foundations for the second building. It is a pity for the American Church of the 1820s that it was clerics such as Hogan and Harold who attracted the newspaper writers.

The disaster left Mount St. Mary's heavily in debt. Immediately Dubois, the other professors, and several of the older students including John Hughes, used the summer recess for begging tours. Old tuition debts were sought along with donations from any kind-hearted people who might be interested in what Dubois appealed for, the "Christian Education of future members of society."[2] Hughes was sent to scour the area around Hagerstown. It was discouraging work. Catholics were held in enough disrepute, as it was, but the papers of late had been filled with the farcical doings in Philadelphia. In one tavern when Hughes entered and asked for contributions a drinker began to ridicule the Catholic Church. He had picked on the wrong mendicant. The uncomfortable young beggar quickly shifted to his more comfortable stance as a figher and lambasted the man in kind. In a college speech class he may have been a bust, but with an antagonist in front of him he was in his proper element. A long, heated argument ensued, and as the barroom debate waxed on the Americans present began to respond to that which Young America always respected in a man: his ability to stand on his own and cut out room for himself. The hat was passed and the seminarian left the place with nearly all present having given him money.

He received encouragement from Dubois who wrote to tell

him that his younger sister (probably Ellen) who remained with the nuns over the summer was doing well. He sent her love and his own best regards to John's parents. Of two men from whom Hughes had received a rebuff when he approached them for apparently expected contributions Dubois wrote: "They are bigotted Presbyterians and no doubt far from wishing success to any Catholic."

These hoped-for contributions he could write off with a passing thought. But the Frenchman was a businessman as well. Of a debtor who refused to make back payments of tuition he gave Hughes directions to open a lawsuit, declaring that the man had broken his word too often to receive special consideration. "These good folks must imagine that I am made up of gold or that I am a great simpleton to put up with such usage."[3]

Dubois was a strange mixture of transcendent faith and hard-nosed common sense. Hughes's other mentor, Simon Bruté, was pure spirit by comparison. There is little to document Hughes's relationship with Bruté during the years at the college, but from his singular and lifelong devotion to the older man afterward it is certain that the relationship was deep and that Bruté was a model of the priesthood that Hughes would have liked to have followed. Any rebuff from Bruté was a blow. When Bruté reprimanded him for an unauthorized visit to his parents in Chambersburg while on school business in a nearby town, he included some frank observations on Hughes's character. Hughes in reply begged Bruté's forgiveness in a manner wholly unlike his correspondence with others. "I must lament that your remarks are too true," he pleaded. "I confess that my example is not such as might be expected from a person in my situation and that my younger brothers may have been scandalized in many instances by my presence as well as absence . . ."[4]

Bruté, it seemed from this and later correspondence written after Hughes's ordination, was one of the few persons, if not the only person, whom Hughes allowed beyond the tough exterior he presented to the world.

His relationship with Dubois, at least on Hughes's part,

never warmed up. The authoritarian "Little Corporal" could and did give the young man the same heavy-handed affection he meted out to Bruté and to all his charges, but John Hughes was not one to forget a past injustice or slight. He would always remember that his entry to Mount St. Mary's had been fought for, and that his eventual acceptance had been no favor from Dubois, but merely "a regular contract between us." The two men were of entirely differing and none too compatible temperaments. John Dubois, so fully paternal, could crawl on his knees with the youngest of the boys to play marbles, haggling over whether a shot was cheated or not. With the ring of the school bell he could immediately become the disciplinarian, assume a stern expression and order the students to class. John Hughes, so separated from his peers by age and background, became more and more inflexible after he donned a theologian's cassock. A portrait captured by a younger student could serve as a description of him at almost any time of his life. ". . . To me he appeared of rather a taciturn disposition, for when he was seated on the benches that margined the first terrace, under the tall poplar trees, I noticed that the occasional visit he had from knots of students, though attended with courtesy and even cordiality, was never long; in fact he appeared to be intimate with one or two seminarians only who occasioned him on his walks. His usual exercise was to pace up and down the garden walks, probably meditating upon the work which was to be assigned him in the future."[5]

Dubois appointed Hughes head prefect of the college, in which role he was to take care of the school's discipline. In the nineteenth century physical chastisement was considered part and parcel of teaching. Just how accepted it was is measured by a polite letter written to the Mount by a father whose son had received what he considered too severe a beating. He notes that he has no objection to a proper flogging but he does feel that "beating a boy about the face with fists is very improper."[6] Hughes, it would seem, was "very improper" during his short stay in office. Dubois relieved him of command after only a few days and one beating. He was too severe for even the stern Frenchman's tastes.

If Hughes needed a fight in order to function well, he would soon have his fill of it. Ordained a deacon in 1825, his time would henceforth be divided between Mount St. Mary's and Philadelphia. There he would become a last-scene actor in the drama that divided the bishop and the Hogan-Harold Catholics of that city.

5

A CLERIC WITH
ONE MEMORIZED
SERMON

With or without William Hogan, the Catholics of Philadelphia were still very much opposed in principle to the powers that the Church accorded any bishop, let alone the cantankerous Bishop Conwell. "The trustees can never admit of Saint Mary's Church being called your cathedral," they informed him. "It was founded upwards of twenty years prior to the appointment of any bishop in this country. The act of incorporation speaks of pastors not bishops. . ."

They brought up an interesting point. The Church in Europe, they argued, had long allowed the sovereigns of nations, as laymen, to appoint pastors and bishops. In the United States it was the whole people who were sovereign. They only asked this same right—the "exclusive right" to appoint pastors. If they gave in on this matter or principle, they told Conwell, "the trusteeship would become a mere nullity." He was, they felt, asking them ". . . in short, to support your unlimited authority."[1]

For almost a year after Hogan's departure, they carried on, dragging behind them as their leader Father Thaddeus O'Meally, who as a preacher was so drab a successor to Hogan he might well have seemed a pallid representative of orthodoxy rather than a threatening schismatic. In droves the partisans of St. Mary's stopped coming to hear him preach. The few who remained week after week at last got rid of him by sending him, in April of 1825, to Rome to plead their cause before the Pope. Thereafter, even without a priest they kept the church open. An observer noted: "Since Mr. O'Meally's departure there are none who attend them but the sexton who appears to be prime minister . . . some of the trustees with a few others, who spend some time in conversation, and then close the doors and retire."[2]

With their backs to the wall the trustees approached Conwell, hat half in hand, and told him that they would be willing to accept Father Harold and "a gentleman unconnected with the present controversy, as pastors of this Church."[3] It was a momentary thaw, and had the bishop been of a sunny disposition he might have warmed them into accord. Instead he triumphantly held that a victory had been won and refused them altogether.

Because of his methods the aged bishop was losing the affection of his friends as well. He was arbitrary and secretive in his dealings with the priests of the diocese, often denying them information they needed to carry on their duties effectively. The new deacon, John Hughes, who arrived in the city shortly after O'Meally left, seemed surprised to find that "those who hate the bishop," were "nearly all Philadelphia."[4] Hughes, who was to divide his last year before ordination between Mount St. Mary's and Philadelphia, was adopted for the time being by Father Michael Hurley, an Augustinian who had already served in the city for over a generation. Hurley took a strong liking to the young Irishman, helped him to straighten out his naturalization as an American citizen, took to clucking about his health and educated him to the difference between a real "knowledge of the world" and the "farfetched cases of conscience" that made up the bulk of seminary studies. ("Pay no more attention than what may be necessary in the exercise of the class, as you would hereafter find them to be useless.") He also had a few tips about preaching sermons, advising Hughes that he should write and keep a stock supply six months in advance, and that he should keep these brief (". . . half an hour or thereabouts will be sufficient").[5]

Possibly because he was still traveling regularly between Pennsylvania and Maryland, and because a six-month supply of sermons as brief as Hurley had directed would have filled a good-sized trunk, Hughes had only got around to writing one. At least that is all he had prepared when the unpredictable old bishop chanced upon Hughes in Chambersburg and abruptly decided that his deacon should accompany him in a diocesan visitation. Happy to relieve himself of duties, and without advance warning, he pushed Hughes into the pulpit at their first stop. The young man preached, and well enough. When they stopped at a second town and Conwell called upon his deacon again, the nervous young man gave the same sermon, word for word. And again at a third stop, and so in every town and hamlet they went through. By the time they returned to Philadelphia, Conwell was referring to the talk as Hughes's "cuckoo sermon." If there was any gift for oratory within this new cleric who dared not go beyond mouthing one memorized piece, it was not born yet. Even so, Conwell began to wax enthusiastically about this attractive immigrant deacon. He and Hughes hailed from neighboring counties in Ireland. The elderly cleric might have mused that had Hughes not emigrated and had he himself properly received the bishopric where he had served faithfully as vicar general for twenty-three years, the two might have met under similar, yet more normal circumstances. Besides, in a diocese filled with so many vain vagabond priests out to make their own fortunes, Hughes exhibited a trait that would always remain constant: a loyalty to the Church's proper chain of command. This young man was the bishop's young man, one of the few in sight who belonged totally to the Church. "Ah, Hughes is the boy, isn't he?" he exclaimed after he had watched his deacon for a while. "He takes all the wind out of our sails. We'll make him a bishop some day."[6]

But Hughes, it seems, was a little frightened by the ugly turmoil in the diocese. While in Philadelphia he lived with Father Hurley at St. Augustine's. The community of the Mount had made a stronger impression upon his loner's nature than he would have cared to admit. Comparing that peaceful community to the rough-and-tumble politics of the diocesan priesthood, he projected upon religious life what he had known at Mount St. Mary's. Quietly he began to make inquiries about joining the Augustinians. His "mysterious course" in doing so worried one friend at the Mount, who advised him to consult his bishop, and to discover how the Augustinians would use him when he entered the order.[7] Whoever did advise him, the idea was quietly dropped. In the fall of 1826 he was back at the Mount to finish his studies for the diocese of Philadelphia.

In the first week of October he left Emmitsburg behind him forever. He departed to become a priest, traveling, so he wrote, "in good company, with the bishop of New York in the stage and three dollars and a half in my pocket." The new bishop of New York was John Dubois. If earthly happiness is important, it is sad that whoever had advised John Hughes to turn down the Augustinians had not advised Dubois to turn down the bishopric and remain at his college. Mount St. Mary's had been his most noble achievement. It was a realm in which he had been deservedly happy. In New York a purgatory of other men's making awaited him.*

The subsequent relationship of the two men makes it ironic that John Dubois wrote to Hughes to congratulate him on his ordination, addressing him as "my ever dear child and Reverend friend," and hoping that "we may reunite one day where we can no more be separated."[9]

---

*A gossip-filled letter written by an Irish priest named Savage, of the New York diocese city of Albany, indicated what sort of purgatory this would be: ". . . We have for a bishop a Frenchman who, I think would be if he dare, a restless little despot, a man with very little learning and less brains has been appointed at the instance of the French party for the most prominent and most respectable see in America, New York. This party for years back has been endeavoring to blacken and misrepresent the character of the Irish clergy to the court of Rome, and they have so far succeeded in their villainous designs that no appointments are now made unless such as emanate from that quarter. In fact the object is to get the whole of this continent into their hands. . . . However, if the Irish be faithful to each other there is no fear. . ."[8]

6

"WHEN TO ME
EVERYTHING WAS NEW"

The first few months of a man's priesthood involve a necessary reeducation about his relationships with others. This is not because he himself has changed but because most other men refuse to treat him any longer as an ordinary human being. Whatever they love or hate about the priesthood in general they project upon the character of the individual priest. Later, Hughes would refer to this period of his life as a time "when to me every thing was new."[1] During his own process of reeducation, suffered in the midst of Philadelphia's fighting Catholics where he had to watch the Church being destroyed not from without but within, he wrote: "I believe no man has ever been found in the beginning of his ministry in such a trying, such a critical, or such a difficult situation . . ."[2]

The week before Hughes was ordained the trustees of St. Mary's had met with Bishop Conwell to effect a formal end to the Hoganite schism. The agreement produced at the meeting amounted to an abdication of spiritual powers on the part of Conwell, and was labeled as "the fatal articles of Peace" by a disgusted Simon Bruté who predicted that "sooner or later, evil would again come out of them."[3]

If the future brought a clash between the bishop and trustees the document provided that: "He, the bishop, shall appoint with himself any two Catholic clergymen not connected with the church of St. Mary's who shall meet a committee of three lawfully appointed by the Board of Trustees. . . . A major-

43

ity of votes on either side shall be respected by the Bishop . . ."
If a tie ensued a fourth person was to be chosen by lots, "whose
vote shall determine the bishop."

As if this contract, signed by the bishop, was not clear
enough, the trustees annexed to it a declaration that was also
accepted by the bishop: ". . . for the sake of peace the Trustees have consented that Dr. Conwell should from this date be a
pastor, but this act done under peculiar circumstances, they
declare, is not to be considered as forming a precedent."[4]

By agreement of both parties William Vincent Harold was
named pastor of St. Mary's, and all involved settled down to
enjoy a supposed future of tranquillity. In the ensuing wave of
Christian harmony, both factions joined to flood Philadelphia
with the good will of a society called: "The Vindicators of the
Catholic Religion from Calumny and Abuse"—presumably
now calumny and abuse that came from outside the Church.
Among the 180 men who signed as members of the society was
the newly ordained Father John Hughes, inconspicuous in the
long list of the city's Catholic notables. He was then living with
Bishop Conwell at St. Joseph's chapel which, though a stone's
throw from St. Mary's, the bishop had raised to the status of a
separate parish and claimed as his own permanent residence.[5]

The young man had every intention of remaining inconspicuous in the confusing situation in which he found himself,
and Bruté wrote firm advice that he keep far away from the entire controversy. This advice was seconded by Father Michael
Egan who had succeeded Dubois as president of the Mount.
Egan also warned Hughes to "keep on the best and most
friendly terms with Mr. Harold, and convince him that you
never meddle or intrigue in any way." His reasoning for this
was clear. Heads were bound to roll when higher authorities
discovered the pact of peace. Egan feared that Conwell, and
possibly others like Hughes who might be drawn involuntarily
to the prelate's side, would suffer. He warned: "There is a
storm, I am afraid, gathering in the Vatican which will burst
on the good old bishop."[6]

The "good old bishop," either from remorse over the articles or from a growing sense of paranoia as to who was friend

or foe, continued to alienate those who were his strongest upholders. He became ever more unpredictable and could not be counted on to acknowledge his own actions. Resentful of Harold, who might fairly be called a foe, he lashed out against him. In December of 1826 he deprived him of his vicar general-ship, claiming that it was "in consequence of your insulting language and behavior to me on several occasions."[7] The bat-tling began all over again. "I demand at your hands some spe-cific charge . . ." Harold shot back, refusing to relinquish his office, "I am unconscious of any word or act of mine, even of intention, to insult you."[8]

In April the bishop determined to get rid of Harold and called together the priests of the city. He asked them to sign a paper denouncing Harold's behavior as being arrogant and domineering. They all signed it except Hughes. Uncertain of himself, feeling bound to obey the sound advice of Bruté that he keep away from the issue, he begged to abstain on the grounds that he was new in the city and had nothing to do with the matter. On the next Sunday Hughes was again commanded by the bishop to attend a clergy meeting where a milder state-ment of the case was presented for signing. This time the clergy were asked to agree that, owing to the reprehensible conduct of Harold, the bishop would not be acting "improperly or un-canonically" if he were to refuse Harold his faculties. From a strictly ecclessial point of view the bishop would have been within his rights in suspending a priest whether there was cause or not. It was not a matter of due process of law. Hughes, how-ever, even with the acquiescence of all of his more experienced peers, still stood firm and refused his signature. At length he was assured that the paper would never leave Conwell's desk unless it was necessary to send it to the proper superiors. He gave in and signed.

Word began to leak out of the meeting. A layman, Joseph Snyder, who had been sympathetic to the bishop all along, vis-ited Conwell with several men of the same mind. Together they asked him not to publish the paper that rumor claimed had been drawn up. The bishop not only denied knowledge of any such document, he expressed anger that any of his priests might have been involved in having written it at all. Within a day after this the paper was in the public eye, and the bishop formally suspended Harold.

Harold at this point played his game differently than had Hogan. Rather than push for a separate "American" Church he avoided talk of schism and accepted his suspension. There was a bigger prize that could be won by staying within the Roman system. Conwell's foolish articles of peace had been sent to Rome for approval. Then the bishop had broken his own agreement and attacked the trustees who in turn complained of this to the Congregation of Propaganda, the Vatican office that guided American church affairs. There was always the chance that Rome would conclude that the obstinate octogenarian was the source of most of the trouble, transfer him back to Europe, and—owing to Harold's undeniable ability and popularity—make him bishop in the hope of achieving the long-sought peace. For the present Harold reacted to the supposed damage done to his public image by the priests of Philadelphia. As if to make an example with one case he picked the least experienced and thus most vulnerable of the signers, one who had not yet built up any public following from which he would draw sympathy. He sued John Hughes for defamation of character.

Harold achieved his desired effect. A graduate of the Mount from Philadelphia, writing to Egan, decried the lost state of tranquillity, the "impolitic act" of suspending "one of the most popular of our confessors," and sadly related: "One week ago, dear sir, how different would have been the story. . . . I could have told you of the growing popularity of Reverend Mr. Hughes, a popularity most richly deserved. But Alas! I must now reverse the picture. I must tell you of the people, almost distracted by their violent passions, crying out for the restoration of Mr. Harold. I must tell you that, blinded by their passions they condemn Mr. Hughes as an enemy to Mr. Harold because it is said that the bishop has put him in the pastorate of St. Mary's in place of Mr. Harold."[9]

With advice to stay where he was coming from his mentors at the Mount, Hughes staved off Conwell's wish that he take over St. Mary's until obedience demanded it. Only then did he move around the corner with a Father O'Reilly as his assistant to become with half a year's experience in the priesthood the pastor of the warring parish. The trustees did not welcome the two priests with open arms. Tolerating their presence for the sake of having someone say Mass, they declared that because neither Hughes nor O'Reilly had been properly hired, the church was under no obligation to pay them any salary.

Hughes put up a brave front. He performed his duties; he preached—subtly taking the congregation over coals with a sermon on "pride and the abuse of human knowledge" ("M. Carey's spectacles were not idle," he noted).[10] He steadfastly refused to discuss any of the ongoing nonsense with laymen. Observing to Bruté that although popularity was "a greater temptation than money," and that "public opinion is against us here," he angrily decided: "But public opinion is credulous; it concludes according to its premises and when it is ill informed its conclusions are rash and oftentimes wrong. . . . It is an idiot—because it has no memory and of course cannot learn wisdom by experience."[11]

Hughes also tried to show an optimistic face about the lawsuit in the civil courts. It was, he wrote to Egan, "all nonsense, because the question will amount to this: whether a Roman Catholic bishop has the right to ask the opinions of his clergy on any measure of an ecclesiastical character. If he had not then the free exercise of religion is no longer tolerated."[12]

But privately there was one man upon whose shoulder he dared to cry. To Bruté, whom he loved, he opened his "almost breaking" heart: "I have been sent to St. Mary's on last Sunday for the first time after having held out against it until the only alternative I had was to obey or else leave the diocese, which I would gladly do if I thought such a step at this moment would not prove injurious to religion here. . . . That paper to which I put my hand against both my head and heart, originated in darkness, and I am sorry to say, ended in treachery. . . . It is hard to do good by preaching, especially when you have to contend with the passions of the audience. . . . I have no spite against anyone, but I have been sorely injured in this business."[13]

It was both a debasing and disheartening experience. In

such circumstances a shallow man might have responded by joining those about him who used the Church as though it were just a game of human politics. A weak man might have become sour and let bitterness affect his religious faith. But Hughes was neither weak nor a man ready to use the Church for his own purposes. Bruté was nearby, and from this man's simple, great heart came counsel. For all of his brilliance Bruté had never become comfortable in English, and when he wished to speak from within his soul he always turned to his native language. He wrote to Hughes in French: "My good friend, God is all in all for a good priest. He serves him with joy and fidelity through infamy and good fame. . . . If [God] permits that he be humbled he can only profit by it personally in merit; penitence for sins; resemblance and union with Jesus Christ." If ugliness in the supposed believers surrounding him was cause enough for breaking Hughes's heart, then, suggested Bruté, rely simply upon work, and above all the Mass for "your true peace, your true happiness. . ."[14]

The intrusion of God into that godless struggle seemed almost out of place, but it was just the advice that helped the young priest to put the whole mess into proper perspective. He had been put into an unwanted role of authority as pastor. Now, gaining a sense of confidence, his natural talents were beginning to show. His awkward homiletic experiences as a deacon were never to be repeated. He gave promise of becoming a powerful preacher. The people in St. Mary's took a second look at him. Lean, attractive and intelligent, this was not a clergyman of whom they would have to be ashamed if they lost the pending judgment from across the Atlantic.

As Hughes's popularity grew, Harold began to back away from his lawsuit, eventually dropping it. If his hopes worked rightly and Harold won the bishopric Hughes might be a power to contend with. Why put himself into the same position with Hughes as Conwell had been in with him and his own followers? The trustees still held out against paying the pastoral salary. After all this was at the very base of their argument with the bishop. Were they to pay Hughes and his assistant O'Reilly they would be admitting the bishop's right to appoint priests over their heads. But for the present, they had a presentable clergyman as pastor, and they were content to wait for a ruling on the principle at stake.

Hughes, however, refused to wait. Taking hold of the reins of leadership, he suddenly twisted the situation into an unexpected route. The prestigious parish of St. Mary's, so prominent in wealth and heritage, had been a prize sought after by every clergyman the parishioners had dealt with as far back as any of them could remember. The fighting had always involved a question as to who was worthy of them. On June 17th Hughes startled them from the pulpit by announcing that as they were people who didn't live up to their obligations he was not interested in being their pastor. His resignation was immediate. He was returning to St. Joseph's and removing his assistant with him.

St. Mary's had no priests. Harold was caught off guard. He was playing the game of orthodoxy for the sake of that prized miter. He couldn't move in without destroying the posture he wanted the hierarchy to see. Bishop Conwell, with a glowing charity that poured coals upon the heads of his adversaries, volunteered to say a single Mass for them each Sunday morning at nine.

It was a coup for which Hughes was singlehandedly responsible, winning for him the deepening affection of the old man (who soon afterward began continually recommending to Rome that Hughes be made a bishop) and the wary respect of the public, who learned that this was a man far above the calibre of the clerical pygmies they thought were representative of the priesthood.

In the summer of 1827 the storm that Egan had predicted thundered back across the Atlantic. The Congregation of Propaganda condemned the agreement between the bishop and the trustees as being "calculated to overthrow the episcopal power"[15] and Conwell, to Harold's possible advantage, was invited to make a trip to Rome, compliments of the Pope. It seems the condemnation caught the trustees by surprise, for their principal champion, John Leamy, the treasurer, immediately resigned to show his disgust. John Hughes was jubilant.

To a friend he wrote: "Their condemnation was promulgated yesterday in all the Catholic Churches in this city—to the inexpressible joy of your humble servant. You see by this that the Court of Rome is determined that the bishop shall be bishop, in spite of him."[16]

If the Vatican decision bolstered the episcopal authority, it made Conwell no less vacillating. He avoided the summons to Rome, complaining that the heat of summer made it a bad time to travel. In October, as if to cover up any tracks of the scandal having happened, he reinstated Harold to St. Mary's along with his constant underling, John Ryan.

In the spring of 1828, a sharper summons from Cardinal Cappellari at the Congregation of Propaganda arrived for Conwell. The administration of the diocese was taken away from the bishop and given to Father William Matthews of Washington. Conwell was told to leave for Rome immediately. Harold and Ryan, at the center of all the trouble, were politely informed: "It will be most agreeable to the sacred Congregation to be advised of your speedy departure from Philadelphia towards Cincinnati. . ."[17]

The command, as if to allow no possible loopholes, was signed by the superior general of their religious order as well as Cappellari. Hughes, who had been so jubilant over the defeat of the principles for which the whole battle had been fought, felt no joy over the public degradation of the warriors involved, even though each one of them had hurt him publicly and deeply. "I feel pity for each. . ." he told Bruté. "They have all preached obedience to lawful authority, but now it is in their power to preach effectively by the practice of their own doctrine. I trust they will. I feel dejected. I was perhaps heretofore hasty and unmerciful in my judgments; but now, and since I heard this news, their faults seem to have escaped my memory, and I am almost tempted to ask (as if I had a right to do so), why are they overtaken by this humiliation? I speak as if you saw my heart. . ."[18]

By early summer the discredited old prelate set sail for Europe. Harold and Ryan, however, continued to bide their time, forestalling their exit from Philadelphia. The "obedience to lawful authority" that they had depended upon had not played out to their advantage. Thus they shifted ground and appealed, as Hogan had previously, to their democratic constituency. Harold wrote to Cardinal Cappellari to explain why they felt bound to do so. Referring to Rome's orders as a "sentence of removal which no foreign prince is allowed to pass on an American citizen," he reasoned: ". . . We could not obey without violating the loyalty we have sworn to the Republic. The most learned lawyers thought that the matter should be referred to the President. . ."[19]

And so it was. On July 2nd, 1828 Harold wrote to Secretary of State Henry Clay and as a citizen asked the government to protect his civil rights against the pretensions of the court of Rome. For once his ever-present shadow could not act with him. Ryan had never become a citizen. Hurriedly he applied for naturalization papers, and as soon as he had done so he dashed off his own plea for sanctuary from within the temple of American liberty.

The result was a furor. There was sympathy for them (beginning with President John Quincy Adams, no admirer of the Romish Church), and against them from men such as Hughes. "Hogan talked about it," he wrote, disgustedly, "but they have done it."[20]

In fact what they had done reduced Hogan's escapades to the level of a side show. Here was the danger of a legal precedent. If the man in the White House believed the Catholic Church was a threat to human liberties, then it wouldn't be difficult to deny the Church jurisdiction within its own proper realm. Hogan had been a vain china doll, hoping to cut out for himself a world the size of a wealthy parish. Failing in this, he had quickly enough became a Protestant and fought against the whole Catholic system. Harold and Ryan, claiming faithfulness to that system, would have held it up to public scorn to satisfy their ambitions within it. Hughes labeled them "diabolical."[21]

The United States acted. There was no American representative at the Court of Rome, since the latter was a universal religious as well as a third-rate civil power. So President

Adams sent directions to the minister to France, James Brown, and instructed him to raise the issue with the papal nuncio in Paris, Monsignor Luigi Lambruschini.

Their meeting in September of 1828 lay in strange new diplomatic territory for the young Republic. Even the names of the two men seemed symbolic of what was involved. The United States, envisioning itself open, free and guileless, sat down with a complicated power whose intrigues in European history represented dark villainy in American folklore.

Brown informed Lambruschini that the government had no desire to interfere in the spiritual relationships of Catholics. It had a duty, however, to protect the temporal interests of these citizens. It was understood in Washington that the two friars involved had been ordered to leave Philadelphia and were to be sent to Ohio where, so they had informed their government, "they would be subjected to grave penances and corporal afflictions." Lambruschini assured Brown that the order involved a simple transfer of ministry and that no evil treatment awaited them in Cincinnati.*[22]

The American ambassador, apparently dubious, continued to argue on behalf of the two priests. President Adams, he said, being a man of letters, had a personal liking for Harold because of his education in literature. What was more, both Harold and Ryan had done a great deal of good among the Protestants of Philadelphia and as highly esteemed as these men were the bishop was generally "hated and despised." Their removal could only cause harm.

The nuncio responded to these character portrayals by pointing out that the bishop had at least shown a marked spirit of humility by journeying to Rome whereas Harold and Ryan had ignored their freely taken vows of obedience. He then moved to the center of the issue. The Church held no civil power over these men. Their vows were voluntary and if they

---

*Official Rome, at that time, was still foggy in its knowledge of American geography. Lambruschini, relating the conversation to Cardinal Cappellari, felt it necessary to again remind the Cardinal (who had, after all, sent the original orders to Harold and Ryan) that Cincinnati was within the limits of the U.S.

wished to leave these vows all that they had to do was walk away from them as had Hogan. If, however, they wished to remain within the Church's structure then they had to obey. It was the same as if they were working for any other employer in the United States; if they didn't care for the way the shop was set up they were always free to quit and move on.[23]

After these interviews Brown related his information to the State Department. Henry Clay received letters as well from the archbishop of Baltimore and from Father Matthews, explaining the Church's position as Lambruschini had. Clay decided that the issue lay fully within the realm of the spiritual rather than civil, and in November forwarded his decision to the friars, enclosing Brown's report from Paris. The further appeals of the two were ignored and the affair was ended as far as the United States government was concerned.

Harold and Ryan still refused to give up. Steeped in the wiles of canonical procedure they found loopholes to forestall their departure while vainly soliciting support from clerics on both sides of the Atlantic, all to no avail. The hierarchy kept silent for a year while the two ranted in Philadelphia. To say anything publicly could have endangered the precedent newly established in Washington. At length the two friars reached a dead end. They couldn't for very long claim loyalty to a Church that refused to speak to them. They had to be either obedient or follow Hogan. Ryan gave in first, leaving not for Cincinnati but Ireland. Finally Harold followed, for once taking the shadow role that Ryan usually played. They both remained thereafter comfortably within the bosom of the Church and spent the remainder of their lives taking potshots at the state of Catholicity in the United States. Writing to Father Thomas Levins in New York a year after his departure Harold warned (prophetically, as it turned out, for the man he wrote to) ". . . the priest who leaves Ireland for that country has to look forward to nothing better than a life of trouble and a desolate death bed." Adding, as a note of encouragement, "I shall try to get you some Irish newspapers."[24]

In Philadelphia a Catholic community demoralized by years of scandal and fighting was still adrift without leadership and without much to be encouraged about for the future. "We remain in the usual way in this city of long standing confusion," wrote Hughes. "We are enjoying the quietude of suspense. How it will terminate, God alone can tell."[25]

7
"A STUPENDOUS TISSUE OF IMPOSITION AND MENDACITY"

When John Hughes was sent to St. Mary's only months after his ordination, an observer added to the complaints against him the question of age. Older people, the observer noted, "feel a repugnance to going to young priests."[1] It was a remark that could have been made in almost any age of the Church's history. A new clergyman, like a new doctor, must prove himself by performance. Hughes took it lightly enough: "They call us boys now and then; but time will gradually wear away this objection," he countered. Then, pointing to the other extreme of their constant complaints, he added happily, "Besides, if it be age they want the bishop is old enough for them."[2]

It is no easy task to measure the success of a man when he deals with the human spirit. But it would seem from the judgment of contemporaries that Hughes was a good parish priest. Bruté, quick to scold him even after ordination, was proud of his work. The priests of the diocese who took to him, who acknowledged him as a kindred spirit—Michael Hurley, Thomas Heyden, Terence Donoghoe—were men whom history acknowledges as being dedicated priests.

Returned to St. Joseph's, Hughes approached his pastoral duties with a rigorous energy. As his reputation for preaching grew so did the numbers of people who came to him for help. He generally had a steady stream of converts under instruction. He would write with satisfaction to Bruté that he and Donoghoe had spent up to seven hours a day in the confessional in preparation for Holy Week, and that the number of those receiving the Eucharist was greatly increasing. He helped in founding an orphanage to take care of destitute Irish waifs and brought the Sisters of Charity from Emmitsburg to help in this work. "I am so incessantly occupied in the affairs of others," he worried in the first flush of his ministry, "that I am discouraged at having so little time to attend to my own."[3]

It was not his busy parish work, however, that was to give him fame or launch him into the hierarchy. It was his jousting in the fields of polemics. From the first time he flexed his oratorical muscles in a barroom argument, this sort of defense of faith was where he felt most himself. If his contemporary Catholics were so stupid as to be destroying themselves from within, he was more concerned with the foe outside the gates.

He had gotten into the habit, while a student, of returning Protestant attacks on Catholicism by dashing letters off to newspapers. In answer to a tract entitled *Protestantism and Popery* he had written a fifty-seven-page pamphlet and had it published under the authorship of "a clergyman of Chambersburg, Franklin County, Pennsylvania."[4] In 1828, his first year in Philadelphia, while living amidst the flying brickbats at St. Mary's, he had encountered a fictional piece with the catchy title: *An Apology for Bible Societies; or, A dialogue between Andrew Dunn and Father Dominick, A Catholic Priest, illustrating the Beneficial Influence of Disseminating the Holy Scriptures in the Vulgar Tongue.* The pamphlet told, in vulgar tongue, the tale of an Irish lad who comes to his local pastor with doubts about his faith. He gets a horsewhipping for having bothered the good man. Understandably smarting from this reception he manages somehow to get a look at a bible, and being thus transformed is able intellectually to trounce the bully of a priest. He ends up a Protestant, happily ever after.

It was badly written—its pious story spilled across the top of each page with explanatory doctrine on the bottom as footnotes—but it was nonetheless popular. Hughes, to counter its effect, turned the plot upside down and rewrote it, apparently to prove that Catholics could write fiction in just as vulgar a tongue. In his version Andrew is a poor Protestant but "a good liver" with "a great horror for cursing, swearing, drunkenness and all such vices." He is unhappy with his faith. His friends notice him going about with his eyes "bathed in tears" and make bold to wonder why ("Oh! Andrew," said they, "excuse our boldness; do tell us the cause of these melancholy looks . . ."). Andrew seeks solace by praying with a Catholic neighbor who is "a very good liver" and who has a talent for citing scriptural references in the middle of his prayers ("Oh Lord . . . who has said, Mark XVI: 16, 'he that believeth not shall be damned'. . ."). This neighbor educates Andrew with all sorts of vital information about the Roman Church including several accounts of faithless priests who had turned their backs on God by becoming Protestant and had all "dropped down dead in the streets." It takes a day or so of such solid reasoning and then Andrew professes himself a Catholic, eventually to die a good and holy death.[5]

Hughes was enthusiastic about his novelette and sent five dollars' worth of booklets to Bruté "at first cost," suggesting that they could be sold at twelve and a half cents apiece. He wanted the book to be carefully disseminated though. "I do not wish the thing to make any noise," he advised, "because the Protestants will take the alarm."[6]

He needn't have worried. No alarm was sounded. For weeks after the book's arrival Simon hedged at returning a critical comment, lamely offering that he just hadn't found time to get all the way through the thing. Months later Bruté was still at a loss as to how he could unload his supply.

This was Hughes's last attempt at fiction.

Hughes had not yet developed the fierce devotion to the United States that he would have in his later years. He still felt, as did many of the emigrated Irish, that he had been forced into an "exile." Protestant England had forced the banishment of people like himself "who were constrained to leave their country because—they loved their country too much." They had become "cast on every distant shore; there, like uprooted plants, to perish unless fostered by the hand of foreign kindness." He admitted to looking back with a "luxury of mingled feelings" to the home of his childhood.[7]

In the spring of 1829 came word that the long campaign of men such as Daniel O'Connell had won a success. England's Parliament had passed the Catholic Emancipation Act, ameliorating some aspects of their tight hold on Ireland. On May 31st a solemn Mass of thanksgiving was celebrated at St. Augustine's where Hughes preached to a packed church. It was a good homily, his first to be published. He took his listeners through a concise and unembellished history of Ireland, described England's domination of the "Island of Saints" and that island's ultimate oppression when the conquering enemies "took their march through all Ireland, bearing liberty in one hand and degradation on the other." The price of such liberty would have been her acceptance of the Protestant religion, "but she saw no reason to believe in its veracity and to profess it would have been hypocrisy." Rather, in the face of persecution which lasted for centuries she chose to hold to her ancient faith as "the anchor of her best and last hope."[8] Hughes placed the blame for Ireland's suffering at another level than mere religious or political bigotry. Instead it lay in a tendency planted deep within the nature of the human animal—the lust for "irresponsible power." Moreover he declared that England was not the only country upon whom such blame could be laid. Holding up a mirror for a young chauvinistic America to see itself he warned: ". . . Pursue [this passion of power] across the ocean to the shores of Africa, and there you will detect it, putting manacles by the same right, on hands that were free."[9]

Some Americans were unhappy to hear of Ireland's emancipation. Philadelphia's Episcopal *Church Register* decried the new freedoms allowed to a "superstitious and corrupt Church." Darkly predicting that a sickly lion was still a lion and capable of regaining "wonted ferocity" it noted: "We shall be sorry for this measure if the revival and dissemination of the trumperies and delusions of Popery are to be the result of it."[10]

Hughes immediately protested against the article, and when the *Church Register's* editor, Reverend W. H. Delaney (later Episcopal bishop in western New York), tried to brush off his objections, Hughes attacked him in several letters to the *United States Gazette*. The letters were in one respect a demarcation in his career. For the first time he felt obliged to change the custom of the anonymous pseudonym and stamped his letters openly with a name that was beginning to be known as standing for something—his own.

During the months that Bishop Conwell was in Rome Hughes felt a strong sympathy for him because of his "constancy and sufferings."[11] He was by no means blind to the foolish old man's defects. He informed his friends at the Mount that the bishop had written twice but had said nothing about the state of the diocese. ("If he knew anything he appears to have studied how he might fill up his paper without saying it.") What he did fill the paper with was news that he had visited the Pope along with 130 other bishops and cardinals "with and without beards." "And," notes Hughes, "he adds in his own way that he was 'as well dressed as any of them.' "[12]

Conscious of the need for a proper chain of command, Hughes worried about the public effects of the bishop's recall while Harold and Ryan had lingered on, apparently triumphant in the eyes of their friends. He wrote to Conwell in January of 1829 before the departure of Harold and Ryan, urging the bishop to return as soon as possible. If the precedent of the American government becoming involved in the business of the Church could be "fatal to religion in this country," he said, the weakening of ecclesiastical authority by the punishment of a bishop would also be an example "which the restless spirit of republicanism so prevalent in this country will appeal to in all future similar occasions."

"The excess of liberty," he noted, "calls all proper authority despotic."[13]

It had been a long time since the proper Catholic authorities in the United States had made any effort to meet and discuss problems—almost two decades. The need of such a council gave rise to a long, bitter argument between the reluctant Archbishop Marechal of Baltimore and Bishop John England. In exasperation England wrote to the archbishop: "You will excuse me for giving the opinion that the Philadelphia case is one which alone would be sufficient to command our attention in a canonical way."[14]

Only when Marechal died and Archbishop Whitfield took his place was the first Provincial Council of Baltimore called. It sounded more impressive than it appeared. There was no ecclesiastical pomp. The council amounted to the gathering of seven missionaries in the house of the archbishop in Baltimore. They were assisted by a number of priests. John Power represented Bishop Dubois of New York. Francis Kenrick attended with the bishop of Bardstown. And John Hughes arrived in the company of Father Matthews who, in turn, stood in place for Conwell.

One of the main problems at hand was, of course, what to suggest to Rome about Bishop Conwell's diocese. Before anything had been decided about this matter, however, the members of the council were stunned and dismayed by a surprise visitor—Bishop Conwell himself.

He had disappeared from view and abruptly resurfaced twice in the previous half year. Rome had not quite known what to do with him. Cardinal Cappellari had set him up comfortably and dangled before him the possibility of retiring to a life of leisure almost anywhere he might choose—in Europe. But without warning he had bolted from the Eternal City in the middle of the night on Easter Sunday, April 19th, 1829. "Everywhere there were rumors," he insisted, "even in America and especially in Washington, that it had been decided to keep me here in Rome for my whole life." Besides, he had property to attend to in the United States, a land that, though he had not been born to it until he was in his seventies, was he felt "my country . . . of whose government I am a citizen."[15]

He turned up in Paris where Luigi Lambruschini did his ablest to detain him. A letter from Cappellari arrived chiding Conwell for disobedience, asking him to consider the harm that might happen to the American Church upon his return, promising him a larger allowance if he would stay. It had no effect. On the last day of August he disappeared again. "We do not know where he went," apologized an embarrassed Lambruschini, who had decided that the old man had "impaired reasoning."[16]

Conwell had set sail for America, and part of his reasoning, impaired or not, was, so he claimed, his spiritual obligations to his "best friend," President Andrew Jackson. There had been a friendly and sympathetic exchange of letters between the two as Jackson assumed office (the one having lost his wife; the other having lost his diocese) and now the bishop felt that "Old Hickory" was ripe for conversion to Catholicism along with his "children and relatives."[17]

A missive from Rome suspending the old bishop had heralded him long before the docking of his ship, and so the men gathered at Baltimore to solve the Church's problems were expecting his eventual arrival. But they didn't expect it then and there when he and his diocese were the primary problems to be solved. They were as irked with him as official Rome had been. He was not allowed to vote at the meetings and rather cruelly not allowed to say Mass. Eventually, however, their sympathies for him returned. He was well into his eighties. He would live, at most, a year or so more. Why not give him a coadjutor and let him end his days with dignity? The bishops wrote to Rome asking benevolence in his regard, noting that he had "suffered much for religion" (and ignoring that he had returned the compliment to religion, with interest). All considered, they begged, "his weak mind is to be blamed, not his ill will."[18]

Rome complied with their wish. Before he had bolted for the U.S. Conwell had insisted to Propaganda that he be returned along with a coadjutor and had given them a list of possible candidates: Gallitzin (Pennsylvania's aged Russian-prince missionary), Hurley, Heyden, Matthews or Hughes. Of this list all were seasoned veterans but Hughes, who was barely two years a priest. Because he was on the bishop's list he was officially considered when an auxiliary bishop was to be named, but only for the moment that it took to note that he was entirely unknown to Rome. Instead, the miter went to the man the Baltimore council had opted for: Francis Kenrick, the gentlemanly Irish scholar who was the head of a seminary at Bardstown, Kentucky. The measure of the worth of this young man (he was the same age as Hughes though he had been a priest since 1821) was that the nomination was singular—no other candidate's name was sent. The only dissent in the nomination was from Kenrick's own bishop who didn't want to lose him in Kentucky. Kenrick assumed his new office in June of 1830. When he arrived he found John Hughes in the midst of an ugly melee with clergymen, both Protestant and Catholic, from New York City.

Hughes had never confined the scope of his work to the size of a parish or even a city. He couldn't have even had he wished. There was always a missionary aspect of a priest's work in the 1820s. A number of parishes in Pennsylvania record John Hughes as being one of the first priests to serve their community. In one town, Manayunk, still raw with newness, Hughes laid the cornerstone of a Catholic church, and in an unusual display of ecumenism, for him as well as his hosts, he accepted the hospitality of the local Presbyterians and used their church building to say Mass.[19] He kept his finger in Mount St. Mary's business; while acting as a sort of agent for the school in Philadelphia he sent opinions as to the governing of the institution: "A regular and unbending discipline should be maintained among the professors as well as among the boys," he decided. "I make this observation because on my visit last year it appeared to me that things had very much retrograded from the time I was there."[20]

His reputation as a preacher was growing steadily. In December of 1829 he was invited to New York to preach a charity sermon in St. Peter's on Barclay Street. There was a new weekly newspaper floating about the streets to greet his arrival in the city. It was called the *Protestant,* soon to be subtitled: *Expositor of Popery.* It had been launched shortly after the British had passed the Emancipation Act, and the winds that filled the paper's sails blew from seventy-three local ministers determined to awaken the American Zion to the dangers of a resurgent Babylon. The number and diversity of ministers in-

volved caused the editors to claim that it was the first nonsectarian religious paper in the country. In one sense it was. If no
Catholics were involved in the writing of the paper, they were
more than included in its content. In issue after issue every
story that appeared from front to back was a denunciation of
popery and a vindication of the Reformation. Most editions
carried woodcuts depicting some historic atrocity committed
by the mother Church. ("Papists sending Christians to heav-
en," read the caption under a festival of tortures depicting the
Inquisition.) Readers flipping through its pages could choose
from such headlines as: "Peter Never at Rome," "The Bible!
The Bible! And Nothing but the Bible," "Popish Relics, or
Lying Wonders," "Canadian Papist Converted," "Mass House
Bells."[21]

In the midst of horror stories dredged from the previous
nineteen centuries, the occasional discovery of Rome's activities close to home seem to have been aimed at something like
comedy relief. The paper noted, for instance, a new and frightening display set forth before native American eyes: a St. Patrick's Day parade. Squeezed amidst accounts of the Crusades,
tyrannous popes, and inquisitions, the alarm was sounded:

> We were surprised last Thursday to see the Nation's
> flags hoisted in various parts of New York. Upon inquiring
> the cause we were told it was done in honor of Saint Pa-
> trick. American Protestants and citizens should pause and
> reflect! What will be the consequences of thus combining
> civic honors with the absurd legends of traitorous Po-
> pery. . . ? There was a procession in true Popish style
> about the streets. President Jackson and O'Connell in full
> display—and this atrocious insult to our citizens being toler-
> ated with impunity. Next year we may have Saint Dominic,
> and Saint Ignatius and the crucifix.[22]

The local Protestants were spared Dominic and Ignatius.
They were to see a good deal more of St. Patrick.

Much like pornography, the paper, though grand fun to
read for a number of issues, quickly waxed repetitious and
tiresome. As with pornography it sold readily to a certain class
of citizenry and embarrassed many others, especially those who
called themselves, in faith, by the all-embracing title of the

sheet. One such Protestant protested: "I looked and when I beheld the names of some whom I once considered men of liberality and learning, and endowed to every generous and Christian like feeling, I must confess I was shocked not a little . . . I took up the paper again and at every word (would that I could have said at every line) I was checked by the torrent of calumny which was vomited forth against a respectable body of my fellow citizens . . ."[23]

New York City's Catholic paper, the *Truth Teller** (the *Protestant* called it "The Lie Teller") sought to stem this tide of abuse with apologetics, but the *Protestant* declared that it would not sully itself in an arena with them: "A debate with those [Catholic] journals could not possibly elicit any advantage because it would be an employ exclusively to repel vituperation and to disprove falsehoods. The whole system of Popery is a stupendous tissue of imposition and mendacity."[24]

Hughes carried the paper back with him to Philadelphia and continued to study its style and content issue by issue. Then in the February 13th issue there appeared a letter signed "Cranmer" urging Protestants to realize their own strength and the weakness of Catholics. Rome's forces, he said, were mere "human paper pop guns which the Protestants will pay back in canister Bible bullets shot from Luther's bomb and Knox's cannon." Cranmer then went on to take some very well-aimed shots at Catholicism's claims of infallibility: "It is still more astonishing that no Popish author has ever yet told us what is the Church in the understanding of the term, and still less have they ever agreed respecting the persons with whom infallibility is lodged. The Jesuits claim it for the Pope, others for a general council, others for the whole hierarchy, others for the Pope and a council, and others for the Pope and all the priests . . ."[26]

It was a good shot, aimed at that which had been a bone of contention within Catholicism for centuries before that time,

---

*The paper reflected the nationality as much if not more than the religion of its subscribers. It ran constant front-page accounts of Ireland's politics and campaigned against local advertisements such as the one which called for: "A cook and a chambermaid. They must be Americans, Scotch, Swiss, or Africans.—No Irish."[25]

and that was destined to be fought about for an indeterminate time into the future. In any event it was a theological issue too refined for the *Protestant*'s readers and caused no ripple. A more pointed headline warned: "Black Nuns from Montreal to Superintend Albany Girls. This is too Scandalous." If mothers in Albany allowed this to happen, the paper warned, their daughters would become "deceitful, lewd and ensnaring tools whom their confessor will employ for the gratification of his own avarice and pleasures."[27]

Then a second Cranmer letter appeared, sharply different in content and style from the first. This one spoke directly to the mentality of the *Protestant*'s readers. Noting that in Philadelphia, from whence he wrote, Catholics numbered more than any other single denomination, he bemoaned: "What would the immortal Penn have thought? The Papists," he reported, "are swarming themselves into every nook and corner of our country . . . the Pope is sending over well-disciplined officers to command his Romish armies and have them in readiness for the signal when the holy crusade is to be commenced against the heretics. . . . If we are to succumb to the pressure of Popery, let it be after a glorious struggle. Let the *Protestant* cry aloud and spare not." Modestly he added, "I am ready to supply all local information."[28]

Supply he did. On March 13th he wrote that the "cool, calculating and crafty" Pope had dispatched emissaries who were "gliding through our ranks, watching the spirit of defection where it exists and bribing it into existence where it had not been before." Proof of this could be seen in the "indefatigable" work of Roman priests and in the large new school of Canadian nuns in Albany. The very buildings of papists attested to their growth "with their display of crosses of iron and of brick and of marble."[29]

The articles were popular. The *Protestant* printed a biography of the original Cranmer, and when there was a lapse of three months without any missives from Philadelphia the paper begged Cranmer to take up his pen once more. He happily complied.

In the June 12th edition he noted that in Philadelphia

four Mass houses were "filled each three times on the Sabbath." This swelling Catholic population, he warned, was "digging a pit in which may be buried, ultimately, both our civil and religious liberties—and those who are standing on its very brink can see no danger at all."[30]

On the 26th of June what turned out to be the last of the letters was published. In it Cranmer called teaching nuns "she wolves" out to devour America's youth. Urging Protestants to fight such dangers he declared: "Let there be no more hanging back, let there be no more palsey in the hand. . ."[31]

A week after this last entry, on July 3rd, Cranmer appearing in the *Truth Teller* ripped off his Protestant mask to stand masked as "A Catholic." Having decided that the *Protestant* was a slander rag "too gross except for the meridian of the fish market" he had thus given them material suited for such, and in doing so had "woven in as many lies as possible." He had cloaked himself in the guise of one of their sainted heroes, although he noted, "If a solitary virtue could bribe Peter at Heaven's gate, Luther and Calvin and the long head roll of reformers could not muster the toll. They virtuous, they meek and ascetical, ingenious and forgiving! I tell you they had all the infirmities which rottenness could lend nature." Then addressing the seventy-three ministers who sponsored the *Protestant* he sneered: ". . . with the exception of about twenty what do we see but the clerical scum of the country."

"You and your sect," he declared, "are impelled by the desire of religious preeminence over your fellow citizens of other denominations. . . . [You] have hit upon the unworthy expedient of raising the 'hue and cry' against the offending papists and representing them as the persons who are preparing to tear up the charter of American liberty. Your object is to send the strong but innocent prejudices of the American people in pursuit of an imaginary game in order that . . . you may cement the bonds of matrimony between Church and state and then regale the weary hunters at the nuptial feast."[32]

The seventy-three ministers, caught with their cassocks down, reeled for a moment and then reacted. In its next issue the *Protestant* figured out that Cranmer had referred to Philadelphia as "that" instead of "this" city, and so looked for Cranmer in New York. They decided it was the *Truth Teller*'s Thomas Levins. Levins, who had once been warned by William Vincent Harold that missionary priests in the United States would find lonely deaths, was the parent of the Irish-Catholic paper. Instead of hitting his antagonists head-on Levins had developed a style, later employed by Finley Peter Dunne, of satirizing them in the conversations of a quaint Irish character named Fergus (sometimes Berkeley) McAlpin. In almost every issue Fergus could be found meeting with his cronies: Malachy McArthur, Neil Sullivan, and Corny O'Hanlon in a Brooklyn Navy Yard tavern—the Sheet Anchor. There the quartet sat, aiming barbs amidst witticisms, hanging the lopped-off heads of their opponents on pikes of humor. It was natural that the *Protestant* should blame Levins. A jape such as the Cranmer stunt would have been right down his dockyard alley. Thus they shot their retorts directly at him.

"A Catholic" had admitted in his confession to a scruple of conscience about printing what he himself called "broad, palpable, grinning lies." But he had rationalized his rightness in doing so: "I was satisfied that no enlightened man would believe a line published in the *Protestant* except he knew from other sources that it was true; and that no modest woman who had read it once by accident would ever read it again by design. I wanted to ascertain whether or not conscience had anything to do with the columns of the *Protestant*. I found it had not. . ."[33]

Somewhat like a man labeled as an "old pervert" who objects to being called "old," the *Protestant* ignored the main thrust of the argument and focused on the phrase "you and your sect." "There are Protestant ministers," the editor snorted, presuming he was addressing Levins, "of ten different denominations who do now strenuously encourage and recommend the paper." Such a glossing over of the nature of Protestantism, he decided, could have arisen only from "profound ignorance," or else "Roman deceitfulness."[34]

"Catholic" quickly answered, calling the editor of the *Protestant* a "vendor of lies. . . Too stupid to invent, too poor to purchase them, he begs their communication and publishes them gratis, provided they are against Roman Catholics." Hughes, then, employed a tactic that was to become almost his trademark in a life filled with public argument. Scoffing at the claim that the letters came from New York he wagered $500 "that there are in the city of Philadelphia not less than four Catholics who have been in the habit of communicating all manner of suitable trash for the columns of the *Protestant.*"[35]

Then, all of a sudden, Hughes found himself under cross-fire. Levins did not care at all for the honor of being branded as the author of the still-anonymous letters. Fergus McAlpin sounded forth from the Sheet Anchor Tavern pronouncing the whole Cranmer escapade as a "petty and childish trick." There was nothing courageous in searching for the conscience of the *Protestant:* "I do not think the discovery merits a national testimonial," Fergus decided. "I thought [conscience] like one of those dandy corsets which checks oscillation to the right or left. But with the Philadelphia 'Catholic' it is universal elastic. It fits every form and yields without pinching to every strain."[36] Then, dropping any trace of banter, he leveled a significant charge: "I now ask him and seriously and sadly I put the question. Could he for an instant so cheat the misgivings of his Catholic heart as to believe that a ridiculous search after the conscience of the *Protestant* and the Calvinistic parsons could authorize the very improper and false accusations expressed against the Catholic Church in his first communication and in his other communications?"[37]

Then the seventy-three ministers, with a sharper second wind in their sails, returned to their own defense. "Catholic" had boasted of perpetrating some twenty "broad, palpable, grinning lies." Well, then they reasoned, "to expose the 'liar' to the contempt and derision of every man of sense it is sufficient to take him upon his own word and exhibit him in that character in which he has chosen to appear before the public . . . a cool deliberate liar."[38]

Hughes was stung by both of these attacks. Hotly, he lashed back at McAlpin, whom he knew to be Levins. It being his turn to play the "old pervert" objecting to the word "old," he ignored McAlpin's severe charge that as a Catholic he had only added ammunition to the stockpiles of bigotry and carped at Fergus for quoting from the first Cranmer letter of February 13th. He denied that this letter, with its reasoned attack on infallibility, was his child: "No such passage occurs in any of Cranmer's letters," he insisted, adding that he denied it so vehemently because it contained "the only falsehood in the whole communication which is important enough to merit a contradiction."[39]

The Sheet Anchor brotherhood, however, refused to let him off their pike. His head was stuck up with the others of their mocking for public display. Corney O'Hanlon took "A Catholic" over long lengths of hot coals, wondering why a boaster of lies should quibble so after having proudly owned up to the letters.

The fight increased in ugliness. "A Catholic" flailed at the brotherhood: "The editor of the *Protestant* knew that I never wrote that passage," he asserted (as if that editor would ever jump forth to verify the discrepancies in handwriting), "I am neither its parent nor its author."[40] Again he made an "appeal to the purse," challenging any to prove that he authored the first Cranmer letter, and laying $1,000 as a wager on his innocence. Corney O'Hanlon was quick to retort: "This is ever the last appeal of vulgarity. A bet with the author of "palpable, broad, grinning lies." I would not become bondsman for a bet with him of a dozen rotten cabbages or half a dozen frost tainted turnips."[41]

Hughes, who had refrained so temperately from tearing at the Church's fabric with the foolish Catholics of Philadelphia, had allowed himself to become involved in a silly public squabble with another priest, his original foe all but forgotten and no doubt smiling happily on the sidelines. At last an impartial observer who paid tribute to the otherwise good characters of the two brawlers pleaded with them in the *Truth Teller* that as "gentlemen" they stop a controversy which "savours much of the rancorous, dirt flinging tendency so frequently practiced by the fierce theologians of the sixteenth century. In polemics, as well as politics," this peacemaker ventured, "Irishmen have ever unfortunately been too prone to fritter away their native energies and intellectual resources which if concentrated for laudable objects should prove irresistible."[42]

And so, dashed with the cold water of polite reproval the hotheaded Irishmen backed away from their fight. Hughes, the worse for wear, learned a few perimeters that had to be set in polemical tournaments, and the Sheet Anchor brotherhood retreated to its earlier stance saying: "The conscientious casuistry of the Catholic Cranmer we consign to the new Bishop of Philadelphia. He will soon purify the theological atmosphere and inform the subtle deviser of the profound plot which probed the *Protestant* whether a mask of evil may be assumed to effect a good."[43]

Indeed the young Bishop Kenrick, so much the scholar and gentleman, had arrived to assume authority over the shambles of his diocese in the middle of this donnybrook. He was not pleased with it.

8

A QUEST FOR A MITER ON A DARK ROAD

"Your tilting with the Reverend Mr. Levins gives me to pain."[1]

Kenrick was writing to Hughes from Chambersburg, and his pain was compounded by a number of afflictions, not the least of which was a fever so great that those attending him feared for his life. He had arrived in the diocese only weeks before, listening to ardent promises of good behavior from the recently forgiven Conwell. "He professes his determination to live with me in perfect harmony and to leave me the free administration of the diocese," Kenrick noted with satisfaction, adding generously, "I am on my part resolved to do everything for his honor, peace and happiness."[2]

Unfortunately the honeymoon was over before the shy young bishop had so much as unpacked his bags at St. Joseph's where he was to live with Hughes, Terence Donoghoe, and Conwell's "innumerable nephews and cousins."[3] All the ecclesiastical authorities (including Conwell) understood that Kenrick was to be the man holding onto the reins, but out of a charity for the old bishop's pride, no public announcement had been made to that effect. The old bishop took advantage of this within a week of his arrival back home. He constantly referred to his auxiliary as "the boy," and broadcasted about that "full authority" had been returned to him.[4] In a city where democratically oriented Catholics had for so long worked on establishing a balance of power within the Church's system, the

71

prospect of Conwell standing ready to throw in his lot wherever it might be to his own advantage frightened Kenrick. His fear was compounded by Conwell's fondness for hiring lawyers and fighting his battles in public courts. "Now," Kenrick worried, "if under some pretext they open a litigation against me before a civil tribunal, I fear that the judges will scarcely be satisfied by what I claim for myself—the Jurisdiction and the authority of the Philadelphia diocese—since the other man is Bishop of Philadelphia and I am named Bishop of Arath."[5]

Whatever condition Arath may have been in, Philadelphia was, as John Hughes saw it, "in a deplorable plight."[6] But rather than stew about Conwell, Kenrick resolutely set out on a visitation of his new spiritual domain. He diplomatically allowed the old man to grapple after the episcopal stipends meant to support the bishop's work, but before he left on his travels (supported by Providence and little else) the bishop of Arath wrote to Rome, explained the dangerous situation, and begged permission to set forth publicly that he was Philadelphia's proper administrator.

For a month he trekked about the state, confirming and ordaining, visiting farmlands, coal-mining areas, canal cities peopled with Irish laborers, seeking Catholics in backwoods areas. The combination of physical stress and the worries about the impending fight for control of the diocese at length became too much for the sensitive man's nature. In Chambersburg, the home of Hughes's parents, he collapsed from a fever. The illness was grave enough not only to frighten those who nursed him, it also moved Kenrick to write a formal statement to the effect that should he die John Hughes was to be entrusted with the temporary care of the diocese.

He and Hughes were never to be friends. They were basically incompatible, and they rarely cared for each other's methods in dealing with matters or people. But they always respected each other's worth and were willing to work as a team for the sake of the Church. Kenrick always shrank from public polemic, convinced that it did more harm than good. He had arrived in Philadelphia to find Hughes happily flushed and sweating from beating upon foe and friend alike. However much this caused him pain he knew that Hughes could be counted on. Dangerously weakened, he wrote to the priest six months his senior whose every action spelled strength and asked for his help. Hughes left immediately for Chambersburg and took over the bishop's duties. He had the deep satisfaction of preaching in those authoritative circumstances to a congregation that included his mother and father.

He remained with Kenrick, and when the young prelate was well enough to resume travel on October 12th they completed the visitation together—joined for a spell by Hughes's friend Father Thomas Heyden. For a month they followed an arduous course, journeying over what routes they could find, in whatever kind of conveyances were available. Kenrick began to learn why his companion was gaining a name for his powers as an orator. Without the flourishes of popular oratory, Hughes spoke directly and intensely to people, never allowing them to drift into inattention because of digressions on his part. In Blairsville, after he had homilized in place of the bishop, a parishioner pumped Hughes's hand as he left the church and pronounced: "Your Reverence has preached a rouser."[7]

For his part Hughes learned that if Kenrick was retiring by nature he was not vacillating. At Youngstown the bishop removed a disagreeable pastor and in Pittsburgh he withdrew faculties from a wandering cleric who belonged in Cincinnati. There was hope for this diocese yet.

At Loretto there was only one seat left on the public coach that was leaving for Newry. Kenrick took this while Heyden and Hughes caught a ride in an open wagon. It was well into evening as they bumped along the road when the discovery was made that the bishop's miter and crozier had fallen out of the baggage. They pulled up and argued about what to do. Hughes was for turning to search for the lost articles. Heyden and the driver insisted that since the night was quite dark and the road dangerous they should keep on. Refusing to take "no" for an answer, Hughes finally yanked the reins from the driver's hands, turned the horse himself, and headed them back. They found the lost items.

As soon as they returned to Philadelphia it was obvious that firm decisions were needed there as well. Kenrick an-

nounced to the trustees at St. Mary's that he would be their
pastor. As Hughes noted, "They kicked immediately." Determined to prove that they still held the ultimate right of appointment, they called a meeting on January 12th, 1831.
Hughes afterward described the encounter to John Purcell.
Perhaps it was because he had feared that the polite Kenrick
would be no real match for the fierceness of the trustees that he
was so exultant in his description.

> Dr. Kenrick attended the meeting himself. His pres-
> ence (in his cassock, and his cross displayed on his breast)
> disconcerted them. He then proved, to the satisfaction of the
> meeting, that the trustees were misrepresenting. He made
> them eat their own words. He told them they must not dare
> to control him in the exercise of his episcopal authority. He
> said he was their pastor and their bishop; that St. Mary's
> was and should be the cathedral of the diocese; and he was
> supported, and the trustees were put down by their own
> meeting—and I may say their own party! . . . He said he
> wished no other trustees, so long as these gentlemen would
> confine themselves within their proper limits, and not pre-
> sume to meddle, directly or indirectly, with his authority.
> There was finally a kind of shaking hands between the van-
> quished and the victor—with what sincerity on their part,
> time only will tell. At all events, it is the first time within ten
> years that an attempt has been made to pluck up the root of
> the schism—and I assure you Dr. Kenrick did it with a
> giant's hand.[8]

The trustees, however, were not finished. They tried to
grease the giant's palm, or at least half grease it. The board
held another meeting—this time just the laymen—and voted to
tempt Kenrick with a fraction of the salary he had been living
without. He refused to reach for it, and curtly informed them,
"You are no board without me."[9]

When the trustees, then, absolutely refused to confirm the
bishop's right to appoint pastors, he interdicted the church and
closed it as had Conwell a few years before. Only this time, in
this elaborate sort of chess game, his adversaries had a piece on
their end of the board that they hadn't possessed before—a
bishop. Conwell suddenly allied himself with his old enemies.

Kenrick worried openly about this new development:

"Now there is great fear lest the Bishop of Philadelphia offer himself as a leader to them; for it is known that for many weeks he had frequently had conferences with them, and on last Friday, when the trustees had a meeting at St. Mary's he was present and for a full hour spoke with them. At that time he showed to them, as they relate, a paper by which he affirmed he still enjoyed the rights of the Bishop of Philadelphia and accused me of usurpation."[10]

There was a different and as yet untried tactic that still could be used against the cathedral parish of St. Mary's. Up until this time it had been the only church in the vicinity considered proper for the use of a bishop, and the trustees had always played upon that presumption. Whenever they had chosen to oust an unwanted prelate, he had been forced to retreat around the corner to Willings Alley and preside from the unimpressive chapel of St. Joseph's. And so, reasoned Kenrick, why not build another edifice worthy of being a cathedral—one whose title would be held by the bishop, with no lay trustees?

He gave the job to Hughes, and Hughes who admired this sort of tactic plunged into the project with characteristically rigorous energy. He secured a lot on Thirteenth Street— which drew complaints from some people that he was building too far outside the city.* He hired a young architect, William Rodrigue, whose family had befriended Hughes, and with the laying of the cornerstone in May 1831 he began construction. Hughes was always the poorest of businessmen, and beyond begging for subscriptions he had no promise of any backing whatsoever. He openly counted himself fortunate to receive the generously given pennies of the laborers from whose ranks he had sprung. This was no way to finance a large building; at that rate St. John's might have been years in construction. Then Mark Frenaye, a wealthy middle-aged merchant, entered the scene. Frenaye had lived a remarkable career. Born in Santo Domingo in 1783, his family had moved to France in time for him to be imprisoned during the Revolution. Mark

---

*It was a complaint that would be registered against him again in another quarter of a century when he began constructing his next cathedral church.

then returned to Santo Domingo where in the uprising of 1803 he was held hostage by the black revolutionaries. He escaped to Jamaica where in 1806 he was sentenced to a prison ship there for refusing to be inducted into the militia. Moving to Philadelphia in 1807, he remained until 1820 when he bought land in Alabama and there lived what he called "a very rough life." He sojourned in Mexico for several years, and while in New York City in 1828 met Bishop Dubois. Dubois brought him back to the faith he had "neglected for twenty-eight years" and under the Frenchman's guidance Frenaye came to see himself as a "new man, no longer of the world."

In 1829 he settled permanently in Philadelphia. Though no longer of the world, he was still in possession of a sizeable fortune of this world's goods. Reawakened to his religion, he developed a strong dislike for what he saw in trusteeism, calling it a "system of Protestantism." John Hughes was his chosen confessor. He watched with growing sympathy as the financially impractical young man floundered about building a church with virtually nothing. If he were left on his own the defeat of St. Mary's might take a generation. Frenaye approached Hughes. "I placed at his disposal," he modestly related, "forty thousand dollars, which was secured by bonds deposited at the United States bank." It created a fury, as Frenaye himself noted. "The trustees of Saint Mary's did all they could to prevent the erection of Saint John's. A meeting was held at St. Mary's parsonage, at which Mr. Joseph Dugan, one of the trustees, was present. Mr. Dugan was much excited and walked up and down the room and with his hand closed shook it at me and denounced me as a speculator."[11]

The laying of the cornerstone took place in May of 1831. With funds at hand, the work moved ahead rapidly. By the end of that month the trustees began to back down, abandoning their long fight for right of appointment, retaining only their claims over the purse and the right of grading clerical salaries. As John Hughes put it: "They were left to themselves and they couldn't stand it." If it was a victory, it was nonetheless an ugly one; Kenrick fell ill again. ". . . I perceive by close observation," wondered Hughes, who enjoyed every minute of these scrapes, "that his mind is of too sensitive a character for such shocks. . ."[12]

Even pastoral work had something of a battleground atmosphere. During two months of that spring of 1831 Hughes carried on a furtive tug-of-war with a Protestant clergyman for the soul of an elderly near-Christian, undecided about which Church he should use to try to storm heaven's gates. Reverend Bedell would show up at the man's deathbed and preach to him as to why he should be an Episcopalian, and then Hughes would show up in an effort to convince him of Catholicism. The poor old fellow—an organist who apparently played music for all denominations—was lost amidst the discordant philosophies played about his head. At the finale he at last committed himself to Hughes, bringing a sense of peace to his own soul (and ears) and to the soul of his last moment's confessor.

Hughes's solicitude for people was authentic. Unfailingly throughout his life whenever he dealt with those who were weaker than he or in need of help he assumed an attitude of protection. In that spring he sent a note concerning a new student at the Mount: "He is excessively timid and diffident, and in order that he may be at his ease it is necessary that attention should be paid to him."[13] Again he showed a touching concern for a Sister Mary Lewis and helped arrange for her departure from the convent, explaining simply: "She was unhappy."[14]

This was time when he needed solicitude for himself. Engulfed in the construction of St. John's, he received word in late September that his mother was dying. The news came without warning. She had been ill for a long time, yet when it became obvious to the family that she was sinking toward death she strictly forbade them to notify John. It was the work of his priesthood that was uppermost in her mind; she would not, she told them, take him away from the discharge of his duties. The Church mattered; not herself. If we know very little about the childhood of John Hughes, this maternal self-sacrifice alone tells much of what made him the man he was.

Only when weakness made death imminent would she allow him to be notified. Upon hearing, he dropped everything, took a steamboat that docked at Baltimore at 2:00 A.M., and then caught the first stage from there, reaching Chambersburg at seven in the evening. Not daring to ask any questions to those who greeted him, he rushed home where he found the family gathered weeping around his mother's bed. He kissed her, knelt down and read the prayers for the departing. She was fully conscious. She prayed along with him and continued to do so until, sometime during the evening, she breathed her last.

For a week he remained with his father, leaving only to join Kenrick for a church consecration in Gettysburg. Then, with family affairs put in order and his father settled with his son Patrick and wife, Hughes returned to Philadelphia to resume his work.

Cardinal Cappellari, who had suffered as much as everyone else from the willy-nilly antics of Bishop Conwell, had just been elected Pope Gregory XVI. Not surprisingly he soon sent a brief to Philadelphia explaining that Kenrick had all jurisdiction within that diocese. This should have left matters cut and dried. It didn't. When the now-powerful coadjutor returned from his second diocesan visitation—at the same time that Hughes returned from his mother's death—it was to see that Conwell had evicted the new bishop and all his belongings from St. Joseph's rectory. It was a public humiliation. Yet rather than use the authority he now held to slap back at the old man, Kenrick bowed still further and quietly took lodgings in another house. This may have kept the peace, but it did little for the prestige of ecclesiastical authority. Furthermore, as if he thrived on humble pie, Kenrick began to woo the trustees of St. Mary's by backing away from his determination to use St. John's as his cathedral.

This was not the way John Hughes would have dealt with disobedience. Authority, in his developing opinion, had to be strong and decisive or it was asking to be disobeyed once more. Hughes was busy with plans for the opening of the church in early spring of 1832, and with impatience bordering on disgust he decided that Kenrick would be the wrong man to do the honors: ". . . The fact is," he judged, "that he does not seem to understand what suits such an occasion."[15]

Hughes saw his new, would-be cathedral through windowed glasses. He spoke lavishly of it, describing it as the handsomest church in the United States. It was hardly this. It was a roomy stone building, well suited to the purposes for which it was built; the only people who expressed any disappointment in seeing it were those who had heard Hughes enthusiastically speaking of it before their own eyes could take it in.

As if to punish the over-conciliatory Kenrick for rejecting this new cathedral, Hughes invited from New York the highly esteemed (and highly self-esteemed) Vicar General John Power. Hughes set the stage well for the occasion, and what seems surprising, he did so with an eye toward a good relationship with the city's Protestants. The mayor was present, as were a number of clergymen of various sects. Hughes would have done well to stick with a speaker of whose diplomatic tone he would have been assured. Power was slated the week after this consecration to meet the New York Protestant Association in a debate. As if rehearsing for the encounter, he ignored the polite group in front of him at St. John's and launched into a long and bitter tirade, defending the "four marks of the true Church" and ridiculing Protestantism.

Hughes was humiliated. When the ceremony was concluded he confronted Power and informed him: "My dear sir, you have ruined me!"[16]

Quite to the contrary. The acrimonious sermon was picked up by the press, criticized by Catholics and Protestants alike. One critic, Reverend John Breckinridge, would within the year decide to take Hughes to task for it. In doing so he would give his Catholic adversary widespread fame.

9

PESTILENCE AND POLEMICS

To atone for John Power's betrayal of his hospitality, Hughes allowed a public celebration held in the new church on the 4th of July, convincing himself that the affair "was not political but purely patriotic." After a band displayed its musical wares, Hughes stood on a platform constructed in the middle aisle. He opened the occasion with an invocation warning against "national pride and arrogance," and then sat down and suffered along with the rest of the audience while a local orator, Charles Ingersoll, marched his listeners through the usual Independence Day fare. It was, as Hughes noted, "a panegyric" of revolutions. "It was foolish and pronounced so by nearly all that heard it," he admitted, "but it was in its spirit such a one as might have been expected, and in this country could do no harm."[1]

Far off in Emmitsburg Bruté was horrified at this laxity on the part of Hughes. There was a constant stern anxiety in the older priest's attitude toward this student he had guided from laborer to priest. Perhaps he worried that the clerical cassock cloaked only a raw Irish immigrant who remained unchanged underneath. He hurried to reprimand Hughes both for the secular ceremony and for what he had decided was too short a time the new pastor had allotted for hearing confessions at St. John's.

Hughes, with a trepidation that he certainly never exhibited toward his bishop, pleaded his situation to his mentor. Re-

81

garding confessions, the hours posted were not meant as limitations to his availability. And as to the Independence Day celebration he promised Bruté: ". . . I do not mean that it shall ever be repeated where I am. Nor would I have granted it at this time (because I look upon such occasions as you do) did I not fear that the refusal would have added to the bitterness of feeling produced by the very harsh texture of an injudicious sermon some months before."[2]

The bitter feelings that frequently existed between native Protestants and immigrant Catholics, however, were held in abeyance during the summer of 1832 by a foe that attacked both groups indiscriminately along the eastern seaboard.

"It seems highly probable that the epidemic which has begun at Quebec and Montreal, "reported Philadelphia's *National Gazette* woefully in late June, "is the Cholera, and was brought from Ireland."[3]

The Asiatic cholera, endemic to the Far East, had never before attacked the Western Hemisphere. In 1831 Americans had watched it spread steadily westward through Europe and fearfully they had speculated that it might be carried across the Atlantic by the ever-increasing flow of immigrants. When it broke out in Canada it was logical that the blame should be placed upon those uprooted peoples. But there was heightened fear in the knowledge that many Irish who traveled to Canada did so only because movement within the British Empire was more expedient; they had the United States as their ultimate destination. Quarantine laws were quickly passed to keep immigrants from entering New York, but both they and the disease made their way southward. In early summer New York was infested. Philadelphians began to feel a sense of panic. Scores of citizens wealthy enough to do so moved from the city. Public officials and the press did all that they could to allay the people's fears. They declared that conditions were such in Philadelphia that there was hope the cholera might pass by them with but a light touch. But fear, along with disease, was in the air. In July the Episcopal bishop called for a day of fast and prayer; Kenrick ecumenically joined him in the plea.

The disease struck full force by midsummer, and when it did there was no quieting the situation. Unlike the previous plagues of yellow fever, which had a lower mortality rate and was more understood medically, cholera struck quickly, painfully, and more often than not fatally. Violent diarrhea, vomiting, and cramps brought most victims to death within a matter of hours. Physicians operated in the realms of guesswork; they flailed about prescribing cures as contradictory and bizarre as might have been invented by medieval barbers. Preventative measures that included the avoidance of strong drink and certain foods were listed daily in the newspapers (items such as watermelon and green corn were highly suspect). Bloodletting and dosages of calomel (a product of mercury and chlorine) were believed to be good treatments for those stricken, and a personnage no less than the president of the New York State Medical Society suggested plugging up the rectum with beeswax or oilcloth to stop the diarrhea.[4]

There was one phenomenon of the disease, however, of which all educated observers were in agreement. Americans could thank the immigrant for its introduction and its spread. The cholera took its firm hold in the lower classes who were crowded into the slums of their own making. Preachers were quick to cite the moral dissipation to be found among these people. In Puritan America with its Old Testament morality, there was common agreement that an avenging God was making a judgment upon their manner of life, their proneness to drink, and their natural squalor.

In Philadelphia cholera first broke out in great numbers at the Arch Street prison. As a last-ditch preventative stand the authorities attempted to break up the overcrowded public facilities; over 500 paupers were moved from almshouses to places outside the city. But the move was too late to stop the mounting death lists. The newspapers abandoned their early reassuring tones and began to report the numbers of victims by streets.

There is little wonder that when those who could afford to desert the hot, crowded city for the safer open country, the clergy shut the doors of their all-but-emptied churches and left as well. There was just as little wonder that the Catholic clergy remained where they were stationed. Critics of Catholicism had always loved to point out that the *ex opere operato* belief in the sacraments meant that the Church could conduct its business, happily, without the presence of any people. But the other side of this jibe was the almost military assumption that the work of the Church had to be carried on regardless of external events. Daily Mass was still to be offered; and more pointedly Catholics believed that when danger of death existed a priest had to be summoned to administer the sacrament of Extreme Unction.

This attitude was clearly reflected in letters written by John Purcell, caught by the siege of sickness in Philadelphia, to his assistant at Mount St. Mary's in Emmitsburg. He stoically anticipated the possibility of his own death and showed strong displeasure that a planned school retreat had been canceled, even though Bruté and several students were ill. As much as it was possible business was to be carried on as usual.[5]

The illness within Philadelphia soon overflowed all existing medical facilities. The Church helped to supplement these. Father Hurley received permission from Kenrick to turn St. Augustine's into a makeshift hospital. The Sisters of Charity in Emmitsburg traveled into the danger zone, passing the carriages of those who were making good their escape. Throughout the summer they served as nurses, and their collective and individual valor—not without its casualties—was widely reported in the secular press throughout the United States. Those Protestant writers who took such notice of the Catholic clergy seemed almost incredulous that these outsiders to the mainstream of American life should be so selfless. "Sacrifices of convenience were made by them," noted one, "even the private dwelling was given up and converted into a temporary hospital for the sick, while the priests themselves assisted as nurses, giving with their own hands the medicines prescribed."[6]

John Hughes did nothing more heroic than any of the others. He simply did his job. The sacramental life of St. John's was carried on without interruption, and Hughes shared the work of caring for those in the hospitals. Years later he would recall that even after the bone-wearying routine of each day a vehicle had to be kept ready at the parish door for the sick calls that came throughout each night.[7]

The comparison between the unified army of priests and nuns and Protestant clergy became a source of embarrassment to some people. "This should be accounted for," demanded one Presbyterian to the sectarian paper the *Philadelphian.* "Some reason ought to be given for deserting their posts at a time like the present."[8]

A reason—in fact several reasons—were offered by Doctor Ezra Stiles Ely, the paper's editor. After denying that any ministers had left town "on account of the cholera," he added that there was no need for them to have remained in any event: ". . . The cholera," he declared, "when it really commences its operation leaves no time for instruction in religious things." Then, mitigating the role the Catholic clergy had played, he insisted: ". . . They have no wives or children of their own, according to law, to whom they could carry home any pestilential disease. We give them all due credit. Of the fact of their superior fidelity we have no evidence."[9]

Reading this, Hughes was immediately up to fight. He resented the nativist canard in Ely's comment about priests with no wives or children "according to law" and dashed it aside, stating: "We appeal to all of those who have been witness of our conduct." So much for defense. Then he attacked. Noting that Ely, a minister, had found it "very convenient" to absent himself from the city, he condescended to agree that, of course, it was not "on account of the cholera." As to there being no need of a clergyman for the rapidly dying victims he could sneer from experience: "If you had conversed with a single patient in a collapsed state you would not have fallen into the mistake." And while the Catholic clergy "had no right to take to themselves the credit of doing more than they were bound to do," if the Protestants were consistent about what they were currently preaching they should have been among their flock, guarding them "against the delusions of that ministry which they are accustomed to denounce as the ministry of the Antichrist."

"Thousands and thousands of dollars have been levied on the pious credulity of the people to keep the Pope out of the 'beautiful Valley of the Mississippi,' " continued Hughes, "and why is it, that the same zeal has not been shown to keep him out of the cholera hospital?"[10]

An astute contemporary once noted a characteristic of John Hughes that separated him from Bishop John England and from the other defenders of the Catholic faith in America. Whereas the others remained behind the walls of gentlemanly conduct even in the face of attacks such as those printed in papers like the *Protestant,* Hughes would accept the gauntlet "only on condition that he was not to remain on the defense, but would be allowed to attack whenever the opportunity should present itself."[11] Hughes himself, commenting upon the "heavy" tone of Catholic apologetics and the effect created upon the American consciousness by anti-Catholic ministers who played to the galleries, had long since decided: "The grand secret in this age is to get, not matter, but readers."[12]

In September, when Autumn weather cooled down the dangers of disease and once again allowed time for the rekindling of intersect sniping, Hughes filled six columns in the *United States Gazette* with a tract blasting Ezra Stiles Ely for his use of the word "Romish" for "Catholic." He took the occasion to review for the public the clergy's behavior over the summer. Protestant ministers, he charged, were "remarkable for their pastoral solicitude so long as the flock is healthy, the pastures pleasant and the fleece luxuriant, abandoning their post when disease begins to spread dissolution in the fold."[13]

This was too much for Reverend John Breckinridge, a Presbyterian minister, fondly described by a friend as a "Calvinist" of the "old school." He was no bible-clutching pulpit pounder. Born on the 4th of July in 1797, the same year as Hughes, he represented the finest in native American stock. His father had been attorney general during Jefferson's administration, and young John had been sent to Princeton to study law. There, "bowed like a bulrush under a sense of his own sinfulness,"[14] he had abandoned the law to enter the ministry and thence had served as a chaplain to the House of Representatives for one year. In 1831 he moved from Kentucky to Philadelphia where he had a full year to observe this upstart immigrant priest before he acted. In the fall of 1832, after Hughes's public criticism of Protestant ministers, Breckinridge used the press himself to question the intelligence of the Catholic clergy. Then he offered to meet with any priest or bishop in the tournament field of "discussion." Hughes rose quickly to the bait: "You have been neither just nor ingenious in your observations," he answered. "Now, sir, I am equally ready to accept this challenge."[15]

Breckinridge could claim an initial victory at this onset, for he quickly informed his adversary that such a response had been exactly what he wanted. ". . . I published that letter," he told Hughes, "impelled to it in part by the frequent and sometimes insolent attacks that were made upon the Protestant Churches—and in part by the very unwarrantable course pursued at the consecration of the house of worship at which you officiate."[16]

Word that there was to be a Roman Catholic-Protestant debate sparked an immediate flurry of interest. The local Episcopal newspaper, counting itself as neutral, announced that it would referee the encounter and astutely advised the public in advance that ". . . if this is to be a popular discussion of the controversy, in appeal to the vox populi, the success of either party will depend more on adroitness than truth."[17]

Breckinridge, whose adroitness had been polished by his aristocratic background, lobbied for an oral debate. Hughes, though he had shown himself effective as an orator, knew the deficiencies of his own education and refused such a forum, telling Breckinridge that he would not become a "theological gladiator for the amusement of an idle promiscuous, curious multitude."[18] Instead, it was finally agreed that both parties would publish their arguments in the pages of their respective Church newspaper. This might have presented a problem to a man of lesser brass than Hughes, for there was no Catholic Philadelphia newspaper. He started one; the *Catholic Herald,* relying upon the editorial talents of an Augustinian, Father

Nicholas O'Donnell, with whom he had earlier that year prepared a report on the feasibility of a diocesan seminary.

In January of 1833 both the newspaper and the debate commenced. The two opponents alternated writing and answering each other's essays, the principal argument being whether or not Christ meant to establish a Church, and, if he did, whether he meant it to be Catholic or Protestant. Week after week throughout the spring and summer of that year a mixture of heavy dogma and even heavier insults was handed back and forth. Without the drama of a face-to-face confrontation, interest in the debate fell, while disproportionately the pedantic arguments of the debate grew heavier and longer, bulging from the columns of the two respective newspapers. After four months of reporting the controversy, the Episcopal referee wearily commented that Hughes and Breckinridge were out to sea and wholly out of sight of land. This fairly neutral observer begged permission to resign his role, expressing a fear that "the debate is likely to outlast the present generation."[19]

On into the hot summer months the two opponents sweated over their manuscripts, shoveling verbiage at each other, endlessly quoting the fathers of the Reformation and Counter Reformation, stopping all the while to accuse each other of misquoting their sources. Hughes, ill equipped on his own, turned for assistance to the ample libraries and intellects of Nicholas O'Donnell, a disapproving Francis Kenrick, and above all to the erratic genius who had educated him. Desperately he wrote to Bruté: "I have not the books; and if I had, not being familiar with them, I should not find time to investigate. I wish you would review from the commencement every reference, and refute, either by a brief quotation from the passage referred to, or by a clear explanation of its meaning in the context. . ." Then, like a child heedless of hurting a parent from whom love is assured, Hughes demanded: ". . . Of all things be clear, for neither myself nor the readers to whom it is to be submitted possess your intellectual discipline and habits of familiarity with books—and for our sakes make everything lucid, even to excess."[20]

One facet of the debates for which Hughes did not have to

depend upon Bruté was the sledgehammer insults he traded with Breckinridge. While Hughes mocked the Protestant clergy for their flight during the cholera epidemic, Breckinridge credited Hughes with "diarrhea verborum" and regretted "to see that you grow less courteous as well as more feeble and prolix."[21] The steady tactic of Breckinridge was to attack the immorality and cruelties of the Roman Church. The constant attitude of Hughes was to acknowledge the sins of this, the "one true Church," and then brush off Protestantism as if it were something that didn't truly exist at all.

Breckinridge wondered how Hughes could approve of Pope Alexander III condemning heretics into slavery while as an Irish Catholic immigrant he wished to adopt for himself Protestant America's Declaration of Independence. In a statement interesting to remember for the sake of the attitudes Hughes would hold a quarter of a century later, the naturalized citizen who had once been forced to oversee slaves snarled at his waspish foe: "When you wished to pay a compliment to our memorable Declaration of Independence were you not rather unfortunate in coupling it with an allusion to the question of slavery? . . . It reminds me of the negro slave, who, on his way to Georgia, shook his manacled hands at the capital and began to sing "Hail Columbia, Happy Land."[22]

In September Breckinridge announced that he had to leave town for several months. In the dust of his departure both men declared themselves the winner, and both vowed to fight yet another day. Still, no admirer of either man claimed that a single convert had been won from the opposition as a result of the debate.*

---

*Even in the flush of battle, John Hughes could sometimes surprise the public with a show of courtly grace. While carrying on with Breckinridge, he wrote a review of the "charge" on the same subject (the "rule of faith") published by the assistant Episcopal Bishop of Philadelphia, Henry Onderdonk. Though the Episcopal paper called Hughes's response inaccurate, it acknowledged that "the style of his review is entirely courteous, and such as becomes the Christian and the gentleman."[23]

10

PANTING TO DO GOOD, WIDESPREAD GOOD

Within the realm of the Church John Hughes was gaining a name as a defender of the faith—a man whose fearlessness and loyalty were beyond question. With a scarcity of such priests in the American Church, Rome was choosing ever-younger men to serve as missionary bishops. The fact that it was Conwell who had first suggested Hughes for a miter was not held against him by the Congregation of Propaganda, and in 1833 he, along with his close friend John Purcell, President of Mount St. Mary's, was considered for the post of bishop of Cincinnati.

Propaganda was making a decision in the dark, for both candidates were virtually unknown to them. The cardinal prefect thus counted it good fortune that John England was in Rome. He approached England for advice, and England, as ever, was happy to give it. "There is one point, Your Eminence," he counseled, "which may deserve to be considered. Mr. Hughes is emphatically a self-made man, and perhaps he would be on that account more acceptable to the people of a western diocese than Mr. Purcell." The next day the prefect happily returned to John England and announced that the affair had been settled. "As soon as I told the Cardinals what you said about Mr. Purcell's being a self-made man," he said, "they agreed upon him at once and the nomination will be at once presented to His Holiness for approval."[1]

When this error was discovered it was, in a manner of

long-established custom, blamed upon the Holy Spirit. A cultured scholar whose self-making had presumably been done in Paris where he had studied for the priesthood was sent to the wilds of Ohio. The belatedly educated laborer remained in the city of brotherly love, there to bully the nation's most eminent Protestant divines.

Purcell's departure left the presidency of the Mount vacant. Hughes had been granted a master of arts degree by the college in 1831, but he was under no illusions about such honors: "I would not add anything to your stock of knowledge," he confided to Purcell, "by telling you they are unwarranted."[2] Still, some considered Hughes as a good candidate to take over the institution. One priest alumnus wrote to Bruté that Hughes's "shrewdness" and "knowledge of the world" recommended him highly. The Breckinridge articles, he noted, "justly or not, give him the repute of a very learned man and powerful writer as well as orator. . . He knows his depth, can conceal his ignorance of some things and support a reputation in spite of it. He is, besides, a man of constant improvement. . . He pants to do good, widespread good. . ."[3]

Bruté was less impressed by Hughes's sudden notoriety. He wrote out his thoughts on the qualifications necessary for a college president. Noting that whoever guided the Mount should be humble, know the temper of the boys, be self-possessed, calm, and not irritable, he added: "There is in my eyes perfect certainty that we cannot have Mr. Hughes, and there is no evidence that he would answer in all respects."[4]

However much his stature was raised in popular esteem, Hughes's fame did not ease his problems on a parish level. Having built a costly edifice, Hughes was hard put to pay for it. ". . . It will be necessary for the pastor of this Church to preach well—or to work miracles," he wrote to Sister Angela, his sister, "I must depend on the former. . ."[5]

Yet, while aware of the necessity of being a crowd-pleaser to attract a more highly educated (and thus more highly contributing) congregation in finicky Catholic Philadelphia, Hughes, who had erected St. John's as a direct slap at the trustees of St. Mary's, never quailed from reminding Catholics that it was high time the Church in the United States was put in order. He warned that those who had helped to confirm the prejudices of those Americans who had studied only caricatures of Catholics should be "cast off." He declared, "Let us respect ourselves and others will respect us."[6]

Thus Hughes, who was poison for nativist Protestants, was equally unpalatable for upper-class native Catholics. After two years there was barely a dent made in the large debt at St. John's. Again Mark Frenaye sought to help. He had spent several years in Mexico and knew the right people there. He suggested that Hughes and he go there on a begging tour. "I will be your pilot," he assured him. "The people are liberal, very liberal, and you will soon collect sufficient funds."[7]

The idea caught fire with Hughes. He dove into a study of Spanish until he was nearly fluent in the tongue. The two booked passages from New York. The day before they were to leave Philadelphia, however, Father Gartland, Hughes's assistant, made an impassioned plea at his Mass for parishioners to prevent the journey. A wealthy man in the congregation was so moved by Gartland's pleadings he stood up and announced that he would begin a subscription fund. The pledges made were such that the trip was canceled at the last moment.[8] Instead, Hughes's travels in 1834 were limited to accompanying Kenrick on another visitation throughout Pennsylvania.

Whether or not the Catholic house was in order during the 1830s, it was certainly under steady attack from without. Anti-popery newspapers that heralded warnings of Babylon's resurgence were having a field day. In 1834 Samuel F. B. Morse took time off from the telegraph to tap out an anti-Catholic polemic: *Foreign Conspiracy Against the Liberties of the United States*. In August of that year Boston mobs inflamed by Lyman Beecher, by Rebecca Reed's broadcasts of escape from an Ursuline novitiate, and by newspaper stories of nunnery dungeons, marched to Charlestown and burned a convent school to the ground (their passions fueled by the mother superior who met them and warned that "the bishop has 20,000 Irishmen at his command in Boston.").[9] In early 1835 Miss Reed, a convert who had indeed spent several months in the convent, published an account of her experiences, and it became a runaway best seller. It was no lurid exposé. It depicted scenes of penitential floor kissing, and a life of bone-bare austerity. ("Our diet consisted of the plainest kind of food, principally vegetables and vegetable soups, Indian puddings and very seldom meat. . . We partook of this diet in imitation of the Holy Fathers of the desert, to mortify our appetites.")*[10] The tale climaxed with the authoress' Gothic mystery escape to freedom while the bishop of Boston and the mother superior made plans to spirit her off to Canada.

To John Breckinridge the public's mood seemed an auspicious opportunity to create victory from the stalemate that had remained hanging for over a year. In New York City in January 1835 he heard that John Hughes was to make an address in Philadelphia before the Union Literary and Debating Institute. Not having time, even with the new railroads, to rearrange schedules on short notice and confront the troublesome priest face-to-face, he wrote a letter challenging Hughes to a debate, ending with the taunt: "I can conceive of only one reason for your refusing, and I hope time has overcome that."[11]

Hughes showed up at the debating society's hall before the arrival of this letter, thinking that he was to give a prepared talk. Instead he was uncomfortably surprised to find himself confronted by what seemed to be a second for Reverend Breckinridge—Reverend William L. McCalla, a Presbyterian minister who had visited Hughes on a number of occasions to seek information about Catholicism. Perplexed and wary, yet afraid of being labeled a coward, Hughes agreed to show up the week after and become that which he had previously refused to be, a "theological gladiator." This time he would have to debate while confined to his own immediate knowledge. He would even be deprived of the remote aid of his mentor. During the previous year Bruté had become the bishop of Vincennes.

---

*On certain gala occasions apple parings were served.

The bishop immediately available to him was thoroughly angered by the prospect of oral debates. Kenrick forbade the *Catholic Herald* to cover the story. In directives undersigned by John Hughes acting as his secretary, he advised Catholics to remain away from such public combats and to respond to bigotry by simply leading virtuous lives.

Under this cloud of disapproval, Hughes arrived at the Debating Society's hall on the 29th of January to face an audience packed predominantly by backers of his adversary. Breckenridge had the upper hand owing to the high tide of nativism and his own cultured background. He took great pains to remind the audience of the latter. Constantly calling Hughes a "foreigner," he declared that it was a trial for such a man as himself to "stoop to such company." He announced that ". . . nothing but the love of liberty as an American, and of truth as a Protestant Christian could induce me to subject my feelings to the coarse and ill-bred impertinence of a priesthood whose temper and treatment towards other men, alternate between servility to their spiritual sovereigns and oppression of their unhappy subjects." Moreover, Hughes was, he decided, ". . . really ignorant of what gentlemen owe to one another."[12]

Hughes, pronouncing such declarations "flourishes of stump oratory,"[13] reminded the galleries that Breckinridge's "gross and abusive epithets" proved that he himself was no gentleman. He objected to being labeled a foreigner, noted that he had resided and preached in Philadelphia for ten years and that he had enjoyed a good relationship with society of all denominations.[14]

Getting down to business, Breckinridge appraised the beneficial advantages of allowing Catholicism to exist freely in any country. "Popery is the malaria of the nations," he warned. "Popery makes the very land to decay while it enslaves and destroys the soil." And thus there was danger in it to the United States: ". . . If the priesthood can but rally from the dark papal states of Europe a full band of their unlettered and deeply subjected militia, then may we see this land ruled by a papal mob, and then these slumbering doctrines will awake for new carnages in this confiding nation."[15]

Hughes attempted to break this image of a Catholicism that cultivated unlettered mobs and pointed out that after the invention of the printing press and before the Protestant Reformation there had been some forty editions of the bible printed in Italy alone. At this point W. C. Brownlee, the guiding spirit behind the *Protestant Vindicator Against Popery* who had traveled from New York for the show, was unable to restrain himself. Bounding from his seat he demanded whether or not these editions were in the vernacular. When Hughes affirmed that they were he yelled out: "I deny it."

Breckinridge flailed away at the medieval union of Church and state and the Spanish Inquisition, and he blamed the Roman Church for the backward state of Latin America. Hughes begged to differ. Reminding Breckinridge that Latin Americans of their own generation had thrown off the shackles of European power and yet freely chose to remain Catholic, he then dragged out a parallel list of Protestant Church-state tyrannies. In the brief 300-year history of Protestantism there was "not a single case in which their doctrines did not drive them to persecute others when they had the power."[16] Since Hughes's list of crimes were as extensive and real as any crimes Breckinridge had drawn up, the Presbyterian retreated a half step and admitted only that: "Our fathers learned to persecute from the Church of Rome. . ."[17]

But Hughes was not so much interested in Breckinridge's fathers as his contemporary brethren. The anti-Catholic laws in Protestant countries were as ugly as anything the minister might dredge up from Spain's Inquisition. Hughes enumerated at length England's anti-Catholic laws, noting: "In Ireland, the code was still more ferocious, more hideously bloody. . ." The man who had watched his sister's body laid to rest without benefit of religion because of England's laws reminded his audience that he spoke from experience about the lack of liberty that his aristocratic opponent knew of only from story books. "I am an American citizen by choice—not by chance," he told them. "I was born under the scourge of Protestant persecution, of which my fathers in common with their Catholic countrymen had been the victims for ages. Hence I know the values of that civil and religious liberty which our happy government secures to all. . ."[18]

Confronted with this escapee of England's penal laws, Breckinridge did well to point out the local autonomy of the American Churches. "The European Protestant Churches are Protestant in regards to Rome," he said. "The American Protestant Churches are so in respect of established religions, as well as in regard to Rome." Breckinridge claimed that if Hughes so loved liberty in the United States he would have to acknowledge one certain premise that "the principle of the American Constitution is Protestantism."[19]

Hughes, in response, built up a series of "ifs." If Protestantism was so tolerant, and if as Breckinridge said Calvinism ought to be preached under the Pope's windows, then Breckinridge ought to feel no hesitancy at inviting Hughes to say Mass at his own Princeton Theological Seminary.

Breckinridge, passing up that opportunity, turned to the topic of Catholic convents, which he called "sinks of idleness if not corruption," and hinted darkly that even in the United States they were built with cellar dungeons "thereby exposing them to the fate of the convent in Boston." Hughes, who could draw upon public memory of the Sisters of Charity's heroism during the cholera epidemic, demanded: "Point to the spot on the map."[20] The spot was not pointed out.

Surprisingly, Breckinridge never utilized what might have been effective ammunition, the Catholic trustee scandals of the previous decade. Instead he looked for sins that Protestant America had been taught to see in Rome. Exhibiting a "specimen"—Bishop Kenrick's advice for examining one's conscience before confession—he read the deliciously lewd list ("Procured pollution in one's self or others. Wanton words, looks or gestures. Lascivious dressing, colours or paintings. Lewd company. Lascivious balls or dressings. . . Ate hot meals or drank hot wine to procure or excite lusts") and then announced "Is not this the vocabulary of a brothel? What but a Roman Catholic priest could have had the pollution to conceive it, or the audacity to give it in a book of devotions to prepare a female to meet him in confession?"[21]

Hughes ignored such flights into the realm of conjecture and urged his opponent to use verifiable facts. Whenever the minister used a source wrongly he insisted on stopping at that point, once even exhibiting his gambler's morality by offering a $500 bet that Breckinridge could not produce the source of a supposed Catholic quote.

If Protestantism was the source of American liberties, Hughes alleged that it was the colonial Catholics of Maryland who educated New England about toleration. He read to the audience from Sewel's *History of Quakers* which depicted the tortures endured by this sect at the hands of Massachusetts Puritans. And then there was that Charlestown convent. Like a fighting dog biting into a jugular vein Hughes grabbed onto it at the beginning of the debates and refused to let the point go. Breckinridge might talk on endlessly about Catholic horrors in Europe's past, but these were as far removed from American life as Greek mythologies. Hughes kept bringing the talk back again and again to that which had filled United States newspapers only months before. It was his strongest point and Breckinridge's weakest. Breckinridge would declare of Roman priests that "the day of their doom is at hand," and Hughes would wonder: "The day of our doom may be destined in the decrees of Calvin to come in the night as was the case of the convent at Boston."[22]

When Breckinridge accused Hughes of fearing Lyman Beecher, Hughes shook him off. "The fact is not so. . . The defenseless females and children of Mount Benedict have had reason to 'fear' him. And yet I do not say that the burning of the convent was the direct motive of his fiery sermons in Boston and Charlestown. The fact is, the doctor wanted money, and like some of his brethren knew that he could extort more by denouncing Popery than by preaching the gospel."[23] Hughes reminded his listeners that Beecher could not be relegated to the European past. "Property has been destroyed—lives have been jeopardized—by the Presbyterian persecution in the United States and in the nineteenth century—for no other crime save that of worshiping God according to the dictates of conscience."[24]

The incident sat like a rock in the center of the platform. Unable to make it go away, Breckinridge took to defending the incendiaries. "I need not, I will not stoop to repel such malignant but powerless thrusts," he declared. "But I will say this, that there are certain kind of houses, which the Pope used to license in Rome, which the boys and mobs in America, taking Judge Lynch's laws, sometimes pull down, not as Protestants against Popery, but as enemies to gross immoralities which we cannot name."[25] The audience seemed unable to fathom the sublety of these immoralities too gross to mention, so the minister reiterated: "If our profession of faith be discredited, the appeal of course must be to facts. The only one he had adduced is that, at Boston, the riotous rabble taking the convent for a _____ wickedly burned it down."[26]*

The effects of the debates were widespread. W. C. Brownlee rushed home to try the same topic on a New York audience. Minus the moderating directives of a peaceminded Bishop Kenrick, crowds of Irish Catholics showed up to listen to the minister. A fight broke out and the auditorium was badly damaged. The recorded Hughes-Breckinridge debates were put into book form, approved by both parties, and the book's ensuing popularity with Catholics rather than with Protestants seemed to show that it was they who found the debates something to be proud of.

John England in his *Catholic Miscellany,* while noting that the book was too long, found it "amusing" to witness the Presbyterian minister fall into such raging passions, and commented that his calling Hughes "rude" was much like "some men who, while in a state of inebriety, imagine everyone about them to be under the influence of liquor but themselves."[27]

This was the crux of Hughes's victory—and that the victory was his was very clear. It was not because he had proven himself superior to his native American adversary but because

---

*The nineteenth-century publisher who later committed the debate to print apparently decided that Breckinridge's language was too precise for public eyes. Readers of another century must fill in the blank for themselves.

his adversary had not shown himself to be as superior as he claimed to be. When a village dandy taunts a local ruffian and provokes him into what becomes a fistfight, the dandy is almost always bound to lose. The ruffian walks away looking no different than he did before the fight. But the dandy's clothes are soiled, his nose is bloodied and his hair is mussed. He has turned himself into an object of ridicule before onlookers who have gathered at his own calling. Breckinridge had entered the fray, pulling his gloves off finger by finger and reminding his audience that he was a "gentleman" forced to chastise a vulgar foreigner. He had staggered away, having proven himself no gentleman and looking much the worse for wear. Hughes, the lifelong scrapper, had walked away dusting off his often soiled hands, perhaps surprised that he had stood up so well on his own without the help of Bruté, and pleasantly surprised to find that he had become rather famous all across the country. "Mr. Hughes," decided John England, "has won unfading laurels for himself in this discussion."[28]

The Hughes-Breckinridge debate, published in book form in 1836, never managed to compete in religious sales departments with a book of convent reflections published earlier that year. It was *The Awful Disclosures of Maria Monk*. Rebecca Reed's slim volume had been selling so splendidly throughout 1835, it must certainly have seemed to Reverend W. C. Brownlee and the ministers of the *Protestant Vindicator Against Popery* to be a work of Providence when an infant-toting woman named Maria Monk appeared at their doorstep anxious to tell the world all about her escape from a Montreal nunnery. Brownlee, writing to Maria's brother John Monk in Canada in order to verify her origins, introduced another interesting character into the proceedings: "She was at my house this morning," he wrote, "in company with a gentleman, a convert from popery, and who had studied for the purpose of becoming a priest. He is now a Christian and a member of the Methodist Church. His name is Hogan."[29]

The man had done more than study "for the purpose of becoming a priest." It was none other than William Hogan, late priest of St. Mary's, now beginning what was to be a life-long career as an anti-Catholic polemicist.

Maria's family was not the source to ask for corroboration. Her mother would steadfastly warn the public that the girl had been a little strange since a childhood accident when she had run a slate pencil into her head. Maria had been a passel of trouble to everybody while growing up and had, indeed, spent time in a Catholic Magdalen asylum.

As colorful as the true version may have been, the gathered ministers enjoyed the story that was spun out by Maria and her cohorts even more. It was set into writing while the *Protestant Vindicator Against Popery* hinted to the public that an escaped nun in New York City was about to divulge the real story about priest-nun relationships. The Harper Brothers, thinking themselves too respectable for the final product, set up a subsidiary publishing house to bring it forth. When the book hit the stands it became an immediate and controversial best seller. It was the very opposite of Rebecca Reed's story of bleak convent austerity (though ironically the American public accepted both versions of convent life as simultaneously true). The kissing done by the Sisters in Maria's book was reserved not for the floors but for parish priests who gained entrance to the convent by secret tunnels from the rectory. The infants born as a result of these relationships were horribly done away with. When any virtuous young lady who had been duped into joining the convent (e.g., the authoress) refused to comply to these evils she was either done away with, or tortured into submission. One hapless victim in Maria's story was placed under a mattress and jumped upon by the mother superior and the visiting pastor. Miss Monk then held aloft her child as proof for the world that she had survived only by making it to the other side of the mattress.

Throughout the year of 1836 she was top ticket on the lecture circuit. Extra editions of the book were rushed off the press, but there just wasn't enough of Maria herself to go around. A second "nun" was added. Frances Partridge ("Saint Frances Patrick," as she was hailed by her sponsors) arrived on the scene, the two women were reunited in an emotional display at a public meeting and they preached to separate audiences while corroborating each other's stories.

The editors of the *Protestant Vindicator* were aching to test Maria before the Catholic clergy. They issued a call in their paper: "Challenge—The Roman prelates and priests of Montreal, Messrs. Conroy, Quarter and Schneller of New York, Messrs. Fenwick and Byrne of Boston, Mr. Hughes of Philadelphia, the arch prelate of Baltimore and his subordinate priests and Cardinal England of Charleston, with all other Roman priests and every nun from Baffen's Bay to the Gulf of Mexico—are hereby challenged to meet an investigation of the truth of Maria Monk's "Awful Disclosure's". . .[30]

Seeing this, Breckinridge dared Hughes to "meet the call like a man or henceforth keep still at St. John's."[31] But the Catholics, including Hughes, kept still on the matter. It was obvious that by facing such inquisitions as were set up by Maria's promoters the Church stood only to become even more an object of their farce. As Hughes noted about the fairness of the proposed inquiries: "The laws for testing the guilt of witchcraft were merciful and just and philosophical compared with the principles laid down and advocated . . . with regard to the clergy and nuns of Montreal. And this . . . in the United States."[32]

Surprisingly, help came from a most unexpected source. William L. Stone, the editor of New York's *Commercial Advertiser,* a firm anti-Catholic then and for the remainder of his life, was too fair a newsman and too respectable a citizen to jump on the bandwagon of those profiting by the "tale of lust and blood." He decided to ferret out the truth. He defended his doing so to his friends by reminding them that there was "an essential difference between taking sides with Satan, and defending him from false accusation." He obtained permission from the sisters in Canada, and with the *Awful Disclosures* in hand he examined every nook and corner of the Hotel Dieu convent, the supposed scene of the story. When he returned to New York he called upon the ministers who acted as the guardians of Maria and Frances. In their presence he grilled the two women. After extensive questioning he stood up and announced to the clergymen present that neither of the alleged nuns could ever have so much as been inside the Hotel Dieu. When he turned to leave W. C. Brownlee remonstrated with him. As Stone remained adamant in his resolve to expose the hoax, Brownlee claimed that it would be a matter of Stone's word against Maria's and then heatedly called Stone a liar. Stone bade them a good day, went home and wrote out his findings.[33]

The short but factual pamphlet he produced never caught up in sales with the lucrative *Awful Disclosures,* but it nonetheless gave Catholics a sense of having been vindicated. Poor Stone suffered from having played the champion of justice, being attacked from almost all sides by the nativist press.

Nor were things going too well for Maria. Fame had not brought her fortune, although the Harpers were rolling in profits. Unhappy over this and unable to get help from the courts who rejected her lawsuit against the publishing house, she fled from New York in midsummer, heading for Philadelphia.

In the eyes of her sponsors, it was a silly-goose thing for the girl to have done. But as there were golden eggs in the goose involved, ex-Father Hogan was sent to convince her to come home to those who truly appreciated her for what she was. She gave in, returned, and in an effort to explain her absence a story was given out that she had been captured by a band of priests. They had brought her to Philadelphia, incarcerating her in an asylum. There on the morning of August 15th Father John Hughes presided over a breakfast at which rum was served and where the priests pondered about what steps should be taken to silence the troublesome ex-nun. ("Damn her," she heard muttered, "we have had enough trouble with her already.") She managed to escape to the office of a physician who harbored her until she was saved by Mr. Hogan.[34]

When this report was given out, the *United States Catholic Miscellany,* stopping momentarily to wonder just who this Mr. Hogan might be, kicked poor Maria's tale to shreds. John Hughes, who had traveled West during the summer at the invitation of Bishop Purcell in Cincinnati, was on the morning of the breakfast described by Maria preaching in the cathedral at St. Louis, Missouri. It would have been difficult for him to have been ladling rum in Philadelphia.

It was just as well that he was probably out of accusation's reach. Maria, who had been brought back to New York to produce more golden eggs, produced instead another baby. By now her credibility was wearing a little thin. Although her book was to live on as a sort of classic in American publishing history, the book's heroine sank quickly into obscurity. After a dozen more years she died in a New York prison convicted of pocket-picking in a whorehouse.

It was public controversy and excitement that the ministers of the *Protestant Vindicator Against Popery* wanted. And if Maria had failed them in that regard after her trip to Philadelphia, they were soon to get all the controversy and excitement they would ever want. Maria's accused rum ladler and captor was moving to New York.

11

SCANNING THE INSIDES
OF MITERS

The clement ecclesiastics of the 1829 Baltimore council had hoped that by allowing Conwell to remain as titular bishop of Philadelphia he might die in dignity—and die soon. As the years passed there was increasing cause for chagrin. Far into his eighties and stone blind, the increasingly addled Conwell was still very much alive and very much kicking. He continually shot off protest letters to Rome, to other bishops, and to any officials, clerical or lay, he hoped would listen, demanding that the rights of office usurped by "the boy" Kenrick be restored to him. It is little wonder that "the boy," so retiring in nature, wanted to retire in fact from Philadelphia. New York was a possible out. Dubois, who felt his age, had asked in 1835 for Kenrick as a coadjutor. Kenrick begged off. Five years of playing substitute for an elderly bishop was enough. Instead, he had a counterproposal for Rome: split the diocese of Philadelphia and create a new See at Pittsburgh with himself as bishop. His place as Conwell's coadjutor could be taken by John Hughes, whose qualifications Kenrick listed: ". . . He is far better fitted than I or any other for the work of governing (the diocese). He is strong in the gifts of nature, he has learning, he is a good man, he has a practical knowledge of affairs, he knows the art of directing souls, he is loved by the people and priests."[1]

Rome was not in the habit of moving swiftly in matters regarding the United States. The matter stretched out over two years. In January of 1836 the Congregation of Propaganda agreed with Kenrick's proposal and sent it to Gregory XVI for approval. Kenrick was to become the first bishop of Pittsburgh. John Hughes would be consecrated coadjutor bishop of Philadelphia. This plan was headed off, however, by John England who wrote to the Pope that he objected to action on Kenrick's plan until it could be discussed by the American bishops. Then, quite independently of England, Kenrick wrote again to Rome. Dubois was waxing persistent in his plea for Kenrick as a coadjutor—or if not him then John Hughes. Kenrick feared that the Frenchman's wishes might eclipse his own. "I would not be pleasing to the clergy [of New York]," he pleaded, "many of whom passed from this diocese to New York, bereft by me of their faculties. Others know of me by report and would scarcely tolerate my rule. . . The same can be said of Reverend John Hughes."[2]

Rather than be caught in an undesired transfer Kenrick agreed with England's view that the whole matter be left until the American bishops could meet together. Kenrick was not only fearful of the future; his sensitive nature had been wounded by intimations both in Philadelphia and in Rome that he simply wanted out of his unpleasant situation, ". . . as if," he complained, "I was abandoning my post in despair."[3] By summer the Pope decided to take the whole stew from the flames and let it cool, as the bishop of Charleston had suggested, until the next Baltimore council should present a collectively agreed upon plan.

Unfortunately, word of John Hughes's supposed appointment had leaked out and had been printed in European, then Philadelphia newspapers. Then further word had arrived that all action had been postponed. To have had a miter placed on his head only to be knocked off was a public humiliation to Hughes. He was no unknown pawn but a well-publicized champion of religion. He didn't shrink from demanding explanations from England or Kenrick. Hughes hurled off testy letters to both bishops. It was a foolhardy thing to have done. His superiors, men of power and influence, were in a position to cut off his ascent to the episcopacy. They both answered him, apologizing for insults not intended; both assured him that his name remained foremost on the list for advancement.

Despite this, however, Kenrick began to nurse resentment toward this strong-willed priest, a man of his own age yet so much more colorful and popular than himself, a man who dared to reproach him as if he were a peer. Within weeks he was writing letters meant to prevent Hughes from becoming a bishop. To the Propaganda Fide he claimed: "On this occasion he showed himself so avid of honor and so seized by evil suspicions that I am not easily convinced that he should be promoted to the episcopacy."[4]

John England, a misplaced natural leader in a rural southern diocese, had never had to compete with an underling who was more a crowd pleaser than himself. He felt no animosity to the outspoken hero whom he himself had crowned with "unfading laurels" after the Breckinridge debates. He did, however, have a candidate of his own for whom he was campaigning— his longtime friend John Power, twice vicar general of New York and a mutinous foe of John Dubois.

After his angry outburst, and with this added factor considered, it is almost a wonder that Hughes didn't spend the remainder of his life applying his poor business acumen to the liquidation of St. John's enormous debt. He claimed not to care, owning that he had "if not humility, at least sense enough" to disregard the temporal glory of seeking a bishopric. "I had studied the inside as well as the outside of a miter," he told Kenrick, "and I regarded him who is obliged to wear it as entitled to pity, not envy."[5]

If, indeed, Hughes had spent time looking at the insides of miters it was probably because he was looking for one his size. As had been observed of him—he panted to do good, widespread good. With his aptitude for leadership this meant a position of command wider than the domain of a city parish. To his friend Bishop John Purcell, who through a bungle of names on the part of the Holy Spirit accidentally occupied the see of Cincinnati intended for himself, Hughes wondered: "Is it a very delightful thing to be a bishop? Are there not difficulties that touch the quick and make it painful to be invested with authority?"[6]

Yet even while playing a rhetorical devil's advocate he sounded as if he were expressing a wish. If so, the wish was soon enough fulfilled. In April of 1837 the bishops met at Baltimore. Hughes was present as a consulting theologian. Dubois had chosen not to attend, but the remaining prelates—including Purcell and Bruté—decided to accede to Kenrick's plan for a See at Pittsburgh. Quashing Kenrick's own hopes for an immediate ticket out of Philadelphia, however, they nominated John Hughes to be sent as coadjutor to New York. The unhappy Kenrick, seeing the strength of approval for Hughes, shrank from entering into a personality clash; he decided to make no mention of the sharp dispute between himself and his secretary. Instead he wondered out loud whether it was fair—in the face of the ever-deepening economic depression of that year —to remove a man responsible for building a church for which there remained a $40,000 debt.* The fact that Hughes had built the church on Kenrick's orders seems not to have occurred to the bishop as he spoke. There was only one actively dissenting voice—that of John England. England was determined that, in justice, the office of coadjutor of New York had to go to John Power, the vicar general who had served as a priest in that city from a time when John Hughes was still digging roads. But such an appointment could have been made only over Dubois's dead body. When the document recommending Hughes went to Rome it went with Kenrick's signature, and without England's. He was the only bishop to refuse assent.

It was a trying time for John Hughes. He was physically ill when he went to Baltimore. For a man of such strong energies he either possessed a constitution more frail than he wanted others to know or else he took poor care of himself. Throughout his adult life he would push himself for long periods of time without proper rest, and then when most busy he would collapse in weakness from an inflammation of the lungs. During the council he was obliged to ask John England

---

*Times were hard enough that when Hughes on one occasion gave a fund-raising sermon—though he was considered a good draw and was at the height of personal popularity—only $20 was taken in.[7]

to preach a sermon he was to have given. Then with all else he received word of his father's death in Chambersburg. He went home, took care of the necessary family concerns, and wrote a comforting letter to his sister who was unable to come home from the convent. To her he admitted, "The doctor says I require rest of mind and body."

Still, as the older brother Hughes would not admit of anything that could slow him down. He waved off even the need of a doctor: "He considers my little attacks nothing more than a cold aggravated by anxiety and fatigue."[8]

He accepted Purcell's invitation to travel to Ohio, to view the diocese that should have been his. Possessed of a Catholic puritan spirit he refused to admit it was a trip meant for relaxation. He wrote ahead to Purcell outlining problems the two could work on when he arrived, and then while out West he swung through Ohio and Missouri on a speaking tour.*

In November official word was received from Rome appointing John Hughes as bishop. Amidst the continued complaints of Kenrick ("The Loss of Reverend J. H. is likely to make the church which he erected bankrupt"[9]), he made preparations to move from Philadelphia where for a dozen years he had been happy and known satisfaction in his priesthood and in his personal life. There were strong personal attachments to that city. Mark Frenaye, whose total dedication in life was now to his Church, had moved into St. John's.** Hughes had all but been adopted by the socially prominent Rodrigue family, the elderly patriarch of which had been a refugee from the slave uprising in Santo Domingo. William Rodrigue had designed St. John's Church, and Hughes, like an older brother, had no doubt helped to fashion the relationship that grew between the young architect and Margaret Hughes. They were married in 1836 and later followed Hughes to New York City. Hughes was hesitant to leave this place, hesitant even to leave

---

*He was on this tour when Maria Monk accused him of having held her captive in Philadelphia.

**He continued to live there until his death in 1873.

the church he had fashioned himself.* This latter sentiment caused one last bone of contention between Kenrick and himself. Hughes had extracted a promise from Kenrick that St. John's would at last be made into that which it had been intended to be—Philadelphia's cathedral. When Hughes told his congregation that this agreement had been made, Kenrick angrily backed off, telling Hughes that nothing should have been said without final approval from Rome. John saw it as a retreat before the untrustworthy trustees at St. Mary's. Betraying his own clerical prejudices, he accused Kenrick of collusion with them: "If instead of treating with laymen, good and pious men, I admit, but yet nothing more than laymen and pewholders only, like so many others [have], you had spoken to me at first your intentions, we should not have been brought to this painful crisis."[10]

In retaliation Hughes refused to sign over the deed of the church unless it would be named the cathedral. It was an irony, for by exercising this temporal legal power in order to enforce his own individual will he had somewhat vindicated the stand for which democratic Catholics had fought all along. He remained adamant. St. John's was built to be symbolic of the destruction of trusteeism, and he would see a total victory in that respect. "I have contended too long," he lashed at Kenrick, "against any lay interference to admit it now in the management of any ecclesiastical matters with which I am concerned." And if Kenrick didn't get the point clearly enough in this missive delivered on December 25th, Hughes finished the letter— and any remnant of friendship that might still have existed—by saying, "If you are so thoughtless as to expose me to suspicion and contempt by the unworthy policy which you have permitted yourself to adopt toward me, I cannot submit to it and in my own defense I shall be constrained to oppose and rebuke it."[11]

Hughes had begun this attack by thanking Kenrick for some small episcopal courtesy extended, adding that he would

---

*While in New York he was still so tied to St. John's as to protest the installation of gas lighting, which he felt ruined the inner decor.

be happy to reciprocate with a like courtesy "when in my power." Quite obviously he did not feel far from power. And yet they were not quite peers; Kenrick had one sharp weapon to use. It was not ecclesiastical but social. Hughes had refused to execute the deed. That was in his legal power to do or not do. But in that case, Kenrick informed him, "the terms of your letters must be my apology for not being present at your consecration."[12]

It was an interesting impasse. If John Hughes, the onetime day laborer, would do no business with laymen, then he could stand publicly ostracized in the clerical world in which he chose to do his temporal business.

In this instance, Hughes exercised a rare movement in his life experience. He backed down. The title of the church was signed over to Kenrick, and the bishop of Arath agreed to be present and to smile upon the consecration of the new bishop of Basileapolis.

PART TWO

The Bishop

12

A FRENCH
ST. PATRICK

As John Hughes was being consecrated a bishop, John Dubois was celebrating his fiftieth anniversary as a priest. The newspapers noted that such an occurrence in the United States was rare, owing to the sufferings and privation that missionaries such as Dubois experienced in their lives. And yet for all that he had endured in his young and middle years no sufferings or privations compared to the ill treatment he received after he had been made a bishop. His elevation had been a mistake on the part of Rome, both for the old Frenchman and for New York. If in the happy world he had created and ruled at Mount St. Mary's he had been caricatured as "The Little Bonaparte," then New York City was his St. Helena.

When Dubois was named bishop of New York, Reverend John Power had been reigning as vicar general of that diocese since the death of the previous bishop two years before. With dark curly hair, blue eyes, and a virile fair-skinned face, he was attractive both physically and personally. A great favorite with the 30,000 Catholics of New York, he awakened an honestly exchanged affection between himself and almost everyone he dealt with—an attribute he possessed until the day of his death. The parishioners of both St. Peter's and St. Patrick's churches in New York had petitioned Rome to make him the new bishop. They were disappointed and an outsider, a Frenchman, was sent to them. It is easy to understand their initial reaction. It is less easy to condone the open warfare that was unleashed and sustained upon Dubois by Power and the mere handful of priests who made up the clergy of the diocese.

The opening barrage was fired during the new bishop's consecration ceremony in Baltimore. Dubois had diplomatically invited Father William Taylor of New York's cathedral to preach on the occasion. This gentleman responded by climbing into the pulpit, complaining to the congregation about the disastrous consequences that resulted to religion from injudicious appointments to the episcopal office, and judged that Dubois's appointment over a people "almost exclusively Irish" was a "bold and hazardous experiment." He finished with the ringing hope that his words "would resound under the dome of the Vatican," then descended from the pulpit and left Dubois with this hostile welcome resounding in his ears.[1]

Although there were some angry reactions from those present, this was no bother to Taylor. The sermon had been designed as his swansong; he left on the next boat to Europe. Yet not without some applause to ring in his own ears. The New York *Truth Teller* run by Power and Father Thomas Levins (of the Sheet Anchor brotherhood) regretted the departure of their brother priest and praised him for the "fearless intrepidy" with which he had revealed "in forcible and explicit terms the present state of the Roman Catholic religion in this country."[2]

A week later, when Bishop Dubois arrived in his diocese, he was installed at St. Patrick's and pleaded that "all party feelings should be buried in oblivion."[3] Then John Power handed over to him the trust he had exercised for two years—"with honour to himself and to the satisfaction of the Catholics of New York,"[4] as the *Truth Teller* phrased it. The paper recounted the bishop's entry to his See, and followed it by an article that regretted the departure of Father Taylor. Dubois's next step was to address his people. He did so in the conciliatory and heavily paternal manner characteristic of his dealings as president of the Mount. He moved directly to the core of the problem. The complaints that he was foreign were complaints, of course, that he was not Irish. This, he felt, should be no problem to a people who each March 17th went all but mad praising a man Dubois believed to be French. He asked them: "Is Saint Patrick less the patron and protector of Ireland for having been born in Gaul?" Even more importantly, he pointed out that it was the purpose of immigrants to become assimilated. He, like they, had moved from another country, but had lived and worked in the United States for thirty-five years. This fact, he pleaded, "would surely give us the right to exclaim we, too, are American." Beyond that, Dubois pointed to a deeper cause for unity: ". . . We are all Catholics. Are not all distinctions of birth and country lost in this common profession?"[5]

The people he served did not accept this explanation. In fact they didn't have the opportunity to accept it. The *Truth Teller,* purportedly a Catholic but more accurately an Irish paper, disdained publishing the pastoral letter.[6]

Dubois was not effective as a preacher. If Power was to be believed, this man who had built a flourishing college spoke the English language so poorly he could not be understood at all from a pulpit. "Hundreds leave the Church," Power insisted, "and actually go into the rum shops while he is speaking."[7]

The attitude of the clergy spread quickly enough to others. The man who, almost four decades earlier, had been handsomely accepted by the Protestant Virginia aristocracy was consistently snubbed by Manhattan's Catholics. A former student regretted the bishop's lack of cosmopolitan graces, saying, ". . . He has a different people here to act with to those at the Mountain. I have been asked what sort of people were the Mountaineers who would be led by such a nonsensical talker as the Bishop. He has not made one respectable acquaintance since he came here."[8]

Even after several months' time when the *Truth Teller* was again asked to print the bishop's pastoral, the newspaper bent backward only so far as to tell the public: "A few copies of this letter remain on hand and can be had at the office of the *Truth Teller,* or from sextons of the various Churches."[9]

Dubois, however, was indomitable. He settled down to work as a bishop—which, stripped of the romance of title, meant administering an unruly clergy and laity who had chosen to hate him before they had met him, doing the work of a parish priest in New York City and doing the work of a missionary throughout New York and sections of New Jersey. In 1828 he undertook an extensive visitation of the diocese. He reached Buffalo, the farthest point of his territory, by route of the Erie Canal, finding several hundred Catholics where he had expected to find less than a hundred. They had no priest. He would have to make arrangements to get them one, from somewhere.

In 1829 he decided to go on an extensive begging tour of Europe. He needed to recruit good missionaries to fill immediate needs and to get funds to build a diocesan seminary. Journeying eastward across the Atlantic he crossed sea lanes with the willful Bishop Conwell, at that time making good his "escape" from the Holy See. The Pope, having so recently listened to an American bishop whose ambitions and worries were all for his own sake, now listened to a man whose deeply felt worries were for the Church in America. Dubois was given free reign to solicit as he might throughout Europe. He had little luck, for Europe, as Dubois noted, was in "a convulsed state." France hadn't changed much. He had fled the country as a young man in the wake of Revolution. In 1830 he walked into another revolution. He left as emptyhanded as he had four decades before. Ireland was too destitute to help New York with its problems. Dubois came home from his trek with a mere $3,000 to show for his efforts. To the Irish in New York it was just one more indication of his incompetence.

"Dubois is old," John Hughes observed to Purcell, adding that the people who surrounded the bishop included "few who will think it a duty to carry his plans into effect."[10] Yet those plans, even in the absence of money, were very concrete. "I have purchased one hundred and sixty acres on the North River at the distance of upwards of 30 miles," Dubois announced to his people, "and of quick and cheap access from the city by steam-boats."[11] It would be his college and seminary—a second Mount St. Mary's.

The buildings went up slowly, commensurate to the bishop's ability to pay, and the project became another subject for his enemies' ridicule. Power complained to Father Paul Cullen, of the Irish College in Rome, that "our aged bishop" had sunk the diocese into debt. "The Bishop will never get any help from the people," Power declared, "because they have no opinion of his prudence." The project, however, was foolish only so long as it was in the hands of the bishop. Power hinted that everything concerned would fit into proper place if only the Sacred Congregation would delegate the responsibility to himself (as, at that time, Kenrick administered Philadelphia for Conwell). "I will," Power promised secretly, "within my own family find funds to complete the work."[12]

John England, Power's protector within the hierarchy, added his voice to the complaints going to Rome. He wrote, "In plain truth this finest city of the Western world commands resources that might, by a man even ordinarily prudent, be drawn forth to such an amount in aid of religion as to make it flourish . . . but with the great portion of his flock and the public at large Dr. Dubois is looked upon as worse than crazy."[13] Power contended that Dubois was not interested in sick calls because there was no money in the matter.* And in general he judged that the bishop "is unpopular, hated. The fault is his own. His favorite theme is abuse of the Irish priests . . . If interference be not interposed, a century will not repair the evils."[14]

Dubois took it all as if he were riding determinedly through a hailstorm. He pleaded for conciliation. "I am aware that it has been spread about that I was averse to employing clergymen from Ireland," he wrote. "I deny the charge as repugnant equally to my feelings and my conduct. I appeal to the many appointments which I have made since I took possession of the see. Are they not all, with two exceptions Irishmen, or the sons of Irishmen? And truly happy do I feel in the selection."[15]

His pleas fell upon ears whose owners had made conclu-

---

*Students of the Mount would, in memoirs, recall incidents such as the occasion when Dubois rode twenty-five miles at night to be with a dying Catholic, returned at dawn, then went immediately to morning prayers with the students and fainted, from exhaustion, in chapel.

sive prejudgments. One of those who most consistently and directly attacked him was Thomas Levins of the *Truth Teller,* whose acid-tipped pen had only a short time before made itself felt in Hughes's first public fight. Levins complained that Dubois was always fluctuating between caprice and visionary schemes, and that, moreover, he was hostile to Thomas Levins.[16] His vilification of the bishop at length became so open that Dubois suspended him. It was not so much a matter of turning to attack but of finally drawing a line that could not be stepped over.

The clever Levins, however, had the trustees of the cathedral in his pocket. They promptly hired him to superintend the Sunday school. Being thus supported he took up residence near the cathedral and worked as an engineer on the construction of the Croton aqueduct to supplement his salary. The bishop was reduced to utter poverty, since the trustees, in announcing their financial support for Levins, told Dubois that they could not be responsible for him as well.

They were not talking to a Conwell bent upon his own comforts and prerogatives. This was a man who had been deprived the greater portion of his life of both comfort and security. Such normal luxuries meant nothing to him. Like Levins the trustees had crossed the drawn line. Without any qualms Dubois could smile at them and say, "Well, gentlemen, you may vote the salary or not, just as seems good to you. I do not need much. I can live in the basement or in the garret. But whether I come up from the basement or down from the garret, I will still be your bishop."[17]

Then disaster struck Dubois's nearly completed college at Nyack. In 1835 it burned to the ground, uninsured. This was the year of the Charlestown convent fire. Immediate rumor and subsequent histories hinted that the fire was the work of a nativist incendiary. If an intensive investigation had been conducted by legal authorities, however, the application of motive might have pointed at suspects closer to home. Dubois refused to quit. He no longer had the stamina to take a pickax and mark out new foundations as he had after the Mount's great fire. But once again he managed to tell others that this was all part of God's providence.

By 1835 Dubois was ready to admit that he needed help—
Irish help. Under no circumstances would he hear of Power
becoming coadjutor. Kenrick was one Irishman who could be
counted upon to be a gentleman, and he was in a desperately
unhappy situation with Conwell in Philadelphia. Dubois wrote
to Rome and asked if he might have him as coadjutor in New
York. Kenrick, who did not know Dubois well, had his fill of
such situations. He politely fought Dubois's requests with his
own counterproposals for a new diocese in Pittsburgh. It was
only after the bishops had met at Baltimore in 1837 and agreed
with Dubois's request that Rome sent him, not Kenrick, but
Hughes whom Dubois had listed as a possible alternate.

There was always a one-sided expression of affection between Dubois and Hughes. The Frenchman had quickly grown
into seeing Hughes as one of his mountain children, never realizing that Hughes did not feel a corresponding sense of son-
ship. While Dubois thought he had graced an Irish laborer first
with education and then the priesthood, Hughes would always
remember their relationship at the Mount coldly as "a regular
contract between us, in which neither was required to acknowledge any obligation to the other."

Perhaps with that in mind, and knowing the relationship
between Kenrick and Conwell, Hughes wrote to Dubois and
voiced more apprehension than joy about their future relationship. The letter hurt Dubois. He wrote a long reply to
Hughes hoping that the younger man saw, as his old mentor
did, that the appointment was an expression of divine will. In
attempting to assuage Hughes's fears he pronounced an ironic
prophecy that would come true in a matter of weeks:

> . . . You surely could not suppose a moment that I
> would encroach upon the rights and privileges attached to
> that sacred office, and I have too great an opinion of your
> merit and affection for me to suppose that you would en-
> croach upon mine . . . That scandals should have arisen be-
> tween Bishop Conwell and his coadjutor, who is ex-officio
> sole administrator of the diocese, is no wonder, with a man
> of the bishop's disposition; but I am neither reduced to the
> nullity of Bishop Conwell—a circumstance rather painful to
> human pride—nor would I be disposed to struggle for the
> mastery if I had been placed in his situation; I would have

considered this nullity as a warning from the divine goodness that henceforth all my time must be exclusively devoted to my preparation for death . . .[18]

At the same time, while celebrating his fiftieth year in the priesthood at an anniversary Mass, Dubois spoke for almost an hour. A reporter recorded his impression of the talk as "touching, delicate and forcible."[19]

There is quite a discrepancy between this view and the report of Power that Dubois's broken English sent hundreds from the churches and into the rum shops. John Dubois deserved better than what had been meted out to him during the first eleven years of his episcopacy. And yet the most painful humiliations were still to come.

13

MASTER OF THE SCARLET-CLOTHED HORSE

John Hughes was forty years old when he entrained for New York as its coadjutor bishop. A lean muscular man, he looked more like a well-tailored fighter than a clergyman. As if conscious of this departure from a common mold he had developed a habit of undoing and spreading into a vee the top buttons of his Roman collar. Only the solid white band encircling his neck could identify him as a cleric. His manners were thoroughly American. If he had ever spoken with a brogue he had eliminated it from his speech early in his adult life. Throughout his career his worst enemies would be able to categorize him with the coarse, general run of Irish immigrants only by reason of his birth. The day laborer had become not only an American but an American of good cultural background. He was physically imposing, attractive without being handsome. His brown, curly hair had begun to recede making his forehead more prominent. His Roman nose, sternly set mouth, and blue-gray eyes which could flash with sharp wit or equally sharp anger made him the sort of man who was often intimidating to those in his presence. The impression given was one of self-assurance and strength.

Nonetheless, forty is a convenient age to mark as man's passage into his middle years, and in fact Hughes traveled northward, hoarse of voice and wracked with one of the heavy

chest infections to which he would become increasingly susceptible. As if fully realizing the chasm that authority would place
between his career as a bishop and what he had known before,
he ignored all other invitations and spent his last night in Philadelphia in the company of a friend he had met while digging
ditches in Emmitsburg. Then he entered a new life.

Only one-sixth of Manhattan, the bottom tip, was built
into a city in 1837. The greater northern part of the Island was
still farmland. Yet this bustling center of some 300,000 persons
(nearly double the community which Dubois had found in
1826) considered itself—as it did almost from the days of the
Dutch—to be the very hub of modern civilization.

Father Augustus Thébaud, an astute young Jesuit who
would eventually chronicle forty years of his memories in the
United States, noted in that same year that "New York was already a great emporium in communication with the whole
world, where you could find at short notice any goods, however
costly, even articles of virtu such as you had thought only
London or Paris could procure." However, if it was finesse one
was looking for, this newcomer added, "I had left Paris two
months before; and I cannot say I found Paris again at the
mouth of the Hudson River."[1]

It was a city of churches—some 150 of them. The leading
denominations were the Presbyterians with thirty-nine and the
Episcopalians with twenty-nine. There were only seven Roman
Catholic churches.

The Irish Catholic community, still a small minority of
the city's population, was almost universally disappointed with
Rome's choice of a new coadjutor bishop. Father Thebaud,
who was just then arriving in the city, remarked on the prevalent mood, observing that "the clergy of New York, particularly of the city, were loudest in their discontent about the choice
which had been made. They had heard and approved of the
great things achieved in Philadelphia by the Reverend Mr.
Hughes. But why was he sent to New York, when some See
might have been found for him in Pennsylvania, and the man
they had always admired in New York for his eloquence, zeal,
and ability, a man known to and loved by all classes of citizens,

might with so much profit for religion have been placed at their head? I have heard that when Bishop Hughes was consecrated in 1837 [1838] there were very few clergyman if any except Dr. Power himself who did not harbor these feelings."[2]

If Dr. Power did harbor these feelings he, already knowing Hughes, wisely kept them to himself. Yet there was one Catholic who made his living by airing his reflections. He was James Gordon Bennett, whose electrifying New York *Herald* was revolutionizing the American newspaper. This crosseyed, aggressive Scotsman was so like John Hughes personally that the two were bound to be enemies. Bennett was the product of a pious family that had pushed both him and his brother to study for the priesthood. Bennett soon enough changed his direction, quit the seminary and sought his fortune in the United States. His brother died in the seminary. Forever after, James, convinced that the death was brought about from austerities imposed by religious superiors, vented a strong hatred toward all ecclesiastical authorities both Catholic and Protestant. Balanced against this hostility, Bennett was a good, thorough newsman. He carefully reported all the "religious intelligence" of the day. He reviewed Sunday sermons almost in the manner of a drama critic, and in general he reported whatever he felt the public should know about the activities of the Churches and the clergy. When they did something he approved of—whatever the denomination—he praised them. When he felt they acted like fools or worse he pilloried them with ridicule. Any particular clergyman (perchance John Hughes) might find his activities praised one week and a week later be pounced upon and torn to shreds. Bennett was hated almost universally by the clergy of New York.

As regards religious beliefs Bennett retained a love for the liturgy of Catholicism, while his opinions of religious authority were Protestant in the extreme (save that he was equally repelled by Protestant dogmatism). Other Catholics—especially John Hughes who in general could not stand having ungovernable people around, and who in particular could not stand having James Gordon Bennett around—would have been very happy if Bennett had formally apostatized. Bennett remained, nonetheless, happy and right square at the fringes of the Church, maintaining that Catholicism was on its last legs, and saying that it was the only Church to which he would belong. "I am a Catholic," he insisted, "I believe our Church. I venerate her absurdities—but I do all this in my own way."[3]

And what was essential to that way? Raising himself up to a majestic plural he vowed ". . . we never would and never will submit our mind's free thoughts to the shackles of any man, or set of men under heaven, calling themselves priests and prelates . . . There is no species of Christianity that could more easily link itself with the higher order of civilization than Catholicity, but it must be Catholicity independent of the old fools and blockheads of the Vatican."[4]

James Gordon Bennett, with these loudly expressed ideas and extensive influence, necessarily intrudes into the story of John Hughes not merely as a journalistic observer but as one of the principal characters. Bennett was fond of John Power—whom he asked to officiate at his wedding—and sided strongly with Power and Levins in their fight against Dubois, whose episcopacy he called "capricious, tyrranical, heartless, oldwomanish and absurd; he [Dubois] has reduced and is reducing the standard of Catholicity to a standard that would make Maria Monk pity it, and Dr. Brownlee say prayers for its safety."[5]

The day after John Hughes's consecration, the *Herald* carried two pieces of religious news, one dealing with the consecration and the other with the consecration of the rebuilt St. Peter's church, under the direction of John Power. Bennett found himself extremely moved by the latter proceedings. It was a perfect expression in Gregorian chant and rubric of that which tied him to the Church of his birth. Protestantism, he pronounced, was "bare"; Catholicism was "the religion of poetry."[6]

Then, lest this put him on the outs with his nativist subscribers, he offered a comic picture of the consecration of Hughes who was now, ex officio, in the power structure and heir to all that Bennett resented in the Church. The ceremony, he told his readers, "beggars description." The cathedral was packed with the curious as well as the faithful, for New York had never witnessed the consecration of a Roman bishop. Even throughout the Mass the aisles were crowded with people and with ushers who noisily clattered out extra chairs, then found them ill-suited to the occasion and dragged them away again. People sat on the windowsills. The windows had been thrown open and determined throngs outside risked at least limb by erecting shaky platforms of piled-up park benches. Contrasted to the sedate ceremony and upper-class congregation ($1 entrance fee) at St. Peter's, Bennett felt that the value of placing an episcopal consecration before the general run of local Irish was like pushing "gold rings through pigs' noses."

Of Hughes he had little to say, only that the presence of a new bishop would give the old woman Dubois the opportunity of going back to making "petticoats for the Blessed Virgin." His main desire had been to weigh the quality of the congregation: "Upon comparing notes outside they found that they had heard a mightily illegant sarmint; their toes had been well pounded and their hats and clothes disordered. But it was mighty illigent and idifying." He saved one small thrust for the pompous trappings of the episcopacy. For those in the democracy who loathed the outward show of Romanism he pointed out: "Over the horses were thrown rich scarlet clothes which called to mind at once the Scarlet Lady of Babylon in all her pomp and pride."[7]

Once Hughes had ridden home on his scarlet horse he prepared to settle down to the everyday business of being coadjutor bishop. How he and Dubois would have gotten along on a routine basis is a matter of conjecture. Judging from Hughes's lifelong fealty to the proper chain of command, their relationship probably would have remained correct, even if strained. As it was, within two weeks after the consecration Dubois suffered a stroke. In another month there was a second seizure, worse than the first.

He didn't know how to remain sick. Hughes, trying to care for him, worried: "He insists on seeing every one that comes to inquire for him, and the consequence is that toward the evening of every day he is extremely feeble both in mind and body."[8] His right side was partially paralyzed, yet as soon as he could he got up to struggle through Mass. By the end of March Hughes was pessimistic and wrote as much to the worried Sisters of Charity at Emmitsburg: "I doubt of his recovery as before—ever."[9]

In obvious confusion about his role, Hughes filled up months meeting the 200,000 Catholics throughout the diocese. The 1830s were a time of constant construction of roads, railroads and canals. Immigrants who had worked on crews settled down in all corners of the state. With barely forty priests of varying background and quality to care for them, and in the wake of the hamstrung administration of Dubois, the 55,000 square-mile diocese of New York had yet to be cohesively organized.

Hughes stood at Nyack on the Hudson, viewed the "splendid folly"[10] of Dubois's ruined college, and, not caring for the place, agreed with Dubois's resigned view that the disaster had been providential. Nonetheless Hughes become as convinced as the old bishop that a college and seminary for New York was a top priority. With this on his mind, the green newcomer to the episcopacy was easy prey for a Catholic businessman he encountered just north of Watertown. A Mr. Lafarge had built himself a lordly plantation house on 650 acres of land and then realized that a mansion in the north woods was no way to show off his wealth. He was looking for a buyer when John Hughes knocked on the door looking for his flock. Mr. Lafarge took shears in hand, reversed roles and fleeced the new bishop. Hughes was easily convinced that the place was a steal at the price of $20,000. It would be a perfect school and could serve also as a house of retreat for the clergy. There was no overstating this latter possibility. A retreat of a few more miles distance would have brought the clergy into Canada.

Hughes bought it, Lafarge escaped, and three priests out of a precious forty were assigned to begin a school at this spot whose one minor flaw was that it was "well removed from all great lines of communication."[11] It opened in September of 1838 with eight students. The disheartened rector soon wrote to Hughes, "We might be compared to a big stage coach drawn by four horses and no passengers."[12]

For a man who had first appeared in New York equipped with a scarlet-clothed horse, Hughes was in poor straits. There was no leadership in the diocese, for Dubois, though almost wholly incapacitated, held on to his episcopal rights "rigidly and cautiously." By October Hughes was thoroughly depressed. He unburdened himself to Archbishop Eccleston in Baltimore, Dubois's and his immediate superior. He repeated the details of Dubois's several strokes, his resulting feebleness, and finished by saying: "I have not been and am not now of any more use in the matter of assisting him than when I was in Philadelphia. He never asks my opinion but on the contrary seems glad of every opportunity to prove to himself and others that he does not stand in need of it."[13]

One could sympathize with both Dubois and Hughes. The Frenchman would not accept the reality that his body had failed him. The new coadjutor was watching the diocese head toward disaster. He needed the power to steer matters, and the old man's hands could not be pried away from the reins.

The clergy, along with some of the laity who were resentful of the new outsider, used a test case to see who was boss. They did Hughes a great favor, for their minor rebellion came at a moment when he was at a loss for direction. A proper fight was just what he needed to plump up his own self-confidence and show New York his true mettle. It was a stupid squabble about the management of the cathedral's Sunday school. The trustees had paid the suspended Levins to remain in charge of religious education, and he had done so for several years, even while working as an engineer and editing a short-lived Irish paper, the *Green Banner*. The clerical Irish had pulled their strings at Rome, and before Hughes had arrived Propaganda had directed Dubois to restore Levins. The Frenchman balked at doing so until the man's actual insubordination had been properly reviewed. Now in the first full winter of Hughes's presence upon the scene Levins decided to oust a teacher Dubois had personally hired. When the young man refused to quit, the suspended priest, to enforce his will against a subordinate, called in the law. On February 10th, 1839 the local constable showed up during religion classes and at Levins's orders ejected the teacher. Though this was certainly colorful enough to keep the attention of the children, the occurrence left John Hughes irate. The next Sunday he spoke at the cathedral Masses and demanded an apology from the trustees. As he did this Levins slipped about between each Mass placing circulars in the pews to explain his and the trustees' position, along with his own declaration that for the sake of his principles he had "drawn the sword and will return it to the scabbard no more."[14]

When no apology was forthcoming in the course of a week, the parties headed for a showdown in which one of them had to lose. The situation was roughly parallel to what Hogan had created nearly two decades before in Philadelphia. Only this time the popular suspended priest fighting the system was not contending with a Conwell or even a Dubois, but with John Hughes.

On Sunday the 24th Hughes unleashed a pastoral address.* In it he acknowledged the right the trustees possessed to control the temporal affairs of the church. To balance this he threatened that if they persisted in their autonomous use of this right all priests would be removed and the cathedral would be interdicted. He cordially invited all concerned to meet with him in the church hall that afternoon.

Between 500 and 700 people showed up, and they got their effort's worth. Hughes was in his best form. He treated his audience as if he and they were allies who had been attacked by the destroyers of religion—in this case by their own trustees. He reminded them of their parents in Ireland who had upheld the freedom of faith "at the sacrifice of all that men hold dear besides . . . assembling in the solitude of the mountain or the dampness of the secret cave around their priest, for whose head the laws offered the same premium as for that of a wolf."[15] Then he brought them to the point of decision. What Protestant England could never accomplish they were now willing to do to themselves. He hammered on, alternating between praise

*Signed for the sake of proper procedure by John Dubois.

and threats. "I again appear among you because you have yourselves undertaken and determined to vindicate those rights of your religion which your trustees have violated," he declared. "Assembled for such a purpose I mingle among you as one of yourselves. But should you be unsuccessful in your noble effort, you will see me in another place, pronouncing or supporting the sentence which will sever Catholics and Catholicity from your temple until the rights of your religion be not only acknowledged by your trustees but also guaranteed against future aggression from them or their successors."[16]

It was, in the most perfect sense of the term, pure demagoguery. He got his audience thoroughly whipped up; then for a finale he offered a series of resolutions, the principal point of which was that when a bishop was exercising his God-given power no Roman Catholic should ever place opposition before him—"no matter how legal such an act may be."[17]

The mesmerized audience immediately adopted his resolutions by acclamation. If there were any dissenting parties they looked around and decided to keep their mouths shut. When the resolutions were subsequently written into records of the cathedral a number of the trustees resigned. They were easily replaced with men willing to accept the new order of affairs. Levins withdrew in silence. John Hughes, owing to his natural attributes, was in full command, and New York Catholics for the first time experienced a religious leader.

He theologized about his victory in a report he hoped Eccleston would forward to Rome. "All that is secular and human shall become dead . . . and what is spiritual shall have its full, free and unrestricted efficacy."[18] To an old friend, Mother Rose White at Emmitsburg, he was more himself. "We have killed the trustees twice," he exulted. "The first time they could not believe they were dead so we had to kill them again."[19]

Now Hughes was holding the reins, but not fully. The old man's hands were still there with his. He was happy for Dubois's sake that his long-time persecutors had been driven into the dust: "The poor old bishop is revenged for their treatment of him," he told a friend. "He can hardly believe it."[20]

In fact Hughes so wanted to make sure that everyone involved believed what had happened he delivered a series of six lectures on the evils of trusteeism. Once again he turned to Simon Bruté for the facts. Bruté, who was ill and who would be dead before the end of June, complied for the last time. Detecting a prideful sense of triumph in his student, he also cautioned Hughes that he now had a "delicate task" of healing to undertake and that it would be undertaken in "piety and charity, with a view to instruct, not to humble, to rail."[21] Bruté was heartbroken at Hughes's description of Dubois. He could not envision the crippled condition of his companion who had handled "so readily and properly the immense correspondence of the Mountain . . . so remarkable for his letters to parents, his views, his manner of treating their sons with their very own affection . . . Ah, Bishop Dubois. Mr. Dubois! What a life! Now I have to wipe my eyes, else I can't write."[22]

The condition of Dubois's health was a constant theme in all of Hughes's letters during this period. When he finally wrote to the Congregation of Propaganda hinting respectfully that he, like Kenrick in Philadelphia, should be given actual control of the diocese, he declared that the aged bishop "is now better, now worse. His faculties of mind and body are impaired: his memory especially fails him . . . ."[23]

Still, even with Hughes's steady flow of insistence, the evidence that Dubois might have been addled is unconvincing. The motor parts of his brain may not have been working well, and he may have been slowed down, but all accounts left by others besides Hughes show him to be the same John Dubois he had always been. In March of 1839 a reporter watched him say Mass. Power did the preaching for him, but for the rest, the reporter observed: "The bishop is aged and appears to be very feeble, but he went through the long service without flinching. His voice is not strong, but yet effective. His singing is very correct and his piety calculated to impress those present with reverence for his person."[24]

In August Archbishop Eccleston received official directives from Rome. The jurisdiction of New York was to be given to Hughes. The order was tempered, however, by an understanding of the personalities involved. Out of respect for

Dubois it was to be announced as if he had asked for it. Moreover, Hughes was to take care that every episcopal dignity was accorded his predecessor. Dubois could celebrate pontifical Mass, administer Confirmation, and ordain men to the priesthood. Eccleston, attempting to be diplomatic, traveled to New York to deliver the instructions personally.[25]

The old man did not take it well. To him the brutal blow was the final triumph of the Irish party that had attacked his authority for years. It also seemed to imply, that he, like Conwell, had been detrimental to the good of the Church. He balked. "What wrong have I done," he pleaded. "They cannot take away my authority unless I am guilty of a crime. I will never give it up, never."[26]

But he did. He had already vowed that if he became a "nullity" like Bishop Conwell he would never "struggle for mastery." Although Hughes, providentially, was visiting in another part of the state, Bishop John Purcell, another of his Mountain sons, was in town. The old man trusted him, listened to his reasoning and, once he had gotten over the initial shock (as he later said), he "obeyed the bit, but not till he had covered it with foam."[27]

He and Conwell both had three more years to live. The latter peevishly continued to hinder Kenrick whenever he had the energy to do so. Dubois retired in gentlemanly silence. He occasionally officiated, visited his friends, and continued living in the episcopal residence with his coadjutor, the bishop of Basileopolis. But there was never anything more than a cool and correct relationship between the two men. Till the day of his death he addressed Hughes and referred to him publicly only as "Mr. Hughes."

Hughes consolidated his authority. He kept John Power as vicar general. Levins had been discredited. Even John England's *Catholic Miscellany* had deplored Levins's "want of common sense" in the recent dispute, and regretted that while his friends had hoped that his conduct would show Dubois to be wrong, it had not. Hughes, perhaps because Levins was seriously ill and losing his eyesight, restored his old enemy of the Sheet Anchor brotherhood to his ministry and sent him to the new parish of St. John's at the state capital of Albany. He would die in three years.

The college in the backwoods of nowhere was admittedly a mistake. Hughes looked around and found a half-built estate he liked. On the last day of August 1839 the *Truth Teller* reported that Dr. Hughes had purchased 106 acres for a college and seminary twelve miles from the city and three miles outside Harlem on the Third Avenue Road. Although this might appear out of the way to some, the notice assured New Yorkers that "a new Albany railroad in process of being graded will pass a mere twenty yards from the building and reduce the travelling time from the city to a mere forty minutes."[28] Hughes, who had already begun an orphanage and opened two churches, all of which he called St. John's, again showed his unbiased liking for the name and christened the new institution St. John's College. In time people would dub the school after the name of the area—not of the actual manor bought, Rose Hill—but of the larger and more ancient manor of which it was a part, Fordham.

In October Hughes took sail for Europe, seeking, as had Dubois nine years earlier, both money and personnel for his college. On this first voyage to Europe he was still something of a rustic. He had come to America barely more than a boy. He had labored in and received his entire education in the rural atmosphere of Maryland. He spent the dozen years of his priestly ministry in a city called the "Athens of America"; but this comparison was more favorable to Philadelphia than to the original. The boomtown that he served as bishop may have been the great seaport of the United States, but as Thébaud had observed it was no Paris. That Hughes still possessed a kind of simplicity in 1839 was registered in the diary entry of George Templeton Strong, an Episcopalian who had little use for the Irish or Catholics (and who in due time would extend that sentiment to their new spiritual leader). Hearing a sermon that Hughes gave he pronounced it "decidly the best, indeed the only rational and decent one I ever heard from a Catholic. His manner is very good—plain, candid, and serious. He is no hypocrite I think."[29]

The nine-month business tour of Europe was to be a tempering experience. It gave Hughes a stronger sense of the Church and of his own position in the Church's structure and in the world of politics. He saw the importance of being the bishop of New York from the vantage point of other men, some of them the most powerful men in the world.

On the trip over he was fascinated by his worldly companions and sat in awe through an earnest dinnertime discussion as to whether the oysters were of better character at New York or at Havre. After two delaying periods of calm at sea a violent gale pitched the ship about for twenty-four hours. Angry with himself that he had slept through the beginning of the storm, the bishop ate a hearty breakfast while the oyster connoisseurs hung over the rails. Then he secured himself carefully on the quarterdeck to watch the grand show. It was, he decided, "worth the whole voyage."[30]

In Paris Hughes met the American Ambassador, General Lewis Cass, with whom he would someday cross swords. The soldier politician was a favorite of the King Louis Philippe, who had spent part of his younger days in exile wandering through the wilds of the United States. Cass brought the bishop of New York to visit the royal family. After a month in France Hughes left for Rome. He met Pope Gregory XVI who made a point of asking after Bishop Dubois and sent the old man his respects. For the next three months Hughes became saturated with a world that had previously been only words and distant imaginings. He fell in love with what he called a "city of the soul." "There is but one Rome," he said. "Other cities are beautiful, if you please, but to me insipid if compared with Rome."[31]

Vienna was a place for him to conduct important business, for Vienna it was the center of the Leopoldine Society, a benevolent organization set up to support missionary efforts in distant, primitive areas such as the United States. For their sake Hughes focused upon New York's primitiveness for all it was worth, understandably laying heavy emphasis upon the needs of German immigrants. Impressed by the young bishop, the society was generous in its response. Before he left Austria he was introduced to a number of notables. One was Monsignor Gaetano Bedini, whom Hughes would someday take in tow for a firsthand tour of just how primitive America could be. Another was Prince Metternich who delighted Hughes by telling him that Catholics and the Protestants in America "are like the iron pot and the earthen pot floating down the stream together: when they clash the earthen pot must be broken."[32] Metternich had survived as long as he had in the world of diplomacy for good reason. Apparently he left it to Hughes, and possibly to any others who were listening, to decide which was earthen and which was iron.

Back in Paris Hughes convinced the Madames of the Sacred Heart to staff a school in New York. He was less successful in acquiring Jesuits for St. John's. He had avoided the Jesuit province that staffed Georgetown for fear his college at Fordham would become a lesser sister to that institution. The provincial of the Paris province read the letters brought by Hughes from the Father General in Rome, and with reluctance refused the request. The order had been restored from its suppression only twenty-five years earlier; there was no way to stretch its limited personnel to the diocese of New York. The province was already overcommitted to the United States with its unsuccessful college begun under Bishop Flaget in Kentucky. Disappointed, Hughes settled by commissioning a few Italian Lazarists as instructors. There was no way of dislodging the Jesuits from their western wilderness. Unless, of course, somebody might talk to them personally . . .

At the end of May he was in London. There was no way in the world that this Irish Catholic could have been (or would have wanted to be) introduced to young Queen Victoria, though he stopped to visit St. Paul's ("which after you have seen St. Peter's," he decided with an open mind, "is only fit to be blown up with gunpowder").[33] The high point of his London stay was a visit with Irish hero Daniel O'Connell, a man whom Hughes admired exceedingly. O'Connell led off the visit by denouncing James Gordon Bennett who had recently run a story alleging that Mrs. O'Connell had hired several of her husband's mistresses as maids in their home in an effort to embarrass him. The Irish statesman was distressed, describing the *Herald* account as "the only attack that was ever made on

Mrs. O'Connell."[34] Pocketing this information for further use, Hughes then brought up a complaint that was frequently heard in America against O'Connell. Of late the Irish leader had been criticizing the United States for the institution of slavery. Hughes, the former slave overseer who as a student had written anti-slavery poetry, had by this time modified his former views. In Philadelphia his intimate friends, the Rodrigues, had escaped from the slave uprising in Santo Domingo; from them he heard horror stories of what had happened during that rebellion. From then on he was opposed to any plan of immediate abolition. O'Connell listened to Hughes's criticism, paused, and said, "It would be strange, indeed, if I should not be the friend of the slave throughout the world—I, who was born a slave myself." Hughes reflected: "He silenced me although he did not convince me.*[35]

After England, Hughes traveled to Ireland. It had been twenty-three years since he had emigrated from his homeland. The condition of life there had not been much altered in his absence. ". . . Poor old Ireland," he said. "Alas for the people of this country; the stripes of their martyrdom are everywhere visible. They have been crushed by an apostate nation, which prospers withal."[36]

Still, his concerns were for the present, not for the past, and his thoughts moved westward ahead of him. Even before he left Ireland he was writing to Felix Varela, Vicar General along with John Power, outlining his plans for when he returned.

As it turned out, events were not entirely in his control. When he got back he would discover that Catholics in his diocese had become embroiled in an acrimonious battle about education which only wanted his leadership to become a full-scale war with the Public School Society of New York. He would return home to make his name a household curse among those who wished to exclude immigrants from the mainstream of American life.

---

*Not long before this, Gregory XVI had issued a tepid denunciation of slavery. Hughes did not record whether or not he took the Pope to task at his private interview with him.

14

THE EDUCATION
OF THE POOR

The children of foreigners, found in great numbers in our populous cities and towns, and in the vicinity of our public works, are too often deprived of the advantages of our system of public education in consequence of the prejudices arising from difference of language or religion. It ought never to be forgotten that the public welfare is as deeply concerned in their education as in that of our children. I do not hesitate, therefore, to recommend that establishment of schools, in which they may be instructed by teachers speaking the same language with themselves and professing the same faith.

Governor William H. Seward was addressing the 1840 New York State Legislature, attempting to share with them the vision of a changing, no longer homogeneous America. This lanky, redheaded native New Yorker had long been interested in improving the state's loosely coordinated school system, and a journey through Ireland in 1833 had deepened his sensitivities in regards to these immigrants who had crossed the Atlantic embittered by memories of England's domination. His interest was pragmatic. Those people, once naturalized, would become voters—possibly voters for himself. It was equally pragmatic for the republic, Seward observed. "Since we have opened our country and all its fullness, to the oppressed of every nation," he said, "we should evince wisdom equal to such

139

generosity by qualifying their children for the high responsibilities of citizenship."[1]

Seward was a lifelong skeptic regarding religion. He had joined the Episcopal Church out of remorse following the death of his infant daughter. But the act was done apparently to please his devout wife. After his outward conversion he wrote to his close friend, the political kingmaker Thurlow Weed, and said, "I may as well be explicit with you—I profess not to have experienced any miraculous change of heart—."[2]

Without an intensity of religious feelings, Seward seemed able to stand a few steps back from his co-religionists and see an increasingly heterogeneous America that many of them were not ready to see. As events were to show, he would never be able to educate the nativest public to his own larger view. Seward would pay a costly price for attempting to do so.

The schools of New York City had developed differently from those in sparsely settled areas of the state. In all other districts trustees were elected to take charge of individual schools. In Manhattan schools gradually came under the monopolistic control of a nonelected philanthropic group of men. This group, the Free School Society, had in 1805 generously begun the task of educating poor children of the city who could not afford private schools. Because the society was already doing the job well enough, the legislature gave it funds that in all other areas went to elected supervisors. Various denominational groups in the city also applied for such funds and were granted monies as well.

In 1824 it came to light that the Bethel Baptist church, while operating several schools, was allocating education funds for the purpose of constructing church buildings. In the ensuing furor an act was passed by the legislature empowering the Common Council of the city to distribute and supervise the use of public monies used for education. Denominational schools were cut off; the Free School Society changed its name to the Public School Society (without changing its character as a private agency) and the Common Council, who were all ex-officio members of the society, gave that society the lion's share of state funds.* By 1840 the society controlled nearly 100 schools in New York City.

Although public schools avoided sectarian proselytizing, they imbued American children with a vague kind of Protestantism. Protestant hymns were sung, Protestant prayers were offered, and the bible was read each day. Yet, by the second quarter of the century this Protestant world was beginning to change, notably along the eastern seaboard where German and especially Irish foreigners continually streamed in to overcrowd the cities. Those Catholic immigrants who sent their children to the common schools soon found that they were in an atmosphere hostile to their religion. None of the textbooks save those in mathematics were free of anti-Catholic bias.

In *Cobb's Juvenile Reader,* for example, the word "mass" was defined as a "a lump, bulk; the service of the Romish church."[3] In another reader, children were offered a fancied meeting between Hernando Cortez and William Penn during which Mr. Penn castigated his Catholic opponent in a debate: "A papist talk of reason! Go to the inquisition and tell them of reason and the great laws of nature. They will broil thee as thy soldiers broiled the unhappy Guatimozin! Why dost thou turn pale? Is it at the name of the Inquisition, or the name of Guatimozin?"[4] History was a selective exercise in such books. Martin Luther was "raised up by Providence."[5] Students were assured that "the cause of learning, of religion, and of civil liberty is indebted to [Luther] more than to any man since the apostles."[6] From a geography book a student could learn:

> Superstition prevails not only at Rome but in all the states of Church. The inhabitants observe scrupulously all the ceremonies of religion omitting nothing connected with form or etiquette, although apparently destitute of true devotion. Confession is a practice which all follow more from custom than from christian humility, and rather to lull the conscience than to correct vice.[7]

---

*Several religious organizations of special character, including the Catholic Orphan Asylum, received funds after 1824 because it was considered that they did the job of public education in their routine work.

In the library of every public school was a book, *The Irish Heart*. Through a character in the story, Phelim Maghee, American children were shown how the Catholic conscience operated:

> When Phelim had laid up a good stock of sins he now and then went over to Killarney of a Sabbath morning, and got relaaf by confissing them out o' the way, as he used to express it, and sealed up his soul with a wafer, and returned quite invigorated for the perpetration of new offenses.

The preface of the book made the author's prejudices perfectly evident. It declared:

> The emigration from Ireland to America, of annually increasing numbers, extremely needy and in many cases drunken and depraved, has become a subject for grave and fearful reflection . . . Should the materials of this oppressive influx continue to be the same, instead of an asylum our country might be appropiately styled the common sewer of Ireland.[8]

Books of this sort did not comprise a hearty welcome for newcomers. They began to keep their children away from school in droves. In 1834 Bishop Dubois entered into a polite series of negotiations with the Public School Society for the sake of ameliorating anti-Catholic conditions. The discussions were ineffective, however, and by 1840 conditions prompted Seward to bring the problem to the state legislature. The eight small and overcrowded schools attached to Catholic parishes were woefully inadequate to fill the needs of the thousands of immigrant children roaming the streets, oftentimes collecting into gangs. Why not, reasoned Seward, run schools that would be friendly to these people, if only for the pragmatic purpose of molding them into good instead of harmful citizens? The state could only stand to profit from such a course.

Lacking a sense of purpose and unity, the Catholics of New York responded to the Whig governor's speech along party lines. The *Truth Teller,* primarily interested in Ireland's politics, generally reserved its front page for stories about that country and England, while local stories were relegated to the back pages. When the paper did cover American politics it supported, as did most Catholics, Jacksonian Democrats. In no way was it ready to support Seward, even if it were to Catholic advantage. Seward's efforts were promptly labeled an example of "political juggling."[9] Felix Varela's new *Catholic Register,* looking directly to the opportunity presented for parish schools, praised the governor. The division of sentiment was further deepened when John Power brought 2,400 copies of Seward's speech from Albany. These were distributed in St. Peter's church shortly before the municipal elections. A howl about politics in Church was raised.

Against this background meetings were held and a formal application for funds was presented by the Catholics to the Common Council. A remonstrance was drawn up by the Public School Society to oppose them, and with little fuss and flurry the application was neatly turned down. Throughout the late spring and early summer Catholics continued their disjointed efforts. The Public School Society, while successfully destroying the Catholic application, had responded to requests by Varela and Power for copies of school books, and the society promised to remove sections that they found objectionable. Power upset these delicate negotiations and succeeded in insulting the society by printing examples of the texts in another Catholic paper which began publication on July 4th of that year—the *Freeman's Journal.*

Power had scheduled a meeting for July 20th to plan future actions. But two days before this the British ship bearing John Hughes as a passenger docked at New York. If there were to be future plans now, there was little question as to who would steer them. Hughes took stock of what had happened in New York throughout the winter and spring, listened to Power whose talents for leadership had not proven astute, and then assumed command. Political divisions had to be forgotten. On this issue Catholics would have to speak with one voice. The voice would be that of John Hughes.

In the remaining weeks of summer Hughes campaigned as if he were running for office. He was popular with his people,

and he knew how to work an audience up to laughter, then to
rounds of applause. His theme was not the defense of Catholic
rights to education funds, but rather the need for an unbroken
front in voicing this right. While time was wasted with political
squabbles, he warned, children's minds were being influenced,
alienated, and imperceptibly drawn from the faith. It was time
for their parents to stop imputing evil motives to one another.
Refusing to listen to a good program offered by an opposition
party was like being hungry and then refusing food from an
enemy at the counsel of a supposed friend.

Before a cheering audience of supporters on August 10th
Hughes read "An Address of the Roman Catholics, to their
fellow Citizens of the City and State of New York." The emphasis in the address was on the word "Citizens." "The education which each denomination might, under proper restraints
and vigilance, give to its own poor," the address said, had
passed and become a monopoly in the hands of the Public
School Society of New York. "In a word," Hughes demanded,
"give us our just proportion of the common school fund and if
we do not give as good an education, apart from religious instruction as is given in the public schools, to one third a larger
number of children for the same money, we are willing to
renounce our just claim."[10]

The address of Hughes had the effect of putting the Public
School Society members on the defensive. Any refutation they
might make against the Romanists worked just as well against
themselves. They were a private corporation which wanted to
keep Protestant teaching a part of the common school system.
Even if they could not bring themselves to admit it consciously,
they knew they were on a tightrope.

A committee from the society met with Hughes and
agreed to furnish him with a set of textbooks, a request on his
part which they "supposed" was "for the purpose of uniting
with the committee in ascertaining objectionable passages."[11]
They supposed wrong. Hughes had no intention of accepting
crumbs from a banquet table that was intended for everyone.
After some time passed, the society again approached Hughes,
asking when he would help them in their labors to rid the texts

of "sentiments obnoxious to the Roman Catholic Church."[12] Hughes responded with an ambiguous note, saying "I am at a loss to account for the supposition, on the part of your committee, that I was engaged in the special examination of the objectionable passages with a view to assist the committee in their laudable undertaking."[13]

Hoping to nullify whatever ammunition Hughes was building up in his arsenal, the society hurried its "laudable undertaking" for the approaching school year. Censoring instruction, along with ink stamps and paste were sent out to the schools. For example:

> *English Reader*—Page 51, strike out paragraph, "the Queen's bigoted zeal," etc. to "eternal welfare"; Page 152, erase, "the most credulous monk in a Portuguese convent."
> *Sequel, Murray's*—The whole article "Life of Luther," Pages 84 and 85, paste up "Execution of Cranmer." Page 279 erase, "anon in penance, planning sins anew".
> *Putnam's Sequel*—Erase the article "John Huss"
> *Maltebrun's Geography*—Page 111, erase first five lines. Page 123 erase last paragraph chapter 134. Page 140 erase five lines from the top "and there is no doubt the lower classes of Ireland are so." Page 145 erase, "inflict the most horrible tortures." Page 148 erase "Italy to be submitted to the Catholic bishop." Page 155, erase, "from their religion" down to "ceremonies."
> *Hale's History of the United States*—Page 11, erase "from the persecution of the Catholics" section 22.[14]

Hughes hadn't overcome all Catholic disharmony. At the end of summer a writer who labeled himself "Irish Catholic" accused Hughes in the *Evening Post* of being the "dupe of a Whig Club in disguise." Hughes immediately dismissed the charge. "When I returned to this city," he said, "I found the Catholics broken up and divided . . . Now, happily that the question has been relieved from all the dead weight of politicians of either side; they've united." With a razored edge of humor, he assured the anonymous critic, "We exclude politics from our deliberations as carefully as religion is excluded from the public schools."[15]

With that degree of latitude allowed, Hughes had already

opened correspondance with William Seward. They had never met, but Hughes must have been impressed with the open-minded governor who had once given orders for a priest to be permitted a private interview with a man condemned to death. Hughes thanked the governor for the stand he had taken on the school issue and hinted at an apology for the fact that so few Catholics were Whigs. "Too many of our people having given up their big, credulous hearts to those who have been most artful in wheedling them by professions of interest and friendship . . ." He prophesied that Seward's talents might someday "adorn the first office in a free nation," and he hoped that when the opportunity was presented to vote him there: "Your name will ever be cherished with a peculiar regard by the Catholics of the present generation throughout the United States."[16]

Seward immediately turned the correspondence to a mutual festival of admiration. ". . . I have read with lively satisfaction your appeals to the people of your charge on the subject of the education of their children . . . I need not assure you of my sympathy in regard to the ultimate object of your efforts, the education of the poor. I content myself therefore with saying that it will afford me great pleasure to consult with you freely on the subject whenever it suits your convenience to make your promised visit in this place, and that in all measures calculated to advance that object you shall have what support it is in my power consistently with other duties and relations to afford."[17]

The first letters between the two leaders were circumspect and guardedly political, each man seeking to ascertain how useful the other might be to his purposes. It was nonetheless the beginning of a lifelong and strongly felt friendship.

In September a second Catholic petition was sent to the Common Council. Quickly upon its heels came remonstrances from the Public School Society and the Methodist Episcopal churches. The council decided that all parties should have a full hearing before a second decision was made. On the last Thursday and Friday of October (29th and 30th), therefore, the matter was debated between Hughes and a number of opposing lawyers and clergymen for a total of thirteen hours—six and a half of which were filled by Hughes. The issues were simple. The Catholic immigrants claimed that the common schools were in fact Protestant schools. Though Protestantism was broken into innumerable denominations, the sum total of these was not a universality of Christianity but denominational—the Protestant denomination. Because of the feelings Catholics held about the error of Protestant beliefs, the inculcation of Protestantism in young children would lead, so they felt, to infidelity. A true neutrality in religious teachings being impossible, the Catholics—who did represent the great majority of the poor children in question—wanted monies to run schools that were as Catholic as the common schools were Protestant.

From the Protestant point of view, the bible by itself was not a sectarian book. To them the ecumenical Protestantism of the common schools was a clear expression of unadorned Christianity. In their belief, the Roman Church was Babylon of the Book of Revelation, the product of Satan and superstition. They felt that Catholics should develop American hearts and allow their children to share in the nonsectarian Christianity of the common schools. Public funds could never be allowed to Catholic schools, for that would result in the support a religion with state money.

The frustrating element of the whole debate was that neither side seemed capable of understanding the limits of their own prejudice or of properly addressing the prejudice of the other. A truly neutral contemporary seeking to follow the thread of logic through the lengthy arguments of either party would have found himself at a loss. What the arguments did present was a potpourri of the religious antagonisms between native and new-immigrant America.

Yet in an age when a halfway decent sermon was considered good entertainment, the debates promised excitement if nothing else. On the 29th of October the corridors of City Hall were jammed with people attempting to squeeze into the council chamber. Those who were directly involved in the proceed-

ing had a great deal of difficulty gaining access themselves. At
4 P.M. the hearings began. The routine procedures of council
meetings were dispensed with. The Catholic petition and the
remonstrances were read. Then John Hughes took the floor.
For two hours he picked over the remonstrances against the
Catholic claim and restated the main points of the Catholic petition. The society had resented the implications cast on its
nonsectarian teachings. Hughes amplified them: "They have
alleged, in some of their documents, that we charged them with
teaching infidelity; but we have not done so. We charge it as
the result of their system . . ."[18]

If the society might point out the contradiction in simultaneous accusations of sectarianism and infidelity, Hughes saw
contradiction in the society's offer to allow censorship of books
that it claimed were inoffensive to Catholics. He asked " . . .
are we to take the odium of erasing passages which they hold
to be true? Have they the right to make such an offer?"[19]

After acknowledging the polite tone of the society's remonstrance, Hughes regretted that he could not say as much
for the Methodists. The ministers of that Church reacted to the
Catholic petition with "surprise and alarm," and feared that
the Catholics wished to develop their own educational system
in order to proselytize "such Protestant children as they might
find means to get into these schools." Hughes responded, saying "I ask these gentlemen again, what authority they have for
such an assertion? I should like to see the argument which gives
them their authority to use language and to make a statement
so palpably false as this."

The Methodists feared that should Catholics be given
money, every Church would ask for it. "I wish they would do
it," said Hughes, "for I believe it would be better for the future
character of the city, and for its fame when this generation
shall have passed away."[20]

Then too, there was the fear of the Catholic bible. "We
cannot allow the Holy Scriptures to be accompanied with their
notes and commentaries and to be put in the hands of the
children, who may hereafter be the rulers and legislators of our

beloved country," the Methodist ministers claimed, "because among other bad things taught in these commentaries, is to be found the lawfulness of murdering heretics . . ." Hughes, who had learned to relish twitting puritan moralists with wagers, offered to pay $1,000 if the truth of such an allegation could be proven. He brushed off their claim that Catholic approval of textbooks would involve censorship by "a foreign Potentate." "Now, we regard him only as supreme in Our Church and there's an end of it," he said. Then he tested the sensitivities of his accusors: "If we could ask you—if we could propose that you take our book—if we should ask you to put out the Protestant scriptures and take ours, with ours, with our notes and comment, do you think Protestants would agree to it?"

When the Methodists spoke of the history books they insisted that it was impossible to describe the ten previous centuries of history without speaking unfavorably of the Roman Church. As proof they drew up a litany of Catholic horrors against Protestants. Here Hughes was on his strongest ground. He countered "What is that to us? Are we the people that took part in that?" The man who could draw upon the embittering memory of his sister's burial had no need to reach back into the centuries for a St. Bartholomew's Day or a crusade against the Waldenses. He dragged before them his own life's experience. If they insisted on speaking of martyrdom, then, he said, "I speak of the Catholics of Great Britian and Ireland." Of the Methodist Church, Hughes bowed, ever so slightly, with becoming respect. ". . . It is a young Church. It is not as old as the Catholic Church and therefore has fewer crimes; but I contend again, it has fewer virtues to boast of."

The niceties of polemic attended to, Hughes finished with a practical warning that his listeners should have heeded. It was a warning that indicated the direction in which the fight would move should the Catholics be denied their "rights of conscience." He declared: "A common education then, as understood by the State, is a secular education; and these documents contend that any religious teaching no matter how slight, will vitiate all claim to participation in this fund. Now the Public School Society, in their reports have from time to time stated themselves, and observe with a consciousness that the jealous eye of the community is upon them—they state, still under this restriction, that they have imparted religion. Now, if this doctrine be correct, they are no more entitled to the common school fund than others."[21]

Hughes spoke for over two hours. When he sat down, Thomas Sedgwick, an attorney for the Public School Society, took the floor and spoke for two hours more. His tone was gentlemanly and his arguments free of prejudice. Nonetheless he could not accept the premise that the common schools taught sectarian Protestantism. He gave a concise history of the use of education funds in the city of New York, and he pointed out that after the "gross fraud" perpetrated by the Bethel Baptist church, the Common Council had cut off individual denominations from receiving monies. If Catholics wanted to change this law, then, they would have to go all the way back to the state legislature.

Ignoring the presence in the city of Jews and atheists, Sedgwick offered an ecumenical solution for the schools. "We are all Christians," he ventured, "either bible is the code of Christ." In Ireland, he pointed out, composite scriptures were being used (though many Irish were unhappy with this compromise and a few of the country's recalcitrant bishops had written to the Pope of their disapproval). "If the whole bible cannot be used," Sedgwick asked, "cannot such extracts from it be compiled as will satisfy all parties?" At present, the common schools were used by Protestant churches for religious instructions on Sundays. This use of the buildings could evenly be extended to Catholics as well. "Nothing surely, can be fairer or more impartial," he pleaded, "then to place all the sects on an equality during the week, and, on Sundays, to use them (the buildings) as they chose for religious purposes."[22]

Sedgwick's openminded fairness impressed even Hughes. Had he been the only man to speak on behalf of the Public School Society, and had Protestants and Catholics attempted to implement his ideas and ended the issue at that point, the history of the American public school system might have been markedly different. He was followed however by Hiram Ketchum, a lawyer who had been on the board of the Public School Society for eighteen years. His polemical arguments made much more exciting press, and his angry righteousness quickly stirred up the fires of prejudice among both parties.

Without any recess for the assembled people who had listened to four hours of oratory, Ketchum wandered through a repetition of Sedgwick's reasonings for the next hour and a half. Lacking Sedgwick's charity he heated his arguments with abusive remarks about John Hughes and Roman motives. He professed to be scandalized that a bishop would take up a political cause, declaring, "When I read of a mitred gentleman being received by the people with 'cheers' . . . I must say there is something novel in the proceeding . . . If I or any other man, had been passing St. James, at the times these meetings were held, we should have supposed that they were political meetings, and that possession of the hall was taken by either the 'Whigs' or the 'Democrats.' "

It was absurd in Ketchum's view to say that any particular religion was taught in the schools. "Who ever went to a common school to be taught religion?" he inquired. "I am in the midst of Americans who have received their education in the common schools of this country, and I ask who ever went to a common school to receive religious instruction?" Twisting the coin about, he showed his audience the other side. Good morals had to be inculcated—"and if we are bound to teach them, we are at liberty to teach those general religious truths which give them sanction." But this was all nonsectarian: ". . . We don't teach religion, we don't teach purgatory, we don't teach baptism or no baptism," he assured his audience. Then, overlooking the sensitivities of Jews and atheists, as had Sedgwick, he added, "We didn't teach anything that is disputed among Christians." The common schools he vowed would remain as they were— free. "I believe a chapter from the bible," he observed, "the Protestant translation without note or comment, is read in some of these schools at their opening every day. Shall we give up this bible, Mr. President? It would be a very hard thing." Referring to Sedgwick's proposal of a common bible he observed that though a majority of Catholic bishops had agreed to such a compromise in Ireland, a minority had appealed this decision to the Pope. This was too much for him to bear: "Sir, such an appeal might be made in this country; and if in all candor I ask whether it does not belong to a foreign Potentate to say whether the Bible shall be read in our common schools? . . . And if there be a foreign power, spiritual or otherwise, to say that the Bible shall not be read, I ask if that power may not say that the Constitution and the Declaration of Independence shall not be read?"

This was too much for Hughes. He broke into a smile, which irritated Ketchum. "The gentleman opposite may smile," he insisted, "but I ask if they can escape from these conclusions?"[23]

Ketchum concluded and sat down. Before Reverend Bond could launch into the Methodist objections Hughes quickly stood to reassert the Catholic claim. He did so briefly, pointing out to the assembly that the conclusions drawn by his opponents meant that one of two things had to happen: "Either the consciences of Catholics must be crushed and their objections resisted, or the Public School System must be destroyed."[24]

One of the Public School Society trustees rose to challenge Hughes's complaints about *The Irish Heart,* claiming that they were not fair. The book had, because of the complaints, been removed from the shelves. Hughes replied curtly that he was not aware that this was so.

By this time it was well past 10 P.M. Rather than let this or any other point be drawn out, an adjournment was called until the next afternoon at four o'clock.

By the time of the weary dismissal, the debate had become a carousel ride for the spectators; the same views had been presented to them again and again. It hardly seemed possible that the public would have shown up for a second long evening around the same route. But they did. On Friday people pressed into City Hall in far greater numbers than the day before. The attraction, no doubt, was in the performers slated to appear.

Thursday the bishop had dueled with lawyers. In this second round "the mitered gentleman" was to face Protestant ministers from several denominations, and this promised a hearty display of polemics.

Long before four o'clock the chamber and corridors were filled with eager people. Seeking larger accommodations, everyone moved to a large courtroom. When an alderman objected to use of the courtroom there was a mad dash to the City Council chambers. At five o'clock, with people standing even in the windows, and the place "crowded to suffocation," the show began.[25]

John Hughes, who was to do all the speaking for the Catholics, was accompanied by Fathers Constantine Pise and John Power. Reverend Thomas Bond, who was to defend the Methodist remonstrance, was seated with a number of Protestant clergymen, including Reverend William C. Brownlee. Bond took the floor. He said nothing new about the school argument (nor did anyone else during the next seven hours). Rather he heated the air with the sort of entertainment the public had fought to listen to.

The Methodists, like the Catholics, would have been glad to see their children educated in the particular tenets of their Church, Bond said, "but we sacrificed all our wishes on this point, all our prejudices, on the altar of the public welfare." He had a score, or rather a wager, to settle with Hughes. "We say in our remonstrance that the Catholic commentaries sanction the murder of heretics. This the Right Reverend gentleman denies, and he offers to bet one thousand dollars that we cannot prove our charge. Mr. President, our Church, as the gentleman says, is yet young, but it is old enough to have taught us the immorality of gambling."[26]

To prove the point of the bet—while declining the money —he held up a volume called *The Rhemish New Testament* and began to read from its preface. "In the year 1816 an edition including both the Douay Old and the Rhemish New Testament was issued at Dublin containing a large number of comments replete with impiety, irreligion and the most fiery persecution . . ."

Puzzled, Hughes interrupted him and asked: "From what

do you read?" Bond allowed that he was quoting from the book's "Introductory Address to Protestants."[27] The bible he was using was reissued in New York by Protestant "gentlemen of the highest reputation in this country" for the purpose of showing what Catholics taught about heretics. It was a counterfeit text. Regardless of this admission, Bond spent the next hour quoting its footnotes as official.

At 6:30 P.M. when he finished, the board moved that anyone else who wished to be heard, might apply to speak. Several of the ministers present opted to add their own remonstrances to what had already been said. Reverend David Reese, a Methodist, felt that Hughes was guilty of "haranguing his people in their public assemblies for the purpose of exciting prejudices against the public schools." Overlooking the problem that had prompted Seward's message to the legislature in the first place —the thousands of unschooled immigrant children wandering New Yorks streets—Reese insisted that "before those prejudices were created, when these people had not yet been taught to look upon them as odious, the Roman Catholics sent their children to these schools and availed themselves thankfully of their benefits. But now many of them have abstracted their children merely because harangues of that kind have been made which are calculated to create disaffection among them."[28]

Reverend Knox of the Dutch Reformed Church announced that "candor would require me to go a little further than many have gone who have addressed you." The Catholic Church, he observed, was "exclusive" in its beliefs of "immutability and infallibility." Its members feared public schools because "there is an influence exerted by a contact with the children in these schools adverse to feelings of reverence for Catholic peculiarities."[29]

Reverend Bangs, a Methodist, offered brief and blunt reasons and solutions. Describing the nonsectarianism of the common schools he said: "If I mistake not, one of the trustees told us that the Scriptures were read every day, and that the children were taught that God made them and that he saw their thoughts words and actions; and these we know, are the first principles of revealed religion, in opposition to sectarianism . . . Shall we exchange this Bible for the teaching of the Roman Catholic schoolmaster?" The minister also had a solution to the problem of unschooled children. He announced that "these little vagrants that are suffered to stroll about the streets and spend their time in idleness, I would compel to enter these schools."[30]

Reverend Gardner Spring, a Presbyterian, brought to a climax the tone of the preceding arguments. The Roman Church being "almost uniformly the enemy of liberty," he resented that Hughes should come to "a community of Protestant citizens, [and] ask for the bounty of the State to support such a system as his!" And he continued, saying: "The gentleman has sought to prove that the present system leads to infidelity. Now Sir, let no man think it strange that I should prefer even infidelity to Catholicism. Even a mind as acute as Voltaire's came to the conclusion that, if there was no alternative between infidelity and the dogmas of the Catholic Church, he should choose infidelity. I would choose, sir, on similar circumstances, to be an infidel tomorrow."[31]

When the Protestant clergy had retreated to their seats Hughes got an immediate revenge by speaking for another three and one-half hours, responding to the attacks of Doctors Reese, Knox, Bangs, Bond and Spring. Of the two lawyers from the previous evening, Hiram Ketchum also drew much of his attention. Ketchum, described by the diarist George Strong as a "foolish fat bag of infragrant flatulence,"[32] was, it seems, a man whom people enjoyed seeing deflated, for Hughes got a great laugh from his audience by commenting upon his prosecuting techniques:

"In fact throughout the speech," Hughes informed his listeners, "he, with peculiar emphasis and a manner which he may perhaps have acquired in his practice in courts of law, fixed upon me a steady gaze—and he has no ordinary countenance— and addressed me so solemnly, that I really expected every moment he would forget himself, and say The prisoner at the bar."

Hughes, the immigrant, offered Ketchum a lesson about the workings of democracy.

"I know he lectured me pretty roundly on the subject of attending the meetings under St. James's Church," said Hughes. "He so far forgot his country and her principles as to call it a 'descent' on my part when I mingled in a popular meeting of freemen. But it was no descent; and I hope the time will never come when it will be deemed a descent for a man in office to mingle with his fellow citizens for legitimate and honorable purposes."[33]

For the bulk of the three and one-half hours Hughes reiterated and expanded a question which to him was "a very simple one." He declared, "We are a portion of this people and we merely ask to be placed on an equality with the rest of our fellow citizens."[34]

Like the other speakers when he was done he had brought nothing novel into the discussion. The hour was approaching midnight. Ketchum, who had earlier claimed the right to rebut anything new which the prelate might have included, jumped to his feet and demanded time to speak "on the precise issue before the board."[35] The chairman refused him, wearily commenting: "That has, I apprehend, been very fully debated."[36] Ketchum disregarded the refusal and launched into a speech. He blustered out questions for another quarter of an hour before he was brought down by the pounding insistence of the chairman that he was out of order. The debates had ground to a halt almost into the next day. The meeting was adjourned just short of twelve o'clock. The audience, along with a great deal of hot air, was released from the council chamber.

The public had awakened to what was going on in the battle over schooling. Newspaper coverage of the debates had been both extensive and editorally predictable. The Catholic press was generally behind Hughes. John England's *Catholic Miscellany* picked up the story from the *Freeman's Journal* and praised the bishop of New York in spite of the fact that he took a novel position "of so secular a character." He had acted "not as a priest or theologian, but as an earnest advocate of a great civil and religious right."[37] One Catholic paper that held back its praise was the *Truth Teller*. Devoted to the Democratic party, it was not about to give strength to a Whig governor's policies, bishop or no bishop.

The secular press in New York, nativist in orientation, had almost universally stood behind the Public School Society. The New York *Herald* offered the most interesting secular commentary. Owing allegience only to a public eager for news, James Gordon Bennett was mercurial in his reaction. He was no friend of the School Society. Before the debates he had suggested letting every religious group build its own schools. During the Common Council meetings he praised Hughes for his own moderation in the face of bigots like Bangs, Bond, and Spring. In the final accounting, however, Bennett was so disgusted with all the parties involved that he ended his coverage of the whole affair by musing "Fanny Wrightism must indeed be looking up."*[38]

Without a doubt the best compliment Hughes received was from the New York *Observer*, a Protestant sheet whose observations on Romanism were as constantly bileful as the *Protestant Vindicator against Popery*. Though, on principle, an avowed enemy of Hughes both then and thereafter, the paper grudged him praise for his performance. "No one could hear him," the *Observer* admitted, "without painful regret that such powers of mind, such varied and extensive learning, and such apparent sincerity of purpose were trammelled with a fake system of religion."[39]

Less than two weeks after the debate America went to the polls and elected William Henry Harrison to the presidency. It was a Whig year, yet in New York William Henry Seward ran behind the national ticket, losing half the margin by which he had won in 1838. Nativist Whigs had been disgusted by his

---

*Fanny Wright, along with Dale Owen, was a tireless preacher for the causes of freethinkers. She crusaded for women's rights, birth control, the colonization of freed slaves. She opposed organized religion, Church involvement in politics, and the institution of marriage.

pro-immigrant views, and the immigrants, held in tow by the traditional friendship of the Democrats, remained within the boundaries of their own party. John Hughes apologized to the governor for his "ignorant and misled people." He laid a good deal of blame at the doorstep of the *Truth Teller* which he branded "a vile print," and promised "I shall make a holy war on these miserable traffikers on their credulity."[40]

Seward, in turn, held onto his relationship with Hughes. When it was suggested to him that the bishop had actually worked Catholics against the Whigs, Seward retorted that such a charge was "totally untrue."

"Bishop Hughes is my friend," he said. "I honor, respect, and confide in him."[41] To Hughes himself he was philosophical, writing, "I am content to abide my vindication . . ."[42]

It would be a long time in coming. The general public reaction to his near loss was a strongly expressed opinion that he had been properly scourged for his opportunism. The *Herald* castigated him for "carrying the Common School fund into the market and offering it to the highest bidder for political purposes."[43]

But the question was far from settled, and as the *Herald* noted it still excited "a great deal of feeling in pious circles."[44] While the Common Council worked itself up to a decision there was a half-hearted attempt at compromises made by both the Public School Society and the representatives of Catholic schools. The society was always willing to expurgate polemical books, but they also insisted that they remain the final authority to be approached for such favors. The Catholics on their part were becoming ever more entrenched in the idea that there could never be a truly neutral ground of religious testing in the public schools, and that they must have their own system. Even before the debates Hughes had written to Archbishop Eccleston in Baltimore: "Whether we shall succeed or not getting our proportion of the public money . . . at all events the effort will cause an entire separation of our children from these schools— and excite greater zeal on the part of our people for Catholic education."[45]

In January 1841 Seward's annual message continued to

urge reform. "This evil remains as before," he told the legislature, "and the question recurs, not merely how or by whom shall education be given, but whether it shall be given at all . . ." The Public School Society might run "excellent" schools, but still he insisted, "no system is perfect that does not accomplish what it proposes."[46]

The Common Council of New York City disagreed, and on January 11th, with one dissenting vote, it turned down the Catholic petitions. John Hughes called a meeting of Catholics. On February 11th, Washington Hall, the largest hall in the city, was filled to capacity. The bishop was greeted with an ovation so great that when it quieted he warned the crowd, "My friends, take care of your cheering; for if the advocate of the school society be passing by he will say this is a meeting of Whigs or Democrats." His admonitions brought laughter, then renewed cheers. "We have come here denied of our rights, but not conquered," he announced. Accounting for the logical progress made by the council, he reviewed the situation for his audience: "It was their province to ascertain if as citizens we had grievances to complain of; and if so to see if there were any applicable remedies. But the Reverend Doctor Spring and the Reverend Doctor Bond and the Reverend Doctor Bangs and company (great laughter) came with an old volume of antiquated theology and in chorus brayed, barked and cried: 'Oh what monstrous, wretched and inhuman creatures these Catholics are!' The Common Council heard and were convinced [laughter] . . . Eight or nine hours were wasted in the discussion of a theological tenet, but not one half-hour was given to the only question which the Common Council should have permitted to come before them—namely, are the rights of this portion of the citizens violated or not?" If Catholics were the only sect vocal about injustice done to them, Hughes told them, they were not the only denomination vulnerable to injustice. "While it is the Catholics today, it may be the Universalists, or the Jews, or the Baptists, or the Unitarians tomorrow who may suffer." He indicated the next step to be taken. "We have an appeal to a higher power than the Common Council—to the legislature of the state [cheers]. And I trust it will be found that the petty array of bigotry, which influenced the Common Council, cannot over awe the legislature [loud cheers]."[47]

No politician could have dreamed of an audience so completely in the palm of his hand. A committee was set up to write a petition, and over the next weeks 7,000 signatures were gathered to be sent with it to Albany. The Public School Society, in turn, made plans to head off the Catholics at the capital. More remonstrances and petitions were drawn up.

In late April, after the Catholic memorial had been presented, Secretary of State (and ex-officio Superintendent of Common Schools) John C. Spencer issued a report to the legislature, reasserting what Seward had said. He observed that more children were unschooled in New York City than the entire rest of the state, and he proposed that elected officials from each ward serve as commissioners for the public school system. This would break the monopoly of the Public School Society and place individual schools under the power of each voting ward.

Barely had the report been dropped on the legislators' desks when Hiram Ketchum appeared to appeal on behalf of the society. In a speech which Thurlow Weed characterized as a "violent harangue," he attempted to ridicule Spencer's proposals, pouncing upon the secretary's estimate of city children roaming the streets. Spencer had figured the total to be 32,194 children. This was erroneous according to Ketchum. By his calculation there were a mere 31,952. He worried greatly about the effect of a ward deciding upon the makeup of a district school. Not seeing that he was describing the present plight of the immigrant Catholics he envisioned, "Now suppose that in any given district there should be about five hundred Roman Catholic children and two hundred Protestant children? These Protestant children are compelled to worship according to the opinions of the majority; that is to say, they are compelled to be taught religion according to the doctrines of the Roman Catholic Church. I ask you gentlemen if that is not the tyranny of the majority?"

And yet Ketchum could not see any objection to reading of the King James Bible in schools. Harrison having just died in office, Ketchum proudly pointed to the late President's avowal of the Christian religion in his accidentally suicidal inaugural address: "The sentiment thus uttered by him was an American sentiment, which will be responded to by a vast majority of the people of this country—for, thank God, we are a Christian land." And for that reason he had come to Albany to protect the Public School Society, declaring, "It is one of the jewels of the country."[48]

At the moment, Ketchum was not a jewel in the Whig party. Thurlow Weed, the governor's mentor, angrily listened to the New York lawyer's reasoning and scribbled a memorandum, "Kill Ketchum."[49] Seward had earlier bowed to political pressure—for he disliked Ketchum—and put his name in for a vacancy in the state circuit court. After this speech he replaced him with another candidate.

In the wake of the Spencer report, Hughes kept studiously silent, feeling that the newspapers would be quick to jump on any move he made. For the moment any move seemed unnecessary. The issue was sailing well enough on its own through the state legislature. Even when Seward suggested to Hughes that a Catholic rally might be propitious he still refused. Such a rally would make a great display of moral support, but garnering moral support wasn't the same as counting votes. It could only rake up a nativist cry at a crucial moment. The situation looked good, and Hughes didn't want to upset anything.

Two bills dealing with the school problem worked their way through the legislature. In the assembly, John L. O'Sullivan, a Protestant, introduced a bill which would have left the Public School Society standing, but would put state funds in the hands of elected district officials who would dole out money to any local society meeting criteria set up by the state. Although it was discussed at length, this bill was eclipsed when the Spencer report was put into the form of a bill in the senate. This latter measure would have extended the statewide district system to the New York City area, effectively ending the private monopoly of the Public School Society. Common schools would be controlled by elected officials of individual wards, thus giving the people in each given area a more direct say in the running of these institutions.

The bill seemed headed for passage when on May 22nd, the day slated for its discussion, the Public School Society devised a last-minute tactic to influence the legislators. David Hale's New York *Journal of Commerce* was bitterly nativist and had recently claimed that priests were pushing for the school fund so that they could get money for themselves. Priests, the paper claimed, "hardly afford the most miserable of the people under them even the consolation of religion in the severest affliction without a fee."[50] On May 20th a writer calling himself "Americus" contributed a long piece in opposition to the Spencer report. Somehow enough copies for the entire senate were rushed to William Rockwell, the society's agent in Albany. On the morning of the 22nd each senator found on his desk a copy of the paper with the article neatly marked out, lest perchance it could be missed.

"Americus" could not bear the idea that Catholics asked for equality, "for none are more exclusive than these self same sticklers for equality, none more bigoted, none more arrogant." Noting Spencer's contention that for Catholics "the transmission of their creed is a most essential part of their religious profession," "Americus" asked, "What are those principles, the transmission of which is so essential? I happen to take the following." In "the following" he introduced, apparently without knowing the connection, a character whose career had touched upon Hughes's since his seminary days. It was the irrepressible William Hogan, who had worn the pathways of St. Mary's smooth for Hughes, and who had later rescued Maria Monk from his rumsoaked clutches. Here, offered as debating material for the senators of New York State, was a purported bill of excommunication lifted from the pages of *Tristram Shandy* and grafted onto the history of Hogan:

Excommunication of Mr. Hogan, Pastor of St. Mary's Church Philadelphia—By the authority of God Almighty, the Father, Son, and Holy Ghost, and the undefiled Virgin Mary, mother and patroness of our Saviour, and of all celestial virtues, angels, archangels, thrones, dominions, powers, cherubims and seraphims, patriarchs, apostles, prophets, evangelists, &c., may he, Mr. Hogan, be damned! May he be cursed in his brains, in his vitals, his temples, his eyebrows, his cheeks, his jawbones, his nostrils, his teeth and grinders, his lips, his throat, his shoulders, his arms, his fingers, his veins, his thighs, his genitals, his hips, his knees, his legs, and feet, and toenails!

"Are not these principles very essential," concluded "Americus," "and their transmission indispensable?"[51]

In fairness to them, most of the senators would probably have been willing to dismiss "Americus" and his allegations. Yet his very presence reminded them of public opinion and of the fact that legislative elections were coming up in November. After a sharp debate and a hopeless division a motion was made and accepted that the bill be held over until the next year. Thus all concerned might run the approaching political gauntlet without having to be beaten over the head with how they had voted on this touchy issue.

Hughes was philosophical about the delay. In an address at Washington Hall on June 1st he found it amusing to watch the "many shifts and devices" of the Public School Society.[52] "Their conduct has indeed been worthy of those men who ushered Maria Monk into the world. I mean not the living Maria Monk but the book Maria Monk [laughter and applause]. The Public School Society were so ignorant or their agents so destitute of sense that they took a mock paragraph written by Sterne in *Tristram Shandy* for his own amusement, for a reality. They took it as a matter of fact, and with imperturbable gravity and with extreme simplicity reprinted it as a fact against the Catholics and distributed it to the honorable Senators."[53] Again the hall rocked with laughter and applause. It was not a lesser part of his talents that Hughes knew how to turn a grave topic into humor for the sake of his audience. It was a talent that often left pompous antagonists sputtering with anger and looking foolish. The antithesis of this talent was embodied in the dour Scotsman William Craig Brownlee who had spent so much of his adult life warning Americans that the Pope's "great toe is already on our shores and his whole foot, nay both feet are expected anon."[54]

While Ketchem and Hughes spent much of early summer nitpicking over each other's speeches, Brownlee announced that it was high time that he himself enter the fray. This was all too much for James Gordon Bennett who wrote, "Bishop Hughes begins tonite at Carroll Hall his famous refutation of Mr. Ketchum's arguments on the school question. Then comes the Rev. Dr. Brownlee's refutation of the Bishop's refutation. Then our refutation of both the refutations. Then anything you please. Great times these."[55]

Brownlee's refutation afforded a great entertainment by any audience's standards. The North Dutch church was filled to capacity, not only with the faithful but with a good-sized mob of Irish who had come from the highways and byways, unwanted and ill suited for such a feast. The doctor launched into his talk, keeping to vitriolic side issues while portions of his audience (presumably the Catholics) yelled: "He's an old liar!" "Turn him out!" "Maria Monk!" Discomfited and annoyed, Brownlee yelled back: "No Protestant interrupted Bishop Hughes. I am surprised at this proceeding." The heckling did not abate.

After ridiculing the belief that a wafer could be God, and after contending that priests charged two shillings to hear a confession, he got to the school question. He quoted a priest who when drunk on wine described how a "splendid establishment" out of town for priests and nuns was going to be maintained. "Oh, the public money we're going to get will support that," the priest is supposed to have said. Howls and catcalls filled the church: "Small potatoes!" "It's false!" "Maria Monk!" "Partridge!" "Turn him out!"

"I have the name of the priest," Brownlee insisted. Fistfights broke out, and several of the Irish were invited to leave. Over the din Brownlee called for respect. "I occupy the same place in my Church as Bishop Hughes does in his." He began to quote a bull of Gregory XVI "not yet of blessed memory, for he ain't dead," but by this time the row had become so great his voice went down in a sea of noise. The presentation ended with him screaming something about Catholicism being "false as an emanation from the bottomless pit."[56]

The next evening, when the doctor arrived for a second talk of what was presumably to be a series, a sizeable crowd was gathered outside his church. They weren't waiting for autographs. A melee ensued, and the embattled minister barely managed to escape uninjured. At that point in his career W. C. Brownlee was probably one of the few bigots in New York who had fully earned the right to be so.

During the first week of August Hughes left on a seven-week tour of the diocese. In fast-growing Rochester he consecrated a church bought from the Methodists and confirmed 200 Catholics. He visited Buffalo where at St. Patrick's church General Winfield Scott and his staff joined the congregation to hear him preach. He toured Lockport, Watertown, Oswego, and LaFargeville where the empty seminary remained as a mission center. He preached every day, often three times a day when not traveling. At the beginning of October he returned to New York where the campaigns for the fall elections were in full swing.

The Whigs had little to lose from the school issue despite the impetus given to it by their own governor. The Whig party was the home of the nativist American, and there could be little fear of mass Catholic defection by the nomination of men unfriendly to their proposals. Horace Greeley, whose *Log Cabin* newspaper had been succeeded by his no less partisan *Tribune,* counseled restraint. "All we have to say is to entreat our Whig friends not to magnify this bone of contention so as to defeat our city ticket in the fall. Why should the Whigs be perpetually discussing it while our opponents, who have more direct interest in it, hardly offer a word?"[57]

Nonetheless there were nativists who wanted to take no chances. Samuel F. B. Morse headed a group calling itself the American Protestant Union which began sounding out candidates to make sure of their views on the question.

It was the Democrats who were on a tightrope. What power the naturalized and native Catholics had at all was lodged in that party which had been courting the immigrant's favor for a number of years. The Democrats tried to balance their ticket. Daniel Pentz, an alderman who voted for the Catholic petition on the Common Council, was nominated for the state assembly. But fearful of a defection of native voters, the

party let it be known that the entire slate of Democrats was opposed to any change in the present school system. The candidates themselves did their best to equivocate on the issue.

On October 25th John Hughes therefore called a general
meeting of a Church Debt Association. The debt he ended up
speaking about was that owed by politicians to a constituency.
"If I am a candidate for your suffrages," he instructed his audience, "I make known my principles and ask for your support." To illustrate the vague commitment of the Democratic
candidates in this regard he drew a parallel, envisioning a candidate with a red-hot iron in his possession.

> But suppose you ask him, what he means to do with that red
> hot iron? He will be sure to evade the question. He will tell
> you of a glorious liberty and equality and the sovereign au-
> thority of the people and all that; but press him for an an-
> swer. Tell him you want to know what he intends to do with
> that red hot iron [laughter]. "Oh," he will say, "I am a lib-
> eral man; I intend to do whatever is right. My friends, you
> know me, do you not? I belong to the party" [great cheering
> and laughter]. But still press him for an answer, and make
> him tell you what his ideas are about the red-hot iron
> [laughter].[58]

Over the next several days Catholic representatives
pressed individual candidates as to where they stood with that
red-hot iron. On the 29th Hughes called another meeting at
Carroll Hall. Significantly he dined beforehand with the Whig
boss Thurlow Weed. Though the two men discussed the strategy of what was to be done, Weed, reckoning that an appearance by him would touch a keg of dynamite to that red-hot
iron, chose not to accompany Hughes but to slip unnoticed into
a gallery. What ensued was a scene worthy of any political convention. Hughes stood before the crowded hall and announced:
"There is but one course for you to take: stand up for yourselves, and—I will be bound for it—public men will soon come
to your aid."[59]

A slate of candidates was presented who were sure of supporting "the justice of our claims." Of the thirteen assembly
candidates ten of the regular Democrats were endorsed, but

three independent names were substituted for the three regulars found wanting. Neither of the two regular senatorial candidates were blessed with approval. Thus five new names were added to the race as specific candidates of the Carroll Hall meeting. The reading of the slate was received with a deafening demonstration of approval. Hughes then stepped forward again and exhorted his people to victory. A reporter present recorded the scene.

> You have often voted for others, [said Hughes] and they did not vote for you, but now you are determined to uphold with your own votes, your own rights. Will you then stand by the rights of your offspring who have for so long a period, and from generation to generation, suffered under the operation of this injurious system? [Renewed cheering.] Will you adhere to the nomination made? [Loud cries of "we will," and vociferous applause.] Will you be united? [Tremendous cheering—the whole immense assembly rising *en masse,* waving of hats, handkerchiefs, and every possible demonstration of applause.] . . . Very well, then, the tickets will be prepared and distributed amongst you, and on the day of election go like freemen, with dignity and calmness, entertaining due respect for your fellow-citizens and their opinions, and deposit your votes.[60]

Weed thought the building would shake with the crowd's cheering.

Others upon hearing the news shook with indignation. The *Truth Teller's* editors, loyally Democratic as ever, refused to mention their bishop by name and buried the account of the meeting behind its usual Irish stories. James Gordon Bennett was livid and warned darkly that if such a convention happened in any city other than New York "this foolish prelate, the abbot of unreason" would be unsafe: "The first effects," he predicted, "will be a complete disorganization of all the old parties in New York, and probably the formation of the Protestant and Catholic factions with all the madness of the last century."

Bennett's anger knew no bounds. For days afterward he whipped Hughes publicly. Reminding the world that the "Bishop of Blarneyopolis" was no more than the "gardener of Bishop Dubois" he raged: "If he meant seriously in a Protestant country to succeed in his project, he took the method that would forever put a barrier between his Church and a claim on the school fund. If Bishop Hughes did not see this view, his mind must be blinded to all facts—to all truths—but the dogmas and drivellings of the Catholic Church in the last stages of decrepitude." He had one final admonition for the Irish. "Send the priests back to saying Masses for the dead, forgiving sins, marrying at five dollars a head and drinking good wine at generous tables."[61]

The nativist *Observer* reflected the deepest fears of American Protestants. It warned that "the foot of the beast was trampling on the elective franchise and his high priest was standing before the ballot box, the citadel of American liberties, dictating to his obedient followers the ticket they must vote . . ."[62]

Samuel Morse's American Protestant Union quickly responded to the Carroll Hall ticket by endorsing a list of candidates themselves. It was a bipartisan grouping almost equally split between the two parties and included those men who had most clearly avowed themselves inflexible on the school issue. This development frightened the Whigs, for whom Democratic disunity was a boon. Horace Greeley angrily disavowed the Protestant movement and counseled that the "Whig ticket, the whole ticket and nothing but the ticket" was the wisest route to follow. There was duplicity in the air, he insisted, and the proof of this was that three of the candidates had managed to get themselves endorsed by both religious groups. Obviously there were deals being made behind closed doors:

"We were assured yesterday by a leading Catholic," he said, "that they had private promises from all these men that they would sustain such an alteration of the school system as Bishop Hughes desires. We believe this is true, and we know that Catholics support them in the full confidence that this is so."[63]

Private promises or not, the Democrats, wobbling on their tightrope, sought to stabilize themselves as best they could. Ten of the thirteen men nominated at Carroll Hall issued a vague disclaimer blaming their troubles on "the scheme and the objects of the present Governor of their state," and opposing any sectarian use of the school fund.

Hughes himself, branded by a large segment of the public as an American Machiavelli, coolly issued a statement disavowing interest on his part in politics. The people who met at Carroll Hall, he claimed, quite properly insisted that in a free election there had to be a choice. Because both parties had committed themselves to the cause of the Public School Society, Catholics provided themselves with candidates for whom they could conscientiously vote.

In the November 3rd election Democrats were victorious throughout the state. In New York City the party regulars endorsed by the Carroll Hall meeting won handily with the party. The Democratic candidates who had bucked Catholic displeasure lost. (This despite a last-minute Irish-front Tammany rally that had portrayed the bishop as being manipulated by Whig chieftains.) The votes polled by the Carroll Hall candidates ranged between 2,100 and 2,500 votes, a clout just powerful enough to decide the Democratic party's fate. The hyphenated American was not yet a great force to be reckoned with in United States politics, but during 1841 John Hughes had done much to teach them that they were not merely a conglomeration of votes, but a unified voice as well.

He won hatred for it—enduring hatred. The aristocratic ex-mayor of New York, Philip Hone, privately branded him as "Generalissimo," and the city's newspapers generally assumed from that time onward that he was a political as much as a religious leader.

Hughes, however, turned the tables on the press and observed that he was not alone in playing this game. Shortly after the election he responded: "When several strong denominations attack one that is weaker in a manner which turns religion into politics and politics into religion, the sentinals of our liberties at the press are asleep. But when that one assailed denomination meets the assault and repels the assailants with the same weapons which the latter had selected, then the danger of mixing religion with politics is for the first time trumpeted in the public ear! . . ."[64]

Nonetheless, privately, to a lawyer friend in Baltimore, Hughes admitted that "if I did not go beyond my episcopal sphere I went at least to the farthest edge of it."[65]

The issue being dealt with, the "corrupt politicians" having been taught "a lesson which they will not soon forget," Hughes in November moved back into his proper sphere. He traveled to Philadelphia where he lectured on "the life and times of Pius VII" before the Mercantile Library Association. Bennett, whose attack the bishop had met with a pious silence, stood sputtering with anger. "Who under heaven here cares about Pius VII?" he demanded. "No one, and Bishop Hughes knows it."[66]

Public disfavor brought the bishop and governor still closer together. "I was chafed and jealous," wrote Hughes to Seward, "when you alone were getting all the abuse to which the exercise of the heart's benevolence entitles good men in this world of selfishness and corruption. But now that I am classed with you in it, I am revenged and happy."[67] In return Seward assured Hughes of his importance to the American scene. "You have, my dear sir, a high vocation here," the governor wrote. "One no less than that of lifting the vast and influential emigrant Catholic population from a condition of inferiority and exclusion to equality and harmony with all other sects and citizens."[68]

In his 1842 address to the legislature Seward maintained his insistence on the need of a school bill to affect New York City. With 20,000 youngsters unschooled there, compared to 9,000 for the entire rest of the state, some sort of action was imperative. Chastised by the Catholic defection in the November elections the Democrats in the assembly spurred themselves into action. William Maclay, son of a Baptist minister and one of the three candidates to earn a slot on both the Carroll Hall and Protestant Union tickets, was chosen chairman of an education committee. A bill reflecting the Spencer report was quickly drawn up, hastened on by a petition from the city endorsed by 13,000 signatures.

Battle lines were again being formed. Hoping to overshadow the ostensibly Catholic petition, advocates of the status quo launched a drive for 20,000 signatures. Public school children were asked to perform before the public as proof of the society's worth. At one such exhibition the mayor of New York presided while students lisped through a series of recitations and a boy delivered an eulogy of the Pilgrim fathers' religion. Hiram Ketchum applauded the youngsters when they were done and praised the common schools as comparable to any in the world, adding "I invite any bishop or layman to gainsay it." It was, moreover, the glory of these schools that the bible was read everyday—"our own bible, our own version, no priest's bible."[69]

On March 16th a gigantic rally was called in City Hall Park to gain the 20,000 signatures. At the given hour some 5,000 people assembled around the platform of dignitaries, but a large portion of the crowd turned out to be something other than what was expected. Pressing close in a phalanx of ten people deep, the *Herald's* reporter counted "a great many of the Catholic Irish." The chairman called the meeting to order while the air was filled with cries of "cock-a-doodle-doo," after which "there was a funny sort of pause." The chairman began again, fighting interruptions along the order of "sit down old square toes," and "hats off." Thomas Fossenden was introduced to present the resolutions. Somewhat intimidated by the unfriendly faces before him he shook as he spoke. "Be Jasus, he got the horrors," a voice cried out. "Better take a drink old boy."

Fossenden ignored a wave of laughter and forged on. It was resolved, he read, that the introduction of school districts would be a deplorable matter. The absence of numbers of children offered no excuse to exchange the present system that was run "without sectarian bias." When he declared that the "thick fog of ignorance" hanging over the city was not nearly as great as the "smoke of prejudice" weighing against the present system, a section of the crowd went wild with "cock-a-doodle-doos."

Colonel William Stone of the *Commercial Advertiser,* who had once befriended Catholics by exposing Maria Monk as a fraud, was a bitter foe of the Catholic participation in the school fund. He followed Fessenden, got booed, and asked for "ayes" to support the resolutions. The response he got, as attempted in print by the *Herald,* was a long sort of "Whooe-hoo-o-o-o-o-ah-a-a-a-a! oh-o-o!" A tall, rawboned fellow in the front of the crowd countered this with his own proposal: "I move that the legislature be let alone—let them handle their own business—we've too many legislators here by a damned sight." He won far lustier approval than Stone had. Laughter, cries, and confusion took over as some twenty rowdies jumped on the platform saying that they should make a speech. Chairs and tables were overturned, and as the dignitaries decided it was time to retire, one lad, holding the water pitcher, hurled its contents at the lot of them.[70]

Back at the legislature, the Maclay Bill passed through the assembly with little opposition, then moved on to the senate where forces were evenly divided. Hughes, wary of harmful publicity, did his best to keep out of the limelight. When Maclay visited him while preparing his legislation, word had leaked out of the meeting and Hughes had to issue a public denial that he was in any way the author of the bill. But if he was silent he was not still. Writing to the governor and marking his letter "Destroy this as soon as read" he advised, "I know not how far the suggestion may be in violation of propriety—but if it be I throw myself on your indulgence—that you and Mr. Weed and other friends true and tried 'through evil and through good report' should use your influence to bring out friends of justice and equal rights on the Whig side as well as the other side of the Senate."[71]

It was the tepid Democrats, however, with their two-vote majority who needed keeping in hand. New York's municipal elections were approaching, and now on their own without Hughes, Catholics threatened to create another independent slate, one which would destroy the party's power in the city. This reactivated the nativists and Methodist churches who invited congregations to attend a meeting in Constitution Hall for the sake of endorsing candidates, as the American Protestant Union had done previously.[72]

The immigrants were speaking in larger numbers, however, and the statewide party hustled to please them. The Maclay Bill, providing for district elected commissioners of education in New York City, was passed and signed into law three days before the April election. The Catholics withdrew their slate of candidates.

On election day it was the nativists' turn to use mob rule. Fighting broke out in the heavily Irish sixth ward. A hotel used as a polling place was attacked and gutted. Battle cries such as "The Pope Rules the Republic" and "Blood will Flow" filled the night air. The angry horde moved on the bishop's house on Mulberry Street behind the cathedral. Only Dubois, ill and bedridden in a back room on the ground floor, was at home. Hughes was in Newark for the evening. Bricks smashed through the windows and doors were knocked in. But luckily for old Dubois, who lay frightened and helpless, the police arrived in time to prevent the place from being burned. The militia was called out. Fifty-six people were arrested and the riot act was read in front of the cathedral. Detachments were sent to protect St. Peter's church on Barclay Street. It was midnight before the crowd began to disperse.

And so the blessings of an elected board of education arrived in New York City. It sounded the death knell of the Public School Society's monopoly on public education. The new law allowed the society to exist, but only under the power of the elected commissioners. The society dwindled for eleven years until the impracticality of its existing within the state system finally caused it to will its own demise. At first the bible, along with hymns and prayers, continued to be used in the schools. But the law was there, and test cases were applied against it. Within a year the city's Jews, who but for one ambiguous petition in 1840 had sat quietly through the fight, made a formal protest against the common schools' Christian orientation.

Gradually Americans were forced to see the bible as a sectarian work. Eventually its use, even as a classic of world literature, would be forbidden. Ironically, the school controversy of 1840-1842 was a decisive and unwanted movement by a religious people leading toward the exclusion of values which almost every United States citizen of that day acknowledged as important. In the most pluralistic society in the world, public education was pushed in a direction where it would be monolithic in its bland values, and would teach children only to become, as Hughes himself described, "nothingarians."[73]

John Hughes had won a significant moral victory. Along with William Seward he had championed the cause of immigrants who had been without any effective leadership and had won their civil rights for them. While acting as a spokesman for Catholics he had publicly voiced an awareness that he was fighting, as well, for Unitarians, Jews, and any other minority group that might be overridden by a self-serving majority within a democratic society. And yet, the battle having been won, Hughes proceeded to toss away the fruits of victory. After gaining for immigrants the right to control their own schools, he turned his back on the public-school system and took his Catholics with him. He built up the fledgling parochial school system. Hughes sought state aid for them, but instead of the hoped-for public monies, he eventually relied upon religious orders that built up an army of teachers. His advocacy of a Catholic school system became so strong that within the decade he declared, "I think the time is almost come when it will be necessary to build the schoolhouse first and the church afterwards."[74] In so doing he entrenched Catholics more firmly in a ghetto that was separated from Protestant America.

A principle had been won by Catholic immigrants against nativists, but neither party could claim any long-range advantage as a result of the fight, and both backed away from the battle with scars of resentment. Ironically, no individual suffered more, on a personal basis, than the man who had fired the opening gun, and who was, himself, free of religious bias.

Eighteen years after the passage of the Maclay Bill, William Henry Seward's consistent friendship for the Catholic immigrant would rob him of crucial support, cost him a Republican presidential nomination of which he felt assured, and place it instead in the hands of a little known dark-horse candidate from Illinois.

15

DAGGER JOHN AND THE PROTESTANTS

John Hughes was not entirely consumed by the school issue during these months. The diocese was heavily in the red. In New York City alone the thousands of immigrants who needed schools were also in need of parishes. Although parishes were opened as soon as limited priestly personnel allowed, they were opened with little more than a prayer for backing. The newly rebuilt St. Peter's on Barclay Street, the first parish in the city, had a vast congregation of the poor—and a vast debt to match. Construction of new churches and the purchase of buildings from Protestant congregations was an ongoing process. In 1841 the annual diocesan debt-service of $20,000 would almost have matched the cost of building a new church each year.

American Catholics adopted the abandoned churches of Protestants and their governing system of lay trustees. They also adopted a source of revenue both strange and repugnant to the immigrants. Pews were rented. The enforcement of this practice—except at prime time Sunday High Mass—varied greatly, but the impoverished newcomers generally refused to buy the system, or the pews. It created odd-looking congregations. "The fact is," observed Hughes, "that while there is space, and even empty pews in the galleries, there are many who would prefer crowding the aisles of the church."[1]

Hughes wanted to consolidate debt payments so that well-off parishes (such as they were) could help those in more pressing straits. He made speeches to the laity about the need for Catholic unity, won pledges of support from his clergy, and despite warnings by the financially wise Mark Frenaye, he waited for Catholic zeal to produce solvency. He received a fast lesson about parochial limitations. After a year's efforts not enough was collected to pay off the annual interest on the debt. Catholics were not prone to see the needs of the Church beyond their own parish borders. Two of the city's ten churches, St. Nicholas and St. John the Baptist, refused point blank to take any part in the venture. Hughes finally wrote off the project as an untimely attempt.

The refusal of the two churches to participate reflected another problem that had to be dealt with—national parishes. Both St. Nicholas and St. John the Baptist were German-speaking, and they saw no reason why they should be caught up in a program to help the Irish. Moreover, like the Irish before them who had resented the French hierarchy, they felt, and would always feel, that their bishop deferred to his fellow countrymen at their expense. Yet this was an accidental more than an intentional circumstance. Hughes could not transform himself into a German for their sake. He had a strong and understandable interest in the politics of Ireland. Finally, the vast majority of those he had to care for were Irish. It was they who won the attention and the lion's share of hatred from the nativist citizenry.

With a flair for politics and an enthusiasm for the equality guaranteed them in a democracy, the Irish wanted to belong to the nativist American's world. The Germans, fearful that a loss even of language would mean a loss of identity, drew themselves into the safety of "little Germanys." Mindful of encroachments upon their culture, they dictated orders to their pastors, and with varying degrees of success to John Hughes.

When a group of German Catholics appealed to Hughes in 1840 for a second parish in the city, it was no easy thing for him to allow. As a naturalized citizen sensitive to the word "foreigner," Hughes constantly preached upon the need of the citizens "by choice" to make themselves patriotic Americans. Because assimilation into the mainstream of life in the United States meant so much to Hughes, he balked at what he felt would be regression into a cultural ghetto. Still, he walked a tightrope. The Germans were, he felt, "exceedingly prone to divisions and strife among themselves,"[2] and they might give fuel to nativists by throwing off his authority altogether. He acceded to their requests for their own parishes, and he looked about for someone to help him govern the German community.

Johann Raffeiner, an Austrian, had lived a life similar to Simon Bruté's. He had been a physician during the Napoleonic wars. After several years of lucrative postwar practice he entered a seminary. Ordained in 1825 he arrived in New York in 1833. With the money he had earned in his medical career he founded St. Nicholas Church and devoted his ministry to the care of Germans throughout John Dubois's farflung diocese. As a pastor he stood his ground against the dictates of trustees, winning their dislike and the respect of Hughes. Hughes appointed Raffeiner as his vicar general, as a liaison with his German flock. It was a providential choice. The Austrian priest served the diocese well for almost thirty years. When he died, less than three years before Hughes, the bishop evaluated the importance of his contribution: "We did not always agree in the details of the course to be pursued, it is true, but his large experience was beneficial to me while his humility and zeal helped me. He was indeed a model for the priesthood, and by him I was guided in all matters pertaining to the advancement of Catholicism among the Germans of my own diocese."[3] Although Hughes refused to promote the idea of national parishes, he agreed to their necessity. And while he was never comfortable with the German immigrants, he was judicious and correct in his relationship with them.

Hughes had not become a bishop through political maneuvering but by public recognition of his oratorical and administrative talents. Moving into New York, he immediately applied his debating skills to erring trustees and nativist politicians. But such activities had been his meat and drink for a decade before this in Philadelphia. He grew slowly into the realm of episcopal authority, even with a sense of hesitancy. When asked about the appointment of a new bishop by Purcell in 1838 he was somewhat nonplussed. "I am really at a loss what to say in reply," he ventured. "I have reflected much on the subject and have not been able to think of one whom I could take upon myself to recommend."[4]

By 1842, however, he was speaking with a sense of self-assurance. In the fall of that year he wrote to the seventy-two priests under his jurisdiction, calling for the first synod in the diocese's thirty-four-year history. No man was excused unless he could offer evidence of harm that would occur by absence from his parish. (Only six failed to appear.) They were to meet at St. John's, Fordham, for a week of retreat, to be followed by three days of meetings, and all were to bring for reference copies of the decrees of the Council of Trent, as well as the decrees of the American bishops assembled at Baltimore.

The rules published after this synod were, in effect, an announcement to Catholics, clerical and lay, that the previously leaky vessel of the Church in New York—the product of haphazard immigrant settlement—would now be a taut ship. "The Bishops of this diocese have tolerated customs which the Church did not approve, but merely bore with until a better order could be introduced," Hughes proclaimed. "That time seems at length to have arrived."[5]

The regulations governed the administration of the sacraments. The Roman ritual was to be used in all ceremonies; priests were to be properly attired for official ceremonies; no priest was to be absent from his parish on a Sunday without permission; marriages were not to be performed without four days' notice; rules were laid down for proper burial of the faithful in consecrated cemeteries.

Secret societies were condemned under pain of excommunication. This seems an unnecessarily strong penalty for joining a brotherhood, but the secret societies were a frightening undercurrent in the world of the Irish immigrant. The natives of Ireland were no more bound to one another in familial affection then were the citizens of any other country. The agrarian labor market of that nation, the impoverished conditions, and the willingness of some migrant workers to labor for less than others had brought men into societies bound by secret oaths and known by such names as "the Corkonians," "the Far-downs," "the Cocks of the North," and "the Boys of the South." Transferred to the United States, the old hatreds enkindled by these societies were stirred up anew and were the cause of bloody gang wars among canal diggers, railroad crews, and inside factories that employed the Irish. The excommunication leveled by Hughes was directed to these men rather than those who might join such fraternities as the Masons (where an Irish Catholic would hardly in any event be welcomed) or the fledgling, and necessarily secret, labor unions.

Lastly, Hughes fired off a few shots at his constant target —lay trustees. "We have known many trustees," he judged, "and we have never known one to retire from the office a better Catholic or a more pious man than when he entered it."[6] This allegation was followed by a list of restrictions placed upon their power. No one in the church—not even the sexton— could be hired or fired by the trustees, nor could sums of money be apportioned without permission of the pastor. Books of parish finances were to be kept for inspection by the bishop. Meetings could not be held without the approval of the pastor. Obviously the regulations signified a centralization and transferal of power into the bishop's hands.

When the pastoral letter on lay trustees was published the newspapers of New York expressed alarm for the sake of democracy. This demagogue who had just marshaled his flock to the polls was now denying them a voice in the maintenance of properties that they themselves had built and owned. Hughes took on the loudest of the detractors. He ignored Bennett who piously told the bishop that he ought to confine himself to pastoral duties and forsake political squabbles. The irreverent editor of the *Herald* possessed at least a modicum of right to complain of his own Chruch. The others were to know that though they might fight with Hughes till blood ran in the political arena, when it came to matters within the realm of the Church's own jurisdiction they were treading into a sanctuary where they had no right.

Hughes addressed himself to "David Hale, Esq., who is a

Congregationalist in religion; W. L. Stone, Esq., who is some kind of a Presbyterian; M. R. Noah, Esq., who is a Jew . . ." informing them that he referred to their own religions "not through disrespect, but in order that the reader may judge of your competency to decide a matter of ecclesiastical policy between a Catholic bishop and his flock." Hale he wrote off as ignorant for his claim that superstitious obedience to a priesthood held Catholics in bondage, and for his assumption that the episcopal signature "† John." meant that Hughes wanted himself to be known as "dagger John." ("It was printed a dagger," retorted Hale, "and I supposed it meant a dagger.")[7] Stone had been courageous in his exposure of the Maria Monk affair, but throughout the school issue he had been bitter in his invective toward Catholics. Hughes commiserated that this "poor man" had won himself so much hatred for this previous honesty that he "must in turn show hostility to win back his former friends." Mordecai Noah belonged "to a religion for the members of which I entertain a melancholy reverence, mingled with other feelings which, I trust, are no dishonor to the human heart." Hughes bluntly asked him what right he had to judge Catholic rules about baptism. In short the domain of the Church was his domain. "With the aid of our own means and judgement we can correct its evils without any help from Jews and Presbyterians," he wrote.

During this same period Hughes had commenced his "holy war" against the Catholic *Truth Teller,* and the paper, no matter what it may have thought of the bishop's directives, withheld comment and stewed in a careful silence. Still, it seemed more than an editorial slip-up when the above letter of the bishop was printed and then followed by a two-line appeal that completed the column of type and seemed a part of Hughes's claim: "Wanted—a situation as wet nurse by a middle aged woman with a fresh breast of milk. Unquestionable references can be given."[8]

Three bishops died in 1842. On April 11th John England, who had been in fact if not in title the head of the American hierarchy, died in Charleston. It was the day after this that the nativist mobs in New York had spent election night hurling bricks and firebrands at John Hughes's house in an effort to burn it to the ground. The bricks that smashed every window in Dubois's bedroom that night nearly frightened the old man to death. But he survived, thanks to his basically sound constitution and to the New York riot police. It was Conwell who succumbed ten days after this event, surprising those Philadelphians who came to believe that he would endure until the Second Coming. He was ninety-four and had lived long enough to win the reverence of older people with short memories. Ever the gentleman, Kenrick eulogized him graciously at his funeral and at long last became the bishop of Philadelphia instead of Arath.

The bishop of New York and the bishop of Basiliopolis still lived, uncomfortably, under one roof. To the credit of both men the public never knew of their mutual discomfort, even though enemies attempted to play one against the other. As a slap at Hughes during the school controversy, the New York Corporation omitted inviting him to a reception for the Catholic Prince de Joinville, whose guest Hughes had once been in Paris. Instead Protestant ministers were invited to officiate. Then, as if to underscore the insult, the ailing but real bishop of New York was officially invited.[9]

Dubois would never have responded to the invitation, even if health had permitted. He remained in quiet seclusion. When he was visited by close friends the old man would admit to pains, but if Hughes chanced to enter his room he would straighten up and declare that he was quite well. Quite well!

With the approach of winter Dubois began to fail. Five days before Christmas he passed away, clear in mind and gently speaking to God. On the day of his funeral James Gordon Bennett, who had been no admirer of Dubois during his active administration, was sensitive enough to express disgust at the "thunders of applause" that had greeted the Presbyterian Reverend George Cheever "denouncing with all the bitterness of vindictive bigotry not only members of the Catholic Church, but every foreigner as unworthy of American Citizenship." Said Bennett, ". . . it is impossible to describe the chuckling and gratified shrugging of the shoulder and gleeful rubbing of the hands which betokened the delight with which Mr. Cheever's sentiments were received." Then, moving to the old Frenchman's funeral, with its elaborate rituals, the *Herald* noted one strange fact: "Of the deceased Bishop Hughes spoke little."[10]

Instead of eulogizing John Dubois the new L.shop of New York explained to the congregation that Bishop Fenwick of Boston was to have preached the homily. Fenwick did not arrive in time and he, John Hughes, did not feel that he had known Bishop Dubois well enough to so honor him. Instead he spoke defensively of the right of Catholics to pray for the dead.

John Dubois's labors had never been repaid with anything that the world might call glory. But if, beyond the veil of death, he could care at all what the world thought, he might have noted with wry irony that Cheever's harangue at the Tabernacle at least gave evidence that he had made some sort of impact with his life. Hughes had lived with Dubois for ten years altogether. He had watched his face while Mount St. Mary's College burned to a shell of stone before him. He had seen him weep in the face of crippling illness and humiliating defeat. But he said he did not know him. His mind had been closed by a rebuff in 1818, and when the relationship between the two men had truly begun in 1819 young John had, in turn, decided it was "a regular contract between us, in which neither was required to acknowledge any obligation to the other."

Dubois's funeral was not Hughes's finest hour.

Except for a minor adjustment in his signature, Dubois's death had no real effect on Hughes's office. The synod during the fall, the manner in which he had called it, and the authoritative pastoral issued at its conclusion, were evidence enough to any who might have been in doubt that Hughes was in full and absolute command of the diocese. With souls to be shepherded over so large a territory, however, and with only a small scattered crew of subordinate clergy, absolute command did not mean absolute control. There were shepherds of differing voices anxious to draw wandering members of Hughes's flock into their own.

Simon Bruté

John Breckinridge

John DuBois

Henry Conwell

This nativist cartoon published during the Church property debate shows Hughes, burdened down with his worldly goods, lamenting "Alas! Poor Roman workshop! We can no longer remit to thee the golden goods of America." Seated at the table, Columbia declares "The state is your bookeeper." *New York Historical Society.*

Maria Monk & Child
Georgetown University

W.C. Brownlee
New York Public Library

Hughes, photographed by Brady
New York Public Library

James Gordon Bennett
New York Historical Society

"Jaime and the Bishop." In this 1844 cartoon, Bennett aims dirty water at Hughes who threatens the editor with his crozier, crying, "With all the power of Holy Church will I assail thee, most reprobate and contemptible viper." A Scotsman, left, prepares to assist Bennett while an Irishman, right, begs the bishop for permission "to slap at him wid the shillaly."

New York Historical Society.

A scene from the New York draft riots, July 1863.

William Seward
New York Public Library

Gaetano Bedini
New York Public Library

Nativist Protestants, faced with the problem of an ever-growing Catholic community, cried out against the presence of these "captives of Babylon" and tried to prevent them from infecting the American Republic with the power of their votes. Still, under the Christian admonition to hate sin and love the sinner they tried to view these immigrants as persons who were held in a bondage of superstitious ignorance by their educated and thus culpable clergy. (The American Tract Society in its 1843 annual report cited the example of one Irish woman who purportedly was convinced that Bishop Hughes had the power to change a beefsteak into a flounder.)[11] As a result of their convictions, the nativists launched a double-edged campaign to discredit Romanism and to convert its members to "authentic" Christianity.

Theodore Frelinghuysen, a United States Senator and an officer in several of the Protestant mission societies ("For myself," noted Hughes, "I look upon him as a sincere, honest, and so far as the two ideas can be associated, honorable bigot."[12]) declared that Protestants had to resign themselves to an America that would never again be the same. "The tide is constantly swelling and breaking over us," he said. "We cannot repel it now if we would . . ."[13]

The Home Missionary Society responded in 1842 with a positive approach to the Catholic immigrants, announcing "Let them come with good or with evil intent, as exiles fleeing from tyranny or as emissaries to spy out and possess the land—let them come. We will meet them on the beach, with bread in one hand and the Gospel in the other . . ."[14]

And so bible and tract societies passed out books to catechize, missionaries went from door to door, and the converted papists—among them the prolific William Hogan—preached the good news to the poor. They reported scant success, for it was all too evident to the newcomers that the native American was clutching a brickbat with his bible, not bread. The failure to convert Catholics, however, was more popularly ascribed to the tyrannical Old-World hold of the Catholic clergy. The Tract Society reported of one courageous man who broke this hold, and in the strength of his new-found faith told his former pastor, ". . . if you lay a hand on me it is at your peril. Thank God you have not got me at home in the bogs of Ireland where you could have my cabin burned over my head, or have me murdered."[15]

Such a report meant little to anyone who had experienced the oppression in Ireland and knew who the real oppressors were. But one story that drifted into New York City at the end of 1842 rang too true to be ignored. In the absence of any communications faster than the canals came word that in Champlain, New York, near the Canadian border, a priest had collected bibles distributed by the Protestant societies and publicly burned them. The clear simplicity of the facts soon made it evident that this was not one of the usual canards; it was the truth. Even the most tolerant Protestants became understandably enraged. Public meetings were organized throughout the state to protest this desecration of "the Holy Bible which our constitution and laws recognize as the will of God to man."[16]

Bennett's *Herald,* cool of the religious prejudices of both religious factions, reported the incident and declared that the uncompromising rejection that Catholics leveled at the King James Bible was folly. "That version does not differ in any material point from that authorized by their own Church."[17] In the 1840s, however, neither group was ready to accept such an ecumenical observation.

The *Freeman's Journal,* which Hughes employed as his own organ, precipitously praised the initiative of the as yet unknown priest and labeled the deed a "praiseworthy act."[18] The paper jumped the gun on Hughes. Though he fought without quarter when defending Catholics against bigoted attacks, he never approved his own people acting as the aggressors in ugliness. Cautiously, he issued a pastoral in which he admitted ignorance of the facts and requested that, at his expense, a commission of Protestant and Catholic laymen should be appointed to investigate the matter. "In this way," he hoped, "an odium which would be as unjust as it is unmerited by the Catholic body of the United States will be repelled, and the individuals who are culpable of the outrage will be held up in their proper names to the reprehension which . . . they so unqualifiedly deserve."[19]

The offer was taken up. Three Protestants and three Catholics traveled north to ascertain the truth. They returned with a joint statement laying the blame at the sandals of a wandering friar named Telman, recently from France and based in Canada. Venturing into New York, he had zealously collected bibles and against the will of the local diocesan priest under Hughes's jurisdiction had destroyed them. Five days after the occurrence the bishop of Montreal went to Champlain and "in strong language" disapproved of the affair. The forty-two bibles burned were "but a small proportion of the whole number distributed."[20] In any event, both the distribution and the destruction of the bibles had been a vain exercise. Few of the villagers involved could read. This mattered little, however. The Champlain Bible Burning quickly took its place in the immediate legends of popery.

On the heels of this incident came another internal problem for Hughes to deal with. At the far western end of his diocese the parishoners of St. Louis church in Buffalo issued a statement wherein they "respectfully declined" to accede to the "request" for tighter diocesan controls issued after the fall synod. By limiting the power of the trustees they claimed the bishop was limiting their rights over their own property. Ironically this particular—and as it turned out long-lasting—fight over democratic processes within the Church came not from sons and daughters of the American Revolution, as in Philadelphia, but from a German congregation. Expressing his surprise, Hughes wrote back to inform them that his "request" had been weightier than a suggestion. "Should you determine that your church shall not be governed by the general law of the diocese," he threatened, "then we shall claim the privilege of retiring from its walls in peace, and leave you also in peace to govern it as you will."[21]

They so determined, and took their fight (as had the parishoners of St. Mary's in the 1820s) to the newspapers. But Hughes had been through it all before. He would not play games. Immediately he went to the ultimate weapon. For three weeks at the end of January 1843 he had a warning read from the pulpit of St. Louis church. When this was ignored he removed the German pastor, leaving them without a priest. He curtly informed the parishioners: "When you are willing to walk in the way of your holy faith as your forefathers did, and be numbered among the Catholic flock of the diocese, precisely as all other trustees and congregations are, then I shall send you a priest, if I should have one."[22]

Difficulties of this kind were not always faced over a desk at the episcopal residence. Hughes spent a great deal of time on the road, consecrating, confirming, and doing a good deal of poking into distant corners to see if things were being run properly. He went on a visitation of the diocese after the synod, rarely deviating from a heavily paced schedule. He arrived, for instance, at Binghamton on one Saturday night; the next day he preached four times, consecrated a church and administered confirmation. Ill on Monday, he nonetheless preached twice and consecrated a cemetery. The day after that he rode thirty miles in an open wagon to Oxford, preached there, and continued on to Utica the same evening.

If one was serious about proper administration, this empire of a diocese was too large a task even for a man with Hughes's energy and love of travel. He continually suggested to his superiors at Propaganda in Italy that the New York diocese was ripe to be transformed into several dioceses. With one such request he impatiently slashed out red boundary lines on a map to show how this should be done and sent it to Rome. After Dubois's death he thought it feasible to ask for an auxiliary bishop. There was a council planned for May in Baltimore. He intended to ask for a man at that time. But who? There were several luminaries in the diocese, any of whom would make a popular bishop. There was Power. Despite his hidden insubordination under Dubois he had been a model of correction with Hughes. Such a choice would satisfy those who felt that the vicar general had twice been unfairly cheated of the New York See. No doubt that is why Hughes quickly passed him over. He wanted no strong factions to deal with.

There was the dashingly handsome Charles Constantine Pise, the only Catholic priest to serve as chaplain to the United

States Congress, the writer of novels, histories, and poetry. He was properly subservient and he would have made an attractive assistant. But Hughes was also a man of letters—having written the fudgy *Conversion and Edifying Death of Andrew Dunn*—and he let the consideration of artistic merit go by the boards. In Hughes's estimation Pise was weak. Assigned to St. Joseph's church when the trustees there had made it known they wanted to retain their former pastor, Pise found the heat of unpopularity too hard to take and asked out of the parish. In his stead was sent the quiet John McCloskey who had been a boy at Mount St. Mary's when Hughes was a seminarian. He had retained the face of a child into adulthood and bore a serious, hurt expression that made him seem as if he were always on the verge of tears. Perhaps that is why the trustees at St. Joseph presumed he would not disrupt their campaign for their old pastor. His looks were misleading. For a year he held firm in a silent battle. The Sunday of his arrival he preached to a church where the center pews were kept purposely empty from the pulpit to the back of the church. The parishioners refused him his salary, refused to give him furniture for the rectory, and resorted to such pranks as bogus sick calls in the middle of the night. McCloskey never reacted, never said a word. He simply held tight to his position and would not let go. After a year the parishioners began not so much to tire of the game (St. Louis in Buffalo was to prove that a congregation could wax healthy on such warfare), as to be ashamed in the face of McCloskey's genuine Christian attitude. He began to win friends, and once having done so he never alluded to past unpleasantness.

John Hughes watched all this and grew in admiration for the younger student he had known as a dogged scholar. Appearances meant nothing. Strength is as strength does. He made McCloskey the first president of his college at Fordham. When he traveled to the Baltimore council in May there was little doubt in his mind as to whom he wanted to work beside him as a bishop.

The Baltimore council finished its business in late spring, nominating nine new bishops (including McCloskey for New York). James Gordon Bennett observed that the "Church of a thousand ages" was gaining new life in America—"let David Hale and Mr. Cheever preach till they wear away their tongues, it will be no avail." Adding a dash of salt to the wounds this might cause, he ventured, "We believe no cardinal has ever been appointed from America. Who knows but Bishop Hughes may have the first head to fit the red hat. We nominate him for the 'eminence.' "[23]

Hughes at the moment was seeking no red hat but some cold hard cash. In June he sailed for Europe with Bishop Purcell, Pierre Desmet (the Indian missionary), and his Whig friend Thurlow Weed. The crucial purpose of his trip was to bail out the parishes of New York by a loan in Belgium.

Philip Hone, who had styled Hughes "generalissimo" in the wake of the school fight, mused upon the wake of the *George Washington* as it sailed out into the Atlantic, and confided to his diary some nativist fears about its passengers. "I do not believe that Mr. Weed is an adjunct to the right reverend apostles of Papacy, or that he is to assist them in preparing a report to the sovereign Pontiff of their successful efforts to introduce the true faith into this susceptible country by means of a judicious exercise of the political influence of their band of foreign dictators. But this I do believe, that he by his late efforts and the late governor by his, have done more to give efficacy to this mischievous foreign influence than any two men in the state. As for Bishop Hughes, he deserves a cardinal's hat for what he has done in placing Irish Catholics upon the necks of native New Yorkers."[24]

They landed in Ireland and passing through Dublin witnessed at Donnybrook one of the "monster meetings" for repeal. Hundreds of thousands of frustrated patriots had been worked to a dangerous pitch by the time Daniel O'Connell stepped forward to speak, but within minutes O'Connell had cooled them down to good humor. Hughes, pocketing memories that would be of practical value, took note of the statesman's ability to calm rather than excite—"like casting oil upon the troubled waters." Still, Ireland depressed him. The poverty and oppression, along with what he saw as a mixture of patriotism, indifference and perfidy, weighed upon him so heavily he found it a relief to escape from the spectacle.

In London he watched the House of Commons "attempting to cope with and defeat one man," Daniel O'Connell. "But, though O'Connell has the right," he worried, ". . . they have the power, and God grant that the crises may not end in adding another blood stained chapter to the history of Ireland's misfortunes."[25]

While in England he happened upon one of his seminarians, James Roosevelt Bayley. The twenty-eight-year-old Bayley had been an Episcopal priest whose path to the Roman Church had wound through the walkways of Fordham and long discussions with John McCloskey. John Hughes was immediately taken with him. It was not just that the attractive young aristocrat was intelligent and had a happy manner about him. His clear good looks were reminiscent of an earlier convert to the Roman Church, his aunt Elizabeth Bayley Seton. The resemblance was certainly strong enough to bring John Hughes back to his own days as a day laborer, and to the memory of the gracious lady who had helped push him past the reluctance of John Dubois and into Mount St. Mary's. If he was not one to forget a rebuff, neither was he one to forget a favor. He took the young man under his wing. They journeyed together during Hughes's short stay in England, and the recent convert was relaxed enough with his superior to admit that he would prefer going to see Scotland than to continue farther with his bishop. They parted with Hughes admonishing Bayley to "keep a sharp look out for all good books."[26] It was the beginning of a lifelong and mutually comfortable relationship.

In Belgium Hughes failed to obtain a loan. Either the financiers of that country had been reading New York newspapers or John Hughes was overly honest in describing the state of his episcopal See. In any event they decided that an investment in the churches built by an immigrant society amidst hostile neighbors was not the happiest speculation they might make. Hughes was back in New York by fall, further in the red by the price of one round-trip ticket to Europe.

Bigotry in the United States had always had its lulls and its seasons of intensity. The school issue, the publicity given to Catholic Church discipline, and bizarre events such as the

Champlain Bible Burning were flames to ignite the gunpowder of resentment nativist Americans felt against the immigrants. For several years after John Hughes's formation of the Catholic party at Carroll Hall this resentment occasionally exploded into anti-foreign, anti-Romanist action.

In the summer of 1843 the Mohawk and Hudson Railroad discharged all Irish employees and hired natives in their stead —an action for which the company was applauded by the public.[27]

John Quincy Adams, the statesman of American puritanism, spoke before the Astronomical Society of Cincinnati near the end of that year, and in a speech reprinted throughout the United States used the condemnation of Galileo as a point of reference for which to attack the Roman Church. He also described Ignatius Loyola, the founder of the Jesuits, as the man who, "moving under the influence of fanaticism, invents an engine of despotic power."[28]

Hughes did his best to dampen such explosive charges. He took the occasion of speaking before the Irish Emigration Society in December to deliver an address explaining "The Mixture of Civil and Ecclesiastical Power in the Middle Ages." The audience he was really addressing was not the Irish, but John Quincy Adams and his America.

The medieval union of the Roman Catholic Church and any civil power in the past was "simply a historical accident." Whether it was good or bad, Hughes insisted, Americans were as foolish to judge past ages by modern standards as they would be to blame Columbus for not crossing the Atlantic in a steam vessel. Admitting an unhappy indictment against all Christians—that after the Reformation "the struggle appears to have been, between Catholics and Protestants, who should persecute the most"—Hughes pointed out that if the marriage of Church and state were feared by Americans, they must still recognize that never was there so tight a union as in the American English colonies. The meeting ground for the present age he hoped would be in the absence of religious entanglement safeguarded by the United States Constitution—"a monument of wisdom, an instrument of liberty and right, unequalled, unrivalled in the annals of the human race."

In the heated atmosphere of intolerance, the address was a masterpiece of extended good will and moderation. And yet perhaps it was too moderate for belief, for Hughes, who had been thrashing lay trustees into silence ever since he had climbed to authority, insisted that "the Church herself, in all her own forms of government, was, as she still is, a model of modified and admirably well regulated democratic jurisprudence. In the Church the principle of suffrage and election has ever prevailed."[29]

From late winter into early spring of 1844, with the luxury of McCloskey as coadjutor to share his work, he bound himself to giving twelve weekly lectures on Catholic doctrine. But there was no chance of remaining within the polite walls of the cathedral while American politics seethed with the topic of religion. It was a presidential election year. Nativist agitation was high. Rallies and petitions called for a change in the naturalization laws. In New York thirty-two public schools had, by this time, had the bible banned from their curricula. The board of education in its yearly report cried out against the trend, once again declaring that the bible "without note or comment is not a sectarian book . . ."[30] Politicians laid the blame for its removal upon Catholics. The theme was so constant that the *Herald* predicted the bible would soon be added to the log cabin, hard cider, and fat coons as a political emblem. Said the paper: "All the old insignia have been cast aside for the Bible. The candidates cease to talk about 'the people' and can say nothing but 'the Bible—the Bible.' Orators no longer shouting about the stars and stripes call out 'the Bible—the Bible'; Minstrels cease their songs about the 'American Eagle' and chant hymns in honor of 'the Bible—the Bible' . . . One thing is now certain— that, whoever is to be President, the Bible will decide it."[31]

Before the April municipal elections Hughes took every means to admonish Catholics against gathering into unruly mobs. If there was to be a repeat of the 1842 election-night rioting he didn't want to see Catholic gangs squaring aimlessly off against nativist gangs. He was more organized about it. He stationed over 3,000 Catholic men—"armed to the teeth"[32]—to protect church property. The nativist gangs again materialized bearng "no Popery" signs and displaying very little good will. But they kept their distance and the night passed without warfare. Apparently the Catholics, busy standing guard, kept their distance from the polls; James Harper, the native American candidate, was elected mayor of the city.

In the midst of all this bile occurred a refreshing incident that proved John Hughes held himself in check from black-and-white attitudes toward Protestants. In an age when bishops went back and forth to Europe to handle routine business and spent an equal amount of time jostling through the backwoods in open wagons, Hughes was not an inaccessible man. Anyone who was intent upon meeting him could easily do so. He was a court of appeals for religious disputes between parishioners and priests, a trusted means of communication for the illiterate immigrants wishing to contact someone back home, and a general catchall for a myriad of human problems. Like all men with a touch of greatness he found time. Pressing, great matters were often mixed with pressing, small matters. Thus for instance a portentious letter of ecclessiastical concerns shared with the archbishop of Baltimore is interrupted by the digression—"I take the liberty of enclosing to your address a letter in which a poor widow of the congregation is much interested . . ."[33]

In the wake of the nativist municipal elections a group of Shakers called on him, having traveled 200 miles for that purpose. They explained that an angel had appeared to a member of their community and had instructed them to print 500 copies of a book containing a celestial message. They were to present free copies of the book to a list of sovereigns, princes, and to Bishop Hughes of New York and the Pope. Hughes spoke with them for a length of time; acceding to their request, he sent one of the volumes to the Holy See. In his accompanying letter he explained about the denomination to Rome, noted that they were ridiculed for their lives of celibacy and that public speculation insisted upon attributing immorality to them—though he discounted the rumors and praised them for their simplicity and self-denial. What is notable about his letter—sent, as he had promised the Shakers, with their book included—is that it was written without the slightest trace of condescension.[34]

In the early months of 1844 Bishop Kenrick in Philadelphia had imitated Hughes by stirring up a bible controversy. His approach was more conservative, however, and he carefully limited himself to pleading that Catholic children be allowed to read the Catholic version of the text. With the precedent of New York's public schools before them, passions ran high in the city of brotherly love. On May 6th at a nativist rally in the heavily Irish Kensington district, fights broke out, shots were fired and a Protestant was killed. The city lunged into three days of civil warfare. Throughout that night of the 6th, gangs attacked homes in Kensington, including the convent of the Sisters of Charity.

The next day some 4,000 people gathered at Independence Square and then, behind a soiled American flag which was coupled to the banner—"This is the flag that has been trampled by Irish Papists"—marched to Kensington. New Yorkers waited hour by hour as express trains carried bulletins from Philadelphia. They learned that an Irish fire company was attacked, and in a pitched battle twelve nativists were killed. The Sisters' convent, attacked the night before, was burned.

John Hughes waited for word with emotions more keenly attuned than most. He had never severed the ties that for over a decade had bound him to the Church in Philadelphia. Terence Donoghoe was probably the closest friend Hughes had in the priesthood. They had been assigned to St. Joseph's together, had weathered the cholera epidemic as a team, and when Hughes was sent to build St. John's Donoghoe was sent to erect St. Michael's in Kensington. He missed Donoghoe. Lonely in authority, he wanted the presence of this friend with whom he could be himself, and he frequently, for the rest of his life, begged Donoghoe to move to New York. "I hope you will come to New York . . ." he wrote that year. "I stand in much need of you at this time . . . I do not know that you ever took my advice in any matter pertaining to yourself; neither do I think this strange, but in this instance try it. I do not think you will ever have an occasion to be sorry for doing so. Write soon, and tell me you are coming to spend, at best, the winter with your old friend."[35]

And so he waited with worry for every scrap of news. On the second day of rioting came word that St. Michael's was in flames. Donoghoe had escaped unhurt, but an eyewitness account printed for New Yorkers was a humiliation to read: "The Natives have entered the priest's house. They are throwing from the window the books of his library forgotten in his [Donoghoe's] retreat. Here comes a carpet waving in the wind as it falls, and now demi johns; a crucifix and some sacred images are flying through the air tossed by the infuriated multitude and carried away by the spectators. A Catholic bible produced considerable contention, but, however, it was at length obtained by one individual who ran off with it. The priest's house is now on fire."[36]

Next St. Augustine's where Hughes had lived as a deacon and that had served Philadelphia as a cholera hospital in 1832 was put to the torch. The 5,000-volume library—Hughes's reference quarry during the Breckinridge fight—was piled in the middle of the street and made into a huge bonfire.

St. John's that he had built, where his friend Mark Frenaye made his home, was the mob's next target. By this time, however, the militia had moved into action and the church was surrounded by artillery.

In New York the *Herald* warned its readers against a scheduled mass nativist meeting "until the country gets calm and tranquil."[37] Hiram Ketchum was not to be checked, however. In the midst of all this he gave an incendiary speech, and told his public: "The question originated here, and so I may perhaps be indulged in stating the origin and progress of the contest for the bible in the schools. Wherever the opposition is made it is true it assumes the same character—whether in Philadelphia, Baltimore or New York." Ketchum spurted out his arguments which the *Herald* labeled a "long and commonplace tirade against, Popery, Papists—the Pope and the devil." Ignoring the burned churches in Pennsylvania, he finally warned: "If the country became Roman Catholic they would burn the bible." He sat down, "amid great applause."[38]

The firewinds blowing from the south heated the tension ninety miles to the north. Kenrick had fled Philadelphia during the riots, and though Hughes said nothing of him he was angry that Catholics had not been organized under strong leadership. "They should have defended their churches since the authorities could not or would not do it for them," he insisted.[39]

Rumors grew that a delegation was bringing northward the enshrined flag "trampled by Irish Papists." A City Hall Park demonstration was being planned by nativists for the occasion. John Hughes issued an extra edition of *Freeman's Journal* admonishing Catholics to stay away from public meetings. He also called on the municipal authorities and bluntly warned them: "If a single Catholic Church is burned in New York, the city will become a second Moscow." The lame duck Mayor Robert Morris asked him:

"Are you afraid that some of your Churches will be burned?" "No sir," Hughes countered, "but I am afraid that some of yours will be burned. We can protect our own. I come to warn you for your own good."

Hughes then demanded that the nativist mayor-elect, James Harper, should be brought in to assume responsibility. These nativists were his people, Hughes declared, arguing that Harper should use his influence to cancel the City Hall demonstration. Hughes also advised that a squadron of horse and infantry be readied, just in case all else failed.[40]

The rally was called off by its leaders. Yet New York remained at a tinderbox for a number of weeks. In June Catholics could bristle from reading in the papers that a man accosted a Sister of Charity on the street, called her a "damn Papist bitch" and struck her across the face.[41] Nonetheless tempers held and there were no great disturbances—even when Philadelphia exploded in a second series of riots in July.

As always in such cases there was a great deal of probing to ascertain the causes of what had transpired. In both cities a number of rhetorical diagnosticians traced the flames back to the bishop of New York. One "Protestant and Native" Philadelphian, appalled at the riots, wrote in a pamphlet: "We are told. 'This is a Protestant Country.' " He then asked if that meant "all must become so, or tamely admit to the dicta of Protestant sectarianiam." While he had always felt that Bishop Hughes was "highly impolitic and that the line of proceeding was equally improper," he still insisted that anyone judging him should "imagine himself in the place of Bishop Hughes— or if every Protestant will honestly ask himslef, if he were a taxpayer in a Catholic country—if he had to contribute to a public school whether he could submit to have children taught out of the Douay Bible." What was more, he said, if nativists objected to political shepherds they should look to their own and see "certain Protestant clergymen at meetings of the native Americans and mark them as amongst the most active, the loudest in their violent addresses . . ."[42]

In New York the newspapers renewed postures they had taken during the school crisis. Horace Greeley, his young *Tribune* growing in prestige, took a moderate course. Citing the nativist assumption that the United States was a "land of Protestant ascendancy," he labeled the riots a "deep dishonor on our country." He was quick to fault the other side as well. "The Irish, too, are too much addicted to taking law into their own hands. Educated in a land where the law is the instrument of their oppressors and where violence is their only resource against injustice, they are a great deal too ready to appeal to the bludgeon and the brickbat in support of their rights." It was against this background, Greeley felt, that the public should measure Hughes's attempt to educate his flock to the proper use of the ballot at Carroll Hall. "The great venom with which Bishop Hughes and this Catholic meeting are treated appears to have been incited rather by the fact that they were successful in procuring a reluctant acknowledgement of their grievances and a blundering attempt to redress them."[43]

David Hale's *Journal of Commerce* laid the blame for what happened in Philadelphia squarely upon "a man calling himself 'John, Bishop of New York.' " Lauding the moderation of the nativists he declared: "We had consented to strike out truth from history, and incidental remarks from moral lessons, and in various ways to cover up the foot of the beast at his desire, but when emboldened by concessions he proclaimed the bible a sectarian book and demanded its withdrawal from the schools we could not consent . . . So now when with restless energy Americans rise to break up the conspiracy, the conspirators cry louder than all others against bringing religion into politics."[44]

Bennett, of course, had a circulation to maintain and was not to be outdone. "Who first raked together the embers of religious animosity and opened the way for the perpetration of those bloody and devastating outrages?" he asked. "Well, in looking back upon the history of the last few years we find that there was a certain assemblage of politicians, of a particular class, in what is called Carroll Hall, and that a Right Reverend Bishop of this city, abandoning his holy calling went down into that arena and harangued the assembled multitude in relation to their political duties at the election of 1841." Bennett concluded that "it was the rash, the erring, and unjustified conduct of Bishop Hughes . . . which supplied the torch to the feelings of bigotry and prejudice against the Irish which had been before that fatal moment, smoldering and dying out in the ashes . . ."[45]

The anti-Hughes campaign was not confined to the press. He received a threat of assassination—"A well sharpened poniard for your breast"—from a man who spuriously claimed kinship with the first native citizen killed in the riots. "The foreigner who dared to attempt to turn our institutions to the ends and aims of that religion that has cursed Italy, Spain, Austria, South America and Mexico" he promised, "shall be made to bite the dust."[46]

Hughes could never let such opportunities pass. Playing Becket from the altar of his cathedral he hurled the letter at the nativist mayor and added to it an autobiographical defense of his own behavior, lengthy enough to fill an entire newspaper page. In fact, so the indignant James Harper protested, it was for the newspapers that Hughes meant the open letter. He hadn't even bothered to mail a copy to City Hall. In the letter Hughes related his own immigrant history. Surprisingly he disassociated himself a hairsbreadth from the Irish by saying that though the Hughes family was of Irish birth they were descendents of Welsh blood. Tracing his climb from a common man to a position of leadership in America, he presented his apologies for the present moment. "I never was, and never will be a politician. I am the pastor of a Christian flock . . . As a pastor I was bound to see that the religious rights of my flock should not be filched away from them under pretext of education and against the Constitution and laws of my country." When, as it turned out in the election of 1841, all candidates were against them, then, said Hughes, "I told them to cut their way through this circle of fire . . . I told [the Catholics] that they would be signing and sealing their own degradation if they voted for men pledged to refuse them even the chance of justice . . . ."

He then singled out Bennett's *Herald* and William Stone's *Commercial Advertiser* for misquoting his original Carroll Hall speech and inflaming the public against Catholics. Hughes noted that during the municipal election the *Herald* had alleged that there were dungeons under St. Patrick's cathedral awaiting Protestants. With 30,000 copies of the allegation on the street, he chided Harper, it is no wonder you were elected. Of Bennett he said, "I regard him as decidedly the most dangerous man to the peace and safety of a community that I have ever known or read of."[47]

In reaction to Hughes's letter printer's ink splattered for weeks. Calling the bishop's logic "clear as mud," Bennett declared that this "politico-religious agitator . . . descends to all sorts of low and vulgar witticisms and squirts all sorts of venom and filth around him."[48] In his open letter Hughes had told about the snub Bennett received from the hands of Daniel O'Connell in repayment for malicious gossip the *Herald* had seen fit to print. In reply, Bennett denied ever publishing a malicious story about O'Connell—or about Hughes, for that matter. Bennett reaffirmed his own Catholic faith, although he admitted it was a type that "differs widely from the Catholicity inculcated and practiced and paraded by Bishop Hughes." The editor went on to say that "Irish Catholicity is the worst kind of Catholicity because it is mixed and mingled with party feeling as exemplified in O'Connell, and may be called O'Connell

Catholicity."[49] In return Hughes coolly published in the *Freeman's Journal* each excerpt from the *Herald* referred to, and he carefully cited the issue in which it originally appeared. Bennett, caught, angrily asked for a file of the *Freeman's Journal* that he might place the conduct of Bishop Hughes before the American people in order "to use up what little is now left of him."[50]

Then William L. Stone, describing Hughes as the man "who styles himself Bishop of New York," defended himself from the sickbed in which he was shortly to die. Reasserting his accusations against the bishop's "Jesuitism," Stone spoke of the fear that he had of Hughes's control over his flock: "A word from you then and even the withholding a word might have wrapped our dwellings in flames and deluged our streets with blood. Our Protestant population have lain down and slept securely beneath the protecting hand of Bishop Hughes. What would have been thought had a Protestant clergy-man claimed this kind of power over the people to whom he ministers?"[51]

Hughes responded with a series of letters that revealed Stone's role in the growth of nativism. Horace Greeley, playing the referee, expressed thorough enjoyment at the trouncing of these two editors who were not among his friends. "We cannot advise the public to read the *Herald*," he gloated, "but we wish all could witness the writhings of its editor under the justice administered to him by Bishop Hughes." Turning to the autocratic *Commercial Advertiser,* the *Tribune* scolded the aristocratic Stone for his narrow outlook. "It is evident from Col. Stone's whole argument that not merely Catholics, Jews, Mohammedans, etc., are aliens from his 'National religion' but those Protestants who are more Protestant than his standards are also out."[52]

Stone's death ended the fight between him and Hughes. The fight between Bennett and Hughes went on for roughly another twenty years.

The polar differences between Hughes and Kenrick were once more made evident. Their reaction to the riots shows

clearly why Kenrick, of the two, had more influence on his
fellow bishops and the internal affairs of the Church, while
Hughes was the bishop whom the public of the United States
acknowledged as the leader of Catholics in America. This was
true even after Kenrick was made archbishop of Baltimore. It
is not to say that one was better than the other. They both
made valuable contributions to the Church of their era. But
they spoke to entirely different worlds. Kenrick's refusal to
sanction armed defense against the nativists—"Rather let every
church burn than shed one drop of blood or imperil one precious soul"[53]—sounds a great deal more Christian, generations
later, than Hughes's threat to turn New York into a second
Moscow. Still, from the perspective of that immediate moment, Hughes's churches remained standing while several of
Philadelphia's were in smoldering ruins.

And too, there was the scope of the audience before whom
each played. The general public in Philadelphia barely knew
Kenrick. Except for the time of the riots his name almost never
appeared in the newspapers during all the years of his administration.[54] In New York any citizen who could read newspaper
print knew precisely who John Hughes was and what he was
doing from week to week. Hughes loved publicity, and with his
talents for drama he made the press not so much his pulpit as
his stage. It wasn't that the American public had a choice as to
which bishop they would listen to; it was usually the case that
nobody else could be heard over the voice of John Hughes.

As matters quieted down in 1844 Hughes returned to his
role as a simple Christian shepherd. In July he dedicated a
church in Perth Amboy, carefully explaining the ceremony for
the sake of the Protestants who were present. To Bennett's
credit, he reported his instance of the bishop's diplomacy respectfully, and even with a tone of reserved admiration.

Hughes then went on a visitation of the western part of his
diocese. In Buffalo, the parishioners of St. Louis had been
holding out for two years without a priest. Reacting perhaps to
the inflexible manner in which their bishop had confronted the
nativist Americans, they capitulated and agreed to make a
public apology to him in the city newspapers. Typically, he
authored their apology himself.

16

IN MY DIOCESE

Whether or not "The Bible—the Bible" did affect the national election, James Polk, heading the Democratic ticket, beat Henry Clay to the White House. After the election Bennett claimed that Thurlow Weed, along with all the Whigs who had tried to woo Catholics to the polls, would now probably turn on them: "As to Bishop Hughes and his Irish they had better look out for the next two or three years. The Whig party attribute all their defeat to them, and in retaliation for that, we have no doubt that they will open their guns upon them and persecute them far beyond anything that has taken place yet."[1]

Hughes, it seems, took the advice seriously. For months he kept studiously out of the limelight. Several friends including Mark Frenaye and Bishop O'Connor of Pittsburgh asked him to write an exposition of Catholic principles by way of offsetting the year's riots. He hedged, arguing that "at this moment the malignity of the opposition will construe it into an evidence of that species of understanding among ourselves and combination for ulterior purposes of which they already accuse us."[2] For once, he even asked the cautious Kenrick's advice as to whether or not he should speak out.

By early 1845 the *Herald* noticed that Catholic leaders were exceedingly quiet. "Even Bishop Hughes seems to have awakened to a sense of the propriety of this conduct . . . Carroll Hall no longer rings with the infuriated shoutings of an excited mob, and the sacerdotal vestments of the Catholic clergy are not now seen sweeping the filthy floor of the political arena."[3]

A renewed flare-up of the bible question couldn't draw him into debate. (The Board of Education held firm against David Reese's campaign for compulsory King James and/or Douay readings.)

The sometimes Welshman went so far as to remove St. Patrick's Day to April 7th that winter, hoping to keep the Irish celebration subdued. St. Patrick's Day on the day he had chosen was indeed subdued, but two days after the Ides of March the police were busy from dawn to dawn.[4] Hughes seemed to want a veil drawn over his public activities. In that same month he expressed to Bennett "a violent opposition to the reporting of his lectures in the newspapers." Headlined "The newspaper press as the ally to religion," the *Herald* offered its defense, printed along with a word-for-word report of a Hughes sermon on Transubstantiation and a review that praised Hughes, saying: "Bishop Hughes in the pulpit and Bishop Hughes in Carroll Hall are indeed, quite different beings. On the political platform he was violent, intemperate, mischievous. In the pulpit he is in his 'right mind'—rather moderate and ambitious only of doing good. Bishop Hughes, indeed, as a controversialist is worthy of much praise. He exhibits a model of calmness, candor and charitable feeling some of his Protestant opponents would do well to imitate."[5]

Right does seem to have been on the side of the *Herald* in this case. None of the clergy cared for his doing so—Bennett claimed it was because it cramped their chances to repeat instead of prepare sermons—but he sent reporters to gather, pearl for pearl, the Christian message as strewn from the city's pulpits. No matter what he might express editorially about the minister or priest involved, he printed the man's sermon whole, doing a better job in this department than the religious papers.

Nonetheless, to balance his honeyed mollification of the bishop, a week after this Bennett told the public that Hughes was "a man who possesses more of the demagogue than the Christian."[6]

The demagogue in question was not so intent upon winning a popularity poll among Catholics as keeping them in good order. Thus he expressed anger when the New York

Courier and Enquirer, on the word of an apostate Franciscan, reported that 200 German Catholics had seceded from the Church and formed their own national denomination. Hughes issued a sarcastic public statement saying that he had checked with all his German pastors and couldn't find the missing Catholics: "If the ex-Franciscan priest be not sounder in his new Theology than in the statement of mere human facts," he said, "I fear he will make a poor apostle after all."[7]

Hughes held his own apostles in tight check. He had lived through the long untidy era when United States Catholics were oftentimes dependent on the wandering friars and unconnected clerics who had left Europe to seek their fortunes. The bible-burning friar at Champlain was only the most recent example. Hughes, as best he could over such a large territory, demanded a military obedience from his clergy. Preparing his own list of priorities for business at the next Baltimore council he decided that he wanted general rules for all the bishops to follow in regulating acceptance of the "beggars, priests, friars and lay-brothers with commendatory letters from bishops . . . These have already done much injury . . ."[8]

No general rules could have been written that were as stringent as those he himself followed, and from his desk flowed a steady number of "It pains me" letters. Generally beginning with the assurance to the priest about to be suspended that the missive hurt its sender even more that it would the recipient the message was to the point. "The painful conviction of my mind," began a typical letter, "is that for a variety of circumstances which have come under my notice, I should be faithless to the awful duties of my state if I left you any longer in charge of souls for whom I must render or discount . . ."[9] For all his strictness, however, Hughes was in general neither unfair nor inflexible. No man had ever even vilified him more sharply in public than had Thomas Levins. Hughes reinstated him to his priesthood after he became ill.

Father John Farnam had led his parish into schism during Dubois's administration and had halted his rebellion only because of financial reverses. Hughes arranged for him to finish his days within the dignity of the priesthood at Detroit, far enough removed from the folly of his earlier ministry so as not to cause scandal.[10]

The necessary aloofness involved in such authority weighed upon him and made him ever more a loner. He had always tended to be such by nature, but now, even if he would be otherwise he had few opportunities for friendship. Cardinal Farley, one of his successors, would recall that Hughes had come to the diocese an unpopular man because of the strong lobby to make John Power bishop. Few priests had shown up for his consecration in 1838. The antipathy to the outsider who had supplanted the local favorite still hadn't abated after almost a decade. "This opposition was somewhat allayed by the appointment of John McCloskey in 1844," remembered Farley, "but even in 1846 it is undeniable that many of the Catholic pastors of New York were openly arrayed in opposition to Bishop Hughes."[11]

In this light, Hughes's letters to Terence Donoghoe, for whom his affection never diminished, reflect a man wasting for want of companionship. He would plead with Donoghoe, now stationed in Dubuque: "Why don't you write to me? Being in the wilderness and having nothing to do but to watch the Indians and the wolves, it seems to me you might spend occasionally an hour in writing to your old friend . . . Let me hear from you soon."[12]

But Donoghoe was, as ever, an independent and spiritual man, deeply committed to his own apostolate. He would occasionally give in and visit New York. Yet with perhaps a realization of what proximity would do to their no longer peer relationship, he opted to remain out West with the Indians and wolves rather than share a lair with his old friend.

In December of 1845 Hughes rushed once again to Ireland, England and France ("as fast as steam can drag and fresh, fair winds waft us along") shopping for religious personnel. He brought with him Father John Harley who because of illness had resigned the presidency at Fordham to James Roosevelt Bayley. With a touching solicitude Hughes took the young priest under wing hoping that "the always glorious ocean" would restore his health. He adapted his own behavior on the

trip to suit the happiness of his patient: "Besides the usual ex-
hilarating effect of the sea on my feelings," he wrote his sister,
"I have to play the hero on this occasion to keep my *compag-
non de voyage* in good tune."*[13]

In Ireland he won commitments for New York from the
Sisters of Mercy and the Brothers of the Christian Doctrine.
Then for the first time since he had emigrated in an embittered
sense of exile from his homeland, he revisited his birthplace at
Annologhan. He walked about the farm that he had worked
with his family, visited old Mr. Moutray to whom he had been
apprenticed as a gardener, and on the Feast of the Epiphany
preached in the cathedral at Clogher before a congregation that
numbered a good many of his relatives.

On this trip, so short a time before Europe was to erupt in
revolutions from one end of the continent to the other, the
bishop of New York's immigrants—who had arrived himself
from the Old World with no possessions and only "a few guin-
eas" in his pocket—took stock of the oppression that had earlier driven himself, and now drove countless others to America's
shores: "The first thing that strikes a stranger in Europe is the
contrast between the poverty and feebleness of the laboring
population, and the power derived from hereditary wealth, with
its vast capacity for self-increase, of the more favored classes.
This produces almost inevitably a tendency to crouching and
servility on the one hand, and a disposition to domineer on the
other. The separation is so wide in fact that it seems hard to realize that the two classes belong to the same country, or even
the same race."[14]

There was an irony to his observation; for as the spiritual
leader of Europe's transplanted poor he had to seek financial
help to build churches and social institutions for his people
from the coffers of the wealthy whom he counted as their (and
his) Old-World oppressors. Still, Hughes was too pragmatic a
man to quibble, and he embarked for home at the beginning of

---

*The voyage did this "dear and esteemed young priest" little good. He
continued to fail, and on December 8th, 1846 died in Hughes's house, under
his constant care to the last.

April happy that on this trip he had succeeded "even beyond my hopes at starting."[15]

Hughes's shopping for personnel had not been limited to Europe. Refusing to take no for an answer he had continued wooing the Jesuits about St. John's at Fordham. The college was expanding at a rapid pace (its buildings designed by his brother-in-law William Rodrigue), but Hughes had neither the priests nor the money to do justice to his dreams for the school. The Jesuits in Paris insisted that they hadn't the manpower either, and they were already overcommitted to the United States, having staffed the languishing St. Mary's College in Kentucky. Hughes began writing to the priests in Kentucky himself, painting an ivy-colored picture of things to come. In 1845 the French Provincial, Clement Boulanger, came through New York during his official visitations. Hughes squired him about showing him the sights, no doubt emphasizing the sights a little up the North River at Fordham. He didn't railroad the order. Nobody railroaded the Jesuits. They saw the possibilities both in the college and in being located in the great city of the United States. Negotiations began to solidify. And yet quietly. The word "Jesuit" alone was enough to start nativist rallies at City Hall Park, but more importantly Hughes was in the process of having the college incorporated as a university through the New York State Legislature. He didn't care to create a problem where one didn't exist.

In 1846 the order left Kentucky and bought Fordham from the diocese for $40,000. Hughes didn't let them have the entire estate. With a Jesuitical touch he kept eight acres through which the Harlem Railroad was seeking a right-of-way, as well as nine acres for the diocesan seminary that the Jesuits would staff. James Roosevelt Bayley assumed the task of bishop's secretary, and the presidency at Fordham was turned over to Augustus Thébaud, S.J. Although John Hughes was not a man to relish the idea of a strong religious order within his domain and not quite under his control, the prestige of having the Jesuits at his college seemed worth the price at that time. And besides, a carefully drawn contract between the bishop and the order seemed to preclude the possibility of any conflict of authority.

Hughes was not willing to pay the same price with other religious orders, especially women's religious orders that answered to male superiors general outside his diocese—priests whose command over the actions of the Sisters was more immediate than his own. Simultaneous with his negotiations to bring the powerful Jesuits to his domain he entered into an imbroglio with the Sisters of Charity that resulted in the division of Mother Seton's Emmitsburg community and a separate new order under his direct control.

The Sisters of Charity were just about the finest thing the immigrant Church had for the sake of public relations. Their heroism during the cholera epidemic of 1832, reported in newspapers throughout the United States, caused them to become legendary even among the most bitter anti-Catholics. During the fight for public monies for Catholic schools, the one exception on the books was an allotment of money to the Sisters of Charity for their orphanage school, an acknowledgment of the public good accomplished by their institutions. In 1846, when Hughes was procuring from the city seven acres (in what would later become Central Park) to expand his charitable institutions, an issue between himself and the order that had simmered for a number of years boiled over into a decisive argument.

Mother Étienne (Mother Seton's successor), directed by her Sulpician Superior General Louis Deluol, informed the bishop of New York in late spring of 1846 that the Sisters would no longer care for the boys in the orphanage. The indelicate task had always been against the Sisters' rule; they had originally taken the care only as an accommodation.

Hughes objected. The 130-140 boys were preadolescents— "mere infants"—and to pull out while he was dickering for more land, would "break us up." He had an alternate plan—to break up the order. The fifty Sisters in his diocese could be given their choice either to stay with Emmitsburg or come into a new group under his direct jurisdiction.[16]

The orphaned boys offered the emotional tug to force the issue to a conclusion. Deluol, being able to argue ex officio on a peer level with Hughes, angrily objected to the proposed division: "We consider this step of yours as calculated to inflict a deep and dangerous wound on the community and if the example be imitated (every bishop in the Union has the same right) we would consider it as mortal." To save the order he informed Hughes that all of the Sisters of Charity in the New York diocese were being recalled immediately to the motherhouse. If any Sister chose to remain where she was "it must be well understood that the separation is to be complete and forever."[17] Hughes retorted that although "I am opposed to it, that I protest against it publicly and privately," he would let the unfortunate orphans pay the price for the Sisters' withdrawal: "I shall take no measure of their departure, that after they are gone I shall apply myself to reconstruct, as best I can the wreck and ruins of the charities of this diocese for the last thirty years, destroyed in an hour by the dash of a pen."[18]

If religious orders are able to run a slippery competition with diocesan structures because of their trans-diocesan structure, Hughes still worked the game to his own advantage. As he had with the Jesuits he made a direct appeal to the personnel involved. His younger sister, Angela, a Sister of Charity, was caught in the middle. She was told by her brother to distribute to all the Sisters a copy of his protest in which he sarcastically insisted upon obedience to Deluol's instructions: ". . . on this point the duty of the sisters is clear. Let schools and asylums fall to the ground. That is not their business."[19] At the same time he made it very clear to them that it *was* their business. A flustered Sister William Anna wrote to her superior at Emmitsburg: "I saw the Bishop yesterday. He is really in trouble . . . I think it is the difficulty of providing for the boys at this moment that causes him to act as he does . . ." If through the Sisters' fault the boys were turned out, the bishop had told her, "they will be sent to a place called the 'farms,' the Protestant asylum."

When Deluol sensed that Hughes was fighting, as usual, without quarter, and that he would, as usual, win, a conciliatory letter was sent "happy to say" that the Sisters might remain in New York as they had before the dispute began if they could work under the system where, as elsewhere, matrons cared for the boys while the nuns supervised. But now it was the principle and not the cause of the dispute that mattered. Referring to Deluol's decree, Hughes noted in response: "The perusal of it gave me to understand to what an extent the peace and prosperity of my diocese depended on your good will and pleasure."[20]

The argument finally spilled out over the cauldron's edges when Mother Étienne sent Hughes a piously worded denial of his rights, telling him the Sisters would be removed from the boys' orphanage by October 1st. ("On this point we are decided") and letting him know where the law lay (". . . it is not in accordance with the spirit of our rules and constitutions to consult the several bishops under whom our Sisters may be placed . . .").[21]

In retaliation, Hughes headed off the actions of Mother Étienne's Sister Visitatrix with a blistering missive that sent her scurrying to the safety of a railroad train back to Emmitsburg:

> Dear Sister:
> I believe all the changes have been made among the Sisters of Charity under my jurisdiction, which it was the purpose of the council to make, on the principle that in such matters the bishop of a diocese is not to be consulted.
> This kind of business has gone far enough.
> Be assured that I mean no personal disrespect when I communicate to you a message which must seem rude, addressed to a Christian and religious lady, viz: that I wish and request, and require that you shall leave the diocese of New York with as little delay as possible. I shall tolerate no officer of a religious community, male or female, exercising without my previous advisement and consent, powers of disturbance and embarrassment, such as have been exercised, conscientiously no doubt, in my diocese of late.
>
> Your obedient servant in Christ,
> †John Hughes
> Bp of New York
>
> P.S. If for this the Sisters are to be recalled, let them go; I shall look for others to take their place.[22]

It was a heartrending decision for the individual Sisters to make. The way Hughes had set it up they would have to walk out the door of the orphanage leaving the children unattended. And yet to remain meant severance with Mother Seton's original community. Finally, thirty-one of the fifty Sisters, including John's own sister, opted to remain on the job in New York at the price of starting a new order directly under his jurisdiction. They elected their new mother superior, and Hughes interfered only so far as to say that he wished his own sister excluded as a candidate.* No Sister has left any record of resentment that might understandably have been felt when Hughes made an admission after the dust from the fight had settled. Despite his threats to leave the children unattended if the Sisters had deserted them, he had quietly made precautions "by which they might have left the keys under the doors; and, with God's blessing, on the same day the orphans should not have gone without their dinner."[23]

In one of the many heated letters that flew back and forth between Maryland and New York during the dispute Hughes had made a reference to conditions "in this diocese"—and then had crossed out "this" to reword the phrase "in my diocese." It was a gesture that pretty much summed up how things were run in New York for a quarter of a century.

---

*Sister Angela Hughes was duly elected superior of the order in 1855, and though this might seem an expression of nepotism there is every indication that she was genuinely loved by the Sisters, and that her election was not affected by her relationship with the head of the diocese. Quite to the contrary, the evidence shows that she was treated with no special considerations. When one of her (and John's) brothers was slowly dying she asked if she might stay with him and his family for the duration and was refused permission by her superior.

17

LITTLE BROWN BROTHERS NAMED O'BRIEN

The Mexican War was a growing experience for the United States, but only in a territorial sense. The nation somehow survived the dismantling of its Catholic neighbors to the southwest without appreciably changing prewar attitudes and prejudices. It was "a Protestant country," and hatred of Romanism was still the dominant passion of American society. As hostilities loomed missionary groups were still weighing the possibilities and dangers of allowing Catholics to hold full American citizenship. Reverend George Cheever told New Yorkers how in the land of the Waldenses where Catholics dominated a young man spent three months in jail for not doffing his hat to a "procession of hosts" during the celebration of "a most idolatrous Service." And what was good for the Waldenses might soon be good enough for Americans. "The whole [Roman] system is a masterpiece of Satan," he warned.[1]

Americans, breathing such air, kept a careful watch on their liberties. In 1843 an army lieutenant named O'Brien was court-martialed for refusing to lead his men in Protestant prayers. When John Hughes was sought for his opinion in the matter he counseled acquiescence, noting that in some circumstances one might have to cooperate materially. At that moment, with the military dwindling in peacetime obscurity, it was of secondary importance that the clergymen appointed as chaplains were required to be Protestant and that Catholics were forced to attend Protestant services. Hughes was still fighting in the battlefields of education. To take on a second issue too quickly might be too large a dose for the nativist public to digest. The issue could only be of immediate concern if large numbers of Catholics were involved—for instance if a war broke out and if joining the army became more than simply a choice of career.

Hostilities with Mexico commenced in the spring of 1846. Immediately it was a controversial war, supported by expansionists and slaveholders but generally unpopular in the Northeast. Horace Greeley's *Tribune* was a voice for moralists who saw the war as a criminal despoilation of another country. The Catholic *Freeman's Journal,* though it fell in line to support the government, nonetheless spoke of the United States' passion for possessing the earth, and pointed out to the immigrants that what was being done to Mexico was not unlike what England had done to Ireland.[2]

As with all wars a propaganda image had to be constructed of the enemy. James Gordon Bennett's principal interest in the war was simply to get the most news about it, and to do so he beat his competitors to the presses by pioneering the use of Morse's new telegraph. Overlooking his own religious affiliation, he warned that a conquest of Mexico would flood the United States with Catholic citizens: "This union would entitle them to twenty-eight senators and to one hundred and forty representatives in Congress, and if added to the three millions of Canadians would give them such a preponderance, a protection and security on this hemisphere as they could never expect while separated."[3]

The Morses' polemicist *New York Observer,* having the advantage of a telegraph in the family, took up the cudgels to let America know what it was in for. Mexico was a land ruled by priests who were "ignorant, indolent and exceedingly loose in their morals . . . not a few of them are infidels." To exemplify Roman avariciousness the paper told the story of a Mexican priest who baptized a corpse two days dead because he knew he would be well paid by the family. Such priests were exhorting their followers to kill American boys in uniform. Said the *Observer:* "What can we expect from these vandals

vomited from hell to scourge the nations when we know that
they worship no God but gold and aspire to no happiness but
the gratification of their brutal passions?"[4]

In a sense the nativists fear of papists in this war was well
held, for the atmosphere of anti-Catholicism made Catholics a
potentially subversive group. Immigrants and the sons of immigrants were being sent to face their coreligionists in battle
and to conquer towns where women and children huddled and
prayed in Catholic churches for safety against the enemy. Yet
within the United States Army the presence of priests was forbidden and Catholic soldiers were compelled to attend Protestant services. It was enough to make any man think. The Mexicans played upon this in messages sent from one camp to the
other, and United States soldiers soon found themselves facing
Irish-Americans gathered into a battalion named San Patricio.

John Hughes was not ready to make the concerns of the
United States government his own. His task was the governing
of the immigrant Church of New York. In May 1846 he left
for that year's triennial council at Baltimore, completing plans
for the reorganization of his diocese to include Sees at Albany
(to which he would unhappily lose McCloskey) and Buffalo (to
which he would happily lose the trustees at St. Louis church to
Bishop John Timon). He was also spurred by Terence Donoghoe before leaving to present a totally spiritual matter to the
bishops—that of declaring the Blessed Virgin as Patroness of
the United States.

These and other matters were accomplished by the council
by mid-May while the *Herald* complained to the world that
such business should not be done behind "closed doors." "It is
rumored, however," Bennett speculated, "that the war in Mexico has occupied considerable attention, and some surprise is
expressed that the Irish Catholic priests, which they at their
last session procured to be stationed on the Rio Grande, had
not deterred the Irish and German Catholic troops from taking
part with Protestant America against Catholic Mexico. They
are now said to be devising means to recommend to the priesthood of Mexico with regard to their future course—to preserve

their property, re-unite and re-establish the country and preserve its religious characteristics."[5]

James K. Polk, a practical-minded businessman who
served as President, moved to defuse this situation. Since the
Catholic council took place in nearby Baltimore, he instructed
Secretary of State James Buchanan to invite one of the bishops
to Washington for a conclave of his own. Buchanan wrote not
to Archbishop Eccleston who was the official head of the
American Church but to John Hughes who held that position
in the minds of most Americans. "I venture to request that you
would pay us a visit in this city," he wrote. ". . . I desire to
advise with you on public affairs of importance; and this will
afford me an opportunity of making your personal acquaintance, which I very much desire."[6]

Hughes traveled to the capital, bringing with him Bishop
Loras of Dubuque. A meeting was held with Buchanan at the
State Department. The most immediate thing that the government wanted to clear up was the ban against Catholic clergy in
the military. If it were to be allowed, could any priests be
supplied to serve the Catholic soldiers? Not only could they be
supplied, but the two bishops rode immediately to Georgetown
where arrangements were made for two Jesuits to travel with
the army.

This accomplished, Buchanan brought Hughes to the
White House, introduced him to the President and left the two
men alone to discuss Catholics and the Mexican War. Polk
expressed to Hughes his hopes that if an influential churchman,
for example the bishop of New York, were to travel to Mexico
he might render a valuable service by alleviating Mexican fears
of a destruction of religion by a Protestant United States.
Mexicans, by Hughes's very unmolested presence, would learn
that Catholicism existed freely in the States and that Catholic
institutions would be respected by an army of occupation.
Hughes at first agreed with enthusiasm to the idea of the journey, assuring Polk that he personally knew the archbishop of
Mexico, and expressed his willingness to cooperate with the
government to whatever extent was in his power. Encouraged
by the visit, Polk noted that night in his diary: "I found Bishop

Hughes a highly intelligent and agreeable man and my interview with him was of the most satisfactory character."[7]

Then Hughes began to weigh all the considerations. The President was indeed a practical man, and like a seasoned politician he was carefully playing to all parties. The priests sent to the front were not official chaplains. They were merely, by order of the President, attached to the army as "persons to perform such duties as appertain to chaplains."[8] The distinction may have been small enough, but on the basis that the government was attempting to show that Catholics in the United States were treated with full equality, the distinction was real and seemed to prove the opposite of what the gesture claimed. Similarly, Hughes was being sent to Mexico by the government to accomplish a service of real diplomatic value, but with no official status. "If the Catholic priests in Mexico can be satisfied that their Churches and religion would be secure," Polk had said, "the conquest of the Northern provinces of Mexico will be easy and the probability is that the war would be of short duration; but if a contrary opinion prevailed the resistance to our forces will be desperate."[9] Nonetheless, Hughes had been asked to travel in a private capacity much like the two Catholic "chaplains." He decided that when he returned to the White House he would insist that if he were to go to Mexico City he would do so not in the dangerous and foolish capacity of a civilian taking a tour of an enemy camp, but as an official representative of his government. In short, he wanted the government to have the courage to properly label the job that was being done.

Word was out of the meetings between the President and the bishop. "The intrigues of our government with the Papal Church have begun," reported the Baltimore *Church Times*. "We know perfectly well that the Church never lets an opportunity slip to mix itself up with the politics of any country. We cannot forget that the prelate who has been applied to is the very one who has shown himself particularly shrewd in political matters already . . ."[10]

It was this latter reaction that Polk feared. When he and Hughes talked again the discussion came to a polite impasse.

There were sound diplomatic reasons for the President not to send a new envoy to the Mexican government. It had been only months since that government had refused to receive John Slidell. For the United States to send another representative after that rejection would of itself be another humiliation. In that respect Polk was on firm ground in wanting Hughes to travel simply as a private individual. Hughes declined the honor, which was not so much an honor as a double-edged political and diplomatic maneuver. The two men parted on friendly terms, however, and both had the grace to keep the substance of their final discussion to themselves.

Even at this, Polk received enough backlash from Protestant America to make him realize his astuteness in not making the bishop of New York a formal envoy. Reverend William McCalla, a Presbyterian minister who had earlier battled against Hughes in the school issue, had a brother who was the second auditor of the U.S. Treasury. Using his connection to gain an interview with Polk, McCalla sat and read out loud a number of letters addressed to the President—without giving them to him. Included as well, but also not surrendered, was a formal petition. "The prominent idea, aside from its abuse of Catholics and its fanaticism," recorded Polk, "was that unless I appointed the Reverend Mr. McCalla a Chaplain, the petitioners intended to go before the public and attack the administration upon religious grounds because of the employment of these Catholic priests."

Polk quickly enough rid himself of the aggressive clergyman, observing at the same time: "I have met with no man during my administration, among the numerous office seekers who have beset me for whom I have so profound a contempt. He has not succeeded in getting the office and I shall not be surprised to be assailed by him in the newspaper."[11]

Polk was not disappointed. McCalla quickly told the press that the President of the United States had made a dangerous admission in conversation with him. The two Catholic priests sent to the army were sent only nominally as chaplains. In reality they were spies. Polk fulminated privately: "I cannot adequately express the horror I feel for a man who can be so base as to veil his hypocrisy under the cloak of religion and state the base flasehood he has done. If I were a private citizen I should have no hesitation in exposing him to the world, but it is doubtful whether as President of the U.S. I should descend from my station to notice him at all."[12]

William Hogan, immigrant priest turned staunch pseudonativist, published his reactions in a book called *High and Low Mass*. "What are you Mr. Polk?" he demanded. "Being a citizen of this Republic I am allowed to ask you such questions as are not forbidden by law. Are you a Presbyterian or a Papist?"

"Americans shan't rule us, says Archbishop Hughes of New York," quoted Hogan, elevating Hughes an ecclesiastical notch in the process. Then, sharing his own fears with his fellow Americans, he asked: "Does President Polk understand, or is he aware of the fact that each of those chaplains as well as each and every individual Roman Catholic priest and Bishop in the United States and elsewhere is bound by a solemn oath to hold no faith or give any allegiance to him as President of the United States; or to any president, king executive magistrate or otherwise who is not a Roman Catholic?"[13]

The war lasted throughout the summer of the next year. The task of assuring respect for the Churches, which Polk had wanted for Hughes, fell to a Protestant general. Winfield Scott had been bewildered and saddened three years earlier when his beautiful daughter Virginia had become a Catholic and entered a convent where she subsequently died of illness. Now he promised the people he had conquered: "We have not profaned your temples . . . We say this with pride and we confirm it by your own bishops and by the clergy . . . We adore the same God and a large portion of our army as well as the population of the United States are Catholics like yourselves . . . The Army of the United States respects and will always respect private property of every description and the property of the Mexican Church."[14]

The bible and missionary societies made elaborate plans for a second United States invasion, one bringing the word of God to the Catholics soon to be liberated from superstition. The nativist papers watched for any sign of capitulation to

Rome. When one of these expressed rage at the rumor that a Protestant officer commanded his men to kneel during a Mexican procession of the Blessed Sacrament, the *Freeman's Journal* noted that, ironically, just the opposite had always been true. Catholics had for years been forced to attend Protestant services in the U.S. Army, and when even whole regiments were Catholic they were assigned Protestant ministers for chaplains. To sharpen Protestant memories the Catholic paper pointed out that it was the same O'Brien, now a decorated hero at Buena Vista, who was the lieutenant court-martialed and punished in 1843 for refusing to attend Protestant services.

In September of 1847 the controversial war ended with the heroic and sad defense of Chapultepec Hill at Mexico City by cadets of a military school. Two months after the capitulation Bennett again reminded Americans of the yoke that they had taken upon themselves should they retain possession of all Mexico. Encouraging the opening of diplomatic relations with the new, apparently liberal-minded Pope Pius IX, he advised: "In a short time we shall have under our dominion ten millions of people in Mexico, all of them Catholics. It is therefore of some importance that our relations with Rome should be on a most friendly footing."[15]

Bennett was, as usual, pulling the whiskers of anyone whose jaw was jutted out. Nonetheless in New York, where John Hughes was the unquestioned leader of the impoverished immigrants, the effects of Ireland's potato blight, beginning with the crop failure of 1845, was bringing what seemed to be tens of millions of that country's starving masses to the shores of Manhattan. Mexicans were far out of reach and soon far out of mind. But these vast numbers of newcomers dwindled by comparison the size of earlier emigrations. One nativist who spoke for many was moved to declare: "If I had the power I would erect a gallows at every landing place in the city of New York and suspend every cursed Irishman as soon as he steps on our shores."

With the war over, emotions were returning to normal.

18

BISHOP AND CHIEF

In the decades preceding the Civil War New York's Protestant missionary and charity organizations published yearly reports that reflected strong organization backed by wealth which amounted to millions of dollars. One such report boasted that while Protestants and Jews cared for their own needy, Catholics, but for the care of "a few orphans," made "no corresponding provision for their poor, neither by their churches or otherwise; nor yet assist, by their contributions those who are engaged in this Christian duty."[1]

The Catholics, however, felt little compunction to assist at the proselytizing efforts of the McCallas, Cheevers, and Beechers—efforts that Hughes branded as "souperism." He complained about "the application of immense wealth for the perversion of our destitute children whom we are unable to take under our protection."[2]

It wasn't a case of whether Catholics wanted to be interested in the poor. They were the poor. During the quarter of a century in which John Hughes administered the diocese of New York over 3 million immigrants—the vast percentage of them Catholic—arrived in the port of that city. Germans, coming from less destitute circumstances and thus better organized before they left their homeland, usually had the means to move westward. The Irish were forced to be less mobile. Contrary to historical legend they did not all pile into dockside tenements. Of New York's 3 million immigrant entrees between 1840 and 1860 only about half a million remained to swell the population of the city. Even if these were all Irish it meant that the great majority of Irishmen moved on. They didn't have the funds to get far, but they followed jobs up the North River to Troy, to Utica and outward to smaller towns. The whole Northeast eventually bore as strong a Celtic stamp as the Midwest would reflect the presence of Germans. "The better class of emigrants," Hughes observed, "those who have some means, those who have industrious habits, robust health, superior intelligence, naturally pass through this city and push onwards . . . On the other hand, the destitute, the disabled, the broken down, the very aged and the very young, and I had almost added the depraved, of all nations, having reached New York, usually settle down here,—for want of means, or through want of inclination to go farther."

Those who remained in the metropolitan area may have included the "depraved of all nations" but predominently they were, as he himself realized, "the scattered debris of the Irish Nation." They arrived—and often remained—hungry, diseased, and oftentimes prone to drown their sorrows in cheap whiskey. The centuries of illegitimacy endured by the Catholic Church under England's rule had left Christianity in Ireland weak, both morally and intellectually. Many of the Irish barely knew the basic rudiments of their faith—"not by any willful apostacy of their own"—Hughes knew. Nonetheless, they had "passed away from the faith of their ancestors."[3]

It was this class of Irish who became a target for nativist fears. Areas of the city such as the notorious Five Points became "little Ireland" slums. Irish street gangs became famous by name for crime and rowdiness. The Irish played stellar roles in large riots fought over such weighty issues as whether an English actor should be allowed to appear in a performance of *Macbeth.*

Spiritually uneducated as they may have been, the greatest social factor in the lives of most Irish was the Roman Catholic Church. It was a symbol of Ireland's costly yet fierce defiance of England. Taxed to support the Protestant state Church, yet disenfranchised over many generations, they took the loyalty the enforced government asked of them and gave it instead to their persecuted religion. The priest was the man to whom they gave fealty. Once in the United States, invited by law if not the native citizens to become involved in government, the Irish worked toward naturalization and a lusty involvement in the democratic process. They were an independent, ever disunited lot. Still, if there was a man who could be a leader in their lives ex officio it was the bishop of New York. If there was a man who could be a natural hero to them it was John Hughes—an immigrant who had arrived like themselves penniless, a laborer who wielded his crosier as once he had wielded a pickax, a man labeled by the most widely circulated newspaper in the world as "more a Roman gladiator than a devout follower of the meek founder of Christianity."[4]

To be on the receiving end of such expectations was a frightening burden. To create facilities to cope with the vast number of immigrants was an assignment to be a "brick-and-mortar" man at a time when there were no bricks and mortar. The first church built in New York was still hopelessly in debt, and Hughes's whirlwind begging tours through Europe were only partially successful ventures. Moreover there was the question as to what should be done for a people whose physical needs were as pressing as their spiritual wants. Churches were needed, but so were bread, medicine and jobs. With absolutely no resources at hand Hughes had to decide upon priorities.

Resentful of the anti-Catholicism of Protestant-managed civic charities, he was astute enough to see that an integral part of the American character was an unquestioning generosity toward those in physical need. "The municipal authorities and the laws of the state," he realized, "which amply provide that no human being shall be allowed to die of starvation or exposure, provided, indeed for the physical wants of this unhappy class."[5]

He directed his priests to care for those in public almshouses and hospitals. When the Jesuits arrived he assigned them to the charity and correction institutes run by the city on Wards Island in the East River. This resulted in an ongoing war with scores of nativist administrators who guarded the turf for the Protestant ministry by blocking entry to the priests.

Hughes knew his rights. With each instance of hindrance he was on the back of the civil authorities, beating them over the head with the same logic he had used in the school issue: Either priests were to be allowed in or every clergyman was to get out. He was not a man easily ignored.

In 1841 he sponsored a group of laymen who created the Irish Emigration Society. He gave lectures to raise funds for the organization and even tried to float the idea among a few wealthy philanthropists that land could be bought out West and parceled in small lots to the immigrants. He was quickly advised that this latter project was "nonsense," a view he eventually accepted himself. Until the government formed adequate immigration procedures in the late forties the Emigration Society did its best to advise the newcomers about work, housing, and the avoidance of those who would prey upon what little substance they possessed.

Hughes started a hospital as soon as means permitted, staffed by the Sisters of Charity. The orphan asylums had existed before his administration, and as was evident in his battle with the Sisters of Charity, he was vehement in his protection of these institutions. In his view children were the most vulnerable targets of a proselytizing, nativist America. The care with which he directed orphanages he channeled, for the same purpose, into the building of parochial schools. If he lost the children, Hughes felt, there would be little hope for the future of the American Catholic Church.

Hughes may have acquiesced, out of necessity, in the physical care of adult immigrants by the state, but he never relaxed for a moment his guardianship over their spiritual lives. The fighting denizens of Five Points, the Corkonians and Fardowns, the murderous B'boys were all his—and so were those wasted skeletons of humans so exhausted in spirit and body from poverty as not to care about anything anymore. Assessing his own responsibility Hughes would later recall:

> My lot was cast in the great Metropolis of the whole country. My people were composed of representatives from almost all nations . . . I had to stand up among them as their Bishop and chief to warn them against the dangers that

surrounded them; to contend for their rights as a religious community; to repel the spirit of faction among them; to convince their judgment by frequent explanations in regard to public and mixed questions; to encourage the timid, and sometimes to restrain the impetuous. In short, to knead them up into one dough, to be leavened by the spirit of Catholic faith and of Catholic union.[6]

Such was his philosophy of action, and it was based upon the idea of spiritual unity—a goal that Catholics were never prone to appreciate. With a choice to erect social institutions or churches, he opted for the latter. In his own native homeland he and his countrymen had held onto their religion even when doing so denied them the most basic of civil rights and forced them to suffer debasing indignities. Had the Hughes family opted for Protestantism the law would have allowed a clergyman to pray at the graveside of John's sister, and a family member would not have had to carry in a handful of blessed earth to sprinkle upon her coffin. In the United States, even in the teeth of nativist bigotry, the Church was free, and Hughes would show the world that it existed freely. He would give his people what they deserved because of their will to suffer for centuries rather than buckle to England's will. Utterly without means, he would build them churches. He would eventually construct over 100 of them during his twenty-five years in office, and in begging funds from European missionary societies he would justify what his program gave to the Irish and to every confused and alienated immigrant: "It is only when he has the consolation of his religion within his reach that he feels comparatively happy in his new position. If on the Sunday he can be present at the Holy Sacrifice of the Mass, if only he can see the minister of his religion at the altar and hear the word of God in the language to which his ear was accustomed from childhood, he forgets that he is among strangers and in a strange country."[7]

The more publicly these people acknowledged that Hughes was bishop "and chief," the more the nativists feared them. *The Mysteries of Popery,* published in 1847, included a story about the power that Bishop John Hughes—"the sturdy defender of Popedom"—had over his people. After a probable murder in an Irish neighborhood, the book related, those involved refused to allow the police to perform an autopsy: "The body had already been waked, about fifty persons of both sexes assembled guarding the corpse, with a cross suspended over her head, a lighted candle at her feet—with a sufficient quantity of snuff and tobacco to neutralize all other effluvia, and declaring with clenched fists that she should not be touched again. Probably she had not got quite through purgatory and they thought it necessary she should remain quiet through her journey . . ." Finally two constables were dispatched to Bishop Hughes, "knowing that one word from him would reverse the scene. The Bishop, however, refused to do anything about it, even to approve of the investigation of the alleged crime!! . . . Now we ask, where is the supremacy of the laws? Here is a sect of superstitious religionists, declaring virtually: 'We know not and are not for law, and mock at your law and officers of government . . .' Patriots! Philanthropists! Christians! Are we safe?"[8]

The absolute power of the Catholic Church would remain legend in American lore. The Catholic hierarchy was autocratic, no doubt, but no one ever moved the great mass of Catholics any place they did not want to go. The only actual power John Hughes possessed was over his subordinate clergy. He was listened to by American Catholics, probably more so than any man of that age. When he took a popular position—as with the school issue—they rallied vocally to his banner. When he preached moral strictures, Catholics—then as ever—limited his effectiveness to the public celebration of the sacraments and rules for fasting. With anything beyond that Catholics nodded assent to his exhortations and continued fashioning their own mores as they pleased. His power at its strongest involved no more than moral suasion. The more established Catholics in the United States, those who had inherited the democratic ecclesiology of a Church without an established hierarchy, fought Hughes tooth and nail over the issue of who was to manage what in the Church. This tug-of-war was waged most often with parishes still run by lay trustees—Hughes's staunchest foes within his fold. No new church was built with lay trustees, and those existing under the system fought to maintain their identity as such. During his tenure several churches in New York City were forced into bankruptcy, and when this occurred Hughes bought the buildings at sheriff's sales, honored the debts (which he did not legally have to do), and gained full possession of the churches. St. Peter's—where John Power and Charles Constantine Pise were stationed— sank into bankruptcy in 1844 under the heavy weight of its immigrant populace. A court injunction brought about by creditors unwilling to lose their investments held the crisis in abeyance for five years while Hughes, as well as the parish's trustees, was plagued by those demanding their money. Finally, with interest mounting the debt to $200,000, he sent word publicly that he was coming to the church to "expose to the people the delinquency of the trustees."

One of the trustees named Benson, a Protestant married to Charles Constantine Pise's sister, threatened that he would horsewhip Hughes if the bishop dared show up. A more docile member of the flock merely suggested, "I hope he will behave well. If he does we shall treat him with respect; but if he does not I shall say to him, 'Bishop, there's the door for you.' "

The bishop did not behave particularly well. He gave his usual performance. With a verbal attack he whipped the parishioners to the back walls, pouring out, according to the *Herald,* "a torrent of indignant scathing eloquence upon the devoted heads of the clergy and the trustees, not forgetting Benson to whom he spoke daggers in sly innuendos."

No one dared move close enough to show him the door. He instead revealed a plan which he eventually followed through to completion. He would purchase the church from the law, voluntarily honor the debts when he could, and "appoint" a committee of management, placing himself at their head to relieve the trustees from their present embarrassment. About the only Catholic who enjoyed this one-man melee was James Gordon Bennett. "Bishop Hughes shows spunk," he decided. "We begin to like his lordship amazingly."[9]

It took spunk to face hostile parishioners. It took constant courage to face the uphill effort of building churches with no available finances. Significantly, Hughes never satisfied himself with simply staving off present creditors. He planned for the future, determined that Catholics would take a role of leadership in society. This explains the establishment of Fordham without "so much as a penny wherewith to commence the payment for it."[10] So too, while he brought in the Sisters of Mercy to care for homeless immigrant girls, he brought in the Madames of the Sacred Heart to begin their elite school at Manhattanville and directed the Sisters of Charity to begin the Academy of Mount St. Vincent. During the 1840s the wealthy Episcopalians, influenced by the Catholic movement within their Church, commenced a Gothic revival and began to erect edifices that reflected the best of that style of architecture. Hughes began to dream of a new cathedral for New York, one that would equal the great cathedrals of Europe and be a fitting symbol of the fact that Catholics had truly arrived in the United States. On several occasions he aired plans for this project, but it was a dream far beyond his reach in the 1840s. Moreover it would have been a false symbol. Catholicism had not yet "arrived."

This period of his episcopacy was one of exhausting activity. He was almost always on tour instructing both Catholic and non-Catholics with his impressive powers as an orator. Yet these tours were also those of an administrator overseeing the business of his own diocese and poking into other dioceses as well. One could read of him speaking in Halifax one week, and the next week pick up the paper and see that he was consecrating churches and confirming children in New Jersey. His long-suffering secretary James Roosevelt Bayley, vainly attempting to track Hughes, managed on one occasion to catch a flying missive: "I have just arrived. The bishop [John Timon] is absent, and I shall push on up the lake. I have heard of you at Oswego and here. Your travels remind me of Telemachus in search of his lost father. I suppose the object was my signature to some document. But the world must take care of itself till I return, which will be, I trust 'in all' of ten days. Until which time, do as well as you can. Respects to all the Rev. gentlemen of the palace. I feel strong, and hearty."[11]

"Strong and hearty" as he may have expressed himself, he often labored under the burden of frequent and long-lasting chest infections—a nuisance generally confessed only in letters to his family. There is little wonder that he loved the sea as much as he did. The times he spent traveling on a ship were the only occasions that he was free from the pressures of obligations from without, and from the constant frenetic drive that pushed him from within.

19

BORN WITHIN GUNSHOT OF TARA'S HALL

Beginning with the crop of 1845 and for the next several years Ireland was afflicted with a potato blight that reduced almost the whole rural population to the point of starvation. Immigration to America became an outlet of escape, and in 1848 the numbers of Irish arriving at New York City jumped from 52,946 of the year before to 91,061. The year after that the number went over 100,000, a level at which it remained until the mid 1850s, with a peak of 163,306 in 1851.

With customary empathy toward people suffering, the United States publicized Ireland's grief and sought to ameliorate its suffering. Newspapers were quick to lay the blame upon England who continued to profit from its rule and export grain from the disaster areas. "If your duty as rulers has been faithfully performed," demanded Horace Greeley, "why are your subjects destitute, turbulent and suffering? Why is Ireland, in the very heart of civilization, herself retrograding, a scandal and a sorrow to civilization?"[1]

Even the anti-Irish New York *Observer* mourned the plight of starving masses. Ignoring the system that had brought about the conditions of famine, the paper praised the Protestant clergy who labored among these people. It also related, by comparison, that the Irish had of necessity taken to stealing from their comfortable priests, so that in such times of dire necessity the clergy's property "which was always considered in a degree sacred is not safe from the hands of famishing thousands."[2]

To set the record straight Hughes gave a well-publicized lecture in which he blamed the famine on England's persistent efforts to eradicate Catholicism in Ireland. He asserted that the majority of the Irish, because of their faith, were systematically denied civil rights and the opportunity to own the land they worked on. Protestant England was the oppressor not the local priest who, said Hughes, was the child of his own people.

Doing what little his own means allowed, Hughes contributed funds collected for the education of young men to the priesthood. ("It is better that seminaries should be suspended than that so large a portion of our fellow beings should be exposed to death by starvation.")[3] He also placed notices in the newspapers for those fearful of safely sending money to relations in Ireland: "The Catholic Bishop of New York, Right Reverend Dr. Hughes, wishes us to say that he will take upon himself to receive and forward with certainty and without delay, according to the directions of the writer, any sums not less than five dollars that may be addressed to him at New York."[4]

In Ireland itself the desperate situation had added fire to the arguments of a party that called itself "Young Ireland." This group had grown impatient with Daniel O'Connell's fight for repeal of English rule within the confines of the law. William Smith O'Brien, himself a member of Parliament, John Mitchel, Thomas Francis Meagher, and Thomas D'Arcy McGee were at the center of a growing storm, and when the winds of revolution swept through Europe in 1848 it seemed as if Ireland too was at long last ready to rebel. The "Young Irelanders" issued as much propaganda abroad as they did at home, and in the United States where the Irish were well fed and strong the talk of rebellion took firm hold. Throughout the spring and summer sympathy meetings drew large crowds. It was a presidential election year, and because the cry of "liberty" was always good for votes these meetings were magnets for party hacks and office seekers. Bennett, in disgust, labeled them "nothing but a sparring ground for a clique of petty politicians." As an alternative, he had a suggestion: "What's to prevent the calling of a meeting in the park or some other spacious place, of the real friends of Ireland? . . . Ireland must and shall be a republic, and when this is effected, England and Scotland will follow her example and then the fate of the English oligarchy will be sealed. Physical force, properly directed will accomplish it."[5]

The baby-faced, balding Horace Greeley, in love not so much with the Irish people as with another moral cause for which to unfurl his banners, moved to the forefront of the movement. His fervor in doing so was in no measure dimmed by his hopes to garner votes for the Whig party, his most deeply loved cause. In his newspaper and at public rallies he urged support of the Young Ireland movement. Denying that he was a fomenter of armed rebellion, he maintained nonetheless: "In case they should be driven into forcible resistence to the tyranny that grinds and crushes them, we are anxious that they should be sustained by the 'sympathy' of our countrymen not only, but by those who in all countries love Freedom and Justice and hope to see wrong righted and injury redressed."[6]

As other rebellions in Europe succeeded, the tension over the situation in Ireland increased. Hughes began to be affected by the hopes of his fellow Irishmen. Reports from Ireland affirmed that the country was only awaiting the call of leadership to rise up in unison. If this year was going to mark the declaration of independance for his native land, he did not want to be left standing with the silent while the editor of the *Tribune* served as America's prophet to that declaration. Horace Greeley and Hughes had been enjoying a brief friendship, born of the newsman's discovery of the Irish cause. In February Hughes had gone so far as to offer the services of a traveling priest to convey "any communication or small package"[7] Horace might wish carried to Rome. On August 14th he allowed himself to be swept into the prevailing mood and agreed to address a rally at Vauxhall Garden. Greeley picked him up at the episcopal residence, and once on the speaker's platform the bishop more than fulfilled the hopes of the New York "Directory of the Friends of Ireland." Earnestly impassioned by his own fondest dreams he exhorted the crowd:

> By the last news it appears that the oppressor and his victim stand face to face. I come among you gentlemen, not as an advocate of war—it would ill accord with my profession.

> My office is properly to be a peace-maker, when it is possible. But I come in the name of sacred humanity; not, if you will, to put arms into the hands of men by which they may destroy the lives of others but to give my voice and my mite to shield the unprotected bosoms of the sons of Ireland. It is not for me to say anything calculated to excite your feelings when I can scarcely express my own . . . My object in coming here was to show you that in my conscience I have no scruples in aiding the cause in every way worthy a patriot and a Christian . . . I am a citizen of the United States, and I would do nothing contrary to the laws of the country which protects me; but . . . let Ireland once go into house-keeping for herself, and then answer me if the American people will not come up to the work as though they had all been born within gunshot of Tara's Hall.[8]

Putting money where his mouth was, he laid $500 on a table before leaving the speaker's platform as his contribution toward Ireland's freedom.

If American enthusiasm and physical strength could have been channeled across the Atlantic, Ireland might indeed have won its independence. Instead, reports filtered back that the Irish were floundering in division. By summer's end it was learned that the rebellion had collapsed. It had ended not in glory but in a comic-opera debacle; its largest battle was fought in a widow's cabbage patch. Except for a few scattered melees, armies had failed to materialize and the leaders of Young Ireland were hunted down and captured as if they were bandits. The people had never trusted the rebel leaders who had for so long opposed Daniel O'Connell. O'Connell's untimely death months before had thrown them into an ungrateful and ugly light in the eyes of many. Moreover, the populace had been beaten into indolence by famine. The revolt was poorly organized and arms were scarce. Viewing these odds, the Catholic hierarchy had spoken out against the leaders (who included some priests). When in midsummer the Young Irelanders called for the nation to rise in revolt, they failed to see that they were talking only to themselves.

The American Irish, too, had seen only the glorious possibilities reflected in Young Ireland's rhetoric. When the news arrived that the insurrection had been quickly crushed—as

Hughes noted, "not by the British army but by a squad of policemen"[9]—there was immediately a general feeling of betrayal and humiliation. "Every Irishman from Maine to Texas, who has taken the slightest interest in the cause must blush and hang down his head for shame," Hughes mourned. "Even in this city professional gentlemen and merchants are afraid to meet their American neighbors, lest they may be jeered at for having sympathized with such a set of Gasconaders."

Deciding that "division, the evil genius that has dogged the path of Irish patriotism for seven hundred years, was still on its track," Hughes wrote to the "Directory of the Friends of Ireland" and asked that his contribution be transferred to the Sisters of Mercy for their care of immigrant Irish girls.[10]

The Gasconaders, meanwhile, began to arrive upon the American scene where they were fated not to become friends of John Hughes. The first of these to arrive was young Thomas D'Arcy McGee. Barely taking time to unpack, he began a newspaper, the *Nation,* and ignoring the myriad of causes for the rebellion's failure—not the least of which was the ill-preparedness of its leaders—he laid the fullness of blame upon the opposition of the clergy.

Hughes went after him, unloading both barrels. He labeled McGee's charge "impudent falsehood" and countercharged: "The clergy would have been faithless to their obligations of religion and of humanity if they had not interposed, seeing as they must have seen, the certain and inevitable consequences of a movement so nobly conceived but so miserably conducted."[11]

When McGee held firm in his charges Hughes labeled the *Nation* "insidious poison"—"anti-Catholic, directly in some instances, indirectly in all," and declared that every home in his diocese should be closed to the paper.[12] The *Herald* cried out in the *Nation's* defense, declaring that "His lordship is attempting to control the press."[13] His lordship tried to say in return that he was free to cancel a newspaper should he choose, but Bennett would have none of it: "It is time that this aspiring and ambitious prelate was stopped in his career," he declared.[14]

McGee's worst enemy, however, was not Hughes but himself. In New York he looked around at what Hughes thought of as "the scattered debris of the Irish nation," and peremptorily told them to shape up. "Here as at home," he claimed, "the social training of our people has been sadly neglected. They were not taught (at least until of late) punctuality, soberness, cleanliness, caution, perserverance, or the other 'minor morals' . . . the Irish in America have had the misfortune to make themselves leaders of second rate demagogues, poor statuettes of O'Connell. These men, mostly of Irish origin, flattered them on election days and despised them all other days; appealed to their passions and bigotries, encouraged their weaknesses and vices."[15] Not surprisingly, the New York Irish did not wallpaper their living-rooms with the *Nation*. After a year of such observations, McGee closed shop and moved to Boston.

In the midst of these pleasantries the long-advented visit of Father Theobold Mathew, the famous Irish temperance priest, came to pass. Temperance societies were not popular with Catholics in America. They were not overly fond of temperance to begin with, and beyond that, the movement was closely married to the Protestant bible and mission societies, and thus bore the taint of nativism. The societies, hearing of Mathew's work, looked over the ocean to Ireland and over the man's Romish priesthood to praise the vast influence he had had on his countrymen's drinking habits. He was dubbed an "Apostle of Temperance," and upon his arrival to the United States he was hailed as a fellow child of the light.

Hughes, his suspicions of lionized Irishmen sharpened by his dispute with McGee, was unhappy to learn that Mathew was "determined on this undesirable visit," so Hughes himself determined to "keep him if possible out of the hands of the Philistines." "I shall speak to him frankly," he told Archbishop Eccleston, "almost harshly if necessary." He saw little hope that the Irish would welcome Mathew with open arms either, for the priest had recently accepted a small pension from Queen Victoria. "On the whole," Hughes decided, "I hope no good and dread much evil from his clerico temperance visit."[16]

In early July 1849 Mathew entered New York City as

civic officials and Protestant ministers lined up to cover his path with palms. A levee was held for him in the governor's room of City Hall (while James Gordon Bennett worried out loud as to how the good man could ever be wined and dined without wine). He was waited upon by representatives of the various temperance societies. Matthew Brady took a daguerreotype of him, and he was put up in the manner of royalty at the fashionable Irving House.

A firm admonition arrived from Hughes who warned Mathew that his given title, Apostle of Temperance, had made him dangerously popular with Protestants, and that his work in a ministry for temperance might end up serving as a "mutual ground between the faith of the Church and the heresies of sectarianism."[17]

The American Temperance Union sponsored Mathew at the Tabernacle, and upon that occasion the Reverend DeWitt of the Dutch Reformed Church opened with a prayer. A number of ministers spoke and then Reverend Marsh, the society's secretary, endorsed for Mathew and for the press an opinion that Hughes had heard enough of from Thomas D'Arcy McGee. "Many of your countrymen," declared Marsh, "upon their arrival in this land of freedom fall into the hands of the destroyer whiskey and soon find that they have escaped from oppression at home only to become the slaves of a more grinding oppression here."[18]

Hughes enjoyed all this just about as much as he did the Champlain bible burning. Feeling that Mathew had compromised himself as a priest he sent for him, meaning to lay down the law as it was to be lived in his diocese. To his surprise he found him "truly a humble man." The reformer apologized for any embarrassment his misunderstanding of the American scene might have caused and left himself open to direction from Hughes.[19] Responsive to this attitude, Hughes did nothing to cramp Mathew's popularity. Instead he channeled the priest's activities so as to give reflected glory to Catholic rather than nativist forces. Mathew's residence was changed from the Irving House to St. Peter's church. Hughes personally squired him about during his stay, took him to speak at his colleges, guided him through the city's Catholic charities, and stamped his episcopal approval upon his temperance efforts. The two got along well enough. Mathew remained two years in the United States, during which time his popularity remained high, and his pledge was administered to some 20,000 people. He carefully checked in with Hughes whenever he went through New York and generally resided at such times at the bishop's house.

John Hughes was reaching a point in his career and personality where people who approached him learned to do so diplomatically if they wished success within a certain sphere, the sphere being the world of Catholic Americans. It is nothing less than a tragedy that while Theobold Mathew, whose work was of passing effect, learned this, the hotheaded yet dedicated Thomas D'Arcy McGee did not. It is tragic as well that John Hughes was by habit of office becoming too autocratic and inflexible to see past the impetuosity of youth. Had Hughes let bygones be bygones or at least been better able to see beyond personalities to the issues they represented, had he properly steered McGee's dedicated efforts to educate and colonize Irish immigrants, the history of the Irish in the United States might have been markedly different and less filled with turmoil than it was.

20

A GIFT FROM CONSTANTINE

There was an irony to the nativist image of the Catholic Church. In the nineteenth century while Americans believed Rome possessed immense, sinister powers, it was actually at the nadir of its temporal existence. The revolutions of the previous century had shorn the papacy of any political strength. Napoleon had made a prisoner of the Pope, and the post-Napoleonic world left the Popes desperately holding onto a narrow portion of land cutting across Italy. The Papal States, ruled as a conservative, even reactionary monarchy, stood in the way of Italian unification, the ambitions of France and Austria, and the liberal ideas of government that were sweeping through intellectual circles in Europe.

In 1846 when Pius IX ascended the throne of Peter he began to liberalize his civil government and declared amnesty for political prisoners. His worldwide flock benefited along with his local subjects. President Polk, still wishing to balance any hard feelings generated among Catholics during the Mexican War, managed to push through Congress a bill establishing a legation at the papal court for the first time. The United States reacted positively to Pius IX's liberal tendencies. In November of 1847 New York's Tabernacle was "crammed to overflowing"[1] with a meeting of American citizens wishing to "express sympathy with the Pope." The meeting was called to demonstrate support for his efforts to establish civil and religious liberty throughout the papal dominion despite the armed intervention of Austria. The mayor of New York sat as chairman, a letter from Martin Van Buren was read, and Horace Greeley sang the praises of Pio Nono.

Bennett was pleased with Pius's performance and lauded him for "bringing back the Church of Rome to the novel position which it occupied in the first three centuries of Christianity, before it was corrupted by Constantine and became a part of the state."[2]

David Hale refused to jump on the bandwagon. He was still determined to show that Romanism's spiritual and physical corruption went hand in hand. When Hughes officiated at the funeral of a priest who had died tending quarantine patients not long after the Tabernacle rally, Hale's *Journal of Commerce* warned: "Bishop Hughes has the reputation of never appearing in public without a motive. Now I should like to ascertain what motive impelled him yesterday to head a procession of priests, they in full dress, he in his most fantastic robes and crowned with a miter, through the principal thoroughfare in Staten Island . . . Are we in this Protestant country to be hereafter favored with the full expansion of Papish mummeries?"[3] Still, it was fashionable that season to toast the new liberal Pope, and that is just what occurred at the Astor House when John Hughes was invited to be the guest speaker at the annual dinner to commemorate the landing of the Pilgrims, an event that was traditionally Protestant in tone. "What strange changes have of late come over the spirit of the times," decided the shocked ex-Mayor Philip Hone. "The sons of the Pilgrims toasting the old lady whom their fathers complimented with the titles of 'Whore of Babylon,' 'red harlot' and such like tender and loving apellations."[4]

The New York *Observer,* staunch to the last, was not so much nonplussed as purple with anger at the "humiliation to see our politicians eulogizing an Italian despot and courting his mercenary priests." At least this paper saw clearly the distinction between the Italian despot's religious and temporal powers. For the sake of insult it chided: "As Pope the sun never sets on his dominion. As civil ruler his kingdom is among the weakest and most limited that now exist."[5]

Catholics, too, had the opportunity to understand this distinction explained by the Pope himself. In May the *Freeman's Journal* quoted his benediction as he sent papal troops against the Austrians in Lombardy. "As head of the Church I am at peace with all the universe," declared the Pope. "As an Italian prince, I have a right to defend Italy my country. I bless you. The cause you go to defend is a holy cause; God will make it triumph . . ."[6]

God did not make it triumph, at least not for the Pope. His small kingdom remained a pawn in a chess game played between France and Austria, even as revolutionaries destroyed the government internally. In November of 1848 his minister Pelegrino Rossi was assassinated. Two weeks after that Pius escaped from Rome in disguise and fled to Gaeta. It was electrifying news throughout the Western world, for one could not hear of the deposition of the Pope without being affected by some feelings pro or con.

Some American Protestants combed through the Book of Revelation trying to decide which chapter and verse the event should fulfill. In their eyes this was, the *Herald* noted discreetly, "the final destruction of the Scarlet lady of Babylon of old, as we must now say, in order not to shock the polite ears of Babylon the new."[7]

Horace Greeley limited his interest to political aspects. He felt that the Pope, having inaugurated reform in the Papal States, did not follow through thoroughly enough. "The fault of Pius IX," he decided, "consists not in that which he did but in that which he left undone."[8]

James Gordon Bennett resolved "We do not think we shall cry very much about it." With casual common sense he declared, "It was not as the spiritual head of the Church but as a temporal potentate that he was dethroned. If the people under his dominion desired a republican form of government and could achieve one by revolution they had the perfect right to do so according to the principle that governors hold rule only according to the will of the governed."[9]

Hughes would accept the distinction between the temporal and the spiritual powers, but he could not admit to their separation. "I do not say it is necessary for the Pope that he should be a sovereign," he preached, "but it is necessary for Christianity that he should be free, and if there is no choice except between sovereign and vassal, then he must be a sovereign."[10]

Politically Hughes was on shaky ground, for he had so recently supported the right of his fellow Irishmen to rebel against what they considered tyranny. Bennett scored him for this narrowness of vision.

> At all events the Bishop should be consistent in his opinions for one year, at least, or if he could not hold out for a whole year, he might try to do so for six months. Has he forgotten the speech he made at Vauxhall Garden last July in favor of the Irish insurrection! . . . On that occasion Bishop Hughes was one of the most ardent democrats of this or any other country. He invoked the spirit of liberty and the spirit of religion in the same breath. He made the crowd of listeners at Vauxhall almost leap out of their breeches by his stirring appeals to their patriotism . . .[11]

The *Freeman's Journal* played up stories of supposed atrocities and sacrileges committed by the revolutionaries in Rome, stories that the *Tribune* claimed contradicted accounts filed by reliable reporters on the scene. When Hughes wrote Greeley and accused him of renouncing his former good will to Catholics, Greeley blandly protested in the *Tribune:* "We do not remember that we ever made any professions of good will to Catholics."[12]

In June when Hughes sent out a circular asking for contributions to aid the Pope, Greeley earned his wrath by reprinting the letter and adding the single comment that the money was being collected for Pius's "present struggle against the Roman Republic." Hughes accused him of putting words in his mouth, but Greeley held firm. "The effect of a contribution made by our citizens at this crisis for the Pope," he said, "would be prejudicial to the cause of Italian freedom no matter what the donor's intention."[13]

Hughes debated politely with Greeley, reminded him that he had only recently addressed the Pope as "venerable father," and then scolded the editor for comparing these rebels with the fathers of the American Revoluton. He demanded "in the name of insulted freedom whether the murderers of Rossi and of the other victims of the Roman Revolution are to be admitted, or rather elevated by Americans, to any species of comparative equality with the tarnished names of Franklin, Washington, Hancock, and their noble associates? Though not an American born, yet I for one feel pride enough in the history of the country to enter my humble protest against it."[14]

Bennett, who was not prone to see any move of John Hughes as being "humble," commented upon his debate with Greeley, saying "St. Hughes beats St. Ignatius himself all to pieces in the matter of writing epistles."[15]

There was a touch of envy in his observation. Publicly ignored by the bishop, Bennett did all he could to bait his hooks in order to get the kind of response the *Tribune* was receiving: "We are in favor of the restoration of the Pope to his spiritual domain," he offered ". . . and that is all." Tempting the bishop to comment, he added ". . . we have no doubt that his eminence Archbishop Hughes, although he might have some slight qualms of conscience at first, would unite and relinquish all those untenable claims to the restoration of the Pope to temporal dominion."[16]

Bennett, like Hughes, swung for the gut while fighting, and Hughes stayed away from him, one added reason being that as bishop he would have been at a disadvantage battling a Catholic who refused to bow to authority. The debate with Greeley, kept on a gentlemanly plane was, however, just as devastating, given the illogic of Hughes's position. In response to the comparison drawn with the American Revolution, the editor of the *Tribune* fired back a blistering salvo. "Whether it is politic in a Catholic Bishop to draw the contrast so broadly in view of the precedent history and the dominant faith of the two countries is a question to be pondered, and at all events, if ten centuries of ecclesiastical sovereignty have left the Romans so wretchedly qualified for freedom, we can hardly wonder that they grow tired of such unprofitable schooling."[17]

Nonetheless the donation Hughes had begged his people for—$6,000 when collected—was sent off with high hopes:

"God will mark by his intervention or by an angel unseen by men, the workings of his providence," Hughes declared, "and you will see how the designs of wicked men who have invaded the authority and place of the Pope shall be brought to naught."[18]

For another year while Pius at Gaeta sought help from Catholic allies he received suggestions to move to more hospitable climes including the United States, the home of so many exiles. One strong opponent to the idea of the Pope's presence in America was Hughes who felt the Pontiff would be insulted by anti-Catholics and by Catholics who knew no proper etiquette and "would gape at him with their hats on or sit in his presence with their heels in the air."[19] Bennett, however, thought it was a capital idea and oft repeated a suggestion that Pius move to New York, now the center of the civilized world as Rome once was in the past. An ideal spot he suggested would be Sing Sing, up the river. Bennett noted that the plentiful marble found there would be perfect for a new Vatican.

In time the "angel unseen by men" took visible shape in Napoleon III, whose armies destroyed the short-lived republic and restored the old order. On May 12th, 1850 Hughes sung a *Te Deum* in the cathedral out of thanksgiving for the return of the Pope: "Give praise O daughter of Sion: shout O Israel . . . The Lord has taken away thy judgment . . ." Hughes preached, exulting: "The Church has triumphed before, and will triumph again over democracy and kings and the people themselves when they imagine vain things." Again he repeated his reason for believing in the temporal sovereignty of the Pope. "If he were the subject of any government, how could he freely speak the truth?"[20]

Bennett was disgusted that Hughes "should sing and shout for joy that the vicegerent of the Prince of Peace, who said his kingdom was not of this world and whose crown was composed of thorns, should wade through rivers of blood to his throne. "Pio Nono attributes his restoration to cannon, muskets and bayonets," he declared, "Bishop Hughes to the prayers and tears of the faithful." As to Hughes's assertion that the Pope had to be personally independent to speak the truth, Bennett responded, "We never heard that Dr. Hughes, who is not as yet a temporal sovereign, was in any way interfered with by the city fathers, by the State government or by Congress in speaking the truth."[21]

Hughes would never have admitted it, even if he had lived to see the final loss of the Pope's temporal power, but James Gordon Bennett's criticism of his bishop during this episode was a remarkable contribution to American Catholicism. Hughes, of course, was wrong, yet his pronouncements represented Catholic teaching to a great percentage of the American populace. It meant little that the Protestant Horace Greeley disagreed with him. But when Bennett, who always claimed (even while ridiculing the Church) to be a representative Catholic, stood up to Hughes it was a different matter. The editor of the country's largest paper gave evidence to America that being a Roman Catholic did not mean handing over one's mind to ecclesiastical authority. Here was one intelligent believer who scoffed at the necessity of the Pope's temporal power. In doing so he certainly helped soften the blow of what had to come about within that same generation's time.

The months of the Pope's temporary banishment at the end of the 1840s had been an occasion of painful growth for the Church. It gave rise to rhetoric detrimental to the acceptance of Catholics by the citizens of a liberty-loving democracy. It had caused John Hughes to act contradictorily, first in regard to the freedom of the Irish, and then in regard to the freedom of the Italian people. If there had not been a lampooning member of the faithful nearby to reduce the weight of his arguments, his pronouncements during this interim might have been remembered far more strongly and harmfully than they were.

As it was—even after this trial—ultramontanists such as Hughes had to undergo a great deal more growth, and the Pope had to undergo a great deal more pain, before the Church was ready to accept the inevitable transition that this first deposition presaged.

21

GROWING PAINS

Hughes was into his fifties and aging fast. He fought it, replacing lost hair with a partial wig so natural as to escape detection by even Bennett, who would have pounced upon such vanity. But the bishop didn't eat well and had fallen into the habit at home and on the road of grabbing food when hungry instead of sitting down to a meal. He was equally careless with the use of his own energies. Bishop Walsh of Halifax, one of his few intimate friends, scolded him, saying, "It seems to me that you have no moments of repose, that you are always swallowed up in a whirlpool of multifarious occupations, and that no one appears to have the slightest pity or compassion for your incessant drudgery. This is cruel." Bidding him to take "an entire day's relaxation in each week," Walsh continued: "I have seen you so exhausted after some of your sermons that I have been alarmed. But I knew well it was not the sermon alone that did this, but the previous toil and incessant occupation of mind and body."[1]

The strain began to tell on his constitution. His lungs, never strong, became increasingly susceptible to inflammation. Rheumatism plagued him. He stopped at Saratoga and its healing baths whenever travel brought him near enough for the luxury, and he made the watering place his routine vacation escape. A spa hotel owner, listening to Hughes laud the curative effects of the place, once wondered if the bishop might be so gracious as to give an actual endorsement. Hughes declined, respectfully pointing out that such an advertisement would be improper. Still the request was indicative that the opinion of John Hughes could be a valuable commodity when set before the public, a possibility he had to learn to be careful of. He made the mistake of publicly praising an exhibit of a panorama of the Isle of Cuba, and the *Herald* quickly pointed out other vistas that might interest the newly promoted archbishop: "There is a wonderful collection of strange and curious articles in Barnum's museum, for example, for which the certificate of the archbishop might be of great advantage in the present crisis."[2]

One person who failed to see the sarcasm in such a suggestion was P. T. Barnum. Mulling over the advantages of an espicopal blessing P. T. sent Hughes a letter assuring him of the wholesome, religious atmosphere of his museum, and included as a bounteous gesture one (count 'em, one) admission. "I enclose a *free* ticket,"* he enthused, "and will esteem it a favor if you will give this establishment a critical examination. If found worthy of support I trust you will kindly recommend it to your friends."[3] If Hughes did tell his friends that Barnum's museum was the greatest show on earth he must have done so verbally, for there is no written record of an endorsement. However he kept P. T.'s letter carefully filed for posterity.

In December of 1847 Congress paid tribute to Hughes's nationally recognized stature, inviting him to preach in the House of Representatives. Bennett, who insisted that Hughes was in Washington "luxuriating in the menagerie of politicians and roguery" in order to manipulate any appointments to the newly established mission to Rome, cast a wary eye at the invitation: "If he preaches there it cannot be with the hope of saving many of the sinners in that department of human life. Bishop Hughes must know the value of a politician's soul too well to think it worth saving at all."[4]

On the day of the talk the press reported that "all Washington yielded itself to the delicious frenzy of a new and strange excitement." The heavy rains of a nor'easter had

---

*The emphasis is Barnum's.

turned Pennsylvania Avenue into a vast puddle. Despite that, the muddy streets were thronged all morning with vehicular and pedestrian passengers wending their way to the Capitol. The floor and galleries of the House were crammed with drenched, umbrella-clutching notables as Hughes stood to speak, attired in cassock and episcopal cross.[5] As on the occasion of the anniversary banquet commemorating the Pilgrims' landing, he addressed a group of staunch Protestants. John Quincy Adams sat before him, as did Lewis Cass, John Calhoun, Stephen Douglas, and a number of other powerful men who had often expressed fear of the Roman Church. As at the Pilgrim banquet Hughes politically addressed himself to the occasion. Taking as a theme "Christianity, the only source of Moral, Social and Political Regeneration," he remained blandly ecumenical enough to please the most anti-Roman of Puritans and to confuse Bennett, who called it "a remarkable sermon in its way, peculiarly characteristic of Bishop Hughes, and possessing some curious facts concerning men and things, not exactly religious." Weighing the happy effect that the talk had upon its listeners, the *Herald* decided that the bishop's career to date "has produced an equal amount of disaster and triumph for the Catholic cause."[6]

Hughes continued to gain widespread popularity and distrust. When the primatial See of Ireland became vacant, the Irish press on the other side of the Atlantic circulated a rumor that John Hughes would be brought home to assume the episcopal primacy in the land of his birth. Conversely, Hughes became more and more prominently pictured as the villain in nativist books such as *Romanism in America* and *Washington in the Lap of Rome.*

Within his own diocese he had reached a level of paternalistic stature in the eyes of his people. As possessive as he was of them, they were of him. If he could be perfectly correct before Congress, he gave evidence of the easy command he enjoyed before large crowds of Catholics. The reporter for the *Freeman's Journal,* attending Hughes's eulogy of Daniel O'Connell given, oddly enough, at the Chinese Museum, caught himself laughing along with the audience at remarks "which when we examined them, really contained no subject of mirthfulness, but which from the very oddity of their colloca- tion provoked the spirit of humor."[7] The incident was clear evi- dence of a communal affection.

And yet, possessing full and easy command of large crowds, he was still a loner. His position of authority made it all the more difficult for him to allow people to get close. He was not popular with his clergy in general, being too autocratic in his policies for that. Nevertheless those who worked and lived with him on a day-to-day basis seemed to have genuinely liked him. "We have a very pleasant household," James Bayley confided to his diary.[8] Bayley carried on a constant campaign to get Hughes involved socially, setting up dinner parties to broaden his bishop's personal acquaintanceships. But whether it was because the bishop was basically unsure of himself with small groups of people or unsure of the people who sought to become his friends he kept more and more to himself. Friend- ship begins most comfortably on a peer level. Hughes, being taciturn by nature and so conscious of the pyramid of hierar- chy in the Church, had few real opportunities for com- panionship. One Sunday in the cathedral he recognized a man with whom he had once worked in the stone quarries at Cham- bersburg. He happily grabbed him, invited him to dinner and spent hours talking with him. The bishop was a lonely man. He wanted friendships, but under the circumstances of his work and personality he was incapable of developing them. And so his life became, almost totally, his episcopal work.

John Hassard, a young convert from the Episcopal Church, was forced by illness to abandon his studies for the priesthood. Working briefly for Hughes as an amanuensis, and becoming fond enough of him eventually to write his biogra- phy, Hassard found himself confused by his bishop's personal disorganization and by the wide range of nonessential matters fielded by the bishop of New York. With a sense of astonish- ment he listed types of letters in the episcopal correspondence:

—Young men in Ireland, whom he never heard of, ask his advice about coming to America. One wants a situation in a bank. Another inquired about the prospects of business in general.

—All sorts of people send him boxes and packages to be forwarded to their relations in all sorts of out-of-the-way towns in America.

—Priests in Europe send him restitution money that has been given them in the confessional by penitent thieves, and beg him to find out (mostly with the vaguest directions) the person to whom it rightfully belongs.

—Emigrants send him money and request him to buy drafts to transmit to their friends in the old country. Poor people in the old country on the other hand, ask him to find out their emigrant friends, whose address they do not know.

—A little army of office seekers besiege him for letters of introduction.

—Pious souls write him letters of eight pages about their worldly and spiritual troubles.

—Protestant clergymen preparing themselves for a terrible assault upon the abominations of Popery request him to state, as clearly as possible, the Catholic doctrine on this or that question.

—One gentleman consults him about the Broadway railroad.

—A great many gentlemen ask for loans of fifty dollars.

—Suspicious, quarrelsome or malicious persons trouble him with every kind of absurd charge against their parish priests.

Most of these are promptly and politely answered; and in the great majority of cases, an effort is made to comply with their unreasonable demands.[9]

In 1849 another severe outbreak of cholera swept through the United States. It was less severe than the nightmare experience of 1832 when the nature of the disease was totally unknown, but it still carried off the high and lowly alike. In June the papers carried news that James K. Polk, having just left office, had succumbed to the disease. In smaller print during August the final episode of Maria Monk's story—this time verified—was published in the press. A North River boatman named McCarthy who had slept with her in a "house of disrepute," accused her of picking his pocket and she was sentenced to the Tombs, the city's prison.[10] There within a fortnight cholera ended her fabled career—her book still famous, but she a forgotten soul.

Henry Clay, who had met Hughes in New York, continued this acquaintanceship in Saratoga near summer's end. Attending Mass on a hot Sunday morning as a compliment to the bishop's preaching abilities, the elderly statesman frightened the cholera-sensitive congregation when he buckled with a "violent pain" during the sermon. Helped out by a physician the embarrassed senator whispered, "My good doctor, be so kind as to apologize to the bishop for me for having left the church so abruptly." Later he sought to compensate for his departure by speaking of Hughes's homily as "a massive chain of the closest and most metaphysical reasoning." The *Herald's* reporter concurred, calling the sermon "one of the most powerful I have ever heard." Bennett, peeved at Hughes during this time, printed his reporter's evaluation but assured his readers: "We fear he has not heard many sermons."[11] The editor accused the bishop of hiding at a summer resort while "the working priests" of his diocese took their (and his) places "in the cholera hospital—at the bedsides of the sick and dying—in wretched hovels, in pestilential dwellings, by night and day." He concluded, "Would that we had a Gaeta in this country to which to banish worthless tyrannical, faithless bishops. We want a great sweeping ecclesiastical revolution."[12]

Bennett's blasts against Hughes were frequently accurate, but not this time. While it's true that he didn't make the rounds of the hospitals, those kinds of duties were no longer his. He carried on fearlessly when he was a parish priest during the 1832 epidemic; he was just as fearless in 1849. He was in the city throughout the cholera siege, except for the time spent at the Baltimore council (where cholera was as much a threat). It had been during the height of the epidemic that he accompanied Father Mathew to the city's charity institutions, when he fought with Thomas D'Arcy McGee, when he carried on the debate with Greeley about the Pope's banishment, and when he campaigned for the fund to support Pius at Gaeta. During the same week that Bennett wished to banish Hughes for having fled to Saratoga the *Herald* began labeling accounts of the illness in the city—"The Cholera Panic subsiding."[13] Hughes had been on the job for the duration, but he was no longer a parish priest; he was the most important bishop in the United States.

It was because of his stature that Hughes lost a battle which, at that time, he and other Catholics insisted upon calling a victory. The New York *Observer* had a regular nativist contributor, a minister who signed himself "Kirwin." Kirwin told his readers that he had been brought up as a Catholic, and because of those credentials he felt fit to address himself to New York's Catholic bishops. He led off by declaring that Hughes was too brilliant a man to believe the Catholicism he preached, and next he complimented the bishop for being able to fight "even when convinced of the utter fallacy of your position and defense. . . . Like the ancient priests of Egypt," he decided, "you must have one class of opinions for the public and another for yourself."[14]

With the *Observer* propped upon newstands throughout the city, its front page boasting an imaginary debate, Hughes said nothing. The paper goaded him by taking quotes from his speeches as if they were answers to Kirwin. For instance it lifted a quote from Hughes's talk on the causes of famine in Ireland (Kirwin's birthplace) to the effect that the Irish would have physically fared better had they succumbed to English Protestantism. This was taken as a "candid admission" that Kirwin was right about Catholic degeneracy. "We have published nothing in many years on the subject of Romanism," claimed the *Observer,* "that has attracted such general attention and so justly awakened interest in the Romish controversy."[15]

But it still wasn't a controversy. It was one man yelling insults. Finally, after a number of the attacks were gathered into a volume entitled *Kirwin's Letters to Bishop Hughes,* the bishop's pugnacious bent got the better of his common sense. He responded in the *Freeman's Journal.*

Hughes refused to address an anonymous adversary. Instead over several months' time he published nine long articles entitled "The Importance of Being in Communion with Christ's One, Holy, Catholic and Apostolic Church." But for one passing reference, Kirwin was ignored. The articles bored Bennett who felt that the letters "are curiosities in their way; not convincing, but curious. His Washington sermon is yet the best thing he has done."[16]

Finally when it was revealed that Hughes was dueling with a fifty-year-old Presbyterian divine from Elizabethtown, N.J., Reverend Nicholas Murray, Hughes went after him in his more customary style, changing the title of his own letters to the more marketable "Kirwin Unmasked." The only interesting historical comment made by Hughes throughout the entire correspondence came at the beginning. It was a reference to the conversion of Murray as having occurred "amidst the numerous defections from the faith which loneliness and poverty entail on juvenile immigrants and orphan boys of Irish and Catholic parentage in this country . . ."[17] Then he bore into Murray himself, asking first of all, "By what right sir, did you assume that I am not sincere in the Catholic faith?"[18] As always when he debated, Hughes found one basic weak point in his opponent's argument; he sank his teeth into it and refused to let go. Murray claimed that he had been raised in religious ignorance by his parents, praying prayers in unknown Latin. When he had come to the United States, by his account, "an infidel," Presbyterians took him in and led him to the Gospel. "On reaching the years of maturity," Murray related, "my mind was a perfect blank as to all religious instruction."[19]

It was this contradiction that Hughes went after. He wondered how Murray came to such a deep knowledge of the Roman Church. Said Hughes: "Of your own knowledge of Popery, as you call it, you know nothing—and you have avowed it. Then you are no more competent to speak or write of it than Dr. Brownlee was. What you know of it, true or false, you, like him, have learned from its enemies." After a series of similar attacks in which the minister's own words were used against him, Hughes stood back and declared: "I doubt whether Christendom could furnish one other instance of such mental nudity."[20]

Bennett, who liked to appoint himself referee of all the bishop's battles, this time declared Hughes the easy winner. He wrote: "Our friend the bishop is too much for the doctor. We would recommend the latter, if he wishes the bishop to go into the matter in earnest, to study logic for a year or two."[21]

The New York *Observer* was happy nonetheless, for at last John Hughes had made himself a target within reach. "Bishop Hughes has addressed another letter to Kirwin," it exulted. "He has not yet reached the argument, being still employed in low scurrility into which, we had supposed, Bishop Hughes never descends."[22]

The *Observer* was not alone in believing that Hughes had come out badly in the exchange. The Princeton *Review,* asserting that "Romanism is a monstrous system of conscious deception," declared of the Hughes-Murray exchange: "We presume there never was a case of controversy in this country where the advantage was so entirely on one side, or as to which public opinion is so unanimous."[23]

The *Review* was right. While Hughes may have won some debating points, he came out the loser. Fifteen years earlier an unknown scrapper named John Hughes had debated a famous dandy in Philadelphia and made himself famous in the process. While he was by no means a dandy now in 1848, he was, as Murray had addressed him, the "bishop of the commercial metropolis of the Western world." It mattered little that he bested Murray. As soon as he climbed into the ring with him it was the other man's victory. Hughes had grown in stature without quite realizing it himself. He allowed himself to argue theology with Protestant Horace Greeley while not deigning to notice James Gorden Bennett, a Catholic. He would slug away for months on an equal level with an unknown Protestant divine while summarily suspending John Maginnis, one of his priests, who had written an anti-abolitionist letter to the bishop's friend, William Seward.[24] It was a period when Hughes seemed uncertain in his own self image.

In October of 1850 he received word from Rome that he was to be an archbishop, with the dioceses of Boston, Hartford, Albany, and Buffalo as suffragan Sees to supervise. Before leaving for Rome to receive the pallium of office from the Pope, he accepted the invitation of Millard Fillmore to dine at the White House. Then as a parting gift to nativist New York he delivered a lecture in St. Patrick's church entitled "The Decline of Protestantism and Its Causes." It was an aboveboard but nonetheless ruthless account of what he saw as the failure of the Reformation. For all the talk of private interpretation, he claimed, no orthodoxy was ever more dogmatic and narrow in scope than the teachings of the Protestant Churches. He cited the failure of North American Protestantism to deal with the American Indian, while Roman Catholicism, he said, "brought South America and all its Indian tribes into communion with herself." Laying judgment upon the whole history of Protestantism, he concluded that it "acquired all it ever possessed in fifty years, in the heart of Christianity, amidst war and civil strife, and after that it became stricken as with sterility."[25]

A historian of a later, more ecumenical age would cite this lecture as evidence that Hughes was insensitive to Protestant feelings. True enough, but it was not an age given to sensitivities. The calibre of this lecture and all his public utterances must be measured alongside the standard fare that nativist clergymen doled out to Americans about Romanism. By comparison Hughes's speeches, though lacking in apostolic magnaminity, were almost statesmanlike.

Bennett reported the lecture as if it were routine: "King Solomon has said that there is a season for everything. History bears him out . . . . Barnum from time to time has opened upon us with a black whale, a Fejee mermaid, a Buffalo hunt, Joyce Heth, Santa Anna's wooden leg, a sickly ourang outang, a spotted negro, a giant or a dwarf, a Calvin Edison or the fat boys, a double-headed calf or a pig with five legs, so that with him the season is opening all the time. Bishop Hughes has opened the religious campaign of the season with a powerful argument on the 'decline of Protestantism' and Dr. Dowling has opened on the other side in a dashing hallelujah upon 'the downfall of Popery.' There is a season for everything and every season must have an opening."[26]

22

THE MEANING OF
THE WORD "CATHOLIC"

James Bennett was cool enough to religion to be impartial. Moreover, he wanted to sell newspapers. As he put it: "It is true we were born and educated a Catholic; and looking backwards, all our race were Catholics . . . but in these latter days, since the invention and discovery of Morse's telegraph and Hoe's printing press, and the establishment of the *Herald,* we have become more liberal and comprehensive in our religious notions, and we now believe in both the Catholic and Protestant faiths, with all their divisions and subdivisions, rejecting only those particular little doctrines of either that conflict and quarrel among themselves."[1]

It is unfortunate that Christian leaders did not similarly feel that they had to sell their product to the general public. Individuals who did convert from one denomination to another were a scandal to the Church they left and a triumph to the Church they entered. Neither Nicholas Murray nor William Hogan would have been given a hearty homecoming by their kin in Ireland. James Roosevelt Bayley was disinherited by his Episcopal family. When Winfield Scott's "eldest and most beautiful daughter" Virginia[2] became not only a Catholic but a nun, the Scotts received sympathy from their friends. "I cannot imagine a more severe trial" commiserated Philip Hone. "I know what it is to resign a beloved daughter to the hands of him whose bounty I was indebted for the precious gift; but the bereavement had its accompanying consolation; she died in the faith of her sorrowing parents . . ."*³

The Oxford movement in England had its parallel in the United States, a movement that divided the Episcopalians into opposing camps of "high" and "low" Church. On its most noble level it was the lonely search of a small minority who felt they needed to discover a real Catholicity in the teachings of Jesus despite the divided state of his followers. On a secondary and more noticeable level it was a tendency on the part of some Episcopalians to adopt the liturgical practices of the Roman Catholic Church. It was this latter aspect of the movement that frightened anti-papists among the Episcopalians. At New York's General Theological Seminary several students fell suspect of being, in effect, Roman Catholics. In 1843 a sensitive young man named Arthur Carey was placed on trial for such leanings. He was acquitted, but at his ordination two clergymen broke the solemnity of the ceremony to protest vocally against him. Bishop Benjamin Onderdonk, presiding, ignored them and proceeded. Carey, oppressed by all the criticism, died not long afterward, mourned by his friends for his saintly character. The incident precipitated a small exodus of fellow students from the Episcopal to the Roman Catholic Church, among whom were James McMaster, Edgar Wadhams, and Clarence Walworth.

In 1845 Onderdonk himself was placed on trial by his clergy and fellow bishops for alleged improprieties with women —charges that many observers felt were fabricated in retaliation for the Carey affair. His suspension from office caused Bennett to compare the disgrace of this all-American bishop to the prestigious immigrant John Hughes. "One bishop is going down," he observed, "another is actually rising up."⁵

---

*The Scotts continued to be plagued by Catholicism within the ranks of their offspring. Diarist George Templeton Strong makes reference to the general's grandchild, Winfield, "of whose baptism by Bishop Hughes Mrs. General Scott gave me a moving account the other night. How first they put oil on him and then put salt on him and she really thought they'd make a salad of the poor little creature and end by cutting it up . . ."⁴

The brutal exercise of a spiritual intolerance, always the sore point with Bennett, caused him to veer from his proclaimed ecumenism for the moment. As opposed to the Episcopalians, he praised Catholicism as the Church of the common man. The Catholic Church, he wrote, "does not deny innocent amusement and recreation to the hardworking mechanic or tradesman on a fine Sunday afternoon after their attendance at Mass . . ." Then, as if to express sympathy with the high church movement, he added: "We like the Holy Roman Church—its mysteries, its ceremonies, its music, its gossiping confessional, its venerable sacraments, and its repudiation of straight-laced, long-faced, cold calculating religion which is enough to give one a fit of chills when he thinks of it. We like the Church of Rome for the same reason we like the Italian Opera—because it inspires us, elevates us, ennobles us."[6]

Roman Catholics of that age were as incapable of discussing the Catholic dimension of Christianity as Protestants were. Even the gentlemanly Bishop Kenrick could respond to the Catholic movement within the Episcopal Church only by affably inviting its adherents to capitulate to Rome. For his part, Hughes was happy to receive converts once they jumped over the chasm, but it was beyond his nature and ability to build a bridge for those still remaining on the other side. This was demonstrated in his dealings with young Isaac Hecker.

Hecker, steeped with transcendentalism at Brook Farm, had returned to his native New York on a quest of faith. Weighing the possibilities of the Episcopal and the Roman Church he made appointments with Dr. Samuel Seabury, the high-church editor of the *Churchman,* and with Hughes. The young man was delighted with the "sociableness and perfect frankness" of Seabury, who felt that the hope of Christian unity lay in an ecumenical council.[7] In his diary Hecker noted, "He frankly acknowledged that he thought that error had been committed on both sides in the controversy of the Reformation between the Pope and the Anglican Church. He recommended me to examine those points which kept me from joining the Anglican or Roman Church before I should do anything further . . ."[8]

This reception was balanced against an interview with Bishop Hughes. The immediate skeptical impression that Hughes formed of Hecker was not enhanced when the young man let it be known that his first decision was to enter a seminary; secondarily he was deciding which Church he would serve. "But you are not a Catholic?" Hughes asked. "No," Hecker said, "I am not as yet sure if I wish to join the Catholic Church, but I am very interested in it." "Well, to enter the seminary," Hughes bluntly informed Hecker, "you must have been a Catholic for two years, and in addition you will have to present testimonials from your parish priest concerning your fitness, character and ability."[9]

Hughes intended this reply as a quick dismissal, but Hecker was determined to have help in resolving his dilemma. He pressed his prospective bishop for details about Catholicism. "The Catholic Church is a Church of discipline." Hughes informed him, by way of an essential description.

Hecker weighed this interview in his diary, observing: "I thanked him for the information that he gave, and said that it was for just such information that I sought him, because he seemed to think I had inborn Protestant notions of the Church. So far, this settles my intention of uniting myself with the R. C. Church. Though I feel not the least disinclined to be governed by the most rigid discipline of any Church, yet I am not prepared to enter the R. C. Church at present." Then, judging Catholicism by the strong-minded Irish immigrant with whom he had spoken, he wrote: "The R. C. Church is not national with us, hence it does not meet our wants, nor does it fully understand and sympathize with the experience and dispositions of our people. It is principally made up of adopted and foreign individuals."

This negative opinion was conveyed to his friend and fellow faith-seeker Orestes Brownson who inquired, "Did you ask him about his view of things social and political?" "I did," said Hecker. "And would that I had at least not asked the latter."[10]

Fortunately for American Catholicsm, both Hecker and Brownson were independent enough to seek answers that transcended personalities. Brownson became a Catholic despite the fact that he was an irascible mental giant seeking answers from men less intelligent than himself. Hecker eventually met Bishop McCloskey, who along with Father Gabriel Rumpler of the Redemptorists offered a kind of spiritual oasis for wanderers seeking answers about the Catholic Church.

Once the chasm was bridged Hughes treated converts no differently than born Catholics. They were elevated to the episcopacy, as in the cases of Bayley and Wadhams, and were made prominent pastors, as was the case of John Murray Forbes. Laymen were also offered positions of authority. The newly converted McMaster was entrusted with ownership of the *Freeman's Journal.* At times, however, the same independent spirit that had made each of them critical and searching as Protestants kept them independent and searching as Catholics. This made an absolute disciplinarian like Hughes uneasy. He was accustomed to giving orders, not explaining them. "Unhappily, as time goes on," he complained, "they sometimes betray the absence of original Catholic discipline."[11]

As a Catholic, Orestes Brownson remained nobody's man. He was as wary of the immigrant Church he had joined as his new coreligionists oftentimes were of him. Having moved in a pure intellectual stream toward the Church he found the actual body he had joined to be quite a different reality. "My great trouble," he complained to Hecker, ". . . is that the mass of Catholics are not Catholics. *Inter nos* I do not like in general our Irish population. They have no clear understanding of their religion."[12]

As intolerant as Brownson could be, McMaster was worse. At his baptism McMaster set a priest on fire with the candle he held. It was a symbolic beginning to his relationship with the Church. Hotheaded and independent, while running a paper that New Yorkers took to be the mouthpiece of Hughes, he was a constant embarrassment to his bishop, until Hughes was eventually forced to disavow the *Freeman's Journal.*

Issac Hecker got into the seminary faster than the two years Hughes had quoted to him. And with his customary independence Hecker ignored Hughes's wish that he enter the diocesan seminary, joining the Redemptorist order instead.

Levi Silliman Ives, the Episcopal Bishop of North Carolina, paid a great price to be the first Anglican bishop since the Reformation to convert to the Roman Church. As a high church enthusiast he had started a monastic community and found himself placed on trial by the Episcopalians for doing so. He briefly recanted his Romish tendencies, but finally he made a decisive move in 1852. Hughes took a view of this new convert that was shared by many of Ives's former churchmen, that he was "generous, impulsive, somewhat erratic." Confiding his skepticism to Kenrick, he expressed little faith in Ives's future as a Catholic. "He is to be treated with at least moderate caution," Hughes suggested, "until time shall have tried his mettle."[13]

The celibacy regulations of Roman Catholicism excluded the married Ives from the ranks of the clergy, but the Church was quick to make provision that his new life would be dignified and comfortable. Hughes set him up as an instructor at Fordham, but this being an age when laymen played subordinate roles in the Church, the former bishop was for the most part consciously ignored. Ives showed an inclination to speak before the public, but not about the merits of Catholic as opposed to Protestant Christianity. Having left a Church composed largely of upper-class citizenry, he embraced the lowest class in his new Church, and he began to preach on such topics as "The Poor in Their Relation to Society."

Hughes could never get himself to trust in Ives. It was almost as if he were waiting for the ex-Anglican to attempt to regain his former episcopal prestige. A full seven years after Ives's reception into the Church Hughes was furious when Father McFarrelly of Annunciation church in Manhattanville invited the convert to speak in his church. He channeled his anger through an order that closed the pulpit to laymen. "No priest in my diocese has ever placed me in a more painful position than you have done . . ." he wrote the unfortunate pastor. "In order to be brief I would say to you that the violation of this rule on your part will be equivalent to a suspension, *ipso facto.*"[14] For all this anxiety on Hughes's part, Ives remained relatively free. His home became a mecca for other converts, and he took an active lead in promoting social agencies for the poor. He became, in effect, the parent of a whole new age of Catholic charities.

John Murray Forbes was one of New York's most illustrious Episcopal rectors. Fortunately, for the sake of his clerical status, he was a widower when he entered the Roman Catholic Church. Hughes sent him to study in Rome and then assigned him to St. Ann's church where he lived with his sons. He had wavered shortly after his ordination to the priesthood, unhappy with the strictures of his new Church. But he quickly regained his footing and penitentially insisted on recanting his brief backslide from the Church in a publicly printed avowel: "Outside of her pale, all is emptiness and sterility."[15]

Forbes became fairly close to Hughes writing him letters from St. Ann's that included expressions of affection of his own sons for the bishop. Throughout the 1850s he won a reputation for being as beloved a Catholic pastor as he had been an Episcopal rector. He worked at recruiting professors for the Catholic University in Ireland, and to his bishop's delight he was one of the few prominent converts to the Catholic movement to develop an absolute enthusiasm for docility.

Eventually the high-church movement within the Episcopal communion lost its allure. Roman Catholics had been incapable of seeing it as an opportunity for true dialogue, and many remaining Episcopalians developed a reactionary fear of high-church Romish tendencies. Christians continued to convert as they had before and during the brief phenomenon, but they did so as individuals. The Christian Churches, as communities, had not recovered sufficiently from the wounds inflicted during the Reformation to begin speaking to one another about the meaning of the word Catholic.

PART THREE

The Archbishop

23

VISITORS FROM ABROAD

There were great expectations and rumors both in Roman and American clerical circles that the Pope, by giving John Hughes the archbishop's pallium, intended to make him a cardinal as well. Eccleston wrote quickly from Baltimore informing Pius IX that speaking for the bishops of the United States he thought the honor would be inexpedient. Whatever possibilities were discussed behind closed papal doors Hughes returned home in July of 1851 without the red hat. Prudently he had never said a word in anticipation, and there was thus no need for him to reflect upon any disappointment. Nonetheless, Bennett twitted him for months. Bennett had already been irritated when the *Freeman's Journal* attempted (briefly) to use the "ridiculous title" His Lordship for the new archbishop, thereby "aping the ecclesiastical humbugs of Europe."[1] Now he looked for any opportunity to mourn the fact that John Dubois's gardener could not wear an ermine cape. When Queen Victoria tightened regulations on Catholics in England and forbade them the right to have public processions, the *Herald* wondered, "We do not know whether his eminence Cardinal Hughes intends to appear in the streets with the red hat and all the paraphernalia of that office which, it is said, he has received secretly, and will soon assume openly. But if he does it will be a funny sight and will draw as great a crowd as the ascent in a balloon on horseback."[2] It was enough to keep a man humble.

There were many other sights to draw crowds of New

Yorkers in the early fifties, not the least of which were the arrivals of exiled patriots from the revolutions in Europe.

Had the Hungarians in 1848 succeeded in their revolt against the Austrian Empire, Lajos Kossuth would have been largely credited with their victory, just as William Smith O'Brien would have been for a victorious Ireland. The Hungarians had come tragically close to success and might have won their independence but for the intervention of Russia. Kossuth had fled. He was held by the Turkish government while stories of his bravery spread throughout the Western world, until at length England and the United States arranged his release. In September of 1851 the *U.S.S. Mississippi* was sent to Turkey to bring him in noble exile to America. After a series of disagreements with the captain, however, Kossuth left the ship at Gibraltar and went to England where he was accorded a hero's welcome. In anticipation of the Magyar warrior's arrival in New York, the newspapers covered each step of his English tour, quoting every available toast and tribute made to him so that Americans might measure and prepare their own tributes in yet greater terms. The speeches of Kossuth were printed in full, and with some of his words the hero began to earn the enmity of John Hughes.

He was not invulnerable to begin with. Kossuth had been a great patriot, but only for the sake of his own Magyar Hungarians. He had cavalierly treated non-Magyar groups, and this in no small measure had hastened the downfall of the revolt. In England he made a mistake similar to one John Hughes had made in New York in 1848. Where Hughes had encouraged revolt in his native Ireland and condemned it in the Papal States, so too Kossuth, crying liberty for central Europe, found the banquets honoring him proper occasions to bless England's treatment of Ireland.

Over America's deafening hurrahs Hughes began to shout an angry protest. Labeling the Magyar's speeches "Hungarian blarney," he demanded to know how Kossuth could be "the very poet of insurrection and rebellion on the continent of Europe" and then become "the teacher of tame submission" in the British Isles. Reminding Americans of their recent sympathy for the Irish rebels, he declared: "Smith O'Brien was as brave a man as ever Kossuth was, and Thomas Meagher was as eloquent; and these men are forgotten. The man who claims to have risked his fortune for principles for which they risked theirs, turns round to bespatter their tyrants with praise."[3]

Horace Greeley had been growing increasingly upset with Hughes. Publicly he wondered if the archbishop's concept of religious liberty meant that he, like the Pope in his domain, "would so arrange matters with due provisions of soldiers and policemen and prisons and other similar persuances as that the Catholic religion should simply flourish and be dominant in this country."[4]

With Kossuth scheduled to arrive any day, the editor of the *Tribune* did not want the archbishop of New York to embarrass America with "his evident intent to excite Irish and Catholic hostility against that noble exile . . ." He demanded that Hughes recognize Kossuth's need to be politic in return for Britain's efforts to free him from captivity. Greeley asked, "Whatever Ireland or America may say against England, his mouth is stopped with regard to her, except when he can speak her praise. Should not these obvious considerations have moved the Archbishop to a more charitable construction of that Southampton speech?"[5]

Hughes thought not, and again he took aim at Kossuth. He granted that, at first, he had imagined that history would remember Kossuth's name "as that of a great man." But, Hughes continued, "when on his release from prison I found him offering the incenses of adulation . . . to the very power that had crushed principles such as he professed to have contended for—in the persons of Smith O'Brien and the other Irish patriots—when I found him unnecessarily flinging insult at the religion of most of the people of Hungary simply because such an insult would be grateful in the ears of his English auditors, I could not help forming the opinion that the stuff was not in him."[6]

Hughes's response to Greeley was polite enough to earn a

like response. Delicately, the *Tribune* editor acknowledged that Hughes had "spiritual powers among us greater than that of any other living man." Yet he confessed that in this case the archbishop's pronouncements "seem to indicate at least a decided leaning to the side which appears to us wrong and pernicious." In an apparent effort to bury the hatchet, Greeley admitted that Hughes's position in the school controversy had been correct. He wrote: "We thought then, and still think, that these religious influences were unjust to Catholics . . ." Then, remembering his own role in that dispute with a bit more color than it actually had, he added: "We fought them together until the Public School monopoly was overthrown."[7]

He might better have held onto the hatchet. Two thousand citizens angrily and immediately cancelled their subscriptions to the *Tribune.*

On December 5th, 1851 Lajos Kossuth arrived in New York to a frenzied welcome, disembarking with another exile of the revolutions, the exotic, sharp-eyed Lola Montez. Miss Montez, whose press clippings about a Spanish background ignored her birthplace in Limerick, was a dancer who had caught the lecherous eye of Ludwig I of Bovaria in the 1840s. Madly in love with her, he had made her a countess (after making her a citizen), and lent himself to her strong political ambitions. She brought about the dismissal of his conservative cabinet, she warred with the powerful Jesuit order, and she won the hatred of liberal students who began to address the king as "whore majesty."[8] In the revolution of 1848 both she and Ludwig were handed their walking papers. Now, opting for a return to the stage, she had set sail for the New World. Neither Lajos nor Lola was happy to be sharing the same ship; he felt she might cheapen his entry and she feared he might overshadow hers.

The latter event occurred. While Lola had to be content with the rude inquiries of a few gossip-mongering newsmen, New York turned out *en masse* to give Kossuth a welcome more thunderous than any the city had ever given. He was hailed as another Lafayette, another Washington, almost a demigod of liberty. Civic, social, and religious groups fought to do him honors while he in return spoke eloquently, in perfect English, seeking funds for the renewal of the Hungarian struggle.

George Templeton Strong drew back from the intensity of the moment and remarked, "I shall not commit myself by hurrahing for Mr. Kossuth, but shall wait patiently for more light."

Aristocratic and reserved by nature, Strong had caught wind of something within the essence of the mob's emotions. "There's a strong undercurrent of No Popery feeling mixed up with the legitimate Hungary enthusiasm," he wrote, adding, "The *Freeman's Journal* has thrown cold water on the reception to the utmost of its ability, the Irish Catholics generally keep aloof from it, and people talk bitterly about Bishop Hughes and accuse him of intriguing and maneuvering to embarrass the 'Kossuth movement.' "[9]

Hughes steered clear of the scene. He was right to do so. The people of the United States waxed enthusiastic in adopting fads, heroes, and causes, only to become apathetic about them in a very brief while. "At least nine tenths of those who are sounding the glories of this martyr in the cause of free institutions . . ." Strong sneered, "would be dreadfully puzzled to find Hungary on a map of Europe without names . . ."[10]

Moreover, as much as Americans might love foreign causes they fast developed an aversion to foreigners who moved in next door. Garibaldi had arrived in New York not long before Kossuth. Discouraged and ill he had brushed aside public tributes, settled in Staten Island, and attempted to live a normal life. As soon as he had regained his health he sought work on the docks, asking for jobs in his broken English. He was refused and humiliated. As a prospective employee he was just another foreigner.

Kossuth toured about the country receiving much the same sort of treatment he had found in New York. At first only the South, fearful of anyone who might encourage internal rebellions, was cool to him. Then the Hungarian began poking into United States politics and foreign policy, telling his audiences how they should vote and why they should intervene in European affairs. He soon learned that Americans resented not only foreigners who came to stay, but foreigners who told them how to mind their business. The press began referring to his manners as pompous. The American Anti-Slavery Society published a 100-page pamphlet denouncing him after he refused to talk about slavery. By the time he returned to New York after several months on the road the public had tired of him and had focused its attention upon other idols, one of them being Lola Montez.[11]

Lola had done her best to capitalize on the political sentiments of the day, bemoaning her struggles with the reactionary Catholic Church in Bavaria. She expressed fear that she might be persecuted in the United States as well. Under the headline "Important, if true," Bennett told of her plight, adding: "Some of the Boston newspapers state that Archbishop Hughes and the Jesuits have formed a coalition with the *New York Herald* to spoil the dancing of Lola Montez. Also that the same high contracting parties have a like coalition to spoil the sale of Kossuth's Hungarian bonds. All very likely. Who knows the contrary?"[12]

Bennett was changing his first enthusiastic opinion of Kossuth, whose "puerile and whining" criticisms of America were now "read with pain by his former friends and admirers. . . . He makes a sorry figure," reported Bennett.[13] But surrendering to the Bavarian-Spanish-Irish dancer he editorially patted the hand of the little lady opening at the Broadway Theater, assured her that neither he nor the Church was capable of spoiling her debut. And, he ventured, "we presume, if there are no Jesuits in the orchestra or the pit, she will succeed in her steps with her usual facility of execution and simplicity of style."[14]

John Hughes could be drawn on occasion to the delights of the theater. Indeed, he had been so romantically enraptured with the music of Jenny Lind that he had paid her a visit at her hotel. There is no corresponding evidence that he took a seat in the pit or paid any tribute to Lola Montez. He did, however, express a deep satisfaction when in July Kossuth jumped on board the steamship *Africa* at the last moment before its departure—slipping out of the United States under the name Alexander Smith in order to avoid his creditors.[15]

Nine out of ten Americans may not have known where Hungary was on a map, but they knew Italy. The peninsula was an arsenal for nativist ammunition. In January of 1853 came reports that the Duke of Tuscany had sentenced a husband and wife, Francisco and Rosa Madiai, to fifty-six months in prison allegedly for conducting a bible meeting. Immediately the Madiais won Kossuth's place in the nation's communal heart.

Secretary of State Edward Everett asked Tuscany for an explanation. President Fillmore pleaded with the duke to release the couple and allow them to emigrate to the United States. Senator Lewis Cass, whose son was U. S. minister at the papal court, proposed laws be enacted to protect the religious rights of United States citizens in Europe. In New York several of the city's leading politicians, including Hiram Ketchum, arranged a sympathy meeting at Metropolitan Hall. A large and enthusiastic crowd, including ministers "too numerous to particularize" and an unnoticed John Hughes dressed in mufti, listened to a list of sympathetic resolutions and heard the Reverend Nicholas Murray explain that "the Jesuits were the rulers of the Duchy and not the grand Duke whose conscience they ruled."[16]

The *Freeman's Journal,* under the editorial care of the new Catholic James McMaster, cried hypocrisy. Catholics had asked for the right to speak at the Metropolitan Hall "religious liberty" meeting and had been denied. While not wishing to defend the "imbecile government of Tuscany for which we have little respect," the paper wondered if those Protestants who anguished over the Madiais's incarceration were aware that no prison could be as squalid as New York City's Tombs.[17]

As always Americans were looking through telescopes to see far-off evils while failing to notice the same evils at home. All throughout the Madiai craze, the newspapers expressed indignation that the polygamist Mormons were not made to toe the line of American morality. Even the usually tolerant Bennett wanted something done about them. He demanded "Can our government permit this unblushing imposture of Mormonism—this outrage upon decency and the social institutions and laws of the land—any longer to exist within the limits of the United States? Is it to be tolerated in civilized society?"[18] No one wanted to see a parallel with the Madiai situation. New Yorkers could also read, if they wished, of a Catholic boy named Crotty, stationed in the army at Governor's Island. A Major Sprague in early 1853 had threatened him with flogging if he refused to attend Protestant services. "These things take place, not in Tuscany . . ." accused the *Freeman's Journal*, "but in Protestant America and in the preeminently religious liberty-loving city of New York."[19]

Horace Greeley caught something of the spirit. He criticized Catholics for trying to whitewash the sins of Catholic countries, but then he walked the middle of the road and insisted upon some "plain talk with our Protestant leaders." Their present enthusiasm he felt, "seems quickened rather by hostility to the Catholics than abstract abiding love for religious freedom." He asked the ministers, "Have we ever had one word of pointed remonstrance from your body against the late intolerant Ecclesiastical Titles Act of Great Britain, adding a fresh indignity and outrage to those already inflicted on the Irish Catholics by those who hold them in bondage?"[20]

Over at the *Herald* Bennett had little interest in the defense created by McMaster. He wanted a more widely known Catholic to enter the lists. "Let our venerable Archbishop Hughes," he invited, "equip himself for the fight."[21]

Hughes seldom needed a second invitation to battle, yet he wondered why an American Catholic should be called to the defense. All that he knew of the case were the muddled stories presented in the newspapers, and he was inclined to think that more had occurred than appeared in the American press. If the story was true, then he was "quite free and quite willing to denounce the proceedings of the government of Tuscany as oppressive, unjust and cruel." But still, he pleaded, "the Catholics of this country had nothing to do with the trial and imprisonment of the Madiais. What good effect therefore will be produced by an attempt through the medium of public meetings to denounce them for an act which they had no power to accomplish or prevent?" However, as long as he was at it, he took a few swipes at the "new national policy" to protect Americans in foreign countries that was broached by Senator Cass. Before the national policy began ensuring religious liberty for its citizens on the other side of the Atlantic, Hughes felt it should make sure such liberty was enjoyed at home. "The Mormons have been obliged to seek retirement in the desert in order to enjoy what they call liberty of conscience," he wrote, "and the liberty they there enjoy would not be allowed them under the toleration of the laws of New York. Is it expected, then, in the project of General Cass, that they too shall have the privilege of exercising liberty of conscience in their peregrinations among foreign states?"

Nor did Hughes like to rake up flames in old ashes, but he wondered if the Duke of Tuscany might respond to Secretary of State Everett's demand for an explanation by asking if the secretary's home Commonwealth of Massachusetts had ever made restitution to the Sisters burned out of their convent at Charlestown.[22]

Cass was so stunned by this attack he fashioned a speech that stretched into the next session of Congress and into fourteen newspaper columns when published. The senator felt that the archbishop had been unfair with his examples, especially the burned convent. That particular outrage had been perpetrated by a mob; the duke of Tuscany was persecuting citizens under law.

Hughes shrugged off the rebuttal, noting that but for the great breadth of the senator's response its depth was such that "a child could wade through it." If anything, he said, referring to the same example, the citizens of Tuscany were better off than the Sisters in Massachusetts. The former had at least been forewarned by the law; the latter had presumed that they had a right to the law's protection. He then chastised the senator with a long fatherly epistle about the liberty of conscience, which was offered, Hughes assured him, "as a humble citizen."[23] Cass dropped the matter.

In April after New York had mistakenly mourned the death of Francesco as reported in the London *Advertiser* ("The Church of Rome has had another victim"), both Madiais were released. Bennett reported that the refugees were leaving for England and would soon be going on tour. He ventured to speculate as to what Francesco might do with the proceeds from the lectures. "Let him save his money and get all he can and come here and settle down in the country and he may yet be in time to be duly naturalized and run by some party or other as a candidate for Congress," advised Bennett. "He might do this, even here, within the immediate jurisdiction of Archbishop Hughes."[24]

The impious Bennett knew well whose beard he was pulling. The Madiais would survive well enough under John Hughes. But as Garibaldi might warn them, New York's native citizenry would love them only so long as they took pot shots at popery from Broadway's Tabernacle and returned from whence they came. If they settled down and tried to get work they would soon enough find themselves forced into the ranks of "the foreign element."

Throughout the spring of 1853 nativist groups such as the Friends of Civil and Religious Liberty and the American and Foreign Christian Union sponsored the visit of another useful foreigner, Alessandro Gavazzi. This dashing six-foot-tall ex-priest was a patriot born in Bologna who had fought in the revolution of 1848. Embittered toward the Church, he moved to England, became a Protestant, and with earnest hatred preached against popery. Had he arrived in the company of a man the calibre of Garibaldi and been moderated by his influence Gavazzi might have gained a broader and more enduring fame. As it was, he was encouraged by his enthusiastic hosts to play the part of a male Maria Monk. Instead of advertising a personalized memoir of the downfall of the Roman Republic, the list of lecture topics offered for the public's appetite included such time-proven lures as "Transubstantiation," "Priests and Nuns," "Confession," and so on.

John Hughes, as he often did, slipped in with the crowds and took an out-of-the-way seat in the Tabernacle's auditorium to judge for himself what the newcomer had to say.

Dressed in the friar's habit of his former religious order and asking "What mind is so vile as that of a popish priest?"[25] Gavazzi declared: "The popish religion is the personification of the monarchical government. In your country this large Irish emigration is intended to overthrow your American freedom. Obedience without discussion, slavery without appeal—these are the edicts of popery."[26] The newspaper accounts of the lecture recorded that his audience broke into his talk repeatedly with enthusiastic applause. Perhaps it was the sight of the one grim man sitting with his arms folded that gave Hughes away. On the occasion of a testimonial weeks afterward Reverend Cox awarded Gavazzi with a $1,000 bonus for a task well done, and avowed that he had felt "deeply honored" to have presented Alessandro to the public. "But how much more should I have felt it had I known, as I afterward did, that Archbishop Hughes was present in disguise. We have no ill-will toward Mr. John than Gavazzi himself . . . It is strange that hospitality if nothing else, should not have brought him here to give this stranger the right hand of fellowship in order to show that he is a friend to universal liberty. But then, as an American myself, I recollect that some foreign officials—some known and some unknown—cannot be naturalized, because to swear allegiance to this government they must foreswear their diligence to the greatest despot in the world!"[27]

John Hughes and his popish priests were certainly down on the mat in the eyes of New York's public. James Gordon Bennett on April 23rd drew back from his usual jibing tone and forgot for the moment that he would make the Catholic Church pay for his younger brother's seminary death. He told the American public why he believed Hughes and his breed would indeed he remembered for a great while:

> Children of Catholic emigrants not infrequently imbibe Protestant and Republican notions together. But this is an exceptional case . . . To our mind the secret of the superior success of the Catholics lies mainly if not entirely in their spiritual zeal. Where a Protestant is lukewarm a Catholic is

red hot. The Episcopal doctor must enjoy his library, his dinner, his cozy armchair; the Jesuit asks for nothing but a crust of bread, a glass of water, and a heretic to convert. The one reluctantly accepts a mission to the heathen. He carries with him his wife and children and claims for them if not for himself comforts which are incompatible with the life of an ardent missionary. A breviary and a string of beads are all the other requires. With these he will travel night and day, at all seasons, suffering with equal fortitude the extremes of cold and heat and inclement weather—subsisting on the meagre fare he can pick up by the wayside, often risking his life for his cause and deeming himself amply rewarded if after a life of incredible toil and hardship he can die a pauper on a bed of straw with the consciousness that he has brought many souls to Christ. Those who have traveled among the Indians in the far West will readily acknowledge the truthfulness of our description . . .[28]

Unlike Greeley whose crusading paper was expected to maintain a consistent moral philosophy and who lost 2,000 subscribers by nodding to Hughes, Bennett was so unpredictable that a lapse such as this was expected of him. Insulted Protestants could salve this burn and rest assured that the editor of the *Herald* would soon again remember himself and go back to roasting Catholics. And they were right.

Gavazzi was another matter altogether. He, too, was making unpredictable remarks. The explosive rebel, firing verbal grapeshot in every direction, sometimes swung the cannon toward his smug audiences. After letting them know that he despised popery, he was quick enough to tell them that he despised them as well. "I am no Protestant," he would announce to stunned nativists. "I am proud to be an Italian; and as such I disdain all Protestant denominations."[29]

By May the papers could report that he was speaking "before a rather thin audience." Like Kossuth he might well have run his course at this point. However, in June he had the accidental fortune to try a tour of more densely Catholic Canada. Riots broke out at Montreal and Quebec when he attempted to lecture. The cause of religious liberty was given a rebirth, and he returned to New York once again the hero of the hour.

At this unpropitious moment Gaetano Bedini arrived.

Rome wanted to appoint a nuncio to the United States, an official representative to handle temporal affairs with the government of the republic and at the same time to act as an ecclesiastical liaison between the Pope and his American bishops.

Apparently not having read the American newspapers, the Holy See decided to test public opinion. Archbishop Bedini had been appointed nuncio to Rio de Janeiro, and on his way he was to stop at Washington to present a personal letter of greetings from Pius IX to President Pierce. He was also to check into the internal affairs of the Church in the United States.

At least one member of the hierarchy didn't care for this procedure at all. Peter Kenrick, the brother of Francis, privately described the nuncio's anticipated visit as "anything but agreeable, being one thing in appearance and another in effect."[30] This confusion was very much at the heart of the problem. No one ever made it clear to the public whether he was a visiting prelate or the emissary of a foreign nation, the difficulty arising from the fact of a religion married to a temporal state.

Bedini's arrival in New York on June 30th, 1853 was immediately preceded by the return of Gavazzi from Canada and the arrival of a ship bearing eighty-two exiled refugees from Sardinia. The archbishop couldn't have picked a more unfortunate place or time to begin his diplomatic mission; but then again, Rome could not have picked a more unfortunate diplomat. The forty-seven-year-old Bedini was a timorous, correct man who had been engaged in papal administrative work throughout his entire priesthood. He had served as governor of Bologna—the home city of Gavazzi—during the time of the rebellions. The Austrian army under command of General Gorzskowsky had declared martial law in Bologna, rounded up the revolutionaries, and some fifty of them had been executed. One of these, Ugo Bassi, was a fellow friar of Gavazzi, and now the lecturing Alessandro turned his vengeful fire on the former governor, castigating him as the "Butcher of Bologna." The nuncio, while able to explain to Hughes that the allegations made against him were "false, wholly false and shockingly false,"[31] was unable to defend himself before the public.

Though Bedini was fluent in German, Franch, and Portuguese (besides his native Italian), Rome had sent to the United States a man who had almost no knowledge of English.

Hughes took him to Washington so he could deliver his letter. The nuncio remained at the capital through July while Hughes returned home to attend business. On the 18th he consecrated Mary Star of the Sea church in Brooklyn. It had earlier been anticipated that Bedini would arrive back in time to officiate at the occasion. As a result, the ceremony was more than usually elaborate. Immense throngs of people occupied the church grounds, and the press sent reporters to cover the event. To everyone's initial disappointment Hughes did the honors. However he was in grand oratorical form. He soon enough had the crowd laughing with his remarks, observing that Catholics enjoyed at least as much religious liberty as did the Mormons. When he finally became serious, the reporters who had gathered to write a story about the papal envoy came away instead enlightened by two facts: first they saw the strong devotion that the common people had for John Hughes, and second they realized that Hughes was seriously ill.

Apologizing that he couldn't speak in a louder voice, the archbishop reminisced about a time when a priest came to Brooklyn once a month to say Mass for some ten dozen Catholics. "And now what a spectacle is around me! . . . I ask you . . . are you ready to stand by this great work till it is accomplished? [Several voices answered "Yes, Yes, we are ready and willing."] Very well, your word is enough. When you say it I know you will do it. And when this church is completed the church itself must be a tributary to another Church [cries of "We are ready for another!"] and to another—and that to another. So I shall put no limits to church building on this Long Island, or anywhere else. And now my dear brethren, I had no intention of detaining you so long when I began, because my chest is weak." The reporter added his agreement to this, jotting at the end of the sermon: "The archbishop certainly looked considerably altered in appearance since we had last seen him."[32]

Bedini stopped at Baltimore where Archbishop Francis Kenrick judged, as his brother had, that there was more to the visit than had been announced. "Although his nunciature is nominally to the court of Brazil," Kenrick wrote, "he is a special envoy to the United States, which, I conjecture, is his real mission. He announces himself on his card, *en mission extraordinaire auprès du Gouvernement des Etats Unis* . . . I do not think that either [he or his secretary] will go to Brazil if our government desire that the Holy See have a representative here, as was the wish of Mr. Buchanan."[33]

In Philadelphia Bedini investigated a trustee problem and moved on in three days. He enjoyed social graces, and the fervent Bishop Neumann had little time for them. He bored the Italian. Returning to New York the nuncio latched onto a whirlwind. Ill or not, Hughes had work to do. He rushed Bedini off to Chicago after one day's rest. The two arrived in Milwaukee on July 30th where Hughes preached at the consecration of the new cathedral. They visited Green Bay and then Detroit where a naval captain invited the two prelates to take a ride aboard his ship. The Detroit *Tribune* raised a hue and cry that the business of the Roman Church was being carried on "at the expense of the United States Treasury."

Happy to stoke the flames of public excitement, Bennett offered a rationale for the incident. "Perhaps," he wrote, "they are in need of missionary enterprise along the lakes, and it would be a sorry thing if the government of this great Christian nation could not afford one little steamer for missionary purposes."[34]

Throughout the entire trip Gavazzi dogged the footsteps of the two prelates, sometimes in print, sometimes in person. On August 13th, the trio arrived in Saratoga, N.Y. for the consecration of St. Peter's church—Bedini consecrating, Hughes preaching, Gavazzi taking care of public relations. (*"Le bestemmie che vomito contra il papa,"* as a Milan paper described him.[35]) Alessandro wanted to stay within yelling distance for the duration, but he wanted no personal contact with the prelates. Somehow the three men inadvertently ended up in the same railroad car when they left Saratoga for Canada. Reports of the event differed sharply. One *(L'Eco d'Italia)* insisted that a man got up and led the excited passengers in three cheers for Gavazzi, then three hisses for Bedini. The actual scene was apparently played out in embarrassed silence—a silence that remained unbroken even when a boy entered the car with papers shouting: "Lecture of Father Gavazzi on the Execution of Ugo Bassi." Both parties ignored one another throughout the journey. At Lake George, Gavazzi left by the rear of the car even though his companions moved toward the front exit along with the two archbishops.[36]

As soon as he deposited the nuncio at Quebec, Hughes, burdened with a fresh cold caught at Saratoga, ended his 3,000-mile escort service and returned to New York. Not long after he arrived at Mulberry Street a man named Sassi, one of the Sardinian refugees, slipped in to the episcopal residence and warned Hughes that Bedini was going to be assassinated. Even at that moment, he warned, Italian nationalists were nearby, armed with stilettos and waiting. Hughes didn't know whether to believe the man or not, but to be safe he informed the police. Within a week Sassi was stabbed to death. Then Hughes believed.[37]

Bedini was hesitant to reenter the United States, having caught word not only of the murder but also of another rumor that Hughes wished him to stay away. Near the end of September he quietly showed up in Boston and was described by Bishop Fitzpatrick as being "in a state of terrible trepidation under the fear of conspirators against his life."[38] He seemed both relieved and joyful when Hughes invited him to consecrate the three bishops assigned to the newly created Sees of Brooklyn, Newark, and Burlington. This ceremony on October 30th was one of the grandest ecclesiastical extravaganzas New York had ever seen. Tickets to gain entry to the Mott Street cathedral went at a dollar a head. (Bedini disapproved.)

Hughes was unable to walk in the procession or take an active part in the ceremony owing to a "severe indisposition," but he preached nonetheless for the Italian archbishop. Feeling that the present state of his health marked the finale of his own career, he drew a brief history of New York's bishops, ending the short list by referring to himself as one "who will soon be removed."

With thoughts of death weighing upon his mind, Hughes hoped for some sort of peace among the Christian Churches. "Just imagine the word foreign," he said, "applied to all professing to be Christian. There are no foreigners in the Church of God."[39] With this utopian hope he sat down and the ceremony stretched into the marathon length of five hours, certainly placing many in the congregation somewhere near the same state of indisposition as Hughes. The next day the city of Newark received James Roosevelt Bayley as its first bishop. Hughes had a great liking for his former secretary and wanted very much to be present on this occasion, but he was too ill to leave the episcopal residence.

Bedini, meanwhile, traveled to Buffalo, adding Rome's weight to Bishop Timon's authority against the still-independent trustees of St. Louis church. This was the last of his official assignments, and he was anxious to be safely out of the United States. Hughes had other ideas. If the nuncio had departed then, crawling away in defeat, it would have meant a victory for the people who had instigated all the hatreds against him. His own plan was for Bedini to remain longer, even in the face of hostility, so that Catholics and well-meaning Protestants might show him the sort of honors "which without any reply in the newspapers would sufficiently put down the calumnies and the menaces of the wretched men who had so desperately assailed him."[40] Hughes might have been a man people complained about, but he was not a man people complained to. Bedini didn't have a chance. Hughes rewrote his itinerary.

In December Bedini went from city to city, greeted by holiday lights and the soft glow of his own image, burned in effigy. In Pittsburgh some toughs pushed out of a crowd and blew cigar smoke in the frightened man's face. In Ohio the Cincinnati *Gazette* hailed "the bloody butcher of Ugo Bassi" and printed his biography which now included the legend that Bedini had caused "the skin of [Bassi's] forehead and the palms of his hands to be peeled off and, he, flayed alive."[41] On

Christmas, while he was the guest of Archbishop John Purcell, a protest demonstration was arranged by the Freeman Society, a predominantly German group led by exiled 1848 revolutionaries. Some 1,200 people converged upon the cathedral carrying signs ("No priests, No Kings, No Popery"), an effigy dressed with a miter, and a gallows. The police moved in and a fight ensued. One man was killed, fifteen wounded, and sixty-three arrested.

Public opinion swung immediately to the side of the congregating freemen. It was Christmas after all, and the society itself declared the affair had been no protest riot but a protest procession. This judgment held firm even when the police attested that they had removed from the arrested persons "two swords, three pistols, one poniard, three canes or bludgeons, one sword-cane, a sheathed butcher knife and a few other weapons."[42]

In Wheeling, the press could boast that Bedini had caused only a "slight disturbance." They reported that ". . . the cathedral was surrounded by a mob while the festival was being held. The mob, however, made no demonstration of violence until those inside the cathedral had retired to their homes when the rioters threw stones, breaking the windows . . ."[43]

By the last week of December John Hughes's health had completely broken down. Father Isaac Hecker, now a Redemptorist, was leaving by steamship for New Orleans to give a mission, accompanied by his fellow convert-priests Augustine Hewitt and Clarence Walworth. Hughes was packed on board with them. From New Orleans he was sent to Cuba as the guest of the bishop of Havana. It was hoped he would regain his health in the warm climate.

This left Bedini without the strong protective shield of New York's combative archbishop. The *Journal of Commerce* had been complaining that when Hughes and the nuncio earlier visited Ward's Island the children there "were compelled to kneel down to the two foreign bishops." The *Freeman's Journal,* in its defense against this charge, forgot Bedini altogether and expressed anger that such a canard was pointed at Hughes, "An American bishop . . . He has been some time longer in this country than we have," wrote McMaster, "and we are natives of it we reckon. He was entitled to all the privileges of a citizen about a quarter of a century before we were . . ."[44]

Even some American bishops were cool to the presence of the nuncio. Peter Kenrick wrote to Purcell saying, "I consider his visit to the States to have been a blunder from every point of view."[45] Bishop Spaulding of Louisville wrote to the same prelate, commiserating with him about the Cincinnati riot, and observing: "I apprehend that one cause of [Bedini's failure] was the ambigious character in which he came. He was neither an ambassador nor a merely private individual. Had he been accredited directly to our government instead of to Brazil it might have been different . . ."[46]

Even John Hughes would later gently remind Rome that Americans liked to be dealt with in a straightforward manner. If one wished to mail a letter to the President there was always the postal system; if a government wished to appoint an envoy, it did so. "I have every reason to think," he admonished, "that if Archbishop Bedini had been commissioned directly to this government, without any previous consultation on the subject, he would have been well received."[47]

Bedini returned to New York toward the end of January to make travel arrangements—not to Brazil, but back to Rome. This time it was he who was following Gavazzi. The ex-friar had left for Rome earlier that month, promising that "the Pope must and would be destroyed."[48]

The *Herald* had been happily stirring up emotions, printing a story headlined "Attempt to Force a Young Girl into the Convent of the Sisters of Mercy at Providence." Readers who worked their way into the smaller print could find that she was a nine-year-old orphan fighting her own sister's attempts to place her in the convent school.[49] Anti-popery meetings were advertised regularly. When word was spread that a protest was to be massed against Bedini, hundreds of Irish remained gathered one night until 3 A.M. to stand guard near Hughes's house. On January 30th both the *Herald* and *Tribune* printed a long statement issued by seventy-seven "Italian Patriots." They alleged that the Italian archbishop had written in his own hand the proscription lists against the revolutionaries in Bologna. "The crime of these brave youths was that of loving the same country which you betrayed," the document protested, "and of delivering it from that religion and political yoke of iron which you fastened upon it and which you are endeavoring to extend even over this republic."[50]

Horace Greeley accompanied the statement with a damning analysis of Bedini's role in Bologna. Since no decisive evidence had been offered to prove or disprove the allegations, Greeley insisted that "common sense" had to be brought in. He described the structure of the papal government and the official secular position of governor which Bedini had occupied in Bologna. It was granted that the executions of Father Ugo Bassi and the fifty or so other rebels had been carried out by the Austrian General Gorzskowsky. Yet this man was acting in support of the papacy. He would not have killed a priest without at least tacit permission of the ecclesiastical authorities. Bedini could have stopped him and in Greeley's opinion he was at least passively responsible.[51]

On the 28th of January Metropolitan Hall, where Gavazzi had lectured, burned to the ground. The rumor spread like wildfire that it had been set on fire in retaliation by Catholics. In Boston on January 31st, word got about that the nuncio was in town disguised and ready to sail from that port. A crowd of some 500 people gathered at the Commons that night and burnt him in effigy. Meanwhile others waited to see him off at the wharf, minus an effigy and perhaps hoping for the original.

Bedini was still in New York, making plans to sail on the *Atlantic* February 3rd. Fearful of a riot, Father Jeremiah Cummings moved him to Staten Island the night before. There Bedini wrote a long letter to John Hughes, only half supressing a deep bitterness at the reception the United States had offered him. It certainly had not helped his feelings that the secular press throughout late January carried reports of Hughes's immense popularity in Cuba. Able to speak Spanish, the New York prelate—as soon as he was well enough—visited churches, preached, and mingled like a celebrity amidst congregations. The nuncio said that he trusted Hughes would find every comfort in a land ruled by a monarchy, whereas, it seemed, a democracy was unable to lawfully protect strangers.*[52]

The next morning word leaked out that Bedini was leaving from the dock of Staten Island. A crowd waited for the three-masted *Atlantic* to arrive and pick up the nuncio. Bedini had been a step ahead of them. Unseen, he and his secretary sat in a rowboat ignominiously drifting a safe distance from shore. At 1 P.M. the small steamer *Active,* chartered by a special deputy of the U.S. Marshal, picked the men up and waited another three hours until the *Atlantic* sailed majestically into view. The smaller boat tied up alongside, and as the papal envoy scrambled on board a single cannon blast—the official diplomatic salute—informed the mob on shore that they had missed their prey.

Before the arrival of Bedini nativist Americans of Philadelphia had lodged a formal protest against the use of a marble block the Pope was sending to be a part of the Washington Monument. If it was to be used in the building of the monument, the group resolved to request that a protest block be placed on top of it ("What a set of blockheads," Bennett observed.[54]) A month after Bedini's departure a mob attacked the monument and broke the Pope's block to pieces.

The nuncio wrote a wounded letter of gratitude to the archbishop of Baltimore and attempted to find reasons for which to thank the United States for its hospitality. Reprinting the note, the *Herald* commented, "He seems to be laboring under the impression that the whole people of America were embarked on a conspiracy to murder him."[55]

For John Hughes Bedini retained a thankful affection. In his official reports he agreed with others that Hughes could be too despotic and too nepotistic, but there was no denying his

---

*Ironically, Hughes wrote to Bishop Blanc the same day Bedini left New York describing the Church in Cuba: "The episcopal authority is restricted in almost every way by civil law," he observed. ". . . There is abundant wealth for the support of the Church, but I would prefer our poverty and freedom from secular restraint."[53]

value. He thereafter urged that Hughes be made a cardinal. "Everyone knows that the Archbishop of New York, Monsignor Hughes, is a skillful orator," he wrote, "and this quality, together with his resolute spirit and his untiring energy, has put him on top not only in the estimation of Catholics but of the whole nation. He enjoys in America the highest regard and influence, and this is due to the pulpit and the press. After him ranks the Bishop of Pittsburgh."[56]

When he had heard of Bedini's humiliating departure Hughes was furious. He was angry not only at the nativists but at the sickness that had prevented him from taking the protective role so natural to him. Writing to Bedini, now safely in Rome, he declared: "If I had been in New York we should have taken a carriage at my door, even an open one if the day had been fine enough, and gone by the ordinary streets to the steamboat on which you were to embark."[57]

The timorous Bedini must certainly have breathed a heartfelt prayer of thanksgiving that John Hughes's illness had kept him safely in Cuba.

24

"I KNOW NOTHING . . ."

In the 1840s nativist American politics was confined to the local and state levels. In the 1850s the rabble of immigrants who gained the power to vote made nativism a respectable sentiment for all classes of people to share, and a national party suddenly mushroomed into prominence. It arose almost mysteriously from underground and was exerting power in elections before it showed its face. When the secret societies such as the Order of the Star Spangled Banner merged into a single political movement, it willingly took for its name the response formerly given by members when questioned about secret meetings—"I know nothing."

Even Bennett with his nose for news was taken aback by the meteoric phenomenon. In 1854 he wrote: "Their mysterious movements of surprising success at several recent local elections have attracted much of the attention of that portion of the public who are not in the secrets of the new organization of native Americans. The leaders of political parties, particularly, are much puzzled to make their calculations as to the probable effect of the future movements of this mysterious order of Know Nothings . . ."[1]

Divisions in the Democratic camp, the lingering demise of the Whig party, and the confusion caused by the abolition and temperance movements caused Americans to reassess their political affiliations. They became more inclined to let their votes speak their prejudices. George Templeton Strong gave vent to his aristocratic and nativist tendencies in September upon hearing of a riot that culminated in the burning of a Catholic church. Overlooking any possibility that the gutted church might signify an innocent victim, Strong wrote:

> Another Catholic-versus-Protestant row at Newark—Irish church gutted; those infatuated pig-headed Celts seemingly the aggressors, as usual. We may well have a memorable row here before the fall elections are over, and perhaps a religious war within the next decade if this awful vague, mysterious, new element of Know Nothingism is as potent as its friends and political wooers seem to think it. I'm sick of Celtism; it's nothing but imbecility, brag and bad rhetoric. If the Know Nothings were only political, not politico-religious, I'd join them.[2]

After the fall elections the movement was less vague and mysterious. The party scored spectacular victories in a number of states, won a virtual monopoly of Massachusetts' government, and sent forty-eight men to Congress. This success conviced a great number of fence-sitters, and the party drew even more adherents.

Horace Greeley, orphaned by the death of the Whigs, didn't wish to besmudge his crusader image with the bigotry of the nativists, but he did allow that he could understand their feelings. "We have seen Irish bands of two or three hundred, armed with heavy clubs, traversing the streets on election day and clearly provoking a fight," he wrote. "We have seen men taken to courts to be naturalized and put through like a sheep washing, when they did not know what they swore and when they were in no condition to take on the responsibilities of citizenship . . ."[3]

Even Bennett gave the new party his blessing. "Calmly examined there is nothing whatever in the native creed that wears a narrow or sectarian character; nothing of which a liberal, large hearted man need feel ashamed." Like Greeley, Bennett blamed the rise of the party upon the riotous conduct of the immigrants, and specifically upon the activities of two men.

> . . . The Honorable William H. Seward, seeking to raise himself to power . . . seduced Archbishop Hughes from his pulpit and his altar and persuaded him to address an Irish

meeting at Carroll Hall, surrounded by grog-shop politicians. This drew the line between Irishmen and Americans . . . From the day the Irish were thus organized as a separate race in America, voting on principles of their own and having apparently no principles or feelings in common with the American masses—a native reaction was inevitable.[4]

One man who didn't buy any of this was John Hughes. In the *New York Daily Times* he prophesied that the Know Nothing party could not endure. "It is not a pyramid resting on broad foundations—it is merely an inverted sugar loaf. It is too narrow at the base to support its top heaviness; and even if it were not, the political heats which it is exposed to bear will melt it down, so that, though it may last for years, still in the history of the nation it will be remembered only as the disappearance of a snow shower which fell toward the end of April."[5]

Besides, Hughes couldn't pay any more attention to it because he had the Church's business to attend to. In October, while a Know Nothing convention gathered at the Odd Fellows Hall, Hughes convoked the first Provincial council of New York and met with his seven suffragans at the cathedral. As if to affront the nativists the archbishop arranged an elaborate clerical group—which numbered, it seemed, every bishop, priest, seminarian and altar boy in the Northeast—and processed them through the streets to the strains of Gregorian chant. Once in the cathedral, however, he preached sternly about political duties, letting his listeners know that even with an adopted nationality a person is "not free to be disloyal." Declared Hughes: "It is the very principle of the Catholic Church that a man's family has a third claim upon him; the second claim being that of his country. And for that country he must sacrifice property, and if necessary life itself . . ."[6]

As soon as the council was completed, Hughes left with several American bishops for Rome, there on December 8th to join Pope Pius IX in the promulgation of the Dogma of the Immaculate Conception. Coming from a place where the Roman Catholic Church was forced to fight for its existance against the powers of soapbox orators, Hughes was overwhelmed in the marble grandeur of Saint Peter's to witness the Church's strength. From the most ultramontane of hearts, he recorded the meeting with his fellow bishops:

> These men who had journeyed thousands and thousands of miles, had but just time to refresh themselves and put on their episcopal robes before they walked into the assembly; they took part in the discussion of the matter before the body in the very hour within which they had arrived. There was no comparing of notes as to what each one believed; there was no question of high doctrine or low doctrine. There was the oneness, the universality of truth—one heart, one faith and language.[7]

From this Mount Tabor of Church unity, Hughes returned to New York in early 1855 to find that he had been personally attacked in the New York State Legislature by the Know Nothing forces who were armed with a petition from the trustees at St. Louis church in Buffalo.

Two years earlier Hughes had attempted to steer a bill through the legislature guaranteeing the right of a bishop, by reason of his office, to inherit the property of his successor. The bill was defeated. Now the determined trustees of St. Louis church, whose appeal had been rejected by Bedini, attempted to overcome the spiritual power of the Church by petitioning the temporal power of the strongly nativist legislature. A bill was drawn up and presented by State Representative James Putnam to ban the ownership of church property by ecclesiastical authorities. The bill stipulated that the title to all such properties must remain in the hands of the lay corporation of each congregation.

Speaking in defense of the bill was State Senator Erastus Brooks, a stern-faced Puritan with deep-set eyes, an editor who had turned the New York *Express* into a Know Nothing mouthpiece. "I shall aim to show," Brooks intoned, "that the political state is Protestant in character—if not in its constitution—that its republican success has been mainly founded upon its Protestant religion, [and] that other systems of faith are not in harmony with true civil and religious liberty." He then went on to educate his fellow legislators as to the manner in which

Catholics were controlled by their overlords. "Let me read extracts from some of these oaths, anathemas and excommunications here," he said, "and let the intelligent judgments of men answer what must be the moral and political effect of a power concentrated all over the world and built upon a foundation of fear, despotism, and ignorance." After concluding his long list of fictional oaths, Brooks gave an example of what could happen when the menace of Romanism finally overran a country. "The seven million French citizens who voted to perpetuate the French dynasty did so with French bayonets on one side of the ballot box and French priests on the other . . ."[8]

Hughes disembarked from the *Atlantic* in late March and within a day was issuing letters to the newspapers. James Gordon Bennett was ecstatic that he was back on the scene. "Our venerable and unterrified Archbishop Hughes returns to us from Rome 'like a giant refreshed with new wine,' " he exulted, ". . . like the war-horse of Job he 'smells the battle afar off,' and like a true Celt, if there is a fight of the factions, you may count him in."[9]

This particular fight of the factions involved within one issue the two great campaigns of Hughes's life. To his mind, Catholics living in a democracy must be taught that democratic principles were not to be applied to the Roman Catholic Church structure. Protestants, secure in their ownership of the United States, must learn equally well that Roman Catholicism had a right to exist in the Republic and maintain its integrity. Without addressing the parishioners of St. Louis he reviewed the history of that Church and branded their petition as "a strange jumble of fact and fiction."[10]

William Le Couteulx, the son of the original donor of land on which the church was built, attempted to challenge Hughes on behalf of the trustees, accusing: "I can conceive your displeasure on finding that some Catholics had been so bold as to seek at the hands of their legislature the maintainence of some temporal rights which they had enjoyed for many years, sanctioned by the civil laws of the country and which you wanted to wrest from them, in virtue of a decree of Baltimore!. . ."[11]

Hughes followed his usual pattern. He refused to answer Le Couteulx. It was not the task of a bishop to debate with his laity. Rather he went after the Know Nothing Brooks. The senator had gone to the pains of investigating the apparent personal wealth of Hughes. In the legislature he described the Roman prelate as being five times a millionaire, judging from the church property assigned to his name—"not to John Hughes, Bishop, nor to John Hughes, Archbishop, nor to John Hughes as trustee for the great Roman Catholic Church, but to plain John Hughes in his *propria persona.*"[12]

Hughes responded to this in the *Courier and Enquirer,* sarcastically lamenting that Brooks had cheated him, for the *Presbyterian* had earlier credited him with $25 million. He generously offered that, if the honorable senator could show where his great surplus of wealth lay, he would be glad to donate a public library for the use of New Yorkers. Brooks wished no levity injected into the issue. "I have no time," he retorted, "to waste in humor, evasion or words . . ."[13] Then followed an avalanche of words—returned in kind by a corresponding avalanche from Hughes. Together the two men roamed through every piece of real estate the Church possessed in New York, weighing its actual value, nitpicking the deeds like two lawyers settling a property dispute.

Bennett grew impatient. He decided the whole matter was nothing more than "a waste of words upon quibbles, catches and technicalities." He advised Hughes to be magnanimous: "Having gained the great cardinal declaration of the Immaculate Conception of the Blessed Virgin he can well afford to lose two or three millions of dollars. Why should he lament this filthy lucre. Let him 'lay up his treasures in heaven where neither moth nor rust doth corrupt' . . ."[14]

Rarely did Hughes and Brooks get away from pricing steeples long enough to look at the issue—The Catholic Church's right to own property in its own name. Hughes declared that the Putnam Bill should have been labeled "a penal enactment requiring Roman Catholics of the State of New York to be governed in the enjoyment and use of their own property set aside for ecclesiastical purposes, not by the discipline of the Religion which they profess, but by the statute of the legislature."[15] Brooks agreed that this was precisely the point. "It seems that the Protestant United States," he said, "are to be the only country in the world besides the Papal States in which the old Middle Ages rights of the Pope are to be maintained, at least according to John Hughes."[16]

As with most other polemical arguments of the day the two combatants thrashed about over acres of newspaper columns. In doing so they offered occasional entertainment to those of the reading public willing enough to dig through haystacks of arguments in search of needling insults. These people could delight to find that Brooks decided of Hughes: "In personality and vulgarity he has reached an elevation to which I do not aspire."[17] And that Hughes, in turn, judged that Brooks "has exhibited himself in the light of a man who has no regard for veracity, and who is therefore utterly unworthy of notice. I take him consequently with covered hands to the nearest open sash of window and send him forth with the single mental observation: 'Go hence, wretched and vile insect, the world has space for you as well as me.' "[18]

The wretched and vile insect—being a wasp—imparted a goodly sting before he took off. In late April the Putnam Bill became law. The *Herald* reported that Hughes had met defeat "unless the Catholics of his congregation are as devoutly submissive to his mandates as Catholics used to be to clerical mandates in the middle ages," in which case "the state may find itself two or three millions richer one of these fine days—a consummation by no means to be despised at a time when canal mismanagement has reduced us to a state of quasi-bankruptcy."[19]

In fact, nothing happened. After all the flurry, Hughes decided that the law was "exceedingly silly and even if carried out would be more annoying than injurious."[20] It remained a dead letter; before a decade passed it was written off the books. What was important, as far as Hughes was concerned, was that he had not remained silent while Know Nothings and disobedient Catholics had publicly held the Church up to ridicule. Of his debate with Brooks, the *Herald* observed, "Both of the combatants retire from the field with colors flying and trumpets sounding, but both at the same time rather damaged by the melee."[21]

Neither warring party seemed to think so. Both issued for the sake of posterity a volume containing the speeches and letters of the dispute—each eliminating the most damaging assaults of the other. Hughes's edition, called *Brooksiana,* carried ads for *Haydock's Catholic Family Bible* and Dunigans's "New and Cheap Standard Catholic Publications." Brooks's publication, entitled *The Controversy between Senator Brooks and '†John' Archbishop of New York*, advertised several books on its back pages, including *The Mysteries of Rome in the Nineteenth Century, The Mysteries of the Jesuits,* and *The Secret History of the Inquisition*—"all illustrated."[22]

That the Putnam Bill had little effect was not owing to the will of its instigators. The meteoric rise of the Know Nothings through 1855 turned into as fast a downfall in 1856. As Hughes had predicted, anti-immigrant and anti-Catholic sentiment had been too narrow a base upon which to build a broad political strategy. Slavery was fast becoming the issue all of America was concerned about. The new Republican party, nominating John Frémont for the presidency, became a home for those former Whigs sympathetic to the abolitionist cause. The Know Nothings, endorsed by the remnant of Whigs who still labeled themselves such, put forward former President Millard Fillmore. Fillmore, desperately ambitious for another crack at the presidency, accepted this nomination, even though he had always been polite to Catholic leaders such as Hughes. At the time of the Know Nothing convention Fillmore was in Rome where his pleasant manners, according to the *Herald,* caused him to be "so graciously received by the Pope as to be exempted altogether from the ancient custom of kissing his big toe."[23] Against these two candidates the Democrats unitied behind former Secretary of State James Buchanan.

At the onset of the campaign, Hughes issued a lengthy denial to all concerned that he was interested in politics, a denial that was received with guffaws by the press. And yet, he was on firm ground. He had been extremely vocal about issues. And when the Church was directly involved, as with the Carroll Hall ticket or the Putnam Bill, he entered the political arena without hesitation. But he steered clear enough of partisan politics. Unlike the mass of Catholics who gathered under the banner of the Democrats, he personally leaned toward the Whig and Republican parties. Nevertheless he avoided entanglements with politicians, and he had voted in only one election—casting a vote for Henry Clay. His friendships with Thurlow Weed and William Seward, begun during the school controversy, were genuine and reciprocal. Both men possessed portraits of Hughes. In 1855 when Weed was working against strong odds to have the New York Legislature send Seward back to the U.S. Senate, a group of Know Nothings were invited to dinner at Weed's residence. Touring the house with Hugh Hastings, a Weed lieutenant in the legislature, the men suddenly came upon the picture of Hughes in pontifical vestments. When they suspiciously asked who it was, Hastings panicked for a moment, then, impulsively, took them to task for not knowing George Washington in his continental robes. The Know Nothings immediately hastened to recognize the general, the day was saved, and Seward was reelected.[24]

In the presidential election when General Winfield Scott was pitted against Franklin Pierce, both parties wooed the Irish vote by playing up the anti-Catholicism of the opposing candidate. Hughes had developed a friendly acquaintanceship with Scott. Still he neutralized the ugly situation by issuing a statement to the effect that the country would be safe in either man's hands.[25]

In 1856 he again had a personal attachment to one of the candidates. The Buchanans, although Protestant, hailed from the same part of Northern Ireland as Hughes's family. It became a basis of friendship when the two men got to know each other during the Mexican War. There is little doubt that Hughes was happy to see the former secretary of state nominated for the presidency. Nonetheless, he remained silent throughout the campaign.

The Know Nothings did their best to eclipse slavery with bigotry. William Hogan, ready as ever to help out, issued a couple of volumes—*Popish Mummeries* and *Popery as it was and Is*. Tammany Hall, Hogan surmised, was merely a tool of John Hughes who was a "demure plotting dunce" as well as a Jesuit. Hughes would soon be running the country. "Witness the difference between B. Hughes of New York and the trustees of a Roman Catholic Church in Buffalo," he warned. The Buffalo affair, he said, was "referred to the Pope who decided the matter without any respect or regard to the laws of this government."[26] Hogan tended to hit below the belt. Illustrated by a picture of a man on horseback, with drawn pistols, chasing after a fleeing priest, Hogan's article fantasized: "Suppose the Popish bishop of New York were a young, athletic, amorous man; suppose he fixes his eye upon a young married woman, or some fascinating lady of his flock. He goes after her. A roving friar absolves all and returns home to Rome. No one here will know. Another new friar replaces him . . . and thus the work of seduction and immorality go on from year to year."[27]

With three parties in the field, rumors began to spread that deals were being made behind the scenes. In September both the *Tribune* and the *Herald* reported that the Democrats were busy manipulating. "Extraordinary bargain and sale," screamed the *Herald*. "The New York Irish Catholics to be sold out to the Know Nothings." In order to secure the state for Buchanan it was supposedly being arranged that the Know Nothing politicos would throw support behind him on the national ticket while the Democrats would give leverage to the Know Nothing gubernatorial candidate, Senator Erastus Brooks. This was a dastardly thing to do to the Irish, reasoned Bennett, for "to be sure he hates the Catholics and their religion as the devil hates holy water." "Where is the venerable father Archbishop Hughes?" Bennett asked. "It is time to wake him up. It is invariably when the shepherd is absent or asleep that the flock is invaded, cut up and dispersed in the wilderness. Awake. Arise, Oh Shepherd! for the wolf, yea, a pack of wolves are peeping through the bars."[28]

Hughes gave no indication privately or publicly that he cared how the sheep might disperse and vote. He certainly loathed Erastus Brooks, but he would do nothing to keep him out of the governor's mansion. His newspaper, the *Freeman's Journal,* was becoming something of an embarrassment to him. McMaster was more and more vehement in his pronouncements. He was bitterly opposed to Frémont. Along with the Know Nothings he supported a whisper campaign that had started against the Republican candidate, spreading the word that when Frémont had eloped as a young man he had been married before a Roman Catholic priest. Did this mean that he had been, or was still in secret, a Catholic? The rumors, denied, were spread all the more widely.

Bennett, who was beginning to tire of the Know Nothings, admonished his readers: "The religion of a candidate is of no more concern to the citizens at large than his views on the plurality of worlds, the age of the old red sandstone, the development theory as applied to acari, or any other highly interesting and warmly controverted question of science. His religion rests between him and his God."[29]

McMaster didn't think so. He declared time and again that Frémont was not playing true. He had definitely avowed himself at one time, so claimed the *Freeman's Journal,* to have been a Catholic. Hughes divorced himself from the paper, asking McMaster to cease mentioning him in its columns. For the sake of the public he issued a card disassociating himself from any of the attacks upon Frémont. Beyond this he said nothing.

Even into the last weeks of the campaign when the question of slavery predominated, a paper as far away as the Charleston *Courier* would write an open letter to John Hughes, asking him whether the Catholics of the United States would sanction disunion.[30] He still refused to involve himself. It was not his business.

Henry Ward Beecher was more than happy to comply to such requests, but Bennett was not interested in his ideas. By way of a fast "Oh shut up" he recorded: "Parson Beecher calls upon the people 'to pray' at the next election. He is an old ass. Vote first, and pray as much as you please afterwards."[31]

As long as Hughes was determined to play the sphinx, the *Herald* decided to settle Frémont's religious status once and for all.

"At last the truth is coming out," the paper announced.

"On evidence given elsewhere it is clearly shown that John Charles Frémont is a Jew. Now if he is not a Jew, let him come out over his own signature and say so; and also let a jury of physicians examine him and report whether or not he has been circumcised."[32]

Frémont—circumcised or not—lost the election to Buchanan. The infant Republican party, however, had done well for itself. In another four years it would be a power to contend with. The Know Nothings, so brilliant the year before, placed a poor third. Erastus Brooks was defeated in the governor's race, and Millard Fillmore carried only one state. The religious issue, though by no means dead, was pushed somewhat to the background as the nation geared itself for a showdown about sectional differences and the United States' peculiar institution.

25

THIS OUGHT TO BE
LEFT TO OUR ENEMIES

John Hughes was a good shepherd to have around whenever wolves endangered the flock. In the absence of external dangers his sheep were not unanimous in appreciating the sound of his voice. With the demise of the Know Nothings, and with the nation turning its concentration to issues that would soon bring about its disunion, Hughes could turn his attention to the unity of Catholicism. His fame, however, both as priest and bishop, had been built upon his defense of the immigrant Church. His nature was geared for polemics; he had little talent for the give-and-take of personal diplomacy.

The Church was moving toward a new tension point. When Hughes was ordained in 1826 the Irish clergy were fighting against the continuance of a French-oriented hierarchy. In the 1850s a budding generation of American-born clergy and laity was sizeable enough to make its resentment of an Irish-born hierarchy felt. John Hughes had served one generation's needs. He was beginning to serve a second generation whose needs were not entirely the same.

In the summer of 1853 the New York daily *Times* edited by Henry J. Raymond ran two long articles setting forth this situation: "Infallibility is scratching its temporal head within the Vatican at Rome . . . Know Nothingism has broken out in the form of Roman Catholic bishops on this side of the Atlantic."

According to the articles there existed a sharp division between the native and foreign-born members of the hierarchy. The foreign-born opposed "with some warmth the well-known desire throughout the country among good Catholics to retain possession and control of the temporalities of their Church." The native-born bishops, on the other hand, disagreed "that the genius of the Roman Catholic Church is eminently monarchical. They are disposed to believe it republican."[1]

Hughes branded the observations as "ridiculous," and stated that the appearances of disunity in the largely immigrant Church were created largely by the Irish revolutionaries of 1848, who after moving to the United States continued to blame their own failures upon the priests who had not rallied the people to their cause.[2]

Hughes held no more respect for the emigrating Irish rebels than he had for Kossuth. He never accepted Thomas D'Arcy McGee, even though by the early 1850s McGee was praising the archbishop for his views on education and strongly urging Catholics to teach their children about religion. Two other prominent Young Irelanders arrived in the United States, Thomas Francis Meagher and John Mitchel. They quickly inaugurated a newspaper—the *Citizen*—in December of 1853. The Protestant Mitchel, who had escaped from British captivity and who traveled in disguise as a priest had been hailed as an almost conquering hero in New York. He began dictating political opinions to the Irish as if he had been on the American scene for decades instead of weeks.

Angry at Hughes who had not mentioned him by name in his response to the *Times,* Mitchel slashed away at the archbishop through a series of six letters, heartily laden with insults. He ranged far and wide, endorsing the political ouster of the Pope whom he judged "a bad prince," and agreeing with the *Times* about the tension within the Church. "Plain people who do not look down from high eminences," he boasted to Hughes, "think it a proof that native Americanism does exist among Catholics."[3]

Hughes kept a stony silence. It was just as well, for Mitchel was defeating himself without any outside help. Among the public positions he had taken was a lusty endorsement of slavery. Ireland's would-be liberator declared that he would be happy to have "a good plantation, well stocked with healthy negroes in Alabama."[4] According to Bennett's *Herald* "The announcement was not what is called in stage dialect—'a hit.' "[5]

Having alienated just about everyone in the whole social spectrum, Mitchel escaped from New York—on this trip opting for street dress rather than clerical garb—and as a parting shot he warned Catholics to keep out of "the hands of Irish priests." He moved to the South where he had pleased at least one faction of the American public, there to seek and hopefully own healthy Negroes. Sometime after this, he reflected about some of the blunders he had made while sojourning in the North. "I would if I could, erase from the page and from all men's memory, about three fourths of what I then wrote and published to the address of Archbishop Hughes," he said. "This I say not by way of atonement to his memory—for he deserved harsh usage and could stand it and repay it—but by way of justice to myself only."[6]

Meagher remained in New York. Like McGee he gradually began to adjust his behavior, a rebel emeritus wishing to be a respectable citizen. Hughes occasionally treated him as an erring Catholic from whom he expected obedience. In turn Meagher would assure his archbishop that he remained always mindful "of the duty I owe my religion and my country."[7] To vent the frustrations from such subservience Meagher went instead after a layman, James McMaster, who attacked him routinely in the *Freeman's Journal*—that paper being in the eyes of most New Yorkers the archbishop's organ ("not the organ which plays the tunes in high Mass," explained Bennett, "but the organ that pitches and plays the tunes in low politics.")[8] Having been forewarned of an attack, McMaster armed himself with a heavy cane and gun. When the two men finally encountered each other on the street Meagher grabbed McMaster by the collar, the latter flailed ineffectively with the cane, pulled the gun out and in the scuffle fired wildly. They were pulled away, neither of them hurt. The two good Catholics, one foreign born, the other native, then gave the lie to the charge that there was no unity in the Church. Neither of them pressed charges.[9]

The *Times* articles had described both Thomas D'Arcy McGee and Orestes Brownson as Catholics with republican tendencies. Both men had accused the Irish of incurring nativist resentments by their bad habits and their refusal to be assimilated into the American scene. Hughes expected as much of McGee. His relationship with Brownson was more complicated. The Yankee convert and the immigrant prelate were both fiercely independent, domineering, larger-than-life characters. They could never have so much as sat in the same room together without dividing it into two camps. For his part Brownson always allowed Hughes the final public say out of respect for his episcopal authority. Hughes never trusted the directions in which Brownson's logical mind might take him, and he was often abrasive in the use of the authority that Brownson allowed him, but through thick and thin he maintained both a respect and a genuine affection for the volatile editor.

Shortly before his argument with the *Times,* Hughes had rebuked Brownson for his strong observations on the Irish and had received a wounded reply. Hughes quickly assured the convert that "I am exceedingly sorry if I have occasioned you any pain—that would be far from my intention." Both men were sensitive to being hurt, even though both could often be guilty of hurling journalistic harpoons into others. Perhaps speaking for both, Hughes admitted the need of talking things over: "The written language is oftentimes liable to be misapprehended by the reader, whereas if the writer were present to explain, the misunderstanding might easily be removed."[10]

Their clashes were to become more increasingly acrimonious. Brownson had moved his *Review* from Boston to New York in 1855. After a short duration of being squeezed into that small metropolis with Hughes, however, he moved across the river in 1857 to the freedom of Newark and the friendly understanding of a fellow convert, Bishop Bayley. "I will suffer no man in my diocese that I cannot control," Hughes had told

Brownson. "I will either put him down, or he shall put me down."[11]

Brownson addressed the graduates at Fordham in 1856, and in the course of his remarks said that the climate of America was ideally suited to Catholicism, for the country's founding fathers had based the American order not on Protestant tenets but on the natural law as expounded by the Catholic Church. Hughes who was present interpreted this to mean that Brownson thought the Church should be "presented to the American people through mediums and under auspices more congenial with the national feelings and habits." When Brownson returned to his seat on the podium Hughes whispered to him that he hadn't liked the spirit of the talk. However he did agree in the hushed debate that nothing had been said which was against Church teachings. Much, then, to Brownson's shock Hughes took advantage of his own few minutes of closing remarks to make "hostile and ironic allusions" to what had been said in the speech.[12]

This needling greatly amused the audience, including Thomas D'Arcy McGee, who took pains to interpret the incident to the readers of his *American Celt* as being a heavier slap at Brownson than Hughes had intended. Embarrassed, Hughes apologized to Brownson: "I repudiate the malicious construction which one of our weekly papers has put upon my observations at the late commencement at St. John's College." He added by way of conciliation, "We have all looked upon you as belonging to the whole Catholic Church."[13]

Brownson was not quite ready to accept the peacepipe. The disputed issue had not been a point of doctrine and Hughes had admitted this to Brownson prior to speaking. Then he had employed an unfair advantage. "It was opposing to me a layman, the opinions of an Archbishop," he said. ". . . There was no equality in the case. It was crushing me with the weight of authority in a matter of simple opinion . . . Your remarks, however intended by you, were an episcopal censure upon me and I can see no reason why the *American Celt* had not the right so to consider them."[14]

If Brownson was wary of episcopal authority, Hughes

worried constantly about the disunity fostered by the Catholic press. By the end of 1856 he wanted nothing to do with the fiercely nationalistic Irish papers. McMaster had been a constant embarrassment to him throughout the presidential campaign. The deeply philosophical Brownson, who had traveled so many routes on his way to Catholicism, was still a question mark to Hughes. Yet Brownson's *Review* spoke the Church's mind to a good number of Protestant Yankees. Wishing to pour oil on the waters, Hughes published in December an article—"Reflections and suggestions in regard to what is called the Catholic press in the United States." In a gentlemanly enough way for a man who wanted no differences of opinion voiced, he cited the various divisions between the "first and second generation of emigrants," the different nationalities, the Yankee and foreign Catholics, the born-Catholics and the converts, the political divisions among editors, and then pleaded for unity—or more precisely unanimity of expression. "In brief," he asked, "are the union, happiness, charity, family ties of a united Catholic people to be disturbed, or even trifled with, at the discretion, or rather indiscretion, either of this editor or of that other? . . . This is unbecoming. This is not Catholic. This ought to be left to our enemies."[15]

But some of his enemies were Catholic. One month after this the New York daily *Times* printed a long, bitter attack against Hughes, almost certainly written by one of his priests, and signed only as "Equitas." Equitas described Hughes as the sort of man who sees a fight and sails into it, beating away with terrible effects on all parties indiscriminately. Then, when asked afterward what side he had been on, he would invariably answer that he never battled for party. He always fought for fun, and generally on his own hook. So Equitas described the archbishop's battle against all the factions of disunity in the Catholic press. But the real goal of Hughes, he alleged, was not to fight disunity. Of real disunity he was unaware, for he never listened to anyone, especially his priests. "He has seldom, if ever, called them together or condescended to ask their opinion or advice on this or any other subject. Or if he did, it was to let them retire under the mortification of knowing that their opinion was of no possible consequence . . ."

Equitas did have a suggestion for effecting Catholic unity, and this he presented at the conclusion of his exposé: "In my opinion, and in the opinion of many good Catholics," he proposed, "the Archbishop would manifest more of the tone and spirit not only of a bishop but of a Christian, by retiring from political strife and devoting the few short days of his declining life to the good of his people."[16]

Conditioned as he was to public attack, Hughes was nevertheless stunned and hurt by the article. He wrote to Raymond, demanding of him to "meet the legal consequences of that libelous article or to make known the writer's name."[17] The latter option, viewed from a purely democratic point of view, would have of course afforded Equitas the perfect opportunity of facing Hughes with the opinions he had theretofore not been able to express "on this or any other subject." Like a good newsman Raymond withheld the name until he obtained the permission of his supposed source—an elderly priest named McElroy, stationed at St. Mary's church in Boston. Only then did the editor learn from a horrified McElroy—so unlikely a candidate for authorship as to be perfect front—that the use of his name had been a forgery. Equitas remained untraceably safe behind his mask. Raymond publicly apologized for having fallen prey to "this criminal mode of striking a cowardly blow . . . and imposing upon the editor of the *Times* so far as to make it the means of giving effect to his double malignity."[18]

Apologies aside, the malignity remained—a portrait drawn of John Hughes for the man on the street as seen through the eyes of his clergy. It hurt deeply, and it put this man who was so totally a loner by nature even more on the defensive. There was no use seeking the villain. Hughes had made more enemies than friends, but his outspoken opponents would never have stooped to such a ruse. Equitas might well have been the most fawning and outwardly contented cleric in the diocese. It made Hughes unsure of himself, much more than the attacks would have if he had enjoyed any semblance of good health. Equitas had made him seem a man of the past, an outdated tyrant who obstructed the best interests of the Church.

He was in this frame of mind when a young priest, Father

Jeremiah Trecy of Nebraska, requested an interview with him in March of 1857. With the blessing of Bishop Mathias Loras of Dubuque, Trecy had come to recruit settlers for an Irish colony in the West. The idea was not new. Several attempts at colonization had failed in the past, including one attempted by John England. Neither the impoverished Irish who arrived and remained on the eastern seaboard throughout the 1840s and 1850s, nor the more established Irish who preceded them, had possessed the means of setting up workable organizations that would bring such dreams to fruition.

In 1854 Bishop Loras began advertising the benefits of western settlement, employing first the Boston *Pilot* and then the *Freeman's Journal*. He wanted to mislead no one. There were advantages to moving West but there were hardships to overcome as well. He warned prospective settlers that two years of privation had to be expected before they might enjoy any comforts. There would be spiritual deprivation too. He had few priests, and he confessed that he had found it necessary to remove a resident priest from one area where the people could not support him. His hope was that the Irish by moving to this land would "make it Catholic." Declared the bishop, "There is no doubt that the Almighty supplies by his divine providence this want of churches and clergymen for a while."[19]

The lack of Church structure was enough to blacken the idea in John Hughes's mind. He had begun his priesthood in a democracy of Catholics who had existed without the hierarchy. It had made Protestant-Catholics out of them. He had spent thirty years of his life battling people who refused to obey proper religious superiors. Nor did he want to see settlers without priests fall prey to the well-financed and zealous Protestant missionary societies.

In 1855, at the same time he was fighting the Buffalo trustees in the New York State Legislature, James Shields, a Mexican War hero and former United States senator, came East to sell the idea of an Irish colony in Minnesota. When he presented his ideas to a group of Catholics in one of New York's churches, the archbishop disputed with him on the spot. When Shields had finished speaking Hughes got up and discouraged any plan that would leave Catholics deprived of contact with the Church. Afterward Shields angrily told Hughes, in private, that he "could not see beyond the length of his nose." The people would build churches, he insisted, adding: "They would not only benefit themselves, but would prove benefactors to your poorly paid and apparently half-fed curates, one of whom they would invite to come and dwell in their midst as their honored parish priest."[20] In Shields's account (the only one extant) this aggressive response ended the conversation. Speechless, Hughes turned and walked away.

In February of 1856 "The Irish Catholic Convention for the Promotion of Actual Settlements in North America" met in Buffalo—bringing together some ninety-five deligates, clergy and laymen. One semiconcrete result of the four-day meeting was a resolution that men of means (wherever they might find them in the Irish community) would buy western lands and sell them in lots to the poorer Irish. The plan was soon blessed by the bishops of Pittsburgh, Dubuque, Buffalo, and Wheeling.

Unfortunately, one of the key figures at the Buffalo convention was Thomas D'Arcy McGee whom Hughes still judged by the light of 1849's battles. In his Boston-based Irish paper, the *American Celt,* McGee pushed the project hard. With his talent for a tactless approach he argued the case by insulting the Irish for being what they presently were, "a horde of hardy, vulgar ruffians, unmatched in any former state of society."[21] It was no way to win over either the members of the horde or their spirited spiritual leader who had spent his adult life telling America that the Irish were not a "horde of hardy, vulgar ruffians."

These arguments, set before the public, caused McGee, his paper, and, sadly, the Buffalo convention to come under the criticism of Hughes. In his "Reflections" upon the Catholic press, Hughes branded such an indictment of his people to be "insolent and untrue." Despite the great numbers of immigrants, he argued, there was another side of the story to be told:

> If the writer of the above extract had been pleased to look around him in the city of New York, he could easily have discovered that neither is the first generation neglected, nor the second lost. He could have reported to his countrymen

in Ireland or elsewhere, that within his own memory, and under his own eyes, colleges, seminaries, convents, schools, altogether ranging from the highest education to the very humblest elements of learning have sprung up around him. He could have reported that within the same circle there are not fewer than two hundred and fifty ladies and gentlemen, the great majority of whom are devoted to God in a religious life, who are directly or indirectly engaged in imparting Catholic instruction, blended with secular and useful knowledge. He could have reported that they had under their care an average of from 12,000 to 15,000 Catholic pupils . . .

He agreed that life in the cities could be harsh upon the immigrants. "But this is incident to their transition from one country to another. And it is but truth to say that their abode in the cellars and garrets of New York is not more deplorable nor more squalid than the Irish hovels from which many of them have been 'exterminated.' "[22]

It was after Equitas had hacked away at John Hughes and his notions of Catholic unity that Jeremiah Trecy paid his call at the archbishop's residence. Trecy had been Bishop Loras's official representative at the convention, and now he was in town to advance the project. His request of the archbishop was a simple permission to say Mass while in his diocese. Hughes gave this readily enough and even discussed the idea of colonization with Trecy. He certainly could not have believed, as he claimed in the "Reflections," that if the emigrants deserted New York for the West there would remain "hardly Catholics enough to keep the grass from growing green in the vestibules of the Churches."[23] Nonetheless he backed down only so far as to admit that he had once hoped for the means to start a colonization project, but having realized that such a venture could only fail, he had encouraged individuals—not groups—to travel westward only when their resources allowed them to do so. Trecy left after this conversation without informing Hughes that he planned to deliver a lecture within a few days time at the Broadway Tabernacle. It was this omission that earned him Hughes's wrath.

The day of the advertised talk James Roosevelt Bayley

ιe Irish had moved West in a steady network, while
ests had moved with them. In his estimation this was
method of assimilation. These immigrants were not
st from the Church, and they were becoming intergrat-
he American community.

ıry J. Raymond left for Europe. In his absence some-
) sounded very much like Equitas wrote two more
ous articles for the *Times*. The new letter declared that
of the Hughes administration the New York arch-
was "a chaos without form and void. Not even an ar-
·al structure worthy of a powerful and wealthy com-
–not an institution of learning that commands respect
. can point to his grace as founder and sustainer." It
ε, the writer concluded, for the appointment of a coad-
ιo might compensate for the inadequacies of John
30

ghes was too stung by the public chastisement to let the
)ass. Using Greeley's *Tribune* he answered the charges
ıvisible opponent. He denied that he was about to be
aside. "The Archbishop of New York has not the
idea of asking for a coadjutor, and that there is not
ttest probability of one being appointed during his life,
t his own request," Hughes wrote. "Then as to resigna-
will take that into serious consideration about the year
his life should be prolonged to that remote period."31
pite this public and unnecessary bravado Hughes was
d by the attack. He could not help but wonder who, or
ny, of his priests found representation in the scathing
f Equitas. And yet his sense of devotion to the Church
n a perspective beyond his own faults. In answer to a
ho had openly and directly criticized him he openly and
responded, "Of course I take to myself so far as I
st, the admonition which it contains. I would observe,
, that a thousand things such as you refer to, pass and
ss unheeded by the Catholic people to whom God has
ε gift of faith, if not of theological education. This is
rotection in spite of our blunders with regard either to

came across the river to inform Hughes that rumors claimed
the archbishop of New York was in favor of the colonization
plan. Angrily, Hughes decided to clear the air with a public letter addressed to the bishop of Newark. After Bayley left he
spent hours composing a draft that "without questioning the
purity of motives" of those who had been at the Buffalo convention judged the plans formed at this meeting to be nothing
more than "silly theories." "Their language" he decided, "is in
substance as addressed to their Catholic fellow countrymen,
'Go you, we stay.' "24 He finally got himself so worked up
against the project he bundled himself up and without saying a
word to anyone stalked off through the wintry streets to the
lecture.

The advance publicity for a talk on colonization had not
set the New York Irish on fire. The *Times* described the audience in the Tabernacle for the occasion as being "rather limited."25 Several priests and Thomas D'Arcy McGee sat behind
Father Trecy as he portrayed the future glories of St. Patrick's,
Nebraska, where streets would be named after cities in Ireland
—Limerick, Dublin, Kilkenny—and where the atmosphere,
freed of nativist hostility, would be of Irish making. He finished his presentation—having informed his audience that
Archbishop Hughes had himself once favored such a plan,
when suddenly a sharp voice turned the attention of the audience to the back of the hall. "Wait a moment," the voice said,
"I have a word to say." A man was standing in the galleries,
his scarf still half covering his face. "Come on the stand then,"
someone shouted. "No I shall not," he answered, removing the
scarf, "I would rather be by myself."

Recognized immediately by the crowd, Hughes employed
the galleries as a pulpit and castigated Trecy for seeking permission to celebrate the divine mysteries while omitting that he
intended to harangue meetings for the pure purpose of land
speculation. Pointing to McGee he said that the project had
been instigated by an editor with "nothing else to write about."
He did not question the goodness of the people at the Buffalo
convention, but still he saw nothing but hollowness there.
"What had those gentleman done for the emigrants?" he

asked. "Oh! They had done the office of—What did they call it?—they had performed the office of signposts and crossroads, but they had done nothing themselves. Was there a priest or layman who had moved West himself? Not one. But some of those who had land to sell were the promoters of this project; they had a bad principle at the bottom of it; there was not truth, there was not sincerity in it."[26]

Angrier at the underhanded invasion of his domain than he was over the project itself, Hughes was swinging wildly, much as Equitas had described him. His blows were pummeling fellow bishops, well-meaning philanthropists, friends, and, if he stopped to consider, foes who were not really enemies. Gradually he moved from the personalities involved to the project itself. He told his listeners not to be fooled by any *"coleur de rose"* portrait of the West. Not only were there hardships aplenty there, but since the passage of the Kansas-Nebraska Act that area had been the focal point of much of the nation's troubles: "The gentleman had said there was nobody to disturb the settler there. But had that been the fact in Kansas, and was there any reason for them to expect better?"

Above all, what Hughes opposed was the creation of any "little Irelands." He had developed a strong sense of patriotism to his adopted nation, and though he never would have admitted it to Brownson he was very close to the reviewer's ideas about the need for Americanizing the Church. He disapproved of national parishes. Much of the difficulties at St. Louis church in Buffalo had come from a reluctance on the part of a German communty to share their parish with the incoming Irish. It had been German nationalists in Cincinnati and Italians in New York who fostered and spurred the nativist attacks on Bedini. John Hughes wanted Catholicism to be a single force, not a chain of disconnected ghettoes, and he wanted to see this unified Catholic community accepted by and socially assimilated into native America. "Suppose they succeed in forming settlements exclusively Irish, and speaking Irish," he proposed to the small crowd in the Tabernacle. "Why, by and by they would become as distinct as the Mormons."[27]

Hughes finished by saying that he approved of individual

emigration to the West, but that he
who worked as agents for land sp
and attempted to say that he had
that he was not a land speculator,
not mentioned the lecture while vi
because he had not thought it nec
He said that the suppression of tr
the spoken lie, and that Trecy's a
according to the *Herald*, "while
overcome their surprise at his grac
and his way homeward."[28]

If Hughes was at fault in cru
when his support would have gi
nonetheless difficult to find where
the movement existed. A propose
low up the Buffalo convention nev
ject, which certainly began well en
John Hughes, dwindled quite apa
organization and funds.

As Equitas had found, John
attack. He had been around a lo
deal of power to himself; he could
and he made a good many mistal
porary critics in this instance w
small dogs yapping at the aging li
fighting for, there should have bee
with the same force that Hughes
believed in—perhaps one of those
stamp of approval on the project
West if they had been given the
rural country with memories of m
life and city politics with a gregari
the masters of eastern city gover
had wallowed in slums. But millio
ing upward and had spread out th
might have stopped and got work
Utica—or they might have gone
Hughes had told the Tabernacle c

which
their p
the be
being
ed into

H
one w
anony
becaus
diocese
chitect
munity
and th
was ti
jutor
Hughe

H
matter
of his
shunte
slighte
the sli
except
tion, h
1879, i

D
depress
how m
words
gave h
priest
directly
think j
howeve
must p
given t
God's

ecclesiastical decisions or philosophical systems. Their practice is but little influenced by our theories . . . It only remains for us, during our brief day, to work together under all the embarrassments of our position, or rather of circumstances in which the Church is placed in this country, provided we do not betray the faith; provided we fight a good fight."[32]

Despite his blunders, despite the carpings of anonymous malcontents, there was something in the character of John Hughes that touched the little people of New York, something that made him very special in their lives. In the midst of the appearance of the *Times* articles John consecrated St. Mary's church on Staten Island. The *Herald* described the effect of his presence upon the bystanders: "As the Archbishop moved around the foundation from one place to another . . . the multitude pressed onward with energy and a most unwarrantable zeal or curosity. Mothers with children in their arms struggled desperately to get a sight of the bishop . . . the person of the archbishop was almost encroached upon by the excessive passion of the people to get near him."[33]

The letters of Equitas had been mailed, mysteriously, to bishops throughout the United States, and presumably to Rome. Hughes set out to do two things. First he wrote an eighty-page autobiographical defense of his twenty-year administration for the benefit of Rome. Secondly, he confronted himself with the idea of resignation. He had earlier declared to a friend, "They may do what they will with the diocese when I am under the ground, but as long as I live there shall be no coadjutor bishop of New York."[34] Now, plagued with bad lungs, rheumatism and enemies, he reconsidered. There was a very practical reason for having a coadjutor: the Putnam Bill, if enforced, could wreak havoc during a time of episcopal transition. Even more to the point, he was tired. He began to write repeatedly, almost insistently, to Rome that he wished "to resign as soon as some one should be prepared and fitted to take my place. . . . I do not wish to die out," he pleaded, "in the same turmoil in which God has so far appointed that I should live."[35]

26

ENDOWED WITH A
TIRELESS ENERGY

Rome reacted negatively to Hughes's retirement plea. Bernard Smith, Hughes's friend and a dogma professor at the College of the Propaganda, listened to the reaction of Cardinal Barnabo, Prefect of the Vatican congregation. He wrote Hughes telling him that his request had caused a treat deal of turmoil. "There is no person as qualified as you are for the present difficulties . . ." he reasoned. "Will you make way for someone less qualified to take your place?"[1] It was promised, instead, that a coadjutor would be considered, a promise that Hughes called to the attention of slow-moving Rome a number of times during the lat 1850s and early 1860s. He was incensed, however, when a layman—outside the proper chain of command—took up the idea. He immediatly wrote to the culprit, saying, "I have learned with astonishment and not without indignation that during your recent visit to Europe you took the trouble to recommend to the Cardinal prefect the expedience of a coadjutor for my diocese . . . This is the most extraordinary proceeding on the part of a layman that has ever come to my knowledge . . . It can hardly be possible that you should have so far forgotten your Christian or Catholic training . . ."[2] And to Barnabo he wrote, "I would much prefer to resign and let such a coadjutor administer the diocese by himself."[3]

Later, when he cooled down, he remembered why he himself had asked for help. "My health is poor and declining," he agreed, "and I think that if I could get a coadjutor, more than once mentioned, it would prolong my days if not years."[4]

Hughes was so stringent in his attitude toward proper authority, he could not approve of anyone in whom strict obedience was not a virtue—and this included even the Church's heroes. This explains his opinion, expressed at this time, about Joan of Arc, who had bypassed the Church's hierarchy in her relationship with God. He wrote, "In my own mind there are serious doubts and misgivings as to the real merits of that illustrious and I might add religiously wild girl of France . . ."[5]

No one in his diocese was expected to heed voices—even the voices of angels—unless the voices were cleared first through the chancery. He continued to distrust religious orders who were able to circumvent diocesan authority to some degree by playing it off against their transdiocesan superiors. "Monasteries are by no means popular in the United States,"[6] he wrote to Cardinal Barnabo, speaking as much for himself as for nativist America. Writing to the Sulpicians of the conditions under which men were to work in his domain, he warned, "There are some things, however, which you know of me and which are necessarily to be understood. For instance, you must have seen my anxiety, at all times, that every religious community in my diocese should live to the spirit and if possible to the letter of its own constitution and disciplines."[7]

Hughes oftentimes found that he had no control over what went on behind friary walls, even when it was to the detriment of the Church. He was unable to stop the squabbles of the Franciscans "in relation to the internal administration of their affairs." Seeking help from Barnabo in Rome, he related his own feeling of helplessness at the behavior of these sons of St. Francis: "This [strife] has led to a great deal of mutual crimination and recrimination on both sides—going so far as to accuse one another of grave immoralities—so that if one were to believe the testimony which many give concerning fellow members of their order one should be led to the conclusion that there are very few truly religious among them . . ."[8]

These dual links of authority—religious and diocesan— both leading to Rome, placed him in an awkward position when the convert priest Isaac Hecker ran afoul of his superiors in the Redemptorist order. Hughes had traveled with Hecker. He liked him and respected the great mission work that he had already accomplished. In the latter part of the 1850s, when Hecker and several other American-born priests in the order found themselves restricted by the German language of the Redemptorists, they sought to start an American house. Both John Hughes and James Roosevelt Bayley gave them encouragement, and Hughes made them the specific offer of a church on Fifty-eighth Street in New York. When the idea was rejected by the Redemptorist provincial, Hecker, acting within the rule of the order's constitution, decided to go to Rome to appeal the idea. As soon as Hughes was convinced of the propriety of this course of action he wrote a recommendation for Hecker, describing him as a "laborous, edifying, zealous and truly apostolic priest."[9]

Hecker quickly collided with the superiors of the Redemptorists. He arrived in Rome on August 26th, 1857, and on August 29th, without allowing the young priest to defend his actions, the general of the order expelled him from the community for having acted on his own. The independent Yankee proceeded to walk a tightrope still higher. Carefully avoiding the image of a rebel, he sought out Cardinal Barnabo, and on his way encountered Archbishop Bedini. The archbishop, as if to show that he harbored no ill feelings toward Americans, championed the young priest's cause. Hecker gained an audience with the Pope and was able to present his case. For months, then, he remained on the tightrope.

Hughes, with his devotion to discipline and to the proper chain of command, did not know what to do. In response to an inquiry by the Redemptorist superiors he cautiously—overcautiously—wrote that he would have permitted an approved English-speaking community in his diocese but denied that he had had "the slightest part either in encouraging or approving the step."[10]

Hecker himself asked Hughes for help, and the archbishop's friend Barnard Smith accompanied this plea with one of his own, telling Hughes that "without trespassing on the province of Religious superiors, Bishops can and sometimes should speak out and say which is just for the good of religion."[11]

The letters, sent in care of Hecker's brother George in New York, were brought to Hughes by Hecker's Redemptorist friends. To them, and later to George Hecker, Hughes said that he had written nothing in reply to the Redemptorist superiors, a statement that they knew to be false, for they had already been told of the nature of his answer. George Deshon, one of the priests present, believed that Hughes was playing the crafty politician. "If we succeed without him, he will be our friend," he said. "If we do not he will be ready to lend a parting kick."[12]

Certainly they had caught him in a lie. Yet Hughes had dealt with the clergy too long not to fear that they might involve him in political maneuvers of their own, compromising everything he believed about authority. For all he knew they could have been planning a backstairs maneuver like the one he had witnessed with the friars Harold and Ryan early in his own priesthood. If they chose to play such games they could destroy any chances of Hecker's vindication. Deshon was also correct in his assessment. Hughes would kick them out if they lost. What Deshon failed to appreciate about his archbishop was that Hughes would kick them out even if it broke his own heart to do so. Hecker had moved out on the tightrope, asking to be judged by an authority who judged prelates and religious superiors equally. If Hecker lost on that level the decision would bind the archbishop of New York to obedience as much as it did young Redemptorist clerics.

Happily Isaac Hecker was vindicated by Pius IX who left him free to join forces with whatever diocese would have him. He returned to the United States in the spring of 1858 and formed the first truly American community for men, the Congregation of the Missionary Society of St. Paul the Apostle— the Paulists. It might have seemed natural that he would accept the invitation of Bishop Bayley rather than that of John Hughes. Yet, he chose to settle his congregation under the jurisdiction of the archbishop of New York. Hughes had his personal limitations, but Hecker would always remain firm in the conviction that the immigrant bishop was a great man, and with this man he chose to cast his lot.

There was an added problem in dealing with the religious orders whose authorities were outside of the diocese. They tended to retain foreign cultures even after a long establishment in the United States. The Franciscans were Italians, the Redemptorists were German, and the Jesuits at Fordham were French. When Hughes waged a war with the Jesuits lasting several years, the Jesuit superior in New York with whom he battled, John Hus, could speak only French and was unable to understand English at all.*

Many Americans presumed that Hughes himself was a Jesuit. In the nativist era the term was branded upon anything that reeked of Roman wiles. His name was often in print coupled with the term "Jesuitical." Nevertheless the order learned decisively in the late 1850s that Hughes was not their spiritual kin.

In 1855 Hughes decided he did not want Jesuits from St. John's College to teach at the diocesan seminary that shared the property at Fordham. He replaced them with diocesan priests. Shortly after this, the Jesuits had their land surveyed and discovered that the actual border line of the college cut closer to the seminary than had been thought. It also cut within inches of the front door of the house of the college's first architect, William Rodrigue. The architect's wife Margaret was the sister of John Hughes. The archbishop was not happy when told of the border-line dispute.

The Pandora's box having been opened, all sorts of irritations flew out which had been building up. The Jesuits were unhappy about a number of circumstances, the most predominant being the "cramping clause" of their original contract with Hughes. This clause stated that should the Jesuits depart from St. John's College the school's title would automatically revert to the archbishop. This prevented them from mortgaging or selling any sections of their land. Added to this complaint, Hughes had promised to give them a church in the city. He had

---

*Hughes, who had a talent for picking up languages, could speak French. To annoy the belligerent Hus on one occasion during this strife Hughes began a conference in French and at a crucial point shifted to English to exclude the Jesuit.

failed to do so. He had made an offer of a church that was in debt, but the Frenchmen, ignoring the fact that almost all of Hughes's churches were heavily in debt, refused the parish on that account. They waited for an offer of a debt-free church. No offer of a debt-free church was made.

Jesuits did control one parish in the city—St. Francis Xavier on Sixteenth Street—but Hughes held onto the title of the building—this, they complained, after they had spent $60,000 out of their pockets building it. Hughes saw the other side of the 60,000 coins. They had not come out of Jesuit pockets but the pockets of the parishioners. Moreover he had been angered by their tactics in soliciting funds. St. Francis Xavier had been their second attempt to start a parish. Their first church had burned. They then asked and received Hughes's permission to seek funds in order to rebuild. Hughes had imagined they would preach a general appeal. To his dismay they canvassed New York from door to door. Then, with this money and with the insurance from the burned church, they angered former parishioners by building St. Francis Xavier in a new locale.

These were the major issues. The minor complaints that had been built upon day by day for a decade involved such concerns as the title of the small territory cut off from the campus by the Harlem Railroad, the number of people who cut across college lawns in order to use the seminary chapel as a parish, the question as to whether Jesuits should be allowed to scandalize New Yorkers by attending the opera during Holy Week, and a "fancy fence" that the railroad had promised to build for the Jesuits along the college's property.

Unfortunately John Hus, who described Hughes as *"un caractère inabordable,"*[13] was at least as *inabordable* himself.

At the beginning of their feud in 1856 Hughes suggested selling the seminary buildings and grounds to the Jesuits, a solution that finally resolved the whole dispute four years later. Hus took no notice of the offer. The Jesuits did, however, hear Hughes loudly and clearly when he threatened that should they cut off access to the seminary he would take them into every court in the United States.[14] Then, although he himself had brought up the issue with the college trustees, among whom were laymen, Hughes was incensed that the Jesuits consulted a lawyer. Angrily he objected, "This appeal to the laity is a new feature in our ecclesiastical discipline."[15]

The issue grew stickier throughout 1857, and the cases against both parties broadened with further examples. Ironically most complaints surfaced through a process of self-incrimination, each side accusing the other of spreading particular rumors and spelling out the rumors that they presumed were being spread. With neither party ready to give in to the other, and the Jesuits firm in their judgment that Hughes had *"un spirit extraordinaire de domination,"*[16] Peter Hargous, a Protestant trustee of the college and a close friend of Hughes, recommended quietly to the Jesuits that they appeal the whole matter to the Pope. He told them that he had known the archbishop for twenty-nine years and had never known him to admit that he could be in the wrong. He would, however, bow to a decision made by his own superiors.[17]

Before this step was taken, the provincial in France wrote to Hughes seeking a mutual agreement. The archbishop had given indication enough that he wanted a face-saving out. He had petulantly rejected an invitation to the college's commencement in 1858, but he arrived unexpectedly at the time of the ceremony. In his remarks he told his audience that he had never meant the seminary chapel to be a permanent parish, and that a new parish would soon be started nearby. In response to the provincial's peace feeler Hughes asked for a meeting, arbitrated by Jesuits from the Maryland province. It was held in late September 1858 in the cathedral sacristy. Over the span of several hours everyone had the opportunity to repeat complaints that had been aired throughout the previous three years. It broke the ice, and after five more months of reconnoitering, the Jesuits surrendered on nearly all points and made a formal apology. They did so without Hus. He refused to back down and accepted instead a transfer that his superiors were only too happy to give him.

Having learned that the best way to deal with Hughes was through appeals for clemency rather than through arguments for justice, the Jesuits reaped rewards from a now-benign archbishop. The seminary lands were sold to them—despite Hus's cries from afar that Hughes was unloading valueless rural property. The cramping clause was ended; and although the archbishop never got around to doing so until his successor acknowledged that such had been his intention and did it for him —the title of St. Francis Xavier church was made over to the Jesuit order. The only happy aspect that can be glimmered from the entire affair is the consideration that all parties involved in the dispute had enough respect for the Church's integrity to keep the issue quiet. The laymen involved were as discreet as the priests, and the only people who knew about what went on were those directly involved in the squabble.

It should be noted that at least one Jesuit had a high regard for Hughes. Augustus Thébaud, President of the college during 1846-1851 and during 1860-1863, would have won agreement even from John Hus with his judgment that Hughes belonged "essentially to the Church militant." Hus could only have begrudged the rest of his evaluation. "His great object," Thebaud said of Hughes, ". . . was to give to Catholic prelates in this country a consultative voice in public affairs; and he certainly succeeded, since Presidents, Secretaries of State, governors and publicists asked him to serve his country, and they consented to all the conditions he imposed to save his ecclesiastical character and his conscientious principles of conduct." And of a personal nature, Thébaud wrote, "What I admired in him at that time was his simplicity in the midst of all his honors. I never remarked any change in him when he came back from Washington or Albany and I met with him either in his house at the old cathedral, or in the cottage of his sister Mrs. Rodrigue at Fordham. He was ever the same affectionate and pleasant companion, ready to enjoy a laugh and to relate an anecdote."[18] It was unfortunate that for the sake of preserving his authority Hughes allowed so few people to see this side of his nature.

Within his own diocesan sphere, John Hughes remained an absolute ruler. During the imposition of hands at ordination his priests could not mistake a touch of iron upon the crown of their heads. By 1860 the Italian community numbered some 5,000 people in New York, and nearly 400 families out of these rented a place for worship under the direction of their priest, Antonio Sanguinetti. When commercial interests closed the building in which they worshiped they appealed to Hughes for a formal Italian national parish.[19] Sanguinetti, without waiting for authorization, collected funds in Irish communities and banked the money in his own name.

Being cool to national parishes that created a hyphenated Catholicism, Hughes hesitated about the petition. Sanguinetti then attempted an end-around play. He left for Italy, and at Rome criticized Hughes as a person who had no sympathy for the Italian immigrants. Hughes quickly let it be known that Sanguinetti would best not show the whites of his eyes within shooting distance of Manhattan. Those in Rome who knew the archbishop convinced the Italian priest to stay on the eastern side of the Atlantic. Hughes reinforced the decision, telling Rome "If Father Sanguinetti should ever return to the city of New York he is liable to be prosecuted for obtaining money under false pretenses and sent to the penitentiary."[20]

In a slightly more compassionate vein he commiserated with an expelled seminarian as he wished him good luck in finding a new bishop: ". . . I feel much for your actual position. It is already known that you were admitted for Holy Orders when the accident, I may call it, occurred which prevented me from promoting you to the ranks of the priesthood . . . I have called it an accident, and I do not wish to speak of it as anything else . . . It should be to you, for all your life, not only a warning and a caution, but a solemn reason to justify you in never tasting spiritous liquors."*[21]

Hughes did not discipline blindly. He checked situations through, and if he decided that a priest was innocent of a

---

*In the years after his death it was whispered that Hughes himself had a drinking problem. In 1860 Francis Kenrick, citing Bishop John Timon as his source, wrote to Rome opposing a cardinal's hat for Hughes saying, for one thing, that the New York prelate once had a drinking problem that he had overcome. However, Hughes's severest critics outside the Church never made mention of such a problem. James Gordon Bennett would have pounced upon the information; the nativists would have loved it. Hughes was too much in the public eye to have hidden it. This writer discounts Kenrick's observations.

charge he actively took up his defense. Father Thomas Mooney
was a consistently imprudent young man who said all the
wrong things to the wrong people at the wrong times. As he
was foolish without malice, Hughes brought him on the carpet
often enough to remind him that priests "ought to be tenfold
more cautious than lay persons."[22] But he had little use for the
bileful detractions of parishioners with nothing better to do
than write to the chancery about the personalities of their assistant pastors. To a physician who chronicled long complaints
about Mooney's every action from the time of his arrival in the
man's parish, Hughes wrote: "I am impelled to the conclusion
that neither the spirit of a good Catholic nor an educated gentleman can be found in either of your letters. Your detractions
of Mister Mooney unconnected with the present affair would
be unworthy of a decent pagan."[23]

The direct and outspoken Father Jeremiah Cummings oftentimes stood squarely in opposition to Hughes. When
Hughes was pushing the growth of a Catholic school system
Cummings decided it impossible to maintain his basement
school at St. Stephen's church. He took the entire student
body, marched them to the public school and enrolled them *en
masse*. Although Hughes remained suspicious of Orestes
Brownson's pronouncements, Cummings became one of the
doctor's strongest and steadiest supporters. Cummings was one
of the rare Catholic priests to become actively involved in the
antislavery movement—a cause that was dominated by the
leadership of anti-Catholic nativists. He was anything but a
"yes" man, and there was little wonder so many people (including Hughes, momentarily) took him to be Equitas.
Cummings found it necessary to write a denial to the
newspapers.

In 1859 however Cummings found himself in an embar-
rassing mess that won a great deal of space in the newspapers
and in the hearts of New York's nativists. A Protestant woman
named Anna Haggerty claimed that Cummings had kidnapped
her son so that he might be brought up as a Catholic. Supposedly the boy was being held prisoner in St. Stephen's recto-

ry. Her sustained hysteria convinced a large enough portion of
the public, and with her large backing she brought Cummings
to trial. Before a densely packed courtroom she claimed that
after she had sought the return of her child, Cummings had
come to her house with the archbishop. The two men had denied knowledge of the whereabouts of her son and then had left
"clapping their hands with great joy."[24]

The trial dragged on through a number of stormy sessions,
Mrs. Haggerty giving testimony that sounded like scenes from
the standard nunnery-prison novels. Hughes might easily have
stayed aloof from the proceedings. As wild and woolly as the
drama might have become, few people would have expected the
archbishop of New York to enter this tawdry arena. He did.
Though it was Cummings on trial and not he, Hughes stood by
this priest and presented himself as a witness.

It made for an interesting scene. A generation and more of
Americans had been fed, as with mother's milk, on stories of
Romanism's atrocities. When occasions were presented to cast
these nightmares with real people from the local community,
the situation was somehow reduced to an occasion of embarrassment and foolishness. Before a standing-room-only courtroom Mrs. Haggerty was asked to point out Archbishop
Hughes. It was not too difficult. He sat next to Cummings
staring back at her with a countenance like the wrath of God—
not exactly the sort of man who would have left her house
"clapping his hands with joy." In a manner markedly more
subdued than her previous testimony she indicated that Hughes
was—"that old gentleman."

The old gentleman took the stand and coldly dashed water
upon the whole story. "I have only to say that all this is as new
to me as if it had occurred in China," he told the court, ". . . I
know nothing whatever about it except what I may have read
in the newspapers."[25] Mrs. Haggerty caught hold of herself
and attempted to revive her accusations. But by this time
her allegations were making a farce out of the whole legal
process. The lawyer who had taken upon himself to defend her
stopped the proceedings, apologized to the court for allowing

himself to be so duped, and the judge dismissed the case. Hughes and Cummings, having stood together against an outside enemy, returned to their comfortable family feuding.

Catholics had always looked with pride upon the individual converts who had been the fruits of the Oxford movement. They were not so quick to point out the failures. The most crushing of these was the reconversion of John Murray Forbes. Ten years after becoming a Catholic he found that the discipline in the Roman Catholic priesthood was beyond what he had bargained for. He decided to return to the Episcopal Church where he remarried and resumed his ministry. He subsequently became dean of General Theological Seminary where the American Catholic movement had received its strongest support in the 1840s.

Hughes was crushed by the defection. He wrote to Forbes, "Neither within the last two years nor at any previous time have I ever refused you anything that would be agreeable to yourself whenever it was in my power to correspond with your wishes."[26] For a week after the apostasy Hughes allowed himself to speak of what happened to those around him. After that time he let it be known that he wanted no one to mention the man's name in his presence. Blaming himself as much as anyone else he confessed to a friend in Rome, "His fall has been to me a blow of chastisement; for I had rashly blamed other prelates for having ordained, too hastily, converted persons. My own turn of humiliation has arrived in the case of Dr. Forbes."[27]

Orestes Brownson was sensitive to the affection that Hughes had developed for Forbes. For a moment he pushed aside all the reasons for which he and Hughes jangled one another's nerves and wrote, expressing sympathy "as a father who has been saddened by the death of his own son." He confessed that "the defection of Dr. Forbes has led me to reflect on myself and convinces me that I have been on many occasions unjust and owe you an act of reparation." Then, perhaps because so kindly a missive might be presumed a forgery, Brownson added that he tended to be unjust because Hughes did tend, on occasion, to be somewhat "capricious, tyrannical, unjust, occupied with your own glory, and anxious to discourage every enterprise and talent which did not reflect honor upon yourself."[28] Nevertheless, in the language the two men spoke Hughes understood and returned a note, philosophizing to Brownson that such an occurrence "teaches all of us a lesson that is found in the inspired writings of the apostle; he who thinks himself to stand, let him take heed lest he fall."[29]

There were very few people with whom he could share his life. His affection for Terence Donaghoe, whom he called "my best friend on this earth,"[30] never dimmed. He depended greatly upon him, looked forward to his letters, and hoped for occasional visits. When Bishop William Walsh of Halifax died in 1858, Hughes was so affected by the death of this friend who scolded him about his self-neglect that he was unable to preach at his funeral. "I know myself too well," he confessed, "to imagine that I could utter my sentiments without being choked with emotion."[31]

After a generation in office he liked to bring together the priests who had served the diocese as long as he had, and referred to them as the "old guard." But they had never been a community with him. He lived essentially alone—and even the billiard table that he added to his rooms became a source only of solitary amusement.

His life was his work, and the love that other men sought from individuals he sought, in a very real way, from the immigrant Church of New York. To the end of his life his office was open to little people: "A poor woman of Brooklyn has just called on me in great distress of mind . . ."[32] begins one typical letter of recommendation. Another letter sent to the bishop of Boston on behalf of some woman's daughter states that the girl was "exceedingly talented but as ugly as a mud fence."[33]

There was one special dream that the archbishop held for his immigrant Church. While the Episcopalians borrowed Gothic architecture to erect buildings such as Trinity church, Catholic churches remained expressions of poverty and hasty construction. Hughes wanted to build a cathedral worthy of anything in Europe, an expression in stone to confirm for both immigrants and natives that the Roman Catholic Church was a part of the United States. Several times during his administration he announced that such a project would soon be started. Lack of funds and more pressing demands would then dictate otherwise, and the plan would again become his own private dream. The site remained set—Fifth Avenue at Fiftieth Street —far enough outside central Manhattan as to evoke sarcastic comments from those who knew better.[34] The proposed dimensions of the building were considered outlandish. "I forget the precise figures, but its alleged length is six hundred and eighty feet!!!," observed George Templeton Strong. ". . . It'll probably be a combination of Cologne cathedral and the Crystal Palace."[35]

Finally in the summer 1858 the commencement of the new cathedral seemed feasible. The laying of the cornerstone was set for August 15th, the Feast of the Assumption. Early on that day all the avenues from Second to Sixth were thronged with dense crowds making their way to the site of construction. Some 60,000 people "at the lowest computation" gathered to create what the New York *Herald* described as "one of the grandest ceremonies that was ever witnessed on this continent . . ." adding that "it was the largest assemblage our reporter ever saw in this city."

A large white wooden cross stood where the altar would someday stand, and near to it a platform for those conducting the ceremony. The American flag floated from a half dozen points, intermingled with what seemed to be the flags of all nations. John Hughes spoke to the crowd, and though only a small percentage had any chance of hearing his voice the whole multitude stood in respectful silence. He paid tribute to the first Catholics of New York, so "very few . . . very poor," who had the courage to lay the cornerstone of the first St. Patrick's cathedral on Mott Street "at a period when it was said that the Catholics of New York were not numerous enough to fill the small church of St. Peter in Barclay Street."[36]

This was only months after Equitas had ripped into his reputation and his heart. Still, he believed in the ideal unity of the Church without faltering. Asking God's help, and "under the auspices of the Immaculate Virgin Mary" he dedicated St. Patrick's cathedral to that unity. "Judging from the past, in which the clergy were at all times loyal and one minded in aiding their unworthy bishop in whatever enterprise he had engaged, so will they be in all times to come—and to them, with the powerful cooperation which they will always have from their devoted flocks, I commend this great work, no matter under whose episcopal auspices it may hereafter be carried on."[37]

At one point while Hughes was speaking, the vast assembly through natural jostling began to press close, swaying dangerously against the platform. As the newspapers reported it, Hughes simply stopped and held up his arms as if to still the surging waves of people. After a minute or so calm again prevailed, and he continued.[38]

If he could have ended his career then, the day would have been a fitting conclusion. Even old enemies attributed greatness to him. The Harper family, who had some twenty-five years earlier sponsored Maria Monk, took the occasion of the cathedral dedication to do a feature article about Hughes in their new *Harper's Weekly*. Describing him as a "self-made man" who "awes into silence any serious opposition," the magazine decided that "no individual, perhaps, in this country, in office or out of it, wields a larger influence over a greater number of minds . . .". The magazine continued, saying, "When we hear of him it is almost always in consequence of some assault upon the policy or interest of his Church. Heedless of any fancied dignity of his position which would interfere with the free use of his tongue or pen, he stands forward as the conspicuous mark for whatever arrows or assaults may be launched against the cause which he defends . . . He seems endowed with a tireless energy."[39]

Yet he was far from tireless. It was at this time that he was seeking permission from Rome to retire, or at least to have a coadjutor. The problems of administration were as strenuous as they had ever been while Hughes was not. He had begun the cathedral which was to symbolize that the immigrant Church was at home in the United States, but it would be a long time before that cathedral, as well as that which it was to symbolize, could be a reality. In two years work came to a standstill when in February of 1860 the workmen struck for higher wages and walked off the job. The outside wall, thirty-five feet high at that point, remained that way until after Hughes's death.

The nation was becoming preoccupied with other problems. Hughes assessed that Know Nothingism was dying out, but only because other evils took its place. Informing a friend in Rome of a "small insurrection on the borders between what we called free states and the slave states," he worried for the future of his adopted country. "The wisest men," he related, "begin to be apprehensive."[40]

27

REAPING THE WHIRLWIND

Garibaldi, having been unable to get work on the docks of New York, eventually made his way homeward to start more revolutions. The small states of Italy had regrouped their ambitions during the previous decade and in the late 1850s began an inexorable movement toward the unification of Italy—a movement that necessarily involved the Pope's ouster as a temporal prince. Hughes had arranged an audience with the Pope for a touring William Seward, and he was embarrassed to hear that Pius IX told the senator that the whole world was against the Pope. This, Hughes felt, was "a melancholy thought to entertain in the breast of the vicar of Christ."[1]

Yet in his own devotion to the papacy Hughes could not conceive of the need to end the Papal States. He once again took up a collection for the support of the Pope. He wrote a pastoral letter in defense of temporal sovereignty (sending a copy to every ruler in Europe except Queen Victoria and Victor Emmanuel), and he anticipated the worst for the Church. "My poor mind is haunted night and day," he wrote Cardinal Barnabo, "with the idea of approaching trials such as have not been seen since the days of Nero and Domitian."[2]

Once again, the Catholic Bennett shrugged off such notions. "In the present century," he editorialized, "the Pope has been three times in exile and within fifty years he has been for a period of five years removed from Italy and entirely stripped of his temporal dominion. The Catholic religion did not fare worse in consequence. Pius IX is probably the last Pope who will reign as a temporal prince." Placing himself at the opposite end of the spectrum from Hughes, Bennett concluded, "When the Church of Rome is purged of its temporalities it will commence its new era of power and greatness."[3]

James Gordon Bennett had a somewhat less laudable reason for this phase of his fondness for the Church. He had little to no use for abolitionists, and to his great satisfaction Catholics had remained almost wholly silent about the issue. "While the Methodists, Baptists and other Churches have broken to pieces on the slavery question," he boasted, "the Catholics have stood aloof and avoided the danger . . ."[4]

The great mass of Irish who came to the United States had little interest in slavery. It had been created in the colonies by an England who had made a slave of Ireland as well. It has been nurtured for profit by a Puritan America, which now opposed the naturalization of the Irish immigrant. Slavery was Protestant America's problem. The Irish believed Protestant America should solve it.

As a young rawboned immigrant, John Hughes had been hired as a slave overseer. He had not sought the work; it was the price he had to pay to gain entry to school. Bewildered and repulsed by the experience, he had expressed his feelings in verse:

> Wipe from thy code Columbia, wipe the stain:
> Be free as the air, but yet be kind as free,
> And chase foul bondage from thy southern plain; if such be
> the right of man, by heaven's decree
> Oh then let Afric's sons feel what it is—to be.[5]

His friendship with the Rodrigue family in Philadelphia greatly tempered those earlier attitudes. Years later he recalled, "When I was a young clergyman . . . I was acquainted with white and colored inhabitants of Haiti and Santo Domingo. They told me much of the horrors connected with what history has settled down to call the Massacre of St. Domingo."[6]

By the 1850s he was wary of the abolitionists who, in the

safe seclusion of northern towns, wished the South to immediately release its huge slave population. When Father Jeremiah Cummings in the early 1850s gave a well-publicized and strongly worded antislavery lecture, Hughes slipped into the back of the hall to judge the proceedings. He never took Cummings publicly to task for his abolitionist stand, but he let it be known that his own views were much more conservative.

In 1854 after his bout with pneumonia he had traveled through the South on his return from Cuba. Upon arriving in New York he expressed an attitude toward slavery that would remain with him for the rest of his life. "While we all know that this condition of slavery is an evil," he observed, "yet it is not an absolute and unmitigated evil." Granted that the black race had been "seized to gratify the avarice and cupidity of the white man." Nonetheless, he claimed, this evil institution had brought great numbers of Africans to civilization, and, more importantly, to Christianity.[7]

Horace Greeley and his pack of abolitionists were quick to lecture him about the Church's teachings against the slave trade, and Hughes was quick to agree. "But where slaves have been introduced into a country," he argued, "she does not require they shall be restored to their primitive condition."[8]

Hughes never took to the stump to defend his views— which were moderately expressed amidst the passionate views of others. Most antiabolitionists in the North expressed themselves in offensively racist terms. The *Freeman's Journal,* professing to be a Catholic paper, wrote about blacks as if they were animals. The *Herald,* the most widely circulated newspaper in the world, could unblushingly headline a story about Frémont's campaign for the 1860 Republican nomination as being "A bombshell among the Nigger worshippers."[9] It was not a sensitive age.

Nor were the American Puritans sensitive toward the Catholic immigrants whom they criticized for not jumping upon their abolitionist bandwagon. They failed to appreciate that the newcomers did not share their righteous sense of historic guilt over America's peculiar institution. The question of freedom for slaves did not take up very much space in the priority lists of Irish Catholic immigrants. They were concerned with finding space to live in the North despite the opposition of the same Puritans who wanted to free the oppressed in the far-off South.

Almost universally the native moralists who were antidrink and antislavery were also anti-Catholic. The members of the Beecher clan, fathered by Reverend Lyman, were the great moral crusaders of the ante-bellum period. Over their desks and pulpits they poured out antislavery novels and antislavery sermons. If John Hughes hesitated to join them in their great cause it might have been because they also produced books such as *The Papal Conspiracy Exposed and Protestantism Defended in the Light of Reason History and Scripture* (authored by Reverend Edward Beecher) in which Hughes was attacked by name. If as archbishop of New York he hesitated to clasp hands with those ministers of the Gospel who wished equality for the slaves, it might have been because as late as 1859 he found it necessary to send a petition, with 2,144 signatures, to the Board of Almshouse Governors "respectfully but firmly remonstrating on the enforced Protestant religious teaching of children in Public almshouses."[10]

The schizoid attitude of nativists was further exemplified by the American tour of the Prince of Wales in 1860. Previously New York welcomes had been staged for European revolutionaries who took potshots at crowned heads (especially if the crown had a triple tiara). Now a turnabout was effected for the benefit of the heir to England's throne—the symbol of oppression in Ireland. As the city prepared to fête the prince the large Irish population boiled in resentment. Those in charge of the prince's travel arrangements nervously approached Hughes for assurance that there would be no disturbances from the Irish. Having been offered no such assurances himself prior to the visit of Archbishop Bedini, Hughes responded with thinly veiled sarcasm about "this immense population which I am supposed to represent." He said, "I have discovered a slight but vulgar disposition on the part of some to forget or even betray the courtesies that are due to the prince. But without venturing to be responsible for the conduct of one or another ruffian in a Catholic population composed of all nations, to a great extent Irish, I think I may venture to say that no manifestation of disrespect will be exhibited . . ."[11]

There were only a few such manifestations. The most notable was the refusal by Colonel Michael Corcoran to march his Irish 69th Regiment in the welcoming parade—an act that cost him his command and won him the undying admiration of the city's Irish.

The immigrant Church could not afford the luxury of fighting for the freedom of others. It had not yet won from native Americans the acknowledgment that it had the right to exist freely itself. Nor did it occur to the nativists that in bypassing the rights of a large foreign-born population in order to secure such rights for the next lower class on the social scale, they might be pushing a lid down on a pressure cooker.

By chance, Hughes was visiting James Buchanan at the White House when a telegram brought news of John Brown's raid on Harper's Ferry. Buchanan was a weak, vacillating President who did his best to placate the slave states, and by his lack of firmness he ended by placating no one. For Hughes decisiveness was a prime virtue. He privately urged Buchanan to take a strong stand on the matter. "I cannot imagine a descendant of the Buchanans that I knew in Ireland who, knowing or believing himself to be right, would ever give way," Hughes told him. ". . . I need not suggest that you be firm."[12]

In 1860 Hughes again traveled through the South. Plagued again by illness during the winter he visited Bishop Patrick Lynch of Charleston, and together they went to St. Augustine in Florida. He returned home still feeling ill. "I feel a cold and stiffness in my limbs," he complained, "which I fear means something more than physicians have accounted for."[13] Though at the time it was not known, he was suffering from Bright's disease, a disorder of the kidney. In May he collapsed while consecrating St. Joseph's church in Albany. The press observed, "Bishop Hughes's discourse was highly interesting. He was unable to complete it, however, owing to feebleness and exhaustion, from the effects of which he recovered in a short time."[14]

Ill or not, he must have been sorely disappointed during

that same week when William Seward, whom almost everyone had expected to be the Republican presidential candidate, was denied the nomination in favor of the unknown Abraham Lincoln. Political observers attributed the defeat to ex-Know Nothing resentment within the party over Seward's constant espousal of the immigrants' cause. The grim Puritan Thaddeus Stevens laid the blame more directly on the senator's public friendship with the Catholic archbishop of New York.

Hughes went South again a month after this. The senior class at the heavily Protestant University of North Carolina voted him as the "divine" they wanted to deliver their commencement address. Suprised, and presuming that the students "no doubt intended it as an evidence of their liberality,"[15] Hughes was nonetheless deeply touched. He wrote to the students that he was "anxious to know what would be proper on such an occasion, and especially, what would be agreeable to your class."[16] His talk at the university was described by a local North Carolina newspaper:

> One saw in the preacher an elderly man in infirm health, of bowed form, yet of striking appearance. He wore a tight fitting cassock, ornamented with a row of red buttons down the front and down the sleeves, and surmounted by a doctor's cape. On his breast there lay a carved cross of gold suspended by a heavy golden chain, and on his finger appeared the episcopal ring, which flashed strange light into the wondering eyes of poor Protestants. The style of the preacher and the services for devotion were simple even unto plainness. He and Father McNeirny* pulled aside the desk which held King James' Bible, so that no screen separated him from his audience . . . He pulled out his big red bandana handkerchief, or his spotless one of linen, with utter indifference. He would spit and scrape with his foot, as if he had never preached in the loftiest Cathedrals of the world. He would call on Bishop Lynch for water, as if in too big a hurry to get it for himself. But then, from the reply of our Saviour to the question of the tempting lawyer, as it is recorded in the 22nd chapter of Matthew, he discoursed on love to God and love to man, as is not often heard in a

---

*Hughes's secretary.

college chapel. The densely packed audience listened with scarcely a stir for an hour and three quarters.[17]

The breakup of the Federal Union in the winter of 1860-1861 created a sense of national paralysis that lasted for months. "Even here in New York," Hughes wrote, "the crisis is felt as the greatest torture that has been experienced within the memory of living men."[18] Privately Hughes expected little of the new administration and told Seward that he considered him "the only one in the cabinet of Mr. Lincoln fit to be at the helm."[19] Hughes felt no animosity toward southerners. He had traveled in the South, made southern friends, and the University of North Carolina had honored him in a friendlier manner than he had ever met in the North. The prospect of the looming Civil War was a nightmare to him. "It will be the most sanguinary if not ferocious war that ever dismayed humanity," he warned.[20]

Even in the last moments of peace the immigrant Catholics in both the North and the South shared a sense of unity. In April Michael Corcoran was being feted by the Irish in South Carolina for his refusal to march the 69th Regiment before the Prince of Wales. As Fort Sumpter was being fired upon Jeremiah Cummings was preaching at a church in Charleston. When hostilities commenced, men who had longed for freedom together in Ireland took up guns for the section of the United States to which they had learned to give allegiance. Hughes's friend Bishop Patrick Lynch offered prayers for the Confederate Army. The bishop of New Orleans blessed the flags of southern troops. Irish regiments were formed in the South, one of them headed by a son of John Mitchel. Some of them carried "Erin Go Bragh" banners that had been stitched together in convents. President Lincoln refused a pass for Sisters of Charity assigned from Emmitsburg, Maryland to Norfolk, Virginia. The Sisters, not to be so easily put down, slipped through the blockade to reach their destination.

In New York John Hughes rattled ecclesiastics both in the North and South by flying the Stars and Stripes on top of the cathedral. Against criticism he defended himself by saying that had he not taken such an initiative "the press would have sounded the report that the Catholics were disloyal, and no act of ours afterward could successfully vindicate us from the imputation."[21] The northern Irish volunteered in great numbers, competing to get into the honored 69th Regiment.* Michael Corcoran was returned to his command; one of the young soldiers who gained entry to the regiment's ranks was Patrick Hughes, John's nephew. Assigning them Thomas Mooney as a chaplain, the archbishop sent them to war with the blessing: "Let the Sixty-Ninth Regiment know that I shall be deeply afflicted if they should be less than brave in battle, less than humane and kind after the battle is over, and above all things, if by possibility, they should bring a tarnish upon their name, their country or their religion."[22]

The war spirit did not push Hughes to take new positions on matters he had dealt with throughout his life. Catholics in the United States military had always been forced to attend compulsory Protestant services, but Hughes had long begged off fighting that issue. In peacetime, with a small army, there had been so many other large nativist battlefronts to choose from. As great numbers of Catholics enlisted in the Civil War, the problem was solved before it was a problem. With Seward as Secretary of State, a tolerant President was encouraged to seek advice from the archbishop of New York ("I am sure you will pardon me if, in my ignorance, I do not address you with technical correctness . . ." began Lincoln).[23] Both Seward and Lincoln must have been pleased when Hughes showed less worry about who led the men in prayer, as he did about the fact that the army led them to prayer like cattle: "In no possible case," he advised, "would I allow either a Catholic or a Protestant commander to require the attendance of those under his authority at religious service unless when he (not the commander but the other party) should feel willing to attend of his own accord."[24]

The archbishop's firm clerical disipline was not relaxed.

---

*Florence Gibson's "The Attitudes of the New York Irish toward State and National Affairs" quotes the statistic that of 337,800 soldiers from New York 51,206 were born in Ireland.

The irrespressible Mooney who had already spent so much time studying the designs of Hughes's carpet was once again at war with propriety. The very proper Kenrick in Baltimore entered a complaint, and he was not to be mollified by Hughes's defense that Mooney was "one of the most devoted priests of my diocese when under proper restraint in presence of his superior." The young man was, Hughes admitted, "given to levity —but that is his natural temperament."[25] Propriety won again, and Mooney was soon the recipient of a letter from his exasperated archbishop: "You have disappointed me in regard to the advice which I gave you in Mullaly's office when you were about to start with the 69th," he scolded. "Your inauguration of a ceremony unknown to the Church, viz; of blessing a cannon—was sufficiently bad, but your remarks on that occasion are infinitely worse . . ."[26] Mooney's remarks were not preserved for posterity; his image was. Matthew Brady captured a shot of him, vested for Mass in front of a tent, and surrounded by the men of the regiment. That was the high point of his military career. Three days after the receipt of Hughes's orders he was on his way back to St. Brigid's parish in New York.

Hughes was proud of the 69th, and when first official reports scarcely alluded to their valor he told Seward that this had caused "wounded feelings" among the Irish. "A slight is for them," he reminded the veteran of the school fight, "worse than a blow."[27] And yet, while sensitive to Irish pride he fought, even with the enthusiasm of wartime, anything that might hinder the assimilation of the immigrant. Other Irish regiments swelled up to compete with the 69th, and there was talk of banding them into a brigade. Hughes wanted Seward to dampen the enthusiastic mood.

"Our papers have paragraphs every day about what is called the 'Irish brigade,' " he wrote. "I think regiments and brigades ought to be distinguished by numbers, and companies by alphabetical distinction. I am of the opinion that if there be Irish brigades, German brigades, Scotch brigades, Garibaldian brigades in our army, there will be trouble among the troops before the enemy comes in sight."[28]

Hughes's own devotion to his adopted country was without qualification. The southern states had helped to create the Federal Union, and there had been no additional legislation that gave them the right to secede. Thus he could not conceive of any negotiations with "the pretended government of the Confederate States." Even after the initial victories of the South he had confidence that a full employment of the Union's energies would bring speedy victory. He wanted the immediate possession of Richmond. "I pray you for heaven's sake," he advised Seward, "not to allow it to be a half battle, but one in which whatever the consequences may be, the South will be taught that it is incapable of coping with the North."[29]

He continued to argue with southern bishops about *Te Deums* sung in the cathedral of Charleston "after the fatal triumph by which unauthorized persons drove the federal troops from Fort Sumpter," and insisted that the southern states were nothing more than rebels against their own constitutional government: "The North has not been required to do any thing new, to take any oath, to support any new flag . . . The South on the contrary has taken upon itself to be judge in its own cause."[30]

The Irish immigrants in the South returned forceful arguments. They asked how Irishmen emigrating from a land that existed under a union enforced by England could fight for an enforced union in America.[31] An immigrant in Mississippi wrote to the *Freeman's Journal:* "What I hate worst of all [about the] North, I see that the Irish Catholics are enlisting. I did not think that they would be the last to come against us. It has not been many years since a powerful party started at the North known as the Know Nothing party and they swept like an avalanche over the North . . ." The Irish Confederate offered the contention that the Know Nothings had been spurned by the South, and that in the southern states immigrants found "equality which we could not get in the old Union." If Irish boys had realized this, he reasoned, "they would never be found cheek by jowl with men who a few years ago were exterminating them for no other reason than because they would stand up for the faith of their fathers. Let the genuine Yankees come; they are the boys we are after. They have sown the wind, and I want them to reap the whirlwind."[32]

Both the *Metropolitan Record* (which had served for a spell as Hughes's official newspaper) and the *Freeman's Journal* parted company with their patriotic archbishop and became openly sympathetic to the southern cause. James McMaster, pursuing an editorial course that would place him behind bars in Fort Lafayette, preached open sedition. "The Irishmen," he lamented, ". . . have rushed into a fight in which no interest of theirs is at stake." He told the immigrants that city officials were closing men out of jobs in order to make them enlist. "The park is closed—the Navy yard is closed, and day by day the employees of the custom house whose relations and even brothers are risking limb and life for their country, are drifted out on the waste, barren cold country."[33]

As casualty lists began to mount, more and more Irish became inclined to agree with McMaster. Observing this, Orestes Brownson decried the tepid patriotism of his fellow Catholics, criticizing both clergy and laymen as "doing all in their power to justify the Know Nothings in their grave charges against the loyalty of Catholics." Continued Brownson: "It is undeniable that no religious body in the country stands so generally committed to slavery and the rebellion, or as a body have shown so little sympathy with the effort of the government to save the unity and life of the government."[34]

At the 1861 commencement exercises at Fordham Brownson made the social mistake of voicing such opinions in the presence of John Hughes. Hughes got up and tore into Brownson, and when Brownson attempted to defend himself the archbishop brusquely ordered him to sit down. At the conclusion of the ceremonies Brownson was ignored by the Jesuits who escorted Hughes into a prepared banquet; as if he were a leper the man sat alone until it was time for his train back to the city.[35]

Brownson did not drop the matter, though. He published his ideas about Catholic patriotism and accused Hughes of favoring slavery. Indeed it sounded as if Hughes did. Living up to Equitas's description of a man who swung wildly and blindly when he fought, Hughes argued with Brownson, saying that the only ugly feature about American slavery was its hereditary character. Reaching far in a hazy logic to fill the pages of the

Metropolitan Record, Hughes described the horrors of African tribal war and declared that the transportation of people from such a land was a comparative good: "We of course believe that no genuine Christian, no decent man—would be engaged in this kind of business; still, we cannot discover the crime, even of the slaver, in snatching them from the butcheries of their native land."[36]

Brownson turned the knife upon Hughes by asserting that his opinion placed him under the ban of Gregory XVI who in 1838 excommunicated those who fostered the slave trade. Hughes's article, written under a pseudonym and in the heat of anger, was such an embarrassment when cooler thoughts prevailed that he lamely attempted for a brief while to disclaim authorship. This only got him into deeper hot water with Brownson who, if he could not shout Hughes down in person, would scathingly comment from a distance, "He remembers to speak the truth only when truth best serves his purpose."[37]

Liar or not, John Hughes had good reasons for wanting to keep the slavery question away from the New York Irish. Writing to Simon Cameron, a more moderate Hughes explained:

> There is being insinuated in this part of the country an idea to the effect that the purpose of this war is the abolition of slavery in the south. If that idea should prevail among a certain class, it would make the business of recruiting slack indeed. The Catholics so far as I know, whether of native or foreign birth are willing to fight to the death for the support of the constitution, the Government, and the laws of the country. But if it should be understood that, with or without knowing it, they are to fight for the abolition of slavery, then, indeed, they will turn away in disgust from the discharge of what would otherwise be a patriotic duty.[38]

Lincoln began to grow in Hughes's esteem, no doubt through Seward's influence. By October of 1861, almost as if the fact surprised him, Hughes admitted to the secretary of state: "I take it that the President is the responsible man of this nation"; adding sympathetically, "no President has ever been so severely tested as he."

He had known better days himself. In the same letter he

told Seward, "I am getting old, and it is time for me to begin to gather myself up for a transition from this world to another, and I hope, a better."[39]

Lincoln and Seward had also decided it was time for the archbishop of New York to make a transition, not to the next world but to the Old World of Europe. Ignoring the fact that Hughes was planning to die, the Secretary of State telegraphed him to come immediately to Washington for a discussion of matters of public concern.

The southern states had succeeded in shipping John Slidell and James Mason through the blockade. In Havana the two commissioners awaited a British ship to bring them to Europe where they hoped to win diplomatic recognition for their government. Lincoln did not want to leave a stone unturned while public opinion on the other side of the Atlantic wavered between support of the Union or the Confederacy. He asked John Hughes to pay an unofficial visit to France while the longtime Whig and Republican party boss Thurlow Weed courted England. Such salesmanship could only help, and was worth the price of passage.

Travel was always an invigorating experience for Hughes. Without so much as a second thought he put off his plans for death, packed his bags, and within two weeks time was steaming across the Atlantic in company with his good friend Weed.* In Charleston, the *Catholic Miscellany* immediately discounted the value of the northern bishop embarking upon such a mission. It wrote: "An Irish Catholic ecclesiastic who subscribed five hundred dollars for Ireland's rebellion, or 'secession,' could never wield much diplomatic influence at the Court of Saint James. The prelate who penned the pastoral of the last New York Council in which the French Emperor's sacriligeous treachery and spoilation of the Patrimony of Saint

---

*Lincoln also sent the low Church Episcopal Bishop Charles McIlvane who had made a practice of spending his vacations in England. The author of *The Oxford Divinity compared with that of the Romish and Anglican Church* did not, however, travel with John Hughes.

Peter were unsparingly denounced, could never be a welcome guest at the Tuileries."[40]

Indeed, Hughes would have been a poor candidate to take up diplomacy with the British. On board the *Africa* he debated with English travelers on Lord John Russell's right to use the nation-status term of "belligerents" when referring to the Confederate States. He insisted that they tell him whether, by the same standards, the world should have called the rebels of Ireland in 1798 belligerents.[41]

Far less belligerent himself within the confines of his stateroom, he composed a letter to Cardinal Barnabo and asked the Pope's blessing "even in this matter so apparently foreign to my sacred vocation as a prelate of the Catholic Church." His role was that of a peacemaker, he explained, and he represented "the interests of the South as well as the North—in short, the interests of all the United States, just the same as if they had never been distracted by the Civil War." Leaping to a presumption of approval Hughes reasoned: "I could not refuse his [the President's] request, and at the same time I imagined if any success should attend my mission, it would redound to the benefit of Catholics, and to the promotion of the interests of the Church."[42]

The travelers landed in Liverpool and dashed through England in two days, stopping overnight in London. There Hughes paid an unexpected call on the American Ambassador, Charles Francis Adams. The Puritan son of a Puritan President informed the Catholic bishop that he was in the midst of dining with friends, gave him eight minutes of his time and then bid him off.

The London *Times* was equally friendly. On November 26th the paper observed: "Mr. Weed and Bishop Hughes, two of Mr. Seward's best friends, faintly disclaim the notion that their voyage to Europe is on diplomatic business." Skeptical of this disclaimer the *Times* suggested that they were sent to balance the effect of Mason and Slidell's mission. Hughes's political credentials, like those of Weed, stood out for all to see: "Bishop Hughes is a Roman Catholic prelate of attainments and political experience, moderate for one in his position, skillful, and anti-English. He has worked the Irish element in the States for a considerable period, and has used it in favor of Mr. Seward."[43] Hughes, who was then traveling in France, raced off a reply. He denied that he was anti-English. He followed the assertion with twenty-four handwritten pages relating why he *might* have been anti-English even though he was not. At one point he bore down with such force that his pencil tore the page.[44] In the end a more truly diplomatic head prevailed (no doubt Weed's) and the letter was not sent.

The two men arrived in Paris in the midst of a cold, windy rain that saturated their clothes and chilled them to the bone. Hughes was ill by the time they reached their hotel at 1 A.M., and a doctor was summoned. Despite this he was up at ten the next morning to pay a call on U.S. Ambassador William Dayton. As with Adams, the professional diplomat Dayton was piqued by the sudden appearance of amateurs who could only diminish the importance of the actual ambassadors. The archbishop's instructions written by Seward were carefully nonofficial, but nonetheless authoritative. Hughes was told simply: "You will study how . . . you can promote healthful opinions." Dayton, as the United States minister, was expected "to receive you as a trusted confidential, loyal and devoted citizen who assumes this duty at much sacrifice to himself and only on the earnest request of the President of the United States."[45]

Instead, while Weed returned to London Dayton kept Hughes at arm's length, and over the space of several weeks he made no move to obtain an interview for him with the Emperor. Apprizing himself of this situation, Hughes set out on his own. In Catholic Paris, as Seward had known, doors would be open to the archbishop of New York to which the ambassador himself had no access. The legislature of France was in session, and the archbishop of Paris introduced Hughes to the cardinals of the empire—they being, as Hughes related somewhat wistfully to Seward, ex-officio members of the senate. He was wined and dined by the elite of Paris, anxious to hear pertinent gossip about the *Trent* affair. Mason and Slidell, who would have been competing for the attentions that Hughes and Weed sought, had never reached Europe. An American warship had stopped a British vessel flying the British flag, removed the two men and brought them as prisoners to the United States. England was aflame with anger. Hughes's friend, "the gallant old soldier" Winfield Scott, left Paris for home insisting "war is inevitable."[46] The French, whom Hughes felt were possessed of "a wide-spread ignorance of the state of affairs in our country," were openly sympathetic to the southerners. Even in socially gracious settings Hughes fed them a hard line. The United States, he told them, had done nothing more than what England had done prior to the War of 1812 and still claimed the right to do. Moreover, if Europe wanted to test the "power and resources of the United States" 24 millions of freemen and patriots there would resist being "subjugated, or reduced, or conquered back into subservient colonies no matter whether the national life is attempted by France, or England or both combined." "You would be surprised," Hughes wrote Seward, "if you could have witnessed the wide opening of eyes among those to whom I made this known after dinner today . . ."[47]

As England insisted upon the release of Mason and Slidell, Hughes hurriedly wrote Seward that the two men should be tried and then pardoned by the President before being set free; this would save the United States from losing face to Great Britain. He also hoped that the French would play the role of mediator between the mother and daughter countries. Having discerned that the policies of the nation he was visiting were made in "neither France nor Paris, but the brain of the Emperor,"[48] he had written on his own for an appointment, and on Christmas Eve Napoleon and the Empress invited him to call. The two self-made men were correct enough in their interview. Louis kept his neutral guard up and made Hughes play the visiting curé when he pressed too close politically. Hughes kept to the subject of United States foreign policy, never once mentioning the plight of the Pope or the fact that he himself had severely criticized France for using the Papal States as a pawn in international politics. Instead he asked Louis to arbitrate between England and France before a war broke out over the *Trent* affair. The Emperor replied that he could do so if the source of dispute was a negotiable point such as a boundary line. But the confrontation involved a point of honor, and that was not something that could be negotiated. He, in turn, asked why the North brought about the war with the southern states by imposing a high foreign import tariff. Hughes suggested that it must have escaped the Emperor's memory that the South had been the first to obtain a tariff from the Federal government to protect itself against West Indies cotton.

The Empress interrupted to ask how the blockade, so unfriendly to France's shipping, could ever be maintained "along so extensive a coast."

"It cannot last," she said. "Napoleon I had that topic in mind during the war with England, and with all his immense capacity he gave it up as impracticable."

"Imperial lady," Hughes replied, turning a very small knife, "if Napoleon I had been acquainted, for maritime purposes, with the power of steam and the velocity of electric communication by telegraph his dynasty would not have suffered an interruption . . ."

Rather than wade deeper into touchy issues between France and the United States the couple brought out their son and turned the affair into a Christmas call from the local parish priest. Hughes was asked to lay a blessing upon the heir to a dynasty that the new Napoleons trusted would not suffer another interruption, and the visit was concluded.[49]

Later, Hughes wrote to Seward and weighed the effect his interview might have had upon the liberal revolutionary who had become imperial dictator. "It is generally thought that certain men are above being influenced. This is a mistake. If there ever was a man of such a type, it would be General Jackson; and yet whilst General Jackson would disregard, under certain circumstances, the opinion of his whole cabinet, General Jackson might take up and reflect upon a phrase uttered by the barber who shaved him."[50] Or the curé who blessed his son.

The tension over the *Trent* affair subsided with the release of the two commissioners, although Hughes, the Irishman, remained convinced that the "awful war between England and

America must come sooner or later." He remained in France throughout the winter, preaching to French have-nots from the pulpit of St. Roch and happily playing an ecclesiastical Ben Franklin for the haves of Paris society. Without shrinking he suggested to Seward that his expense account might be enlarged and that he be authorized to peddle the Union cause in other European capitals, like St. Petersburg.[51] Seward's delicate reply showed why he deserved the state department. President Lincoln, he assured Hughes, "directs me to say that while highly appreciating the services which you have already rendered . . . he thinks that, as at present advised, the public interests do not require that your direction should be complied with."[52]

Hughes drew less polite fire from a Paris newspaper that had picked up his anonymous debate with Brownson. The *Journal Des Debates* accused the archbishop of being proslavery. He vehemently denied it but still asserted that he was antiabolition. "Slavery is the sick man of the United States," he insisted. ". . . The abolitionists of the North where slavery does not exist look at the conditions of the sick man through a telescope. Everything to their eye is magnified, and they would prescribe for him accordingly . . . There are in the southern states four millions of slaves. Abolish slavery all at once and what is to become of them? What is to become of their masters? What is to become of those articles which are the produce of their toil and which Europe so much needs? The abolition party in North America make but little account of this."[53]

Defending the South on this point, Hughes had to balance himself. He prepared the French government for John Slidell's arrival with a document he drew up to show that the southern states had always coveted Cuba for the purpose of extending slavery. The politics of France, he had noticed, were formed not in one brain, but two. The Empress was Spanish, and the fate of Spain's colony would be a subject about which she would be "naturally sensitive."[54]

In early February he traveled to Marseilles and sailed for Rome. There, despite the comparative warmth of the Mediterranean climate, he encountered a decided chill in the atmo-

sphere. Several American prelates had complained of the archbishop of New York's secular diplomatic jaunt, and Hughes
found himself very much on the defensive with the Pope, with
Pius's Secretary of State, Cardinal Antonelli, and Cardinal
Barnabo of Propaganda. Optimistically he took note of every
polite smile and decided "they all approved of my conduct, and
instead of censuring me, showed a disposition to confer additional honors."[55] The additional honors—a cardinal's hat—did
not materialize. Yet Hughes almost penitentially resurrected
his ultramontanist fervor and focused monk-like attentions
upon the interests of the papacy. He cancelled plans for a trip
to the court of Spain and instead whispered his support for the
Federal Union to the Spanish ambassador in Rome.

Pio Nono had issued an invitation to the world's bishops
to attend the canonization of twenty-six Japanese martyrs on
the Feast of Pentecost in June. Hughes decided it would be improper for him, being so close, not to remain for the celebration. He joined in the Holy Week ceremonies at St. Peter's and
officiated at the Stations of the Cross in the Coliseum. Indeed
he became so thoroughly enveloped in the world of the Church
he ended one diplomatic missive by assuring a presumably anxious Seward: "The Holy Father and all the Cardinals are in the
enjoyment of good health and apparently peace of mind."[56]

He did not completely forget the purpose of his travels.
Americans from the Confederacy were also in Rome and
Hughes fought the European tendency to sympathize with the
southern cause. Repeatedly he pointed out not only the rights
of the North but its "physical powers," and he predicted that
because of this latter, "the strife must soon come to an end."[57]

Hughes's rheumatism was beginning to cripple him severely. He took heated sulpher baths during his stay in Italy.
After the canonization ceremony in early June he went northward to England, but stopped at Aix-les-Bains in search of
relief from pain. In Ireland, during July, whatever adverse effects the damp climate might have had upon his joints were
burned away by the fire he felt within himself at experiencing
his homeland's oppression. Freshly energetic, he preached at
the laying of the cornerstone of Dublin's Catholic University

and spent a week in that city being treated as if he were a visiting head of state. His speeches bristled with animosity toward England. "When America sent her charities by shiploads to assist the starving thousands of your people," he reminded his listeners, ". . . England required a duty on the bread of Charity, and that for the principle that . . . the regular channels of trade should not be interfered with."[58]

The national dignity of the United States had been attacked by England during the *Trent* affair, he assured audiences, and Americans had "treasured up the memory of that attack with a feeling of revenge."

With an intensity that would convince a Confederate agent that the archbishop was attempting to recruit soldiers for the Union, Hughes made the Civil War into a training ground for future rebellions. He declared: "The Irish have, in many instances, as I have the strongest reasons for knowing, entered into this war partly to make themselves apprentices, students as it were, finishing their education in this, the first opportunity afforded them of becoming thoroughly acquainted with the implements of war."[59]

Being so caught up in his hopes for an Irish revolt, Hughes received a group of young men from Nenagh. He did not know that they were members of the Brotherhood of Saint Patrick, a secret society forbidden by the Church, but he certainly knew they were ardent revolutionaries. A reporter was present and took down the entire conversation—a conversation that would cause Hughes excruciating embarrassment when it was printed in newspapers. While the reporter scratched away unnoticed in a corner, Hughes opened a barrier to his inner self and reminisced.

> Now [continued his grace with a smile] I will confess to you gentlemen, that when I left this country for America—then a young man—I had a kind of spite against priests and bishops [much laughter]. Remember how long ago that was. Well my spite against the priests and bishops was based on the false impressions that they stood between our people and their liberties—that but for them Ireland would be free. [applause and laughter—We cannot convey to our readers any notion of the quiet humor and graceful gentlemanly

tone, with which this was said, and the effect it produced upon his grace's audience.] But you know, I was mistaken. There was one bishop, of whom I never heard anything but was bad [laughter]—in fact he was reported to be a regular government man [renewed laughter]. You may be sure I did not like him; but, let me confess it. I found out afterwards that he was one of the best friends of Ireland. You know, his was the time of what is called the revolutions of '98—a movement in which after all the means were not equal to the object proposed—and that is everything.

With the memories of 1848 still fresh, Hughes warned the young men:

If you undertake a revolution and have not so measured your strength you commit a great crime. You will not do— however just the cause—to undertake to fight a great empire with a few rusty muskets and a commissariat contained in your carpet bag [applause and laughter]. Such rash proceedings only insure ignominious failure and settle the tyrant more firmly in his saddle . . . But if the time comes, it will not be the redress your wrongs merely—for the world is selfish [laughter] and nations take care of themselves—it will originate in an effort to settle other and more general grievances. Through them, no doubt Ireland may have her opportunity.[60]

The next day he traveled to Cork and upon his arrival found his remarks staring back at him from newsprint. Informed that the deputation had been representatives of a secret society, he felt as if he had been manipulated. He could not deny that the words were his and did not back away from the sentiments he expressed. Rather, as he apologized to the archbishop of Dublin he tried "to put myself right in the estimation of the good Catholics of Ireland" and accused the young men of tricking him by a false representation of themselves. As much as he disliked throwing the friendly lads over he had a damaged reputation to salvage. "Though a bishop should be humble and forbearing," he regretted, "he is not bound to be trampled upon by virtue of his humility."[61]

Humble and forbearing John Hughes arrived back in New York on August 12th, 1862. The patriotic service he had rendered for his country made him the object of gratitude offered by all levels of government. The Common Council of New York, which had battled him tooth and nail a generation before, drew up a resolution of congratulations and thanks. There was a present waiting from the governor of the state. The Putnam Bill had been written off the books by the legislature in Hughes's absence, and the pen that had done so was sent as a gift to the archbishop of New York. Three days after his arrival, Hughes went to Washington to confer with Seward. The Secretary of State gave a banquet in the archbishop's honor on a Friday night, and in doing so gave Washington society a taste of being Catholic for the evening. The main course was fish. No meat was served. This consideration was, to Hughes, "the most delicate compliment I have ever received."[62]

On Sunday he was back in New York and preached at the cathedral. Reminding his congregation that "next to religion, men are taught by religion itself to love and serve their country," he pleaded that all force be used to restore the United States unity:

> Volunteers have been appealed to, and they have answered the appeal; but for my own part, if I had a voice in the councils of the Nation, I would say, let volunteers continue, and the draft be made. If three hundred thousand men be not sufficient let three hundred thousand more be called upon, so that the army, in its fulness of strength, shall always be on hand for any emergency. This is not cruelty; this is mercy; this is humanity—anything that will put an end to this draggling of human blood across the whole surface of the country. Then, every man, rich and poor, will have to take his share; and it ought not to be left to the Government to plead with the people, to call upon them to come forward and to ask them if they will permit themselves to be drafted. No; but the people themselves should insist upon being drafted and be allowed to bring this unnatural strife to a close.[63]

This plea, made into a reality, would spill yet more human blood across the country within the year, most drastically in New York.

Thomas Mooney, who was not a man to harbor bad feelings, arranged a gathering of orphans and school children to welcome the archbishop home. Hughes was touched by the demonstration and, in his thanks to the Common Council for their resolution, alluded to the children's welcome in order to distinguish the differing roles he played in life. "Theirs was a welcome to the archbishop while yours is a token of regard to me as a citizen and bishop, for I do not consider the one compatible with the other. My being an archbishop has not prevented me from accepting the kind testimonial offered to the citizen."[64]

Within the Church there were others who took note of this duality in Hughes's life, and who cared little for the archbishop's activities as a citizen. Agreeing with the *Courier des Etats Unis,* which had called Hughes another Peter the Hermit rallying for war, Francis Kenrick's organ in Baltimore, the *Catholic Mirror,* called Hughes the "champion of desolation, blood and fratricide."[65] Father Thomas Heyden used his newspaper in Bedford, Pennsylvania to attack the fellow priest who had been his close friend in the 1820s, and a hurt Hughes responded by discarding Heyden's opinions as those of a "country parson."[66] One elderly priest, intimate enough with the archbishop to scold him directly to his face, told Hughes: "I do not see how you could find a confessor to give you absolution during your journey in Europe. I did hope that during this sad contest the Catholic clergy would have kept their skirts clean from blood."[67] And then Barnard Smith, Hughes's informant in Rome, provided piecemeal accounts throughout the fall that weighed the effects of his diplomatic stay at the papal court.

> There is a great change here with regard to the North . . . I understand the reason for the change. Your exertions were felt and all parties meant to put you down. Your work in Ireland can never be forgotten in America and England can never pardon you. I know they are writing from every quarter against you . . .
> In my last letter I referred to the impressions that were made against you on account of a sermon you preached on your return. The Archbishop of New Orleans censured it

very much. He thinks it was not becoming your high dignity.[68]

Hughes's secular mission had served only to remind the
papacy of the indignities heaped upon Rome by generations of
Yankee Americans. "Here public opinion is against the
North," relayed Smith. "I was lately asked by a Cardinal why
the President recognized the Italian kingdom if the cabinet
were friendly to Catholics."[69] Hughes had warned Europe not
to provoke the nascent force of the United States. Rome, in
turn, decided that the Union would be "too great and powerful" if victorious. The Pope was quoted as saying, "I think it
would be better for the States to remain now as they are . . ."
In October came a letter from Pius IX to Hughes, phrased in
the pious sort of admonitions that Hughes could easily trans-
late as a rebuff. Ignoring any question of justice in the Union
cause, the Pope instructed the archbishop of New York to pray
along with his fellow bishops, North and South, for the cause
of peace.

The trinkets of flattery that Hughes had received from the
nativist politicians were small comforts. The rejection by his
episcopal peers and superiors in the realm of the Church
burned any laurels to ash. In November Hughes wrote to the
one politican who was truly a friend. "It is now more than
twenty-three years since I had the pleasure of being introduced
to you on the railroad train between Albany and Utica," he
told Seward. Then having braced the Secretary of State, and
himself as well, he dropped the optimism that had filled his
travel reports and gave his honest impression of what Europe-
ans thought of the New World and its problems. "There is no
love for the United States on the other side of the water. Generally speaking on the other side of the Atlantic the United
States are ignored, if not despised—treated in conversation in
the same contemptuous language as we might employ towards
the inhabitants of the Sandwich Islands, or Washington territory, or Vancouvers Island, or the settlement of the Red River or
of the Hudson's Bay Territory."

Nor did he retain any illusions about his own popularity.
Of his homecoming talk he confessed, "some have called it not

a sermon but a discourse, and even a war blast in favor of spilling blood."[70]

Throughout that winter into 1863 he retreated not merely into seclusion, but into isolation. He had caught a cold in October while administering Confirmation to Catholic soldiers in the chill open air at Staten Island's Camp Scott. This, with his rheumatism and discouragement, made him into an invalid. Living now with the Rodrigues on Madison Avenue instead of with his priests at the cathedral rectory, he lay on a couch, heavily clothed in a vain attempt to keep warm. Even on days when he felt well enough to be up he remained alone in his room rather than join in family gatherings.

He began to rally toward winter's end. His mind, still strong, battled with the weakness of his body. Diocesan discipline remained firm. A priest who overstepped his authority within his parish received a rebuke colder than the February weather: "You are . . . an assistant . . . nothing more nothing less," Hughes wrote. "The pastor is bound to see that you shall not usurp either his prerogative or mine . . . If this is too much for you I shall put no obstacle in the way of your leaving my diocese."[71]

Levi Silliman Ives, who campaigned for Catholic Charities tirelessly—as far away from a suspicious Hughes as possible—drew the archbishop's fire when he attempted to extend the care of a school for wayward girls to include youngsters who were poor. Hughes's principal objection seemed to be that Ives and his associates had not informed him in advance of the plan. He wrote to Ives, saying, "You and they, with no doubt the best intention, have interfered in a way which as Archbishop of New York, I cannot permit or tolerate . . ."[72]

The suffragan bishops of Boston, Hartford, Albany, Buffalo, Newark, and Brooklyn found themselves taking an unexpected springtime trip when Hughes, as though he were asking them to travel from different sections of the same city, ordered them to meet in Troy, New York, within a week's time of his invitation. He wished them to view and discuss a recently purchased Methodist school that he planned to convert into a provincial seminary.

Hughes was determined to resume a strenuous life. In

March he spoke at the commencement of Bellevue Medical College. In a well-ordered speech pertinent to the occasion, he used his experiences during the cholera epidemic of 1832 to give evidence of the continual need of growth in medical knowledge. In April he delivered an address for relief of the poor in Ireland at the New York Academy of Music, but this time his illness got the best of him. After a few sentences he lost any power to project his voice, and only those within close range could hear him. His own words on the sufferings of the Irish choked him with emotion. "I cannot bear it," he whispered, while a crowd accustomed to his powerful oratory watched an old man, suddenly as piteous as his topic. "We cannot think of it patiently; it is too bad."[73]

In May he confirmed students at Mount St. Vincent, but he remained seated while he preached, and the Sisters noted that his voice "usually so strong, trembled and faltered."[74]

A visit to Fordham was usually enough to stir up Hughes's adrenaline. During June commencement he found the energy to criticize the valedictorian's speech. The young man had spoken strongly against the Federal government and had freely used the word "despotism" referring to its activities. Hughes immediately took him to task for his incendiary statements; he retorted that the United States never needed rebellions to solve its problems as long as it had the "safety valve" of Presidential elections to release pressures.[75]

Severely criticized as he might have been after his return from Europe, Hughes had not backed away an inch from his sense of patriotism. When a European newspaper erroneously reported that his relief for Ireland speech had been part of a "democratic peace meeting" attended also by General McClellan, the New York *Tablet* declared: "No two men in America would be less likely to speak at a democratic peace meeting than the two eminent individuals just named."[76]

The war pervaded all aspects of life and of Hughes's episcopacy. He wrote a consoling letter to Michael Corcoran, assuring him that his authority had made it his necessary duty to execute an insubordinate officer. In June a plea for help came from Mount St. Mary's which, within the month, would lay in the path of Lee's army. A student from Louisiana, Maurice Byrne, had written home that he was "as good a Confederate as ever trotted a horse."[77] His letters were intercepted. He was arrested and sent to prison in Baltimore. Hughes decided that this action had been "childish to the extreme, and unworthy of a government which has any confidence in its own strength."[78]

He wrote directly to Lincoln, described Byrne as "a puny and delicate boy of fifteen years," and reminded the President that Mrs. Lincoln had recently visited with him while in New York and had been accompanied by "her interesting little son," the much-pampered Tad. Without making reference to the undisciplined behavior the President's son was wont to exhibit, Hughes pointedly observed, "I should think it at once cruel and undignified to take advantage of any expression of loyalty or disloyalty which the interesting boy should have made use of on such an occasion." So too, with the case of Byrne: "To detain such a captive seems to me too small for so great a government as that at the head of which your excellency has been placed by the American people."[79] Maurice Byrne was released and returned to Mount St. Mary's. When he turned sixteen he ran away, joined the Confederate Army and ten days afterward was killed in his first battle.

In June of 1863 Hughes preached his last formal sermon. Disheartened by a war that seemed to be an endless bloody stalemate, he pleaded: "We must pray—I do not say for peace, which appears at this moment ridiculous . . . We must pray to the Almighty to bring matters to a conclusion. One side can make war, but it requires two sides to make peace."[80]

In the week following the Battle of Gettysburg Hughes, though he complained of "exceeding weakness in my lower extremities," distributed diplomas at three commencement exercises on three successive nights. On the last of these evenings, he had just arrived home when he received a telegram announcing that Archbishop Francis Kenrick was dead.[81] The news stunned him. He and Kenrick had never been friends, and Kenrick had joined his detractors after the European trip. But they were the same age; they had shared work and lodgings thirty and more years before in Philadelphia and had weathered the long nativist era together. His death made Hughes's own passage from life seem all the more imminent. He insisted upon going to Baltimore for the funeral and stayed at a hotel rather than a rectory or a private home, saying that his failing health would be an inconvenience to a host. He knew he could never endure the long requiem solemnities; so on the morning of the funeral he began to say a Low Mass at a side altar of the cathedral. He was too feeble and began to fall. Several attendants ran to him; he was placed in a chair and his vestments were removed. Though he would again on several occasions attempt to say Mass, he was unable to stand for the length of time necessary. Thereafter he attended Mass celebrated by his secretary.[82]

Even in failing health Hughes knew the mind of the Irish. He had warned the Secretary of State that the immigrants would fight for the Union but not for what he saw as the nativist cause of abolition. The Emancipation Proclamation was a shock to him. "No President excepting even Washington," he wrote, "has been more honest or patriotic than Abraham Lincoln, but according to my weak opinion, Mr. Lincoln is deficient in reliance upon his own judgement . . ."[83]

The *Freeman's Journal* and the *Metropolitan Record* had long since parted company with the Irish archbishop, but they spoke the language and minds of many an Irishman on the street. These newspapers both reflected and encouraged a growing hostility to the war. While the *Record* told its readers that they would soon be taxed to support the freed Negro, the *Journal* assured the Irish that emancipation would cost them their jobs.[84] "The Abolition party is working wonders for the laboring white men of the North," wrote McMaster, who had already been jailed once for his seditious views. ". . . [They] will soon have to be looking out for homes in the far west to make room for the colored emigrants . . . after the first of June when 3,500,000 darkees are let loose, declared to be 'then, thence forward and forever free!' God bless Massa Linkum"[85]

The newspaper injected strong doses of racism into the reasonable fears of the Irish labor force. The word "nigger" was common to New York prints, but the *Freeman's Journal* embellished the slur to a point far ahead of contemporary bigotry. A typical example was the report that "three big ugly female niggers" had arrived in the city to join a growing band of beggars, all of whom complained, "You white people in the Norf told us to run away from our masters an you would treat us like brudders . . ."[86]

In March the city newspapers publicized the tactic of a shipping company that had brought Negroes to break a strike of Irish laborers. Resentments seethed.

When the President signed into law the nation's first enforced military draft the *Freeman's Journal* called the act an "outrage on justice and decency." "Congress," announced McMaster, "has authorized Abe Lincoln to say, as the Roman monster Caligula wrote to his mother 'I have power in all things, and over all persons.' "[87] Nor did it help matters that the law allowed an exemption for any man drafted who could buy his way out with $300. From the view point of the impoverished Irish this meant that nativists—who had fought the presence of immigrants and who had begun the abolitionist crusade—would sit comfortably at home while the poor man went to fight a war that was not of his making. A seething cauldron, the lid of which had been pressed down for over two generations of time, was being heated to the point of explosion.

On July 4th in the wake of Gettysburg, the Democratic Governor Horatio Seymour inflamed New Yorkers with an Independance Day speech directed against Washington's latest tyranny. "Remember this" he explained, "that the bloody and treasonable, and revolutionary doctrine of public necessity can be proclaimed by a mob as well as a government."[88]

Throughout the week the newspapers had printed the casualty lists from the battle—and the lists were heavy with Irish names. It was an inappropriate moment for Horace Greeley to give vent to his dislike for the Irish. On July 9th he published an open letter to John Hughes in response to the archbishop's declaration that Irish immigrants had played no part in bringing about the Civil War. As if the Irish had been an influential portion of the American populace for generations, Greeley lectured Hughes, claiming that "your people" had helped cause the war by their adhesion to the Democratic party, in the election of Polk in 1844, by supporting the Mexican War, and by the refusal of priests to preach abolition of Negroes. "Your people," he scolded, "for years have been and today are foremost in the degredation and abuse of this persecuted race."[89]

On Saturday July 11th, with whatever military forces the city possessed still absent in Pennsylvania, the draft began. The timing could not have been worse. Yet, no one expected trouble. On the morning of the first drawings the *Tribune* decided: "The people generally appear to consider the draft as a matter of course." For once Bennett agreed with Greeley. "The people have become used to its hitherto somewhat dreaded name," he said, "and now look upon the ordeal as a necessary consequence of time and age in which we live."[90]

Throughout the day crowds stood outside the draft boards. *Herald* reporters took note that the people who crowded the curbs and streets were "composed exclusively of laborers and mechanics who seemed unable to raise the amount required to exempt them from the law."[91] They took the proceedings well enough. There was almost a carnival atmosphere as each name called drew hoots and sarcastic cheers.

But the next day was Sunday. A hot humid day with nothing to do but drink and talk about the rich man's war and the poor man's fight.

On Monday morning when the business of conscription was to resume the police expected no serious trouble and assigned only routine protection to the draft centers. As the day began, crowds of men began to gather seemingly without plan, and as they walked in herds up Fifth and Sixth avenues they merged and grew into a formless army. At Forty-sixth Street they turned and headed toward Third Avenue where the drawings would take place. Some of them, as if by plan, began pulling down the telegraph poles used for communication by the city police. Arriving at their destination they watched the proceedings for a few sullen minutes. Suddenly a rock was thrown, breaking a window, and the crowd charged the building, easily pushing aside the meager protective force.

It was the unleashing of a pent-up volcanic force that

would spill fire and blood over New York City for four days. It divided Irish against Irish—for this immigrant group with one foot up the social ladder was divided between respectability and slums, between law enforcement and rioting. Significantly one of the first objects of the mob's hatred was the Superintendent of Police, John Kennedy. On his way to the office of the provost marshal he had seen the massive crowd and left his carriage to investigate. He was recognized, attacked and beaten savagely. Pulling himself away from his attackers he ran blindly across a Forty-sixth Street lot where again he was caught, hurled to the ground and stomped. A passing politician who knew Kennedy managed to appeal to the last flicker of the mob's mercy and saved the man's life. The police rushed small forces to the scene, using what telegraph equipment still worked to relay communication. At the same time an electric communication beyond sense filled the hot July air, and in all precincts the city's poor erupted into a single huge riot. By midday tens of thousands of humans filled Third Avenue searching for a means to express frustrations and hatred. The combined forces of the military and the police mustered barely a thousand men.

An armory became the scene of a battle. A small force of police held it for a time, then retreated through a back window. The mob took it, emptied it of weapons and set fire to it. "No Draft" placards appeared. Hotels, stores, and private homes became the objects of pillage. Railroad tracks were torn up. The city's blacks became the hapless objects of revenge. They had been the cause of the war whether they wished it or not. They were the cheap work force that the abolitionists would use to replace already ill-paid Irish labor. Male Negroes who could not hide or escape from the city were brutally attacked, beaten, lynched and even burned to death. The orphan asylum for blacks on Fifth Avenue was attacked. The superintendent managed to get the children out through a back door before the building was broken into, sacked and burned. One small girl who had hidden under her bed was beaten to death.

The police, as small a force as they were, still had the advantage of discipline over the rioters, and as the day waxed they managed to hold their own in confrontations. Horace Greeley's *Tribune,* the clarion of the abolitionists, was attacked in the evening of the first day. The building was broken into and the ground floor torn apart, but the police managed to beat the crowds back.

Greeley, awed and frightened by the magnitude of what was occurring, reported that this was "not simply a riot but the commencement of a revolution organized by the sympathizers in the North with the southern rebellion."[92]

The Confederacy, after the crushing defeat at Gettsyburg, caught wind of the turmoil in New York and hoped that Greeley was right. The Richmond *Examiner* prophesied that "this excellent outbreak may be the opening scene of the inevitable revolution which is to tear to pieces that most rotten society and leave the Northern half of the old American Union a desert of blood-soaked ashes."[93]

New York was well on its way to becoming just that. The second day of riots involved pitched battles between police and mobs. In a fight on Second Avenue in which the state militia was led by a Colonel Henry O'Brien, howitzers were fired into the crowds. A wire factory containing 3,000 carbine rifles was held only with difficulty by the city forces. The mob sought to give itself direction. "All we want is a leader," cried one man who had climbed atop an awning, "and then we shall go to victory or the devil."[94]

In Washington Secretary of War Stanton ordered first the 7th Regiment, and then after hearing more direful reports, five militia units to rush back to New York.

Governor Seymour arrived in the city and attempted to make up for the harangue he had delivered on the 4th of July. He asked John Hughes, "Will you exert your powerful influence to stop the disorder now reigning in this city?"[95] Greeley seconded the request, reminding the public that Archbishop Hughes was the first man in New York who had publicly urged a draft. He urged Hughes to do something now.

Anguished by the disgrace the Irish were bringing upon themselves, Hughes first attacked Greeley for the hypocrisy of his position. The *Tribune* had consistently defended the right of rebels in Rome to overthrow the temporal rule of the Pope. What was different about the city of New York? Then he issued a statement to the rioters:

> In spite of Mr. Greeley's assault upon the Irish, in the present disturbed condition of the city, I will appeal not only to them, but to all persons who love God and revere the holy Catholic religion which they profess, to respect also the laws of man and the peace of society, to retire to their homes with as little delay as possible, and disconnect themselves from the seemingly deliberate intention to disturb the peace and social rights of the citizens of New York. If they are Catholics, I ask, for God's sake—for the sake of their holy religion—for my own sake, if they have any respect for the episcopal authority—to dissolve their bad association with reckless men, who have little regard either for divine or human laws.[96]

Hughes's priests were on the streets working against impossible odds to stem the avalanche of mindless force. Father Treanor of Transfiguration parish saved a family of blacks from being lynched. The Paulists walked neighborhood streets, attempting to bring calm. Father McMahan of St. John the Evangelist parish dissuaded a crowd from attacking Columbia College by convincing them that it would be a disgrace to destroy a school housing a chapel. Father Quarter talked a gang out of setting fire to a house.

Colonel O'Brien of the state militia was foolhardy enough to return to his home neighborhood. He was attacked, beaten and tortured. Father Cloury attempted to get his murderers away from him. "The man is already dying," he told them. "He can never recover. You have done your worst; now pray let me remove his body, and render to him the last offices of our Church." A moment's truce, but not an obedient peace, was sullenly granted. "You can do your office here," the leader of the mob replied, "and we will protect you in it but no one shall remove the man from where he lies."[97] At that point the mob was still a force that could be momentarily held back, but not stopped.

On Wednesday, the third day of pitched rioting, Governor

Seymour declared the city to be in a state of insurrection. On Rikers Island 300 recruits rebelled and locked up their officers. Only the threat of a bombardment from a gunboat brought this mutiny to order. Within the city the military had taken to repeatedly sweeping mobs with howitzer fire to hold them off.[98]

Greeley still insisted that Hughes himself should be on the streets. He pointed out that the archbishop of Paris in 1848 had lost his life at the barricades while pleading for peace. "That was an act of sublime devotion," he said. "We think the great personal influence of Archbishop Hughes could be used to advantage among 'his people' by his riding among them and speaking to them on their duties."[99]

"Mr. Greeley treats me as if I were a head constable," said Hughes. ". . . It is for the civil authorities to take care of all the people. If they cannot do this they are incompetent to take care of themselves or protect us, and they might as well give us public notice of the fact and then go to bed."[100]

It was not a question of courage. The wildest of the rioters would have respected his person even as they ignored what he said. What Hughes could not bring himself to do was endorse Greeley's use of the words "his people." The rioters may have been nearly all Irish and Catholic, but there were hundreds of thousands of Irish Catholics under Hughes's jurisdiction who were not rioters and who were stigmatized by Greeley's characterization. "His people" were those who obeyed the Church's law and loved their country. He had been forced throughout the nativist era to arm Catholics to protect churches when civil authorities ignored "anti-popery" rioters. Now a tide of brute force had returned to the nativist population the evils that they themselves had sown. Hughes said the same things now that he had said in the 1840s. The civil government had the obligation to preserve civil peace.

It was not a matter of vengeance. The riots crushed him. He was a father whose children had betrayed his trust in them. They had ruined their own name. They had made true all that the nativists had preached about them for years. The military was arriving in the city—4,000 soldiers by Thursday with 2,000 more on the way. If it were a potential revolution it would be quickly put down. Brute irrational force would be stopped with force. Hughes in his sorrow could not see that America had been spoken to in the only language that could interrupt its train of prejudiced thought. Just as the blacks would do in another century, the Irish had taught those above them on the social ladder not to respect them for the sake of justice, but to fear them as a potentially dangerous force.

On Thursday Hughes placed posters throughout the city.

To the Men of New York who are now called in many of the papers Rioters:

Men! I am not able, owing to rheumatism in my limbs, to visit you, but that is not a reason why you should not pay me a visit, in your whole strength. Come then, to-morrow, Friday, at two o'clock to my residence, northwest corner of Madison Avenue and 36th Street. I shall have a speech prepared for you. There is abundant space for the meeting around my house. I can address you from the corner of the balcony. If I should be unable to stand during its delivery you will permit me to address you sitting. My voice is much stronger than my limbs. I take upon myself the responsibility of assuring you that in paying me this visit, or in returning from it, you shall not be disturbed by any exhibition of municipal or military presence. You who are Catholics or as many of you as are have a right to visit your Bishop without molestation.

†John Hughes,
Archbishop of New York.[101]

Ironically, there were many who doubted the authenticity of the notice because Hughes for the first time in many years had signed his last name to a document. There was irony as well, that after such strong insistence that he speak, he was criticized for doing so. The *Times* declared that he was overstepping himself when he promised that his visitors would be undisturbed by the authorities. "Such an assurance implies the assumption of a power superior to that of the law; and whatever the Bishop might feel, we did not think he would be unwise enough openly to proclaim the possession of such a personal or official supremacy."[102]

The *Post* decided the authorities should do just the opposite of what Hughes promised. Agreeing that there were two classes of Irish—"the rioters and the orderly and industrious" —the paper warned:

> Their shepherd has summoned the wolves. Let not the sheep attend also . . . The Archbishop's call, if it is generally obeyed, will draw together a crowd of such miscreants, assassins, robbers, house burners, and thieves. Such a congregation of vicious and abandoned wretches is not often got together. The police should be on the look out there; they may catch many an incendiary, many a murderer, many a highway robber; and we cannot conceive that the Archbishop's safeguard could extend or that he would lend his protection to such malefactors.[103]

Some 5,000 people came to Hughes's residence. Appearing on a balcony, he was too weak to stand. He sat in a chair while addressing them. It was not a prepared speech. For an hour he rambled on, almost hesitantly, much like a parent attempting to make peace with a child after a deed too despicable to discuss and analyze openly. "They call you rioters," he began, "but I cannot see a rioter's face among you . . ." Such may have been the case. The reporters on hand observed that there was little to indicate that the multitude present had been through any pitched battles during the previous four days. "If I could have met you anywhere I should have gone, even on crutches," he assured them. Whereupon they applauded, and several voices cried out "God bless you." The archbishop continued, "But I could not go. My limbs are weaker than my lungs . . ."

"For myself, you know that I am a minister of God, a minister of peace, a minister who in your own trials and in years past, you know, never deserted you." He was interrupted by hearty applause, and cries of "Never, never." He went on. "With my tongue and with my pen I have stood by your fortunes always, and so shall I to the end, as long as you are right, and I hope you are never wrong. . . . If you are Irishmen, as your enemies say that the rioters are, I am an Irishman, too . . . and I am not a rioter." They laughed for him and he began to speak more intimately. "In this country the Constitution has made it the right of the people to make a revolution quietly every four years. Is that not so? . . . I am too old now to seek another home or another country. I want to cling by the old foundations of this, and I want the men who shall constitute the architects of the superstructure to be the right kind of men . . ."

A man in the crowd interjected: "Let the nigger stay south." Another silenced him by yelling the word: "Order!"

Hughes stopped, paused a moment to show his displeasure, and said: "I am not a legislator . . ." And then he spoke of the violence. ". . . A man has a right to defend his shanty, if it be no more, or his house, or his church at the risk of his life; but the cause must be always just; it must be defensive, not aggressive . . ."

He recalled to them a phrase that he had always incorporated proudly into his St. Patrick's Day sermons. The Irish were great fighters, and Ireland had never mothered a coward. But they defended, they never attacked. "Look here men," he pleaded, "the soil of Ireland was never crimsoned or moistened by a single drop of martyr's blood, and that is what no other nation can say . . ."[104]

But "his people" had made a lie of this. The reporters took down his words for a public that would make them into a bitter joke. He had spoken those words so proudly year after year. He spoke them now for the last time, his heart weighed by their hollowness.

Hughes went inside. The crowd cheered until, at length, he came out again. Someone asked his blessing. He gave it. The entire gathering made the sign of the cross in unison. He told them to go to their homes. Like school children, they obediently answered "We will," and began to disperse.

It was his last public appearance. The effect of the riots upon his spirit only intensified what was his last illness. He suffered from Bright's disease. His rheumatism and the advent of cold weather brought the usual heaviness to his chest.

In October he received a letter from Patrick Lynch, the Bishop of Charleston. Although the war had separated them in politics they still remained together in faith and friendship. Lynch had heard of Hughes's collapse at Kenrick's funeral and was worried. He knew that with the war Charleston was out of consideration. But why not consider a trip to Cuba? He assured Hughes that his own health was good. "I take things as quietly as I can. The only thing that startles me is a couple of hours without the sound of a cannon."[105]

Everything remained undone. The war raged on. The immigrants had thrown up new barriers to their assimilation. Even St. Patrick's cathedral, which was to be a symbol of their acceptance and the acceptance by America of the Catholic Church, stood incomplete, its walls, only one-story high, left deserted for the previous three years. And yet he had no more strength to continue the work. By December he was bedridden, cared for by his sisters—Margaret and Sister Angela. Four days after Christmas his vicar general told him his doctors advised that he be anointed. "Did they say so?" he asked.[106] They were his last words. He drifted into quietude and died, peacefully, on Sunday, January 3rd, 1864.

The *Herald* noted that respect was paid to Hughes upon his death "which has never been accorded to any other ecclesiastic in the country since the Declaration of Independence."[107] The Common Council ordered all offices of the city closed. Flags on public buildings were flown at half-mast. A good number of private businesses were closed. Some 100,000 people massed around the cathedral for the funeral, causing a great deal of disorder and confusion. Dignitaries such as General McClellan were present because it was the right thing to do. Others such as Thurlow Weed came because Hughes had been —for one reason or another—an important part of their lives. Amidst the dignitaries, unable to stand without assistance, was Hughes's seventy-six-year-old brother Michael from Chambersburg.

The *Freeman's Journal,* ostensibly a Catholic paper, relegated Hughes's death to a one-column notice on the back page situated underneath a two-line "Conundrum": "Why is gold like freemen? Answer—Because under Old Abe, it is either locked up or quits the country."

McMaster editorialized: "As priest and as bishop the deceased had spoken so much through newspapers and been so much spoken about through them, that on this account rather than for the eminent place he filled officially, it was natural that newspapers and readers of newspapers should be affected by his death."[108]

Horace Greeley, still peeved by his latest run-in with the archbishop, gave more prominent space to an article headlined "Recital of pews in Henry Ward Beecher's church," than to Hughes's death. The *Tribune* noted that "An account of the funeral of Archbishop Hughes, including the sermon by Bishop McCloskey is given on our second page. On the same page is an interesting letter about how colored recruits are got and how they are treated." On the editorial page Greeley said of Hughes that "His public services during the Rebellion are too recent to require attention."[109]

The *Times,* without editorializing, gave front-page coverage to Hughes's death and funeral as proper to a man of his official importance.

In Pennsylvania the *Franklin Repository,* in which Hughes as a student had published his first public argument, remembered him somewhat differently than the New York press. The paper reminded its readers that Hughes "was engaged with his father and brothers in grading and piking our streets, making excavations and performing other work of a similar character."[110]

And then there was James Gordon Bennett. "Archbishop Hughes," he said, "was loved by a simpleminded, religious, and intensely earnest race with a sentiment scarcely short of idolatry." He continued, saying, "Rightly constituted and rightly ruled the power of the Church for good or evil in the State is almost without limit, as the history of the Church shows. . . . When it is presided over by a man of intellect—a man whose opinions upon great questions are regarded as weighty in the counsels of the nation—its importance is seen and felt in every circumstance that affects it and cannot be overlooked by anyone who looks with his eyes open . . ."

John Hughes, decided James Bennett, his longtime foe,

"stood as the champion of that Church and as the champion of its people, by whom he was so greatly admired. In his death the Catholic Church of America has lost its best friend, and as remarked above, the country one of its purest patriots."[111]

It was all in the word "champion." Bishop McCloskey, who would be John's successor, preached the funeral homily. There were certainly many nods of pious agreement among the laity, some muted smiles from those who knew him well, and perhaps a few sighs of relief among the clergy as McCloskey began his sermon by quoting St. Paul: "I have fought the good fight . . ."

Notes

PRELUDE: THE BATTLEGROUND
1. W.H. Bennett, *Catholic Footsteps in Old New York*. New York, Schwartz, Kirwin, and Fauss, 1909, pp. 352-353.
2. Norbert H. Miller, "Pioneer Capuchin Missionaries in the United States," *Franciscan Studies*, March 1932, p. 191.

1. THE PRICE OF A BAPTISM
1. John Hassard, *Life of John Hughes, First Archbishop of New York*. New York, Arno Press and The New York Times, 1969, p. 18.
2. *Ibid.*, p. 20.

2. A MOUNTAIN WHERE MEN MET GOD
1. Bishop John Connolly to Propaganda, Feb. 26, 1818. (N.Y.)
2. Mary Meline and Edward McSweeny, *The Story of the Mountain*. Emmitsburg, Md., The Weekly Chronicle, 1911, Vol. I, p. 91.
3. *Ibid.*
4. *Ibid.*, p. 99.
5. Sr. Mary Agnes McGann, *The History of Mother Seton's Daughters*. New York, Longmans Green & Co., 1917, Vol. I, p. 134.
6. Hassard, *op. cit.*, p. 23.
7. *Ibid.*, p. 36.
8. *Ibid.*, p. 24.
9. Meline and McSweeny, *op. cit.*, p. 99.
10. Hassard, *op. cit.*, p. 40.

3. THE EMPEROR OF CHINA AS BISHOP
1. Bishop John Connolly to Propaganda, Feb. 26, 1818. (N.Y.)
2. Joseph Kirlin, *Catholicity in Philadelphia*. Philadelphia, American Catholic Historical Society, 1909, p. 216.
3. Martin Griffin, "Bishop Conwell," *American Catholic Historical Society Records*, Vol. 24 (1913), p. 36.
4. Hugh J. Nolan, *The Most Reverend Francis Patrick Kenrick Third Bishop of Philadelphia*. Philadelphia, American Catholic Historical Society, 1948, p. 67.
5. Kirlin, *op. cit.*, p. 227.
6. Griffin, *op. cit.*, Vol. 23, p. 308.

4. TRANSFORMATION
1. Meline and McSweeny, *op. cit.*, p. 117.
2. *Ibid.*, p. 120.
3. Dubois to Hughes, July 29, 1824. (Mt.)

4. Hassard, *op. cit.,* p. 35.
5. Meline and McSweeney, *op. cit.,* pp. 140-141.
6. Graham William to Michael Egan, Nov. 3, 1827. (Mt.)

5. A CLERIC WITH ONE MEMORIZED SERMON
1. Griffin, *op. cit.,* Vol. 26, p. 157.
2. *Ibid.,* Vol. 28, p. 82.
3. *Ibid.,* Vol. 28, p. 154.
4. *Ibid.,* Vol. 28, p. 245.
5. Hassard, *op. cit.,* p. 47.
6. *Ibid.,* p. 56.
7. Michael Egan to John McCaffery, undated 1826. (Mt.)
8. Father J. Savage to Father John Leaky, Dec. 13, 1826. (N.Y.)
9. Dubois to Hughes, Oct. 1826. (N.Y.)

6. "WHEN TO ME EVERYTHING WAS NEW"
1. Hassard, *op. cit.,* p. 50.
2. Hughes to Bruté, May 7, 1827. (Mt.)
3. Bruté to Hughes, undated. (N.Y.)
4. Kirlin, *op. cit.,* pp. 249-250.
5. *Ibid.,* p. 255.
6. Hassard, *op. cit.,* p. 58.
7. Kirlin, *op. cit.,* p. 249.
8. *Ibid.*
9. Peter Maitland to Michael Egan, April 5, 1827. (Mt.)
10. Hassard, *op. cit.,* p. 60.
11. Hughes to Bruté, May 7, 1827. (N.Y.)
12. Hughes to Egan, May 13, 1827. (Mt.)
13. Hughes to Bruté, May 7, 1827. (N.Y.)
14. Bruté to Hughes, May 14, 1827; May 22, 1827. (Mt.)
15. Kirlin, *op. cit.,* p. 258.
16. Hughes to Heyden, July 22, 1827; quoted in Hassard, *op. cit.,* p. 63.
17. Griffin, *op. cit.,* Vol. 28, p. 327.
18. Hughes to Bruté, May 14, 1828; quoted in Hassard, *op. cit.,* p. 68.
19. Griffin, *op. cit.,* Vol. 28, p. 335.
20. Hughes to Heyden, Oct. 21, 1828; quoted in Hassard, *op. cit.,* p. 70.
21. *Ibid.*
22. Nolan, *op. cit.,* p. 75.
23. *Ibid.,* pp. 74-76.
24. William Harold to Thomas Levins, Sept. 3, 1830. (N.Y.)
25. Griffin, *op. cit.,* Vol. 28, p. 347.

7. "A STUPENDOUS TISSUE OF IMPOSITION AND MENDACITY"
1. Peter Maitland to Michael Egan, April 5, 1827. (Mt.)
2. Hassard, *op. cit.,* p. 64.
3. *Ibid.,* p. 85.
4. *Ibid.,* p. 49.
5. John Hughes, *The Conversion and Edifying Death of Andrew Dunn; or, a guide to Truth and Peace*—included in *Complete Works of the Most Rev. John Hughes, D.D.,* edited by Lawrence Kehoe. New York, The

Catholic Publication House, 1864, Vol. I, pp. 664-691.

6. Hassard, *op. cit.*, p. 82.
7. Hughes, *op. cit.*, Vol. I, p. 40.
8. *Ibid.*, p. 39.
9. *Ibid.*, p. 40.
10. *Church Register*, June 6, 1929; quoted in Hassard, *op. cit.*, p. 92.
11. Hughes to Bishop Conwell, Jan. 29, 1829. (N.Y.)
12. Hughes to John McGerry, Jan. 2, 1829. (Mt.)
13. Hughes to Bishop Conwell, Jan. 29, 1829. (N.Y.)
14. Nolan, *op. cit.*, p. 84.
15. *Ibid.*, p. 91.
16. Cardinal Lambruschini to Propaganda, June 12, 1829; quoted in Nolan, *op. cit.*, pp. 82-83.
17. Conwell to Propaganda; quoted in Nolan, *op. cit.*, p. 80.
18. Nolan, *op. cit.*, p. 91.
19. Thompson Westcott, "A Memoir of the Very Rev. Michael Hurley, D.D., O.S.A." *American Catholic Historical Society Records*, Vol. I, p. 188.
20. Hughes to John Purcell, Dec. 21, 1829. (Mt.)
21. *Protestant*, Jan. 2, March 13, July 10, 1830.
22. *Ibid.*, March 19, 1831.
23. *Truth Teller*, Jan. 23, 1830.
24. *Protestant*, Jan. 2, 1830.
25. *Truth Teller*, Sept. 4, 1830.
26. *Protestant*, Feb. 13, 1830.
27. *Ibid.*, Feb. 20, 1830.
28. *Ibid.*, Feb. 27, 1830.
29. *Ibid.*, March 13, 1830.
30. *Ibid.*, June 12, 1830.
31. *Ibid.*, June 26, 1830.
32. *Truth Teller*, July 3, 1830.
33. *Protestant*, July 3, 1830.
34. *Ibid.*, July 10, 1830.
35. *Truth Teller*, July 17, 1830.
36. *Ibid.*, July 17, 1830.
37. *Ibid.*, July 27, 1830.
38. *Protestant*, July 24, 1830.
39. *Truth Teller*, Sept. 11, 1830.
40. *Ibid.*, Oct. 2, 1830.
41. *Ibid.*, Oct. 9, 1830.
42. *Ibid.*, Oct. 9, 1830.
43. *Ibid.*, July 17, 1830.

8. A QUEST FOR A MITER ON A DARK ROAD
1. Kenrick to Hughes, Oct. 2, 1830. (N.Y.)
2. Kenrick to Purcell, June 24, 1830; quoted in Nolan, *op. cit.*, p. 150.
3. Kirlin, *op. cit.*, p. 266.
4. Nolan, *op. cit.*, p. 108.
5. *Ibid.*, p. 120.
6. Hassard, *op. cit.*, p. 98.

7. *Ibid.,* p. 110.
8. *Ibid.,* p. 118.
9. Nolan, *op. cit.,* p. 119.
10. *Ibid.,* p. 120.
11. Martin Griffin, "History of the Church of St. John the Evangelist," *American Catholic Historical Society Records,* Vol. 20, p. 352.
12. Hassard, *op. cit.,* p. 115.
13. Hughes to Purcell, June 8, 1831. (N.Y.)
14. Hughes to Purcell, Jan. 12, 1831. (N.Y.)
15. Hughes to Bruté, Feb. 21, 1832; quoted in Hassard, *op. cit.,* p. 128.
16. Hassard, *op. cit.,* p. 129.

9. PESTILENCE AND POLEMICS
1. Hassard, *op. cit.,* p. 131.
2. *Ibid.*
3. *National Gazette,* June 19, 1832.
4. Charles E. Rosenberg, *The Cholera Years.* Chicago, The University of Chicago Press, 1962, p. 67.
5. Purcell to Jameson, July 3, 1832. (Mt.)
6. *United States Gazette,* August 26, 1832.
7. *Tablet,* June 6, 1863.
8. *United States Gazette,* August 26, 1832.
9. *Ibid.*
10. *United States Gazette,* Sept. 3, 1832.
11. Augustus Thebaud, *Three Quarters of a Century; A Retrospect,* New York, The United States Catholic Historical Society, 1904, p. 290.
12. Hassard, *op. cit.,* p. 112.
13. *United States Gazette,* Sept. 7, 1832.
14. William B. Sprague, *Annals of the American Pulpit; or Commemorative Notices of Distinguished Clergymen of Various Denominations.* New York, Robert Carter and Bros., 1859, Vol. IV, p. 646.
15. *Controversy Between Rev. Messrs Hughes and Breckinridge on the Subject: Is the Protestant Religion the Religion of Christ?* Philadelphia, Eugene Cunmiskey, 1862. Hughes to Breckinridge, Oct. 3, 1832; quoted in Preface.
16. *Ibid.,* Breckinridge to Hughes, Dec. 3, 1832.
17. *Protestant Episcopal and Church Register,* February, 1833, p. 78.
18. *Controversy Between . . . .* Breckinridge to Hughes, Dec. 3, 1832.
19. *Protestant Episcopal and Church Register,* May, 1833, p. 184.
20. Hughes to Bruté; quoted in Hassard, *op. cit.,* p. 142.
21. *Controversy Between . . .* p. 86, p. 80.
22. *Ibid.,* p. 214.
23. *Protestant Episcopal and Church Register,* Aug. 1833, p. 281.

10. PANTING TO DO GOOD, WIDESPREAD GOOD
1. Hassard, *op. cit.,* pp. 146-147.
2. *Ibid.,* p. 120.
3. McCaffrey to Bruté, April 25, 1833. (Mt.)
4. Meline and McSweeny, *op. cit.,* Vol. I, p. 290.
5. Hughes to Sr. Angela, Nov. 28, 1832; quoted in Hassard, *op. cit.,* p. 133.

6. Hughes, "A Sermon on the Festival of Saint Patrick," included in *Complete Works*, Vol. II, p. 169.
7. Griffin, "History of the Church of St. John the Evangelist," *loc. cit.*, pp. 373-374.
8. *Ibid.*
9. Ray Billington, *The Protestant Crusade: 1800-1860.* N.Y., The Macmillan Co., 1938, p. 75.
10. Rebecca Reed, *Six Months in a Convent.* Boston, Russell, Odiorne, and Metcalf, 1835, p. 83.
11. Hassard, *op. cit.*, p. 155.
12. *John Hughes, John Breckinridge, A Discussion of the Question: Is the Roman Catholic Religion in any or in all its Principles or Doctrines, Inimical to Civil or Religious Liberty? And of the Question: Is the Presbyterian Religion in any or in all its Principles or Doctrines, Inimical to Civil or Religious Liberty?* Philadelphia, Carey, Lea and Blanchard, 1836, p. 59.
13. *Ibid.*, p. 87.
14. *Ibid.*, pp. 47, 206, 509.
15. *Ibid.*, pp. 348, 527, 231.
16. *Ibid.*, p. 465.
17. *Ibid.*, p. 63.
18. *Ibid.*, p. 274, 20.
19. *Ibid.*, pp. 299, 36.
20. *Ibid.*, pp. 168, 170.
21. *Ibid.*, pp. 544-545.
22. *Ibid.*, pp. 419, 442.
23. *Ibid.*, p. 365.
24. *Ibid.*, p. 510.
25. *Ibid.*, p. 339.
26. *Ibid.*, p. 345.
27. *U.S. Catholic Miscellany*, Sept. 3, 1836.
28. *Ibid.*
29. Letter dated Feb. 1835; printed in *U.S. Catholic Miscellany*, Sept. 7, 1837.
30. Hughes, *John Hughes, John Brekinridge, A Discussion . . .* p. 537.
31. *Ibid.*
32. Hughes letter, undated (c. 1836). (N.Y.)
33. William L. Stone, *Maria Monk and the Nunnery of the Hotel Dieu.* N.Y., Commercial Advertiser, 1836, p. 31.
34. *U.S. Catholic Miscellany*, Sept. 16, 1837.

11. SCANNING THE INSIDES OF MITERS
1. Nolan, *op. cit.*, p. 195.
2. *Ibid.*, p. 200.
3. Hassard, *op. cit.*, p. 168.
4. APF American Center, Vol. 12, Feb. 6, 1837. Letter 1688.
5. Hassard, *op. cit.*, p. 167.
6. *Ibid.*, p. 171.
7. Wescott, *op. cit.*, Vol. I, p. 187.
8. Hassard, *op. cit.*, p. 174.

9. *Ibid.,* p. 179.
10. Hughes to Kenrick, Dec. 25, 1837. (N.Y.)
11. *Ibid.*
12. Nolan, *op. cit.,* p. 219.

12. A FRENCH ST. PATRICK
1. *Truth Teller,* Nov. 4, 1826.
2. *Ibid.*
3. *Ibid.,* Nov. 11, 1826.
4. *Ibid.*
5. John Dubois, *Pastoral Letter,* New York, John Doyle Pub. 1826, p. 7.
6. John Talbot Smith, *The Catholic Church in New York.* New York, Hall & Locke Co., 1905, Vol. I, p. 75.
7. John Power to Bishop Conwell, Jan. 30, 1827. (N.Y.)
8. James Rooney to Michael Egan, June 7, 1827. (Mt.)
9. *Truth Teller,* March 3, 1827.
10. Hughes to Purcell, Dec. 14, 1831. (N.Y.)
11. Dubois, *Pastoral Letter.* New York, John Doyle Pub., 1834.
12. Power to Paul Cullen, Sept. 15, 1833. (N.Y.)
13. John England to Paul Cullen, Sept. 26, 1833. (N.Y.)
14. Power to Cullen, July 23, 1834. (N.Y.)
15. Dubois, *Pastoral Letter,* 1834.
16. Thomas Levins to _____ , Jan. 13, 1831. (N.Y.)
17. James Roosevelt Bayley, *A Brief Sketch of the Early History of the Catholic Church on the Island of New York,* N.Y., U.S. Catholic Historical Society, 1973, p. 112.
18. Hassard, *op. cit.,* p. 180.
19. *U.S. Catholic Miscellany,* Oct. 14, 1837.

13. MASTER OF THE SCARLET-CLOTHED HORSE
1. Thebaud, *op. cit.,* p. 94.
2. *Ibid.,* p. 287.
3. *Herald,* Jan. 10, 1837.
4. *Ibid.,* Jan. 5, 1837.
5. *Ibid.,* Sept. 9, 1836.
6. *Ibid.,* Jan. 8, 1838.
7. *Ibid.*
8. Hughes to Frenaye, February, 1838; quoted in Hassard, *op. cit.,* p. 187.
9. Hughes to Mother Rose White, March 20, 1838. (St. Jos. Archives, Md.)
10. Hughes to Frenaye, March 22, 1838; quoted in Hassard, *op. cit.,* p. 188.
11. Hassard, *op. cit.,* p. 189.
12. *Ibid.,* p. 191.
13. Hughes to Eccleston, Oct. 29, 1838. (N.Y.)
14. *Ibid.,* Feb. 13, 1838. (N.Y.)
15. Hassard, *op. cit.,* p. 195.
16. *U.S. Catholic Miscellany,* March 30, 1839.
17. Hassard, *op. cit.,* p. 195.
18. Hughes to Eccleston, undated, 1838. (N.Y.)
19. Hughes to Mother Rose White, March 20, 1838. (St. Jos. Archives, Md.)
20. Hughes to Frenaye, March 20, 1838; quoted in Hassard, *op. cit.,* p. 196.

21. Bruté to Hughes, April 19, 1838. (N.Y.)
22. *Ibid.*
23. Hassard, *op. cit.,* p. 199.
24. *Truth Teller,* March 9, 1839.
25. Propaganda to Eccleston, June 1, 1839. (N.Y.)
25. Hassard, *op. cit.,* p. 199.
27. *Ibid.,* p. 220.
28. *Truth Teller,* Aug. 31, 1839.
29. George Templeton Strong, *The Diary of George Templeton Strong,* ed. Allan Nevins and Milton Halsey Thomas. N.Y., Macmillan, 1952, Vol. I, p. 102.
30. Hughes to Frenaye, Nov. 16, 1839; quoted in Hassard, *op. cit.,* p. 210.
31. Hassard, *op. cit.,* p. 211.
32. *Ibid.,* p. 215.
33. Hughes to Frenaye, June 1, 1840; quoted in Hassard, *op. cit.,* p. 219.
34. *Ibid.,* p. 218.
35. *Ibid.,* p. 216.
36. Hughes to Frenaye, June 1, 1840; quoted in Hassard, *op. cit.,* p. 220.

14. THE EDUCATION OF THE POOR
1. William Bourne, *History of the Public School Society of New York,* N.Y., Geo. Putnam's Sons, 1873, p. 179.
2. Glyndon G. Van Deusen, *William Henry Seward,* N.Y., Oxford University Press, 1967, p. 74.
3. *Truth Teller,* Aug. 5, 1843.
4. Baron George Lyttleton, *New York Reader;* quoted in Vincent P. Lannie, *Public Money and Parochial Education.* Cleveland, The Press of Case Western Reserve Univ., 1968, p. 105.
5. Lindley Murray, *Sequel to the English Reader,* in Lannie, *op. cit.,* p. 106.
6. Putnam's Sequel in Hughes, *Complete Works,* Vol. I, p. 72.
7. Conradt Molte Brun, *A System of Universal Geography,* quoted in Lannie, *op. cit.,* p. 109.
8. *The Irish Heart:* quoted in Hughes, *Complete Works.* Vol. I, p. 109.
9. *Truth Teller,* Jan. 16, 1840.
10. Hughes, *Complete Works,* Vol. I, p. 50.
11. Bourne, *op. cit.,* p. 326.
12. Joseph B. Collins to Hughes, Sept. 15, 1840; quoted in Bourne, *op. cit.,* p. 344.
13. Hughes to Joseph B. Collins, Sept. 15, 1840; quoted in Bourne, *op. cit.,* p. 344.
14. Bourne, *op. cit.,* p. 348.
15. Hughes, *Complete Works,* Vol. I, p. 79.
16. Henry Browne, "Public Support of Catholic Education in New York, 1825-1842." U.S. Catholic Historical Society, Vol. 61, p. 34.
17. Seward to Hughes, Sept. 1, 1840. (N.Y.)
18. Bourne, *op. cit.,* p. 203.
19. *Ibid.,* p. 208.
20. *Ibid.,* pp. 209-210.
21. *Ibid.,* pp. 212-219.
22. *Ibid.,* pp. 231-238.

23. *Ibid.,* pp. 247-250.
24. *Ibid.,* p. 230.
25. *Herald,* Nov. 2, 1840.
26. *Ibid.*
27. Bourne, *op. cit.,* p. 258.
28. *Ibid.,* p. 269.
29. *Ibid.,* pp. 272-273.
30. *Ibid.,* p. 275.
31. *Ibid.,* p. 277.
32. Strong, *op. cit.,* Vol. I, p. 250.
33. Bourne, *op. cit.,* p. 285.
34. *Herald,* Nov. 2, 1840.
35. Bourne, *op. cit.,* p. 313.
36. *Ibid.,* p. 315.
37. *U.S. Catholic Miscellany,* Nov. 14, 1840.
38. *Herald,* Dec. 31, 1840.
39. *Observer,* Nov. 7, 1840.
40. Hughes to Seward; quoted in Browne, *op. cit.,* pp. 35-36.
41. Lannie, *op. cit.,* p. 121.
42. Browne, *op. cit.,* p. 36.
43. *Herald,* Nov. 18, 1840.
44. *Ibid.*
45. Hughes to Eccleston, Aug. 27, 1840. (N.Y.)
46. William H. Seward, *The Works of William H. Seward,* ed. George Baker, New York, Redfield, 1853, Vol. II, p. 280.
47. Hughes, *Complete Works,* Vol. II, pp. 242-244.
48. Bourne, *op. cit.,* pp. 388-397.
49. Lannie, *op. cit.,* p. 156.
50. *U.S. Catholic Miscellany,* March 20, 1841.
51. Bourne, *op. cit.,* pp. 485-486.
52. Hughes, *Complete Works,* Vol. I, p. 265.
53. *Truth Teller,* June 5, 1841.
54. Mother Mary Peter Carthy, *Old Saint Patrick's.* New York, U.S. Catholic Historical Society, 1947, p. 61.
55. *Herald,* June 16, 1841.
56. *Ibid.,* July 8, 1841.
57. *Tribune,* July 26, 1841.
58. Hughes, *Complete Works,* Vol. I, p. 273.
59. *Ibid.,* p. 280.
60. *Ibid.,* p. 283.
61. *Herald,* Oct. 30, Nov. 1, Nov. 3, 1841.
62. *Observer,* Nov. 6, 1841.
63. *Tribune,* Nov. 1, 1841.
64. Hughes, *Complete Works,* Vol. I, pp. 290-291.
65. Hughes to W.G. Read, Nov. 6, 1841. (N.Y.)
66. *Herald,* Nov. 17, 1841.
67. Browne, *op. cit.*
68. *Ibid.*
69. *Truth Teller,* Feb. 26, 1842.
70. *Herald,* March 17, 1842.

71. "Correspondence between Archbishop Hughes and Governor Seward," *U.S. Catholic Historical Society,* Vol. 23 (1912), pp. 36-40.
72. Lannie, *op. cit.,* p. 230.
73. Hughes, *Complete Works,* Vol. I, p. 182.
74. *Ibid.,* Vol. II, p. 715.

15. DAGGER JOHN AND THE PROTESTANTS
1. Hughes to Frenaye, May 17, 1841; quoted in Hassard, *op. cit.,* p. 256.
2. Jay Dolan, *The Immigrant Church,* p. 90.
3. Thomas Meehan, "Johann Raffeiner," U.S. Catholic Historical Society, *Records and Studies,* Vol. 14, p. 174.
4. Hughes to Purcell, Aug. 6, 1831. (N.Y.)
5. Hughes, *Complete Works,* Vol. I, p. 318.
6. *Ibid.,* p. 320.
7. Quoted in *Truth Teller,* Nov. 19, 1842.
8. *Truth Teller,* Oct. 29, 1842.
9. *U.S. Catholic Miscellany,* Jan. 1, 1842.
10. *Herald,* Dec. 24, 1842.
11. Clifford S. Griffen, "Converting the Catholics; American Benevolent Societies and the Ante-Bellum Crusade against the Church," *The Catholic Historical Review,* Vol. 47, p. 307.
12. Hughes to L. Prentiss, July 22, 1844. (N.Y.)
13. Griffin, *op. cit.,* p. 332.
14. *Ibid.,* p. 333.
15. *Ibid.*
16. *Truth Teller,* Jan. 14, 1843.
17. *Herald,* Dec. 24, 1842.
18. Robert Leckie, *American and Catholic.* Garden City, N.Y., Doubleday & Co., 1970, p. 131.
19. *Truth Teller,* Jan. 14, 1843.
20. *Ibid.,* July 15, 1843.
21. Hassard, *op. cit.,* p. 261.
22. *Ibid.,* p. 263.
23. *Herald,* June 7, 1843; May 29, 1843.
24. Philip Hone, *Diary of Philip Hone,* p. 659.
25. *Truth Teller,* Aug. 26, 1843.
26. Sr. Hildegarde Yeager, *The Life of James Roosevelt Bayley, First Bishop of Newark and Eighth Archbishop of Baltimore 1818-1877.* Washington, 1947, p. 71.
27. *Herald,* July 1, 1843.
28. *U.S. Catholic Miscellany,* Dec. 2, 1843.
29. John Hughes. Lecture: "The Union of Church and State." New World Press, 1843, pp. 3-18.
30. William L. Stone, Jr., *The History of New York City.* New York, Virtue and Yurston, 1872, p. 508.
31. *Herald,* Oct. 13, 1844; Oct. 25, 1844.
32. Hassard, *op. cit.,* p. 275.
33. Hughes to Eccleston (undated). (N.Y.)
34. Hughes to Cardinal Brunelli, Propaganda Fide, April 26, 1844. (N.Y.)
35. Hughes to Donoghoe, Jan. 1844. (N.Y.)

36. *Herald,* May 9, 1844.
37. *Ibid.*
38. *Ibid.,* May 11, 1844.
39. Hassard, *op. cit.,* p. 276.
40. *Ibid.,* pp. 277-278.
41. *Herald,* June 26, 1844.
42. No author, "The Olive Branch," Philadelphia, 1844, p. 11.
43. *Tribune,* May 10, 1844.
44. *Journal of Commerce,* May 15, 1844.
45. *Herald,* May 11, 1844; June 24, 1844.
46. *Freeman's Journal,* May 25, 1844.
47. *Ibid.*
48. *Herald,* May 22, 1844; June 1, 1844.
49. *Herald,* June 20, 1844.
50. *Ibid.,* June 5, 1844.
51. *Tribune,* May 27, 1844.
52. *Ibid.*
53. Nolan, *op. cit.,* p. 320.
54. *Ibid.,* p. 202 (footnote).

16. IN MY DIOCESE
1. *Herald,* Nov. 11, 1844.
2. Hassard, *op. cit.,* p. 280.
3. *Herald,* Jan. 21, 1845.
4. *Ibid.,* March 13, 1845.
5. *Ibid.,* March 8, 1845.
6. *Ibid.,* March 15, 1845.
7. *U.S. Catholic Miscellany,* Dec. 26, 1846.
8. Hughes to Archbishop of Baltimore, Nov. 24, 1845. (N.Y.)
9. Hughes to Father Philip O'Reilly, May 19, 1845. (N.Y.)
10. Smith, *op. cit.,* Vol. I, p. 71.
11. Farley, *The Life of John Cardinal McCloskey,* p. 150.
12. Hughes to Donoghoe, Oct. 10, 1844. (N.Y.)
13. Hughes to Sr. Angela; quoted in Hassard, *op. cit.,* p. 282.
14. Hassard, *op. cit.,* p. 283.
15. *Ibid.,* p. 285.
16. Hughes to Father Louis Deluol, June 7, 1846, quoted in Hassard, *op. cit.,* p. 290.
17. Deluol to Hughes, June 17, 1846; quoted in Hassard, *op. cit.,* p. 293.
18. Hughes to Deluol (no date); quoted in Hassard, *op. cit.,* p. 293.
19. Hughes to Sr. Angela, June 21, 1846; quoted in Hassard, *op. cit.,* p. 296.
20. Hughes to Deluol (no date); quoted in Father Joseph B. Code, *Bishop John Hughes and the Sisters of Charity,* offprint of the Miscellanea L. Van Der Essen. Les Presses de Bélgique, 1947, pp. 997.
21. Mother Etienne to Hughes; quoted in Hassard, *op. cit.,* p. 298.
22. Hughes to Sr. Rosalia; quoted in Hassard, *op. cit.,* p. 299.
23. Hughes to Deluol, Jan. 1, 1846; quoted in Hassard, *op. cit.,* p. 302.

17. LITTLE BROWN BROTHERS NAMED O'BRIEN
1. *Herald,* Nov. 17, 1845; May 12, 1846.

2. *Freeman's Journal*, Dec. 11, 1847.
3. *Herald*, Aug. 20, 1846.
4. *Observer*, June 5, 1844.
5. *Herald*, May 21, 1846.
6. James Buchanan to Hughes, May 13, 1846. (N.Y.)
7. James Polk, *The Diary of A President, 1845-1848*, pp. 97-98.
8. Thomas F. Meehan, "Archbishop Hughes and Mexico," U.S. Catholic Historical Society, Vol. 19 (Sept., 1929), p. 35.
9. *Ibid.*, p. 37.
10. Quoted in *Freeman's Journal*, May 27, 1846.
11. Polk, "Diary" quoted from Meehan, *op. cit.*, p. 39.
12. *Ibid.*
13. William Hogan, *High and Low Mass.* Jordan and Wiley, 1847, pp. 193, 66, 45.
14. *Observer*, June 5, 1847.
15. *Herald*, Nov. 23, 1847.

18. BISHOP AND CHIEF
1. Robert Ernst, *Immigrant Life in New York, 1825-1863.* Port Washington, Ira J. Friedman Inc., 1949, p. 39.
2. Hughes, "1858 Recollections." (N.Y.)
3. *Ibid.*
4. *Herald*, April 23, 1846.
5. Hughes, "1858 Recollections." (N.Y.)
6. *Ibid.*
7. Hughes to Leopoldine Society, quoted in Hassard, *op. cit.*, p. 212.
8. Rev. C. Sparry, *The Mysteries of Popery.* C. Sparry, 1847, pp. 81-85.
9. Hassard, *op. cit.*, p. 353; *Herald*, Oct. 12, 1849.
10. Hughes, "1858 Recollections." (N.Y.)
11. Hassard, *op. cit.*, p. 317.

19. BORN WITHIN GUNSHOT OF TARA'S HALL
1. *Tribune*, June 6, 1848.
2. *Observer*, March 6, 1847.
3. Hassard, *op. cit.*, p. 303.
4. *Freeman's Journal*, Jan. 2, 1847.
5. *Herald*, June 22, 1848.
6. *Tribune*, May 19, 1848.
7. Hughes to Greeley, Feb. 1848, "Letters of Bishop Hughes," U.S. Catholic Historical Society, Vol. 22, p. 39.
8. Hughes, *Complete Works*, Vol. II, pp. 792-793.
9. Hassard, *op. cit.*, p. 307.
10. *Ibid.*
11. *Ibid.*, p. 310.
12. *Freeman's Journal*, Jan. 13, 1849.
13. *Herald*, Sept. 11, 1849.
14. *Ibid.*, Sept. 9, 1849.
15. *Nation*, August 1849; quoted in Gibson, *op. cit.*, p. 29.
16. Hughes to Eccleston, April 16, 1849. (N.Y.)
17. Hughes to Theobold Mathew, July 9, 1849. (N.Y.)

18. *Herald,* July 4, 1849.
19. Hughes to Eccleston, July 22, 1849. (N.Y.)

20. A GIFT FROM CONSTANTINE
  1. *Herald,* Nov. 30, 1847.
  2. *Ibid.,* Nov. 29, 1847.
  3. Quoted in *Freeman's Journal,* Feb. 26, 1848.
  4. Hone, *op. cit.,* p. 831.
  5. New York *Observer,* Jan. 15, 1848.
  6. *Freeman's Journal,* May 20, 1848.
  7. *Herald,* May 13, 1848.
  8. *Tribune,* Jan. 14, 1849.
  9. *Herald,* Jan. 17, 1848.
  10. Hughes, *Complete Works,* Vol. II, p. 19.
  11. *Herald,* Jan. 12, 1849.
  12. *Tribune,* June 27, 1849.
  13. *Ibid.,* June 25, 1849.
  14. Hughes, *Complete Works,* Vol. II, p. 27.
  15. *Herald,* June 27, 1849.
  16. *Ibid.,* Feb. 4, 1849.
  17. *Tribune,* July 9, 1849.
  18. Hughes, *Complete Works,* Vol. II, p. 19.
  19. *Herald,* Feb. 4, 1849.
  20. Hughes, *Complete Works,* Vol. II, pp. 32-33.
  21. *Herald,* May 13, 1850.

21. GROWING PAINS
  1. Hassard, *op. cit.,* p. 331.
  2. *Herald,* Oct. 30, 1850.
  3. P.T. Barnum to Hughes (undated). (N.Y.)
  4. *Herald,* Dec. 13, 1847.
  5. *Tribune,* Dec. 14, 1847; *Herald,* Dec. 14, 1847.
  6. *Herald,* Dec. 14, 1847.
  7. *Freeman's Journal,* Nov. 13, 1847.
  8. Yeager, *op. cit.,* p. 74.
  9. Hassard, *op. cit.,* pp. 318-319.
  10. *Herald,* July 17, 1849.
  11. *Ibid.,* Aug. 8, 1849.
  12. *Ibid.*
  13. *Ibid.,* Aug. 9, 1849.
  14. *Observer,* Feb. 6, 1847; March 6, 1847.
  15. *Ibid.,* June 26, 1847.
  16. *Herald,* Feb. 14, 1848.
  17. Hughes, *Complete Works,* Vol. I, p. 637.
  18. *Ibid.,* p. 638.
  19. *Ibid.,* p. 639.
  20. *Ibid.,* pp. 643-644.
  21. *Herald,* Sept. 17, 1848.
  22. *Observer,* July 15, July 22, Sept. 9, 1848.
  23. Quoted in *Ibid.,* Oct. 28, 1848.

24. Hughes to Cardinal Franzoni, Sept. 18, 1850.
25. Hughes, *The Decline of Protestantism and Its Causes*. Edward Dunigan & Brothers, 1850, p. 24.
26. *Herald*, Nov. 14, 1850.

22. THE MEANING OF THE WORD "CATHOLIC"
1. *Herald*, Jan. 9, 1847.
2. *Ibid.*, Oct. 13, 1844.
3. Hone, *op. cit.*, p. 694.
4. Strong, *op. cit.*, Vol. II, p. 104.
5. *Herald*, Jan. 16, 1845.
6. *Ibid.*, Nov. 25, 1850.
7. Walter Elliott, *The Life of Father Hecker.*N.Y., The Columbia Press, 1894, p. 136.
8. Katherine Burton, *Celestial Homespun.* London, Longmans Green and Co., 1943, p. 87.
9. Vincent Holden, *The Early Years of Isaac Hecker.* Washington, Catholic University of America Press, 1939, p. 202.
10. Burton, *op. cit.*, pp. 91-92.
11. Hughes, "1858 Recollections."
12. Hugh Marshal, *Orestes Brownson and the American Republic,* Washington, Catholic University of America Press, 1971, p. 79.
13. Hughes to Kenrick, Dec. 28, 1852. (N.Y.)
14. Hughes to Father McFarrelly, Feb. 7, 1859. (N.Y.)
15. *Freeman's Journal*, March 26, 1853.

23. VISITORS FROM ABROAD
1. *Herald*, July 30, 1849.
2. *Ibid.*, June 20, 1852.
3. Hughes, *Complete Works*, Vol. II, pp. 745-746.
4. *Tribune*, Nov. 14, 1851.
5. *Ibid.*, Nov. 20, 1851.
6. Hughes, *Complete Works*, p. 468.
7. *Tribune*, Nov. 24, 1851.
8. James Eastwood and Paul Tabori, *'48, The Year of Revolutions.* London, Meridian Books Ltd., 1947, p. 66.
9. Strong, *op. cit.*, Vol. II, pp. 75-76.
10. *Ibid.*, p. 75.
11. *Herald*, July 22, 1852.
12. *Ibid.*, April 21, 1852.
13. *Ibid.*, Feb. 22, July 22, 1852.
14. *Ibid.*, April 30, 1852.
15. *Ibid.*, July 15, 1852.
16. *Tribune*, Jan. 8, 1853.
17. *Freeman's Journal*, Jan. 15, 1853.
18. *Herald*, Jan. 28, 1853.
19. *Freeman's Journal*, Jan. 29, 1853.
20. *Tribune*, Feb. 22, 1853.
21. *Herald*, Jan. 16, 1853.
22. Hughes, *Complete Works*, Vol. II, pp. 480-481.

23. *Ibid.,* p. 499.
24. *Herald,* Jan. 26, 1853; April, 1853.
25. Alessandro Gavazzi, *Father Gavazzi's Lectures in New York.* Dewitt and Davenport, 1853, p. 99.
26. *Ibid.,* p. 78.
27. *Ibid.,* pp. 280-282.
28. *Herald,* April 23, 1853.
29. Gavazzi, *op. cit.,* p. 80.
30. Peter Kenrick to John Purcell; quoted in Conally, *op. cit.,* p. 160.
31. Peter Guilday, "Gaetano Bedini, an Episode in the Life of Archibishop John Hughes," United States Catholic Historical Society, Vol. 23, p. 145.
32. *Herald,* July 18, 1853.
33. Guilday, *op. cit.;* p. 109.
34. *Herald,* Aug. 16, 1853; Aug. 18, 1853.
35. Guilday, *op. cit.,* p. 110 (footnote).
36. *Freeman's Journal,* Nov. 16, 1853.
37. James F. Connally, "The Visit of Archbishop Gaetano Bedini to the United States of America, June 1853-February 1854." Rome, Serves Facultatis Historiae Ecclesiastiae Libreria Eatrice Dell' Universita Gregonanci, Vol. 109, 1960.
38. Guilday, *op. cit.,* p. 112.
39. *Herald,* Oct. 31, 1853.
40. Hughes to Bernard Smith, Nov. 25, 1853. (N.Y.)
41. Quoted in *Freeman's Journal,* Jan. 1, 1854.
42. *Freeman's Journal,* Jan. 1, 1854.
43. Quoted in *Freeman's Journal,* Jan. 11, 1854.
44. *Freeman's Journal,* Jan. 1, 1854.
45. Connally, *op. cit.,* p. 161.
46. *Ibid.*
47. Hassard, *op. cit.,* p. 359.
48. *Tribune,* Jan. 7, 1854.
49. *Herald,* Nov. 19, 1853.
50. *Ibid.,* Jan. 30, 1854; *Tribune,* Jan. 30, 1854.
51. *Tribune,* Jan. 30, 1854.
52. Bedini to Hughes, Feb. 2, 1854.
53. Hughes to Blanc, Feb. 3, 1854.
54. *Herald,* March 9, 1852.
55. *Ibid.,* April 2, 1854.
56. Connally, *op. cit.,* p. 163.
57. Guilday, *op. cit.,* p. 159.

24. "I KNOW NOTHING . . ."
 1. *Herald,* May 29, 1854.
 2. Strong, *op. cit.,* .Vol. II, pp. 182-183.
 3. *Tribune,* June 15, 1854.
 4. *Herald,* Nov. 17, 1854.
 5. *Times,* Aug. 4, 1854.
 6. *Herald,* Oct. 2, 1854.
 7. Hassard, *op. cit.,* p. 372.

8. John Hughes and Erastus Brooks, *The Controversy Between Senator Brooks and ✝ John, Archbishop of New York,* arranged by W.S. Tisdale, N.Y., Dewitt & Davenport, pp. 13-22.

9. *Herald,* April 23, 1855.

10. John Hughes and Erastus Brooks, *Brooksiana, of the Controversy Between Senator Brooks and Archbishop Hughes.* Edward Dunigan & Brother, 1855, p. 65.

11. *Ibid.,* p. 70.

12. Hughes and Brooks, *The Controversy . . .* p. 47.

13. *Ibid.,* p. 34.

14. *Herald,* May 12, 1855.

15. *Ibid.,* March 31, 1855.

16. *Ibid.*

17. Hughes and Brooks, *The Controversy . . .* p. 47.

18. *Ibid.,* p. 51.

19. *Herald,* April 14, 1855.

20. Hughes to an unnamed bishop, April 28, 1855. (N.Y.)

21. *Herald,* May 12, 1855.

22. Hughes and Brooks, *The Controversy . . .* (Back-page advertisements).

23. *Herald,* June 5, 1856.

24. Thurlow Weed, *Memoirs,* Vol. II, pp. 222-233.

25. *Post,* Sept. 27, 1852, quoted in Gibson, *op. cit.,* p. 56.

26. Hogan, *Popery as it Was and Is.* Silus Andrus & Son, 1856, p. 361.

27. *Ibid.,* p. 611.

28. *Herald,* Sept. 12, 1856.

29. *Ibid.,* July 23, 1856.

30. *Ibid.,* Oct. 7, 1856.

31. *Ibid.,* Sept. 21, 1856.

32. *Ibid.,* Sept. 12, 1856.

25. THIS OUGHT TO BE LEFT TO OUR ENEMIES

1. *Times,* July 31, 1854.

2. *Ibid.,* Aug. 4, 1854.

3. *Ibid.,* Sept. 19, 1854.

4. Gibson, *op. cit.,* p. 64.

5. *Herald,* May 31, 1854.

6. John Mitchel, *Jail Journal.* DuBlin, M.H. Gill and Son, 1914, p. 396.

7. Hughes to Meagher, Feb. 15, 1853; Meagher to Hughes, Feb. 19, 1853.

8. *Herald,* March 6, 1857.

9. *Ibid.,* July 29, 1854.

10. Hughes to Brownson, July 7, 1854. (N.Y.)

11. Theodore Maynard, *Orestes Brownson; Yankee, Radical, Catholic.* N.Y., The Macmillan Co., 1943, p. 248.

12. *Ibid.,* pp. 248-250; Hassard, *op. cit.,* p. 383.

13. Hughes to Brownson, Sept. 17, 1856. (N.Y.)

14. Maynard, *op. cit.,* p. 250.

15. Hughes, *Complete Works,* Vol. II, pp. 701, 690.

16. *Times,* Jan. 9, 1857.

17. Hughes, *Complete Works,* Vol. II, p. 504.

18. *Times,* Feb. 21, 1857.
19. Henry W. Casper, *History of the Catholic Church in Nebraska.* Bruce Press, 1960, Vol. I, p. 68. Henry J. Browne, "Archbishop Hughes and Western Colonization," *Catholic Historical Review,* Vol. 36, p. 276.
20. Browne, "Archbishop Hughes," p. 264.
21. Hughes, *Complete Works,* Vol. II, p. 691.
22. *Ibid.,* p. 692-693.
23. *Ibid.,* p. 690.
24. Browne, "Archbishop Hughes," p. 270-271.
25. *Times,* March 27, 1857.
26. Hughes, *Complete Works,* Vol. II, pp. 752-755.
27. *Ibid.,* pp. 754-755.
28. *Herald,* March 27, 1857.
29. Hughes, *Complete Works,* Vol. II, p. 754.
30. *Times,* July 18, 1857.
31. Hughes, *Complete Works,* Vol. II, p. 511.
32. Hughes to Rev. J. O'Callaghan, March 3, 1859; quoted in Hassard, *op. cit.,* p. 411.
33. *Herald,* April 27, 1857.
34. Hughes to Hargous; quoted in Hassard, *op. cit.,* p. 411.
35. Hassard, *op. cit.,* p. 399.

26. Endowed with a Tireless Energy

1. Hassard, *op. cit.,* p. 398.
2. Hughes to Binsse, undated (c. 1860) (N.Y.)
3. Hughes to Barnabo, July 19, 1860. (N.Y.)
4. *Ibid.,* summer of 1860; quoted in Hassard, *op. cit.,* p. 400.
5. Hughes to Bishop Gillis of Scotland, Sept. 2, 1859. (N.Y.)
6. Hughes to Barnabo, Nov. 1857. (N.Y.)
7. Letter draft in Hughes's handwriting. Undated. (N.Y.)
8. Hughes to Barnabo, 1860. (N.Y.)
9. Vincent Holden, *The Yankee Paul,* p. 242.
10. *Ibid.,* p. 358.
11. *Ibid.,* p. 356.
12. *Ibid.,* p. 360.
13. Francis X. Curran, "Archbishop Hughes and the Jesuits," *Woodstock Letters,* Vol. 97, 1968, p. 13.
14. *Ibid.,* p. 12.
15. *Ibid.,* p. 17.
16. *Ibid.,* p. 10.
17. *Ibid.,* p. 22.
18. Thebaud, *op. cit.,* p. 290-291.
19. Jay P. Dolan, *The Immigrant Church.* Baltimore and London, The Johns Hopkins University Press, 1975, pp. 22-23.
20. Hughes to Barnabo, undated. (N.Y.)
21. Hughes to P.A. Malot, Oct. 19, 1858. (N.Y.)
22. Hughes to Thomas Mooney, May 7, 1860. (N.Y.)
23. Hughes to Dr. Brady, undated, 1858. (N.Y.)
24. *Herald,* Aug. 23, 1859.
25. *Ibid.*

26. Hughes to Forbes, March 11, 1859.
27. Hughes to Kirby; quoted in Hassard, *op. cit.,* p. 425.
28. Brownson to Hughes, Oct. 31, 1859. (N.Y.)
29. Hughes to Brownson, Oct. 31, 1859. (N.Y.)
30. Hughes to Terence Donoghoe, Oct. 14, 1850. (N.Y.)
31. Hughes to Bishop Connally, Sept. 3, 1858. (N.Y.)
32. Hughes to an unnamed bishop, May 17, 1858. (N.Y.)
33. Hughes to Fitzgerald, Sept. 5, 1859. (N.Y.)
34. John Talbot Smith, *op. cit.,* Vol. I, p. 179.
35. Strong, *op. cit.,* Vol. II, p. 310.
36. *Herald,* Aug. 16, 1858.
37. Hughes, *Complete Works,* Vol. II, pp. 265-267.
38. *Herald,* Aug. 16, 1858.
39. *Harper's Weekly,* June 26, 1858.
40. Hughes to Bernard Smith, Dec. 11, 1859; Feb. 1859.

27. REAPING THE WHIRLWIND
1. Hughes to Bernard Smith, Aug. 1858, (N.Y.); quoted in Hassard, *op. cit.,* p. 416.
2. Hughes to Barnabo, Jan. 3, 1860. (N.Y.)
3. *Herald,* July 2, 1859; Feb. 15, 1860.
4. *Ibid.,* Aug. 16, 1858.
5. Hassard, *op. cit.,* p. 42.
6. Hughes to Seward, undated, 1862. (N.Y.)
7. *Citizen,* May 6, 1854.
8. *Ibid.*
9. *Herald,* April 16, 1857.
10. *Ibid.,* April 12, 1859.
11. Hughes to Lord Lyons, Sept. 12, 1860. (N.Y.)
12. Hughes to Buchanan, March 8, 1858. (N.Y.)
13. Hassard, *op. cit.,* p. 422.
14. *Herald,* May 14, 1860.
15. Hughes to Bishop Mullock, June 1860. (N.Y.)
16. Hughes to Senior class, University of North Carolina, Nov. 10, 1859. (N.Y.)
17. Hassard, *op. cit.,* pp. 428-429.
18. Hughes to McCosky, Jan. 1861.
19. Hughes to Seward, undated, 1861. (N.Y.)
20. Hughes to Bishop McNally, Ireland, May 22, 1861.
21. Hughes to an unnamed Bishop, May 7, 1861; quoted in Hassard, *op. cit.,* p. 439.
22. Hughes to 69th Regiment, undated. (N.Y.)
23. Lincoln to Hughes, quoted in Hassard, *op. cit.,* p. 445.
24. Hughes to Seward, July 18, 1861. (N.Y.)
25. Hughes to Kenrick, July 3, 1861. (N.Y.)
26. Hughes to Mooney, July 5, 1861. (N.Y.)
27. Hughes to Seward, Aug. 13, 1861. (N.Y.)
28. *Ibid.,* Sept. 12, 1861. (N.Y.)
29. *Ibid.,* June 18, 1861; quoted in Hassard, *op. cit.,* p. 441.
30. Hassard, *op. cit.,* p. 439.

31. *U.S. Catholic Miscellany*, July 6, 1861.
32. *Freeman's Journal*, June 1, 1861.
33. *Ibid.*, June 15, 1861.
34. Maynard, *op. cit.*, p. 321.
35. *Ibid.*, p. 322.
36. *Metropolitan Record;* quoted in Hassard, *op. cit.*, p. 436.
37. Maynard, *op. cit.*, p. 322.
38. Hughes to Simon Cameron, Oct. 2, 1861. (N.Y.)
39. Hughes to Seward, Oct. 15, 1861. (N.Y.)
40. *U.S. Catholic Miscellany*, Nov. 23, 1861.
41. Hughes to Seward, Nov. 20, 1861. (N.Y.)
42. Hughes to Barnabo; quoted in Hassard, *op. cit.*, p. 449.
43. Quoted in unpublished letter to Dublin's *Freeman's Journal*, letter dated Dec. 1, 1861. (N.Y.)
44. *Ibid.*
45. Seward to Hughes; quoted in Thomas Meehan, "Lincoln's Opinion of Catholics," U.S. Catholic Historical Society, Vol. 16, p. 90.
46. Hughes to Seward, Dec. 10, 1861. (N.Y.)
47. *Ibid.*, Dec. 5, 1861. (N.Y.)
48. *Ibid.*, Dec. 1861. (N.Y.)
49. *Ibid.*, Dec. 27, 1861. (N.Y.)
50. *Ibid.*, Feb. 1, 1862. (N.Y.)
51. *Ibid.*, Aug. 1862. (N.Y.)
52. Seward to Hughes, Jan. 9, 1862. (N.Y.)
53. Hughes to *Journal des Debates*, Jan. 3, 1862. (N.Y.)
54. Hughes to Seward, Feb. 1, 1862. (N.Y.)
55. *Ibid.*, March 1, 1862. (N.Y.)
56. *Ibid.*, March 8, 1862. (N.Y.)
57. *Ibid.*, June 12, 1862. (N.Y.)
58. Hughes, *Complete Works*, Vol. II, p. 769.
59. *Ibid.*, p. 764.
60. *Metropolitan Record*, Aug. 16, 1862.
61. Hughes to Cullen, Dec. 5, 1862; quoted in Hassard, *op. cit.*, p. 484.
62. Hassard, *op. cit.*, p. 485.
63. Hughes, *Complete Works*, Vol. II, p. 373.
64. Hughes to the N.Y. Common Council, quoted in *Metropolitan Record*, Oct. 25, 1862.
65. *Baltimore Catholic Mirror*, Oct. 18, 1862; quoted in *Metropolitan Record*, Oct. 25, 1862.
66. *Tablet*, July 25, 1863.
67. Hassard, *op. cit.*, p. 489.
68. Smith to Hughes, Aug. 9, 1862; Sept. 27, 1862. (N.Y.)
69. *Ibid.*, Sept. 27, 1862. (N.Y.)
70. Hughes to Seward, Nov. 5, 1862. (N.Y.)
71. Hughes to Rev. Mr. Joslen, Feb. 7, 1863. (N.Y.)
72. Hughes to Levi Silliman Ives, June 11, 1863. (N.Y.)
73. Hassard, *op. cit.*, p. 498.
74. *A Descriptive and Historical Sketch of the Academy of Mt. St. Vincent on the Hudson*. D. Appleton and Co., 1884, p. 76.
75. *Tablet*, June 6, 1863.

76. *Ibid.,* May 23, 1863.
77. Maurice Byrne to his father, May 21, 1863. (Mt.)
78. Hughes to McCaffrey, June 16, 1863.
79. Hughes to Lincoln, June 1863.
80. Hassard, *op. cit.,* p. 498.
81. *Ibid.*
82. *Ibid.,* p. 499.
83. Hughes to Seward (undated draft of 1862).
84. *Metropolitan Record,* Jan. 17, 1863.
85. *Freeman's Journal,* Nov. 1, 1862.
86. *Ibid.,* Sept. 20, 1862.
87. *Ibid.,* March 21, 1863.
88. Adrian Cook, *Armies of the Streets.* The University Press of Kentucky, 1974, p. 53.
89. *Tribune,* July 9, 1863.
90. *Ibid.,* July 11, 1863; *Herald,* July 11, 1863.
91. *Herald,* July 14, 1863.
92. *Tribune,* July 11, 1863.
93. *Tablet,* Aug. 1, 1863.
94. Cook, *op. cit.,* p. 129.
95. *Ibid.,* p. 160.
96. *Herald,* July 18, 1863.
97. *Ibid.,* July 15, 1863; *Tribune,* July 16, 1863; *Tablet,* July 25, 1863.
98. Cook, *op. cit.,* p. 159.
99. Tribune, July 16, 1863.
100. *Herald,* July 18, 1863.
101. *Tablet,* July 25, 1863.
102. *Times,* July 18, 1863.
103. Quoted in the *Herald,* July 18, 1863.
104. Thomas F. Meehan, "Archbishop Hughes and the Draft Riots," U.S. Catholic Historical Society, Vol. I, Part II, p. 171.
105. Lynch to Hughes, Oct. 19, 1863. (N.Y.)
106. Hassard, *op. cit.,* p. 501.
107. *Herald,* Jan. 7, 1864.
108. *Freeman's Journal,* Jan. 9, 1864.
109. *Tribune,* Jan. 4, 1864; Jan. 9, 1864.
110. *The Franklin Repository,* Jan. 7, 1864.
111. *Herald,* Jan. 7, 1864.

INDEX